Drama as Therapy

Second edition

This new edition of *Drama as Therapy* presents a coherent review of the practice and theory of dramatherapy. With a unique combination of practical guidance, clinical examples and research vignettes, this fully revised second edition considers developments in the field over the last decade and researches the impact of the 'core processes' on clinical practice.

The book shows how dramatherapy can be used with a wide range of clients and applied to their individual needs. Therapists working in different parts of the world contribute examples of their practice, alongside their research interviews demonstrating the effectiveness of dramatherapy. The book draws on studies ranging from child survivors of the tsunami in Sri Lanka to teenagers living with HIV in South Africa, from elderly clients dealing with psychosis in the UK to women in a refuge in Malaysia. Divided into four distinct parts it provides:

- definitions of core processes at work in dramatherapy
- research into how dramatherapists understand what they offer clients
- clear descriptions of the structure and content of dramatherapy
- a wide range of clinical research vignettes from all over the world.

Drama as Therapy offers insights into how experienced dramatherapists understand their work with clients. It will be of great interest to dramatherapy students internationally, as well as professionals working with dramatherapy.

Phil Jones, Reader, Carnegie Faculty, Leeds Metropolitan University, has held the posts of principal lecturer and course leader in the arts therapies at Postgraduate and Masters level. He has lectured across the world and written extensively on the arts therapies: his books have been translated and published in Chinese, Greek and Korean.

Drama as Therapy

Theory, practice and research

Second edition

Phil Jones

Routledge
Taylor & Francis Group

LONDON AND NEW YORK

First published 1996 by Routledge
Second edition published 2007 by Routledge
27 Church Road, Hove, East Sussex, BN3 2FA

Simultaneously published in the USA and Canada
by Routledge
270 Madison Avenue, New York, NY 10016

*Routledge is an imprint of the Taylor & Francis Group,
an Informa business*

Typeset in Times by RefineCatch Limited, Bungay, Suffolk
Printed and bound in Great Britain by
TJ International Ltd, Padstow, Cornwall
Paperback cover design by Sandra Heath
Paperback cover image from print by Neil Walters

The publication has been produced with paper manufactured to strict
environmental standards and with pulp derived from sustainable
forests.

British Library Cataloguing in Publication Data
A catalogue record for this book is available from the British Library

Library of Congress Cataloging-in-Publication Data
Jones, Phil, 1958–
    Drama as therapy : theory, practice, and research / Phil Jones.
– 2nd ed.
        p.; cm.
    Includes bibliographical references and index.
    ISBN 978-0-415-41555-2 (hbk.) – ISBN 978-0-415-41556-9 (pbk.)
1. Drama – Therapeutic use. I. Title.
[DNLM: 1. Psychodrama. WM 430.5.P8 J78d 2007]
RC489.P7J66 2007
616.89′1523 – dc22

                                          2007007576

ISBN: 978-0-415-41555-2 (hbk)
ISBN: 978-0-415-41556-9 (pbk)

This book is dedicated to Neil Walters (1963–2005).
It owes its existence to him.

Contents

List of plates	xi
List of figures	xii
List of boxes	xiii
List of vignettes, research vignettes and research conversations	xiv
Preface to the second edition	xvii
Acknowledgements 1st edition	xix
Acknowledgement 2nd edition	xx
How to use this book	xxi

PART I

1 What is dramatherapy?   3

Introduction 3
Drama as necessary to living 6
Basic tenets of dramatherapy 7
Dramatherapy and meaning 13
Building blocks: creativity, play, drama and healing 15
*Therapeutic change and dramatherapy: how psychological
    disturbance is construed 16*
The contexts of dramatherapy 18
Past and current models of dramatherapy 20

Part II

**2 From amphitheatre to operating theatre? Drama, theatre and
    therapy – a history**   23

Introduction: three histories 23
Healing, drama, theatre 24
*The meeting of drama and therapy: a twentieth-century
    context 26*
Context: hospital theatre 27

Context: twentieth-century theatre and therapy 29
Context: early pioneers – Evreinov, Iljine, Moreno 32
Context: dramaturgy – doing is being is acting 40
Context: play and drama in education 42
Summary 44

3 The emergence of dramatherapy   45

Introduction 45
The emergence of dramatherapy: an overview of documented
  practice from 1939 46
From individuals to profession 50
Interview with Peter Slade 51
Interview with (Marian) Billy Lindkvist 52
Interview with Sue Jennings 54
Training and associations 56
Orientation and the changing face of health care 57
Summary 58

4 Dramatherapy and philosophy: belief and proof   59

Introduction 59
What is philosophy? 61
Useful perspectives 62
Postmodernism and co-construction 71
A third way? Phenomenology and after 71
Identity: selves in relation? 73
Conclusion 78

Part III
5 Dramatherapy: therapeutic core processes   81

Introduction 81
Dramatic projection 83
Playing 88
Role playing and personification 94
Dramatherapeutic empathy and distancing 95
Active witnessing 101
Embodiment: the dramatic body 112
Life–drama connection 117
Transformation 119
Summary 134

Part IV

6 Dramatic projection   137

Introduction 137
Projection: a psychological perspective 139
Dramatherapy–projective techniques 144
Summary 154

7 Play and playing   155

Play in dramatherapy 161
Meaning and play 162
Cultural factors in play 163
Play and dramatherapy 164
Overview: key concepts 165
Dramatherapy practice and play 167
The use of play space in dramatherapy 168
A developmental approach and the play–drama continuum 176
The play–drama continuum 176
Sensorimotor play 178
Imitative play 180
Pretend play 181
Dramatic play 182
Drama 183
Summary 191

8 Role   192

The enacted self 192
Contexts for role in dramatherapy 203
Dramatherapy practice and role 212
Summary 222

9 The dramatic body   223

Introduction 223
Background to the dramatic body 226
The dramatic body in dramatherapy practice 228
Summary 239

10 Symbol and metaphor   241

Introduction 241
Symbols and metaphors in dramatherapy 253

Dramatherapy practice and the connected world 256
Connection and assimilation 266
Summary 269

11 Dramatherapy and ritual   272

Introduction 272
Drama, theatre and ritual 273
Efficacy and ritual 274
Dramatherapy and ritual 275
Dramatherapy practice and ritual 277
Reframing rituals 277
The creation of dramas using ritual forms 281
Summary 283

12 Assessment, recording and evaluation in dramatherapy   285

Introduction 285
Approaches to assessment and evaluation in dramatherapy 289
Why assess? The problems with assessment and evaluation 291
Assessment methodologies 291
The media within dramatherapy 295
Jones's adaptation of scale of dramatic involvement 295
Projective techniques 297
Role-playing tests 314
Johnson's role-playing test 314
Play-influenced assessment 315
Adapting assessment methods 316
Recording sessions 317
Written dramatherapy recording sample 317
Summary 321

Appendix: Research vignettes and conversations   323
References   331
Name index   349
Subject index   353

Plates

1.1   Tsunami   4
9.1   Schlemmer's body transformations in theatrical space   224
9.2   Schlemmer's body transformations in theatrical space   224
10.1 Sleeping Beauty   244
10.2 Open the Door for You Mother Said the Wolf   245
10.3 The Bird from Tree to Tree   245
10.4 The Tower with the Window   247
10.5 The Three Doors in the Tower   247
10.6 The Prince with the Door Key   248

Figures

6.1   Peter and dramatic projection   142
6.2   Dramatic projection in dramatherapy   153
7.1   Sensorimotor play   178
7.2   Imitation   180
7.3   Pretend play   182
7.4   Dramatic play   183
7.5   Drama   183
8.1   Dramatherapy and role   208
8.2   Pattern of role taking in dramatherapy   213
10.1 The Prince in the Tower: two dramatic metaphors   250
10.2 The metaphoric connection   255
12.1 Social atom   298

Boxes

1.1   Dramatherapy – the basic shape   12
6.1   Dramatic projection in dramatherapy   144
6.2   Dramatic projection and small worlds   145
6.3   Dramatic projection and World Technique   145
7.1   Dramatherapy guide – discovering play language   167
7.2   Key aspects of play–drama continuum   177
8.1   Enrolement factors   213
8.2   Pre-role checklist   214
9.1   Main areas of concern – the potential body   229
12.1   Parten's social participation scale   316

Vignettes, research vignettes and research conversations

Vignettes that are part of the research undertaken for the second edition are titled 'Research Vignette' and 'Research Conversation'. All other vignettes are from the first edition of this book.

Vignettes

Sylvester's dream	49
Thomas	64
Jake	66
Girls with eating disorders	74
Peter and the helmet	140
The falling man	155
Girl's play in Silwa	162
Ellen	178
Objects	179
Facial/bodily imitation	180
Imitation of gesture	180
Theresa	181
Amy	182
Developmental play	184
Ballet dress	194
The prince in the tower	242
Barbed wire circle	251
Easter cake	279
Menstruation ritual	281
Assessment in dramatherapy	292

Research vignettes

Child survivors of a tsunami in Sri Lanka	4
A woman in a group for older people who hear voices in England	5
A group for adolescents with HIV in South Africa	5

A teenager in a school for pupils with emotional and behavioural
    difficulties in England   5
A woman in individual therapy in England   5
A child from Sierra Leone   6
Brenda   84
Colette   89
Zandile and Nomsa   97
Bill, Ahad and Ileem   105
Witnessing   108
Maya   115
Lynne   122
Abui   127
Sarah   146
Jilly   148
Children and the tsunami   157
Two weeks left   170
Joe   185
Island   195
Women with BPD who self-harm   199
Patrick   209
Grace   217
What the thunder said   230
The potential body in action   233
Biomechanics workshop   235
Bilal   257
Kia   261
Beth   267
Suraya   299
John, second assessment session   302
John, later session   303
Mountain climb expedition   306
Desert journey   311

Research conversations

Jo Van Den Bosch   86
Jay Vaughan   91
Kirsten Meyer   99
Jan Stirling Twist   106
Mario Guarnieri and Emma Ramsden   109
Shu Ling Lin   117
Christine Novy   124
Roya Dooman   132
Jo Van Den Bosch   150
Debra Colkett   160

Jo Rogers	174
Clare Powis	189
Clare Hubbard	198
Debra Colkett	202
Nancy Secchi	210
Lili Levy	220
Madeline Andersen-Warren	231
Anna Seymour	237
Ruth Goodman	259
Sarah Mann-Shaw	264
Christine Novy	268
Vanitha Chandrasegaram	301
Clare Hubbard	304
Jay Vaughan	309
Naomi Gardner	312

Preface to the second edition

Having been through six reprints and translation and publication in Greek, Korean and Chinese in its ten years of life, I wanted to see how *Drama As Therapy* was doing in the world. To this end, my research has involved in-depth qualitative interviews through vignettes and narrative research analysis from therapists who have used the core processes in their work. This has enabled me to review the ways in which the original text has been responded to in publications, and in clinical practice. The Appendix gives a summary of the research approach and method, and explains the nature of the research vignettes and conversations contained within many of the chapters. The vignettes contain narrative images of practice which dramatherapists have selected to represent the value of their work, and the ways in which they see the core processes within dramatherapy benefiting clients. The conversations are selections of the material created in researching into the way that the therapists see the value of their work. As the Appendix says of their presentation in *Drama As Therapy*:

> The edited versions of the research conversations within this book are deliberately left in more or less the form they emerged in. The editing process was one of selecting particular sections of the conversations, not polishing the words. A part of their value as a research tool was in validating the spontaneity of interaction, the improvisational properties of this mode of enquiry.

A rough image for my rewriting has been that the book went out on one tide and, ten years later, I have tried to find out what the tide has brought with it on its return. In a way, what I've found has turned the book inside out. I've included many vignettes showing how people have used, adapted and challenged the original. The book is changed by them – the ideas and processes originally here have been altered and refined by their experience.

The initial book was my attempt as a practitioner and researcher to move from my own experience and those of my colleagues, in their published accounts of practice and research, into formulating descriptions of processes and practices that were at the heart of change in dramatherapy. At that stage

I wanted to try to gain a sense of coherence for myself, and to communicate it to others – for them to use in benefiting clients. The research that this book contains shows how those ideas and practices have been taken, used and changed.

In its turn, this new edition will be in the hands of clients and practitioners as they develop and work with its contents to change it further. I wish them well together with, the new edition of this book in its new life.

Dr Phil Jones
Spread Eagle House
Settle
North Yorkshire

Acknowledgements to first edition

I would like to thank Neil Walters for his support, editing skills and insight. Without his assistance this book would not exist.

This book was written in London, and during a sabbatical in Xania and Athens. I would like to thank my friends in Greece for their support whilst I lived there. This book owes a debt to Annie and Frank Nowak, Nicos Marinos and Giorgos Sirnou, Manolis Filipakis, Jannis and Gogo Bolaraki.

A number of people have helped in the research and writing through interviews and commentaries on my work. I would especially like to thank Peter Slade, Sue Jennings and Billy Lindkvist – both for the interviews they offered and for the documentation they have provided from their personal collections. Alida Gersie, Robert Landy, Ditty Dokter and Rea Karagiourgiou-Short have given me valuable assistance by their comments on my developing text. Alida Gersie, Hank Guilickx, Ana Palma and Cristina Calheiros assisted with the writing of the history section. Ann Cattanach and Dorothy Langley also must be mentioned in terms of their contributions to the field and to the development of my ideas within *Drama as Therapy*. Helena Ivins, Margaret Walters, Deborah Loveridge and John Convey have all assisted in the preparation of the book. Similarly I must thank the many students whose views have helped hone my ideas and research – from the Division of Arts and Psychology through to the Postgraduate Arts Therapies programme at the University of Hertfordshire. Penny Dade and the School of Art and Design's library services have also greatly assisted my research. Many thanks also to Edwina Welham, Alison Poyner and Nikky Twyman.

The practice described in this book has been supported by a number of organisations and funders. I would like to give special thanks to the creative and financial input of Mike Sparks and the Sir John Cass Foundation. The Calouste Gulbenkian Foundation, the European Community's Horizon Frogramme and Greater London Arts also supported some of the work. I would also like to thank my co-workers Lesley Kerr Edwards, Pat Place, Ayad Chebib and Rosemary Sanctuary.

The first edition of this book was dedicated to my parents, Esther and William Jones

Acknowledgements to second edition

This second edition owes an enormous amount to the therapists who contributed to the research into the core processes within dramatherapy, and to the clients whose work they describe. I would also like to acknowledge the support of the British Association of Dramatherapists who helped offer the opportunity to contribute to this second edition, and to thank those therapists who sent good wishes but who couldn't provide research vignettes. In addition, I would like to thank therapists whose work I have analysed within the text in developing the response to the first edition of *Drama as Therapy*. In alphabetical order, I warmly thank Madeline Andersen-Warren, Jo Van Den Bosch, John Casson, Vanitha Chandrasegaram, Anna Chesner, Debra Colkett, Ditty Dokter, Roya Dooman, Naomi Gardner, Martin Gill, Ruth Goodman, Roger Grainger, Diane Grimshaw, Mario Guarnieri, R. Heymann-Krenge, Richard Hougham, Clare Hubbard, Vicky Karkou, Dorothy Langley, Lili Levy, Shu Ling Lin, Sarah Mann-Shaw, Maggie McAlister, Kirsten Meyer, Steve Mitchell, Christine Novy, Clare Powis, Emma Ramsden, Jo Rogers, Sarah Scoble, Nancy Secchi, Genevieve Smyth, Jan Stirling Twist, Jay Vaughan. This second edition would definitely not be the same without them, and they have profoundly changed the original text which it is based on.

The new material on philosophy draws on conversations with my partner, Neil Walters. Chapter 4, 'Dramatherapy and Philosphy: Belief and Proof', is both a very inadequate gesture towards the PhD on art and philosophy which he would never finish, as well as unfinished conversations with him.

Editorial thanks to Joanne Forshaw, Jane Harris, Dawn Harris, Penelope Allport and to Lola Miller for her help with the book's cover.

21 February 2007

How to use this book

Drama as Therapy is divided into four parts. The first gives an overview of the definition of dramatherapy and reviews dramatherapy's main forms and formats. Included in this is a guide to the structure of dramatherapy processes and sessions. Part II describes the history of dramatherapy. The third part of the book is formed by a definition of the core processes which are at the heart of dramatherapy's efficacy. Part IV considers the main areas of theory and practice. Each area is given a specific chapter which includes a theoretical background, an illustrated guide to practice with clinical examples, along with a summary or definition of the area.

Part I

1　What is dramatherapy?

Drama is mimetic action, action in imitation or representation of human behaviour.

Esslin, *An Anatomy of Drama*

Introduction

There are two perceptions at the heart of this book. The first is that drama and theatre are ways of actively participating in the world and are not merely an imitation of it. The second is that within drama there is a powerful potential for healing.

The term 'dramatherapy' refers to drama as a form of therapy. During the twentieth century developments in a number of different fields such as experimental theatre and psychology have resulted in new insights into the ways in which drama and theatre can be effective in bringing about change in people: emotional, psychological, political and spiritual change.

This book will offer definitions and examples of what dramatherapy is and research into what it offers clients. It will draw on different sources from theory and professional practice all over the world: from England to Taiwan, from Canada to Sri Lanka. Theoretical definitions and those arrived at by professional associations and health care providers offer one kind of answer to 'What is dramatherapy?' but the following moments from vignettes contained in the research undertaken for the second edition of this book draw us straight into the heart of the question, by taking us to where the meaning of dramatherapy matters most: within work with clients. In this place, adolescents tell each other for the first time that they are HIV positive, a woman walks through a landscape that holds her life, cloths create the experience of tsunami waves that destroy homes and families, helmets shut out the world and a child creates a head that represents the man who shot his brother.

Child survivors of a tsunami in Sri Lanka

I had placed a blue cloth in the centre and waited to see what would emerge. The children began to move their arms up and down and we all began to sway spontaneously. The energy began to build and a section of the circle lunged into the centre and then another section. There was a lot of laughter, the lunging became more intense and I requested that the translator ask, 'What is the sound to this movement?' Then it came: 'Whoosh!' Others joined in. We were running in and out of the circle, hands linked: 'Whoosh!' The energy and the noise built further, bouncing off the temple walls, a sort of contained chaos. 'What's happening?' I shouted above the din. They told my translator, 'It's tsunami! Tsunami coming!'

(Debra Colkett, Chapter 7, p. 157)

A woman in a group for older people who hear voices in England

Jilly chose a roaring lion and placed it among all the other animals, where it could see everyone else and was ready to pounce. After a while she laid a lamb at its feet. She spoke about the symbolism. She spoke about her voices as being like the anger of the lion which smothers her. She told the group that her voices constantly swear at her and tell her she is responsible for all the world's disasters. She said she identified with the lamb.

Plate 1.1 Tsunami

She said she felt very vulnerable and as if her life had been sacrificed to her voices. She was also able to make a connection with her own anger which she had split off and was perhaps placed in the voices/lion.

(Jo Van Den Bosch, Chapter 6, p. 148)

A group for adolescents with HIV in South Africa

It was very quick role play. Both were sitting on chairs. Nomsa turned to Miriam.

Nomsa: Can I trust you?
Miriam: Yes.
Nomsa: I am HIV positive.
Miriam: [Giggles with hand over her mouth]
Nomsa: Did you hear me?
Miriam: Yes.
Nomsa: Well?
Miriam: Just don't tell anybody else.

(Kirsten Meyer, Chapter 5, p. 97)

A teenager in a school for pupils with emotional and behavioural difficulties in England

A boy of 13, Peter, stands under a spotlight. He is dressed in a cloak and is covered by a mask in the form of a shiny, totally black helmet, twice the height of his head. In appearance it is not unlike those worn by medieval jousting knights. The previous week he had spent over 30 minutes colouring the helmet's card in several layers of vigorously applied black wax crayon. No part of his face is visible. There is only a small slit for an eyehole. A flap is hinged over the hole, and this is attached to a string which the boy can pull down to cover his eyes completely. As he turns round slowly to the group, he says, voice muffled, 'No one can be seen unless they kneel down first in front of me.'

(Phil Jones, Chapter 6, p. 140)

A woman in individual therapy in England

The landscape came from a poem which Kia brought to therapy. She explored the feelings it engendered in her, we explored those feelings of despair, death, foolishness and failure and also explored the contrasting feelings of hope, life, laughter and trying. From this engagement Kia spent the next few sessions creating a huge painted and collaged landscape, which I witnessed. As the landscape took shape I encouraged her to tell me its story. It was split into two definite sides. On one side there was a huge slate cliff with barren trees and a dark and dangerous cave which often flooded. This place held memories of pain and tension and a large and powerful waterfall separated it from a more gentle and containing landscape. On this side the water followed more gently and within the hills there were caves to keep her character (which we had yet to meet) safe and dry. These caves also kept the character hidden as he or she did not like to be seen by people.

(Sarah Mann-Shaw, Chapter 10, p. 261)

A child from Sierra Leone

The next session Abui wanted to make a mask. He cut out a large head, stuck on wild hair and called it 'evil'. He talked quite a lot this session, decorating the mask, then trying it on himself, as if freed from the fear that this evil could harm him now.

Abui spoke of a man with powers to do harm to people in the villages, the man people feared most back home. Using the name of 'holy spirit' or 'The Dr'. The man who decided who would die and left people to burn on rubber tyres. This was the man who shot his brother in front of the whole family. I was a witness to part of the horror Abui had experienced. How could I reflect back to him anything that didn't overwhelm us both with the enormity of what he was telling me?

(Roya Dooman, Chapter 5, p. 127)

These moments from clinical work occur continents apart, with clients at the beginnings and ends of their lives. Therapists, within the research which this book draws on, provided vignettes from their practice that were followed up by analysis of the ways in which they saw the core processes at work in the therapy. As later chapters reveal, their contexts could not be more different: from dramatherapy taking place in a temple within the ruins of a tsunami-devastated village to a large National Health Service run mental health hospital in the UK, from a small school in a deprived area of a major city to a refuge for women in Sri Lanka. What unites all of these is the way drama becomes a vital part of clients encountering their lives, transforming their experience of themselves and the way they participate in the world they live in. This book and its research into the core processes at work within dramatherapy will show ways of understanding and describing why and how drama can be allied to therapy in a way of working which is as powerful as these moments illustrate.

Drama as necessary to living

In the past one hundred years the theme of drama and theatre as 'necessary' to healthy societies and healthy individuals has re-emerged. Evreinov says that theatre is 'infinitely wider than the stage' and not just for entertainment or instruction; it is 'something as essentially necessary to man as air, food and sexual intercourse' (1927: 6). This phrase is echoed across the century. Forty years later, Peter Brook seeks a theatre that is as 'necessary as eating or sex' in *The Empty Space* (1968). Schechner says of the special world created in performance, 'no society, no individual can do without it' (1988: 11). But *why* should theatre be so essential? *How* can theatre be necessary?

The general theme is not a new one. However, many societies in the twentieth and twenty-first centuries have understood its implications in particular ways. This understanding considers that participating in drama and theatre allows connections to unconscious and emotional processes to be made. Participation is seen to satisfy human needs to play and to create. The festive act of people coming together through drama and theatre is seen to have social and psychological importance. Theatre is both an activity set apart from everyday reality, while at the same time having a vital function in reflecting upon and reacting to that reality.

A theatre has been sought by practitioners such as Grotowski, Brook and Boal which can bring people together and can comment upon and deeply affect their feelings, their politics and their ways of living. I consider that dramatherapy originates from these beliefs, which see theatre as being necessary to living. This book will explore one particular way in which drama and theatre processes are essential, a part of the maintenance of well-being or a return to health.

At the beginning of the twentieth century, drama was used as a recreation, as an adjunct to the main therapeutic ways of working with people in care or health settings. The key aspects of the therapy remained outside the clients' experience of drama. Drama was seen only as a way of making stays in hospital more enjoyable, or sometimes as an opportunity to raise emotional material which would be dealt with later in the hands of the psychologist or psychiatrist.

Over the past four decades a change has come to be fully acknowledged: that the drama itself can be the therapy. This change marks the emergence of dramatherapy as it is currently practised. There are two main aspects to this change or development. One is that the dramatherapy session can deal with primary processes involved in a client's change rather than being an adjunct to other ways of working, such as psychotherapy or clinical psychology. The other is that the root of this process is in the drama. Dramatherapy is not a psychotherapy group or behavioural therapy programme which has some dramatic activities added to it. The drama does not serve the therapy. The drama process contains the therapy.

Basic tenets of dramatherapy

Definition of dramatherapy

Definitions of dramatherapy have been developed by national professional associations and regulatory bodies, by local settings meeting the specific needs of particular clinical contexts and by theoreticians (Lewis and Johnson

2000; Jones 2005; Karkou and Sanderson 2005). The broad definitions fulfil the need to define key or basic requirements that provide a general outline of what the therapy offers, to define standards for practice and training or expectations which clients can expect to be met. The local definitions create a much more tailored sense of what dramatherapy aims to be and to offer. In these the specific goals for different client groups can be seen: for example, a setting offering dramatherapy for people with autistic spectrum disorders, or for seniors dealing with dementia. A one-size-fits-all definition would ill serve clients with very different needs and capabilities. Theoreticians provide definitions which tend to connect practice with theoretical models and systems of ideas, useful in understanding the nature and identity of the therapy from a different perspective. The following material gives examples from these differing perspectives and then draws out connections between them.

The British Association of Dramatherapists offers this definition: the 'intentional use of healing aspects of drama and theatre as the therapeutic process. It is a method of working and playing that uses action methods to facilitate creativity, imagination, learning, insight and growth' (BADth 2004: 1).

US dramatherapist Emunah parallels aspects of this:

> Drama therapy is the intentional and systematic use of drama/theatre processes to achieve psychological growth and change. The tools are derived from theatre, the goals are rooted in psychotherapy. Although drama therapy can be practised within the theoretical framework of almost any existing school of psychotherapy, it also has its own unique heritage, conceptual sources theatre, psychodrama, dramatic play, dramatic ritual, role play.
>
> (Emunah 1994: 3)

Dramatherapy is involvement in drama with a healing intention. Dramatherapy facilitates change through drama processes. It uses the potential of drama to reflect and transform life experiences to enable clients to express and work through problems they are encountering or to maintain a client's well-being and health.

Clients make use of the *content* of drama activities, the *process* of creating enactments, and the *relationships* formed between those taking part in the work within a *therapeutic* framework. A connection is created between the client's inner world, problematic situation or life experience and the activity in the dramatherapy session. The client seeks to achieve a new relationship towards the problems or life experiences they bring to therapy. One client, for example, reported that dramatherapy 'helped me to think about other perspectives on situations', offering 'understanding . . . reframing . . . support' (Barry 2006: 8). The aim is to find in this new relationship resolution, relief, a new understanding or changed ways of functioning.

Who is dramatherapy for?

Dramatherapy is practised with groups and individuals in care settings such as clinics and hospitals and specialist centres such as adolescent units. It is also offered as an individual or group therapy available outside institutions. Work is undertaken with both adults and children.

Dramatherapists are employed in family centres, prisons, special schools and educational units, centres for young adults with behavioural problems, in mental health and rehabilitation settings, community centres and within alcohol or substance abuse programmes. Individual or group dramatherapy is offered to people in the community who are dealing with emotional difficulties through GP, social worker or self-referral. Karkou and Sanderson (2005: 198) report on the range of settings and contexts within the UK, Lewis and Johnson (2000) in the United States and Canada. Dramatherapy is often offered alongside other arts therapies, as part of a multidisciplinary approach.

A defined space is protected through areas such as consent, confidentiality and professional containment, as the dramatherapist operates within an appropriate code of conduct. Langley (2006: 39–49) summarises these well, emphasising the need for clarity in relation to issues such as boundaries and ethics: 'These are to ensure that the clients know what will happen, what will ensure their personal safety and that they consent to the process as a whole . . . necessary on both ethical and legal grounds' (2006: 39).

What happens in dramatherapy?

A facilitator, the dramatherapist, works with groups or individuals over a number of weeks for sessions lasting between 40 minutes and one and a half hours. Each session usually consists of a warm-up phase which develops into an active exploration of areas which are problematic for clients, followed by a closure. The kinds of issues which can be dealt with and the form of the sessions are extremely varied. The main process involves the client engaging with a problematic area through dramatic form and working with the group and/or therapist. Closure often takes the form of discussion and reflection upon the work undertaken within the session. Dramatherapy takes place within clear boundaries which protect the therapeutic space.

The basic processes of dramatherapy

A number of key processes lie at the heart of dramatherapy and they are the main ways in which therapeutic change occurs. The original edition of this book (Jones 1996) proposed them as a way of describing how dramatherapy is effective. These are discussed in detail in Chapter 5. The vignettes and analysis which follows them throughout this book have researched the way in which therapists see and use these core processes. Examples are 'dramatic projection', 'transformation' and 'playing'.

Through *dramatic projection* the client becomes emotionally and intellectually involved in encountering issues brought to therapy in dramatic forms such as characters, play materials or puppets.

Transformation describes the ways in which the client's experience of the expressed problems changes during dramatherapy work. This change is due to the use of dramatic processes to express and explore (to transform) the client's material. Transformation also comes about through experience of the relationships formed during the dramatherapy, both with the therapist and with other clients if the work is in a group. Christine Novy reflects on this in the research vignette Lynne (Chapter 5, pp. 124–125) concerning work with women who have come into conflict with the law. She talks about the profound effect that drama can have on the very way in which people see themselves. She works with the women to develop stories and characters based within the idea:

> that people's lives and identities can be represented in different ways and from varying perspectives; that the stories we or others tell about us are creations and, as such, they can be created or constructed differently. Participants in the project were invited to step out of their everyday lives and into a play space where they might creatively explore personal life stories. The process concurred with Jones' ideas about transformation in dramatherapy: 'The everyday, usual ways of experiencing the self and events are altered by the use of dramatic language ... The dramatic language can transform the experience as it opens up new possibilities of expression, feeling and association' (Jones 1996: 121).

The process can open a number of creative, altered ways of dealing with and experiencing the problem. A number of dramatherapists, such as Novy, link the efficacy of dramatherapy to another core process – *playing*, a part of which is succinctly summarised by dramatherapist Jo Van Den Bosch in the research into her dramatherapy practice, also in Chapter 5. Like Novy, she talks about the 'play space' where a client can 'try things out without consequences, and (which) ... enables both therapist and client to explore the material'.

The expressive forms of dramatherapy

Dramatherapy sessions include a wide repertoire of dramatic expressive forms. These have different therapeutic potentials as illustrated within the vignettes throughout this book. They include:

- the use of created or scripted roles and characters, or playing oneself in a fictional reality, in order to explore life experiences

- the use of materials such as objects, small toys and puppets to play out and work with problematic feelings, relationships or experiences
- the use of the body in dramatic form through disguise, masking, mime or performance art to explore the self, image, relationship
- the use of scripts, stories and myths to evoke and act out themes, personal issues or archetypal material with a view to the exploration of problems
- the creation of dramatic rituals to work through areas of life experience
- moving through different developmental stages in drama to assist in the development of new ways of relating to oneself and to others.

As the research conducted for this book indicates, dramatherapists work within and across the full expressive range of drama and theatre forms, summarized in Chapter 7 as the *play–drama continuum*. Within this research dramatherapist Clare Powis summarises the approach well and, stressing 'the fluidity of the play–drama continuum,' she says:

> This fluidity in the continuum lends itself to the path of a client's therapeutic process: sometimes the client will go one step forward – and in the next session s/he'll be two or three steps back. Confronting a difficult, hitherto unbearable feeling may result in a self-protective withdrawal or regression. And often it may be comforting to return to an early stage of sensorimotor play where there's a familiarity, and where strength can be gathered, in order to face the next challenge or process this one. Hence access to the full continuum helps to inform the therapist where the client is in his or her process. The therapist can then respond accordingly.

The basic shape

Dramatherapy is practised in a series of sessions. The aim of the shape of the session is to find a form for feelings to be explored with the intention of achieving personal change. The content of a single dramatherapy session usually happens within a basic shape or form. In any session it is necessary to find a way in which the therapeutic needs and creative potentials of the group or individual can connect with the expressive forms and processes of dramatherapy.

Some work is highly structured. Aims will be set and the dramatherapy session, content and process will be agreed with the group. Other approaches see the content and process emerge spontaneously as material brought to the session by the group or individual emerges. However, as work develops over time a dramatherapist will often have some prepared ideas based around what the group or individual has done to date; it is important to remain sensitive to the group's immediate needs and situation:

We might start with a very structured session which we might have to change on the spur of the moment, because we have to work according to the needs of the special populations. There are patients who want to perform; there are patients who want to sit and do nothing.

(Schaffner and Courtney 1981: 144)

A usual form for dramatherapy is a basic shape which divides into five sections or elements, as Box 1.1 illustrates.

The *warm-up* is an activity that helps an individual or group prepare for dramatherapeutic work. It usually takes the form of a variety of exercises that concern the emotions of the group and/or the group's use of dramatic processes or language. The warm-up often helps to mark the start of the creation of a special dramatherapy space. Langley refers to the variety of these activities: 'warm up is a prelude to "action" but action comes in many shapes and sizes' (2006: 67).

Focusing is a period when the group or individual engages more directly with the area or areas to be worked on – the subject or content of the work. Whereas the warm-up section may be general, the focusing section usually involves a move towards more specific areas. Focusing can be said to be the way in which clients arrive at a state where they are ready to explore an issue in some depth and with involvement. This section often includes negotiation as to the work which can be included within the session. It may include specific warm-up activities or preparations linked to the development of a main activity.

Within most dramatherapy sessions there is a period of time which marks an intensity of involvement. This *main activity* can involve different aspects of drama as described above in 'expressive forms'. The ways in which the intensity is shown varies between groups. For a group of people with severe learning difficulties it might be marked by an increased concentration in their work with an object – from a lack of interest to a three-minute period of focus. For another group it might be a period of sustained improvisation.

The main activity might take the form of:

• one or more individuals dealing with an issue
• a group as a whole working together with a specific theme or focus

---

Box 1.1 **Dramatherapy – the basic shape**

• Warm-up
• Focusing
• Main activity
• Closure and de-roling
• Completion

- all members of a group working on their own material with each other in small groups, pairs or in the large group.

The *closure and de-roling* phase marks the ending of the main active work involving dramatic forms. It is usual for there to be a clear point at which individuals leave or disengage from the dramatic space or activities and the ending of any audience/performer divisions. This closure period includes 'de-roling' exercises if character, role or improvisation are used. If materials such as play objects are used, this phase includes an opportunity for individuals to shift their engagement with the materials – to leave the direct, dramatic involvement. As Lili Levy says, in one of the research conversations in Chapter 9: 'In Dramatherapy we work in the connection between fantasy and reality, so it is fundamental after the client finishes exploring and enacting their fantasies, to de-role; that means to find a way to leave behind and separate themselves from the role he or she has played in order to prepare herself/himself face the reality or outside world.' If group activities have taken place then 'closure' is a time for group dramatic relationships to be ended.

Completion is a crucial aspect of dramatherapy. It is an activity separate from the immediate disengagement from the main involvement in drama which constitutes the closure stage; it is also separate from de-roling. Completion has two main components. The first is a space for further integration of the material dealt with during the main activity. The second is the preparation for leaving the dramatherapy space. Integration can take a purely verbal or a dramatic form such as a reflective game or activity. In some cases it might involve discussion of the work: the making of personal connections and sharing of perceptions and feelings. In Chapter 12 (p. 313) the research into the core processes in Naomi Gardner's work stresses how important this can be for some clients: 'It would perhaps have been difficult for them to make connections with their own lives while they were still in role. However, on discussing the differences and similarities they shared with their roles, after the drama, the group began to assimilate the different aspects of themselves as seen within their characters.' For some groups completion might be a time of internal reflection, so the period might be spent partly or wholly in silence.

The length of each section varies according to the way a group uses dramatherapy. In many cases the warm-up and focusing will take up a third of the time, the main activity another third, and closure, de-roling and completion the last third. However, as a group develops the warm-up time may be reduced. The description of the session in Chapter 12 (p. 317) can be seen to illustrate these different elements at work.

Dramatherapy and meaning

Drama and theatre are social activities. As O'Neill and Lambert have said, an important facet of drama is social and involves 'contact, communication and the negotiation of meaning' (1982: 13). The discovery and communication of meaning in dramatherapy is a key concept within my analysis of, and research into, how dramatherapy is effective for clients. Important aspects of the relationship between dramatherapy, meaning and the client include the ways in which:

- life experiences are given *added validity* by depicting them dramatically with, and in front of, others
- an individual's dramatic work is *recognised and understood* by others; the feelings and experiences they depict are empathised with and responded to by others
- the process of dealing with life problems through enactment leads to the creation of a *vital relationship between the client's life experiences outside the dramatherapy and the enactments they take part in within the therapy*.

By establishing a link between the client's life experiences and the dramatherapy, the possibility is created of finding new meanings in their lives through the playful, experimental space of dramatherapy. This is described in detail in Chapter 5 within the 'Life Drama Connection' section. Laurel of the Japanese Atari Research Division, has documented the positive potentials of virtual reality through computer graphics. She sees this in terms of the relationship between the process of finding meaning and the creation of dramatic worlds. Laurel argues that virtual reality creates access to areas of:

> meanings that are only rarely afforded by the real world. Dramatically constructed worlds are controlled experiments, where the bare bones of human choice and situation are revealed . . . If we can make such worlds interactive, where a user's choices and actions can flow through the dramatic lens, then we will enable an exercise of the imagination, intellect and spirit of an entirely new order.
>
> (Laurel 1991: 14)

This can be seen to be parallel with the qualities attributed to drama and play by many authors (e.g. Casson 1997; Langley 2006). Pitruzzella (2004: 70), for example, summarises this way of looking: 'Dramatic reality, which possesses a "transitional" quality founded upon "as if", is the physical and mental place where mimetic relationships can be enacted without irreversible consequences for the life of the person.' Emunah (2000: 75) states that 'central to much dramatherapy work is the idea that the space, relationships and activities within the drama [*is*] a rehearsal for life'.

Ruth Goodman, in the research into her practice contained within the vignette 'Bilal', (Chapter 10, p. 260), sees her work in a way that echoes Laurel:

> I think, essentially, therapy is about the presence of a willing witness/ listener. It is also a continuous creative process of trying to find meaning through and within the therapeutic relationship. The connections made

between Bilal and myself enabled him to begin to reconnect with dislocated parts of himself, his feelings and experiences. The wonderful thing about dramatherapy is that, as well as being witnesses, we can also be co-creators, playmates and engage creatively with whatever roles we are cast into or choose to play for a particular purpose. When someone has been traumatized, the recovery of meaning can take a long time. I believe that although my role was to help Bilal find meaning in his story, it was fundamentally to stay alongside him through the processes of telling and all the complex feelings that emerged.

This aspect of constructing dramatic therapeutic 'controlled experiments' is an important way for the client to find meaning in their world and to deal with problems they are encountering. Many clients' accounts referred to in this book echo the properties within dramatherapy which enable people to create experiments, alternative ways of looking at themselves and their lives. The women working with Christine Novy, described in the research into dramatherapy practice in Chapter 5, for example, bear testimony to this as they say: 'I don't see things in the same way', 'I am beginning to take my life back in hand', and, 'to make choices that suit me' after their work playing fantasy roles.

Building blocks: creativity, play, drama and healing

Dramatherapy builds upon the healing aspects that are present in dramatic and theatrical activities. Generally speaking these healing aspects are based in the processes of creativity, playing and acting. Klaesi (1922) and Müller-Thalheim (1975) have put forward the idea that creativity has within it inherent self-healing processes. Müller-Thalheim discusses this specifically in relation to people in psychotic states, but considers some general implications. These include the Freudian notion that creative products are formed from elementary impulses from the unconscious, rather like dreams. However, he goes further than framing creative expressions as symptoms, which Freud seems to consider as the main quality of art. Müller-Thalheim sees 'inspiration, change, new combinations, new actions' (1975: 164) as inherent to much creativity, and claims that these are central to health and to development from ill health or problematic conditions. He indicates a natural healing process involved in art making. As an example he discusses Ernst Josephson's use of a few symbols in painting: 'His paintings seemed not only to reproduce his difficulties, but also to free him from them' (1975: 165).

His faith here is in the natural healing potential within the artistic medium and process. This lies in the healing value of creative expression and the value of playfulness as a way of creating new insights. In addition he suggests that expressing problematic material and emotions through the arts changes the relationship to the problems or feelings. For example, 'Real fear is being converted into fictional fear' (Müller-Thalheim 1975: 166) and is, therefore, more able to be faced, talked about and dealt with. He believes in the arts as a counterbalance of 'sense and order' against the 'nonsense and disorder' (1975: 166) which many people experience in distress or illness.

Whilst his notions of artistic activity and experience are romantic and culture specific, there are a number of points here that have been developed by empirical research and which are pertinent to dramatherapy: the emphasis upon the healing potential inherent in creative processes; the notion of playfulness; the creation of imaginary or fictive representations of emotions as being useful in the healing process of therapy.

Drama and therapy have been linked by a number of people from different disciplines. Peter Elsass, for example, notes an 'apparent similarity' between the work of the actor and that of the psychotherapist. He identifies this connection as the aim of creating new insights or making implicit knowledge explicit for audience or for patient (Elsass 1992). Antinucci-Mark notes that theatre and psychotherapy are 'from similar roots and meet similar needs' (1986: 15). She notes that both involve an interplay between fantasy and reality, the manipulation of internal objects and images and the creation of an 'as if' scenario in terms of time and place (1986: 15).

However, such connections do not usually go beyond acknowledging a parallel in order to understand aspects of theatre or psychotherapy. For example, Antinucci-Mark does not take her exploration beyond noting the parallel. Elsass uses it as a point to begin a consideration of shamanism. Indeed, he says in his conclusion that theatre 'is not like therapy' but that it is a useful analogy to make (1992: 342).

Dramatherapy is more than an acknowledgement of the connections between therapy and theatre. It takes the parallels or similarities and actively seeks to bring about a new form of therapy which builds on the relationship, as this book and the research into dramatherapy practice it contains will show.

Therapeutic change and dramatherapy: how psychological disturbance is construed

One of the simplest definitions of therapy is that it is a form of intervention aiming to bring about personal change. The nature of this change within dramatherapy practice in part reflects the setting of the work and the orientation of the dramatherapist. In research the major influences cited by dramatherapists reflected the variety of ways in which dramatherapy is practised. Dramatherapists cited group dynamics theory, psychotherapy, theories of play, the work of Jung, Winnicott, Rogers, Freud and Klein, for example. Psychodrama is cited as an influence 'which many dramatherapists now see as a sub-division of dramatherapy' (Fontana and Valente 1993: 63). Dramatherapy's capacity to connect effectively with different approaches to therapeutic change is reflected in the literature. Examples of this aspect of dramatherapy's variety range from work in conjunction with cognitive behavioural therapy (Rubenstein 2005) to a psychoanalytic approach (Chaplin Kinder 2005), from practice rooted in Jung and ritual (Hougham 2006) to role theory (Landy 1994).

This diversity is also noted by Dokter. She asserts that differing cultural notions of drama and healing result in different treatment orientations based on culturally specific concepts of illness (1993). In developing a critique of dramatherapy in different contexts, she critically comments upon a tendency to see dramatherapy within an 'either/or' framework. This sees it either as 'a form of psychotherapy' or 'a creative healing art form in itself' (1993: 89). In line with Dokter, I do not see the division as necessarily present in the way that dramatherapy is practised. Currently, dramatherapy functions within a number of theoretical and therapeutic paradigms. As the book will demonstrate, it serves within behavioural frameworks as successfully as it does within family therapy, or within dynamic psychotherapy contexts. Hougham talks about the context in the following way:

> We notice a leaning towards short term interventions and cognitive and behavioural solutions. All can be important, necessary and effective. But if we ... address some of the underlying factors in psychological disturbance through looking at culture, religion and myth, we may find some deeper causes.
>
> (2006: 4)

He points to the tradition of drama as therapy influenced by Jung in working towards a therapy that moves 'beyond technique and towards a study of the soul and the religious function' and by theatre practitioners such as Grotowski and Schechner typified by him as seeing the stage as 'less a representation of the world, and more a place to explore myth and the inner images of the self' (2006: 4).

As the points made by Dokter and Hougham suggest, the ways in which psychological disturbances are construed vary widely. It could be that at some point in the future dramatherapy theory and practice might develop or work with one particular model of the mind, or become attached to one particular school of thought concerning the ways in which the individual or group experiences psychological distress. This is not the case at the moment.

Authors such as Ciornai (1983) and Canda (1990) have stressed the importance of cultural and socio-economic factors in considering change within the arts therapies. Ciornai places emphasis upon the need to orientate work within the cultural and social background of the client. She notes the possibility of areas such as oppression, discrimination and poverty being overlooked in therapeutic approaches which focus exclusively on intrapsychic factors. The need is to balance internal and external factors affecting the client's life (1983: 64). Both authors emphasise the necessity for therapists to be conscious of their own cultural assumptions about the expressive forms used within the arts therapies. Clients' expressions and intentions through dramatic form may operate within cultural traditions which differ from those of the therapist. Ciornai and Canda both advocate the necessity for arts therapists to 'provide service in a manner that is accessible and meaningful to the client' (Canda 1990: 58). This entails the need for the therapist to be 'culturally literate', contextualising the work within accurate cultural knowledge, positive regard for cultural diversity, practical cross-cultural communication skills and familiarity with relevant artistic expressive forms and traditions (Ciornai 1983: 65; Canda 1990: 58).

As Chapter 5 illustrates, key processes in dramatherapy are constant and there are basic assumptions about how dramatherapy can facilitate change. The task of the dramatherapist is to comprehend how these basic processes and expressive forms connect with the context of the work. This context includes the situation within which the client lives – the impact of factors such as poverty and oppression, the ways in which the client presents or sees an issue or difficulty and the philosophy or ethos of the setting or framework in which the therapy will be undertaken.

The contexts of dramatherapy

Kirsten Meyer's work in South Africa with children and teenagers who are HIV positive, as the research in Chapter 5 shows, demonstrates the social and political diversity and complexity which dramatherapy encounters. In addition, her practice reveals the challenges as well as the importance of trying to respond to local needs and contexts. Her work involves group therapy as part of a project that was set up between Zakheni Arts Therapy Foundation, a funding body HopeHIV (UK based) and a perinatal HIV research unit. Meyer says:

> What we found at the end of the year was that it is not possible to work with children unless we are also working with their caregivers. There is a large amount of stigmatisation of HIV in South Africa. Our government has denied it for a long time. Disclosure is a big issue and many people are very frightened of talking about it. In addition it is against our constitution to divulge anyone's status without their consent, and children need their guardian's consent. One child I worked with was basically driven from his community with his mother because she openly disclosed their status. The caregivers are often frightened, as they do not know how to answer the questions the children may ask. Sometimes a child will find out his/her status by mistake, or just put two and two together: often much to the relief of the caregiver as she/he does then not have to deal with their questions. Another child who had been disclosed to was open about her status at school. Before this she was often bullied by other children who used to take her sandwiches away. After her disclosure she thought the others liked her more now, because they no longer took

her food, but in fact their caregivers had told them never to touch her because she was HIV. Needless to say, the work is complex.

We decided to run children's groups alongside caregivers' groups (which are run by a social worker and an HIV counsellor). This seems to work much better as the caregivers are given a space to dialogue around disclosure and their feelings surrounding their status if they are HIV positive. Most of the caregivers are grandmothers and aunts, as many of the children's parents have died of HIV, and sometimes they need a space to express feelings around the loss of their own child before they can engage with their grandchild's/niece's status.

Here is very directly illustrated the ways in which practice is connected to the nexus of poverty, political and government attitudes towards HIV and people who are positive, the legacy of apartheid, western government and drug industry involvement, cultural attitudes and intergenerational attitudes, alongside processes such as bullying and stigmatisation. As Meyer points out, the impacts are varied and far reaching, with the therapist and the organisations facilitating the therapy responding to these needs as best they can:

> Providing psychodynamic therapy in deprived and under-resourced communities in SA often means rethinking aspects of the therapeutic framework. With this particular group it was necessary, in setting up the project, to provide transport money for caregiver and adolescent to and from the clinic, as well as sandwiches and juice. This raises many questions for therapists (providing money and food), not to mention difficult countertransference issues, but the reality of working in our country is that unemployment is high, and when such basic needs are not met, how does one begin to work with emotions? Secondly, antiretroviral medication has many side effects and it is important to manage nutrition as well. Thirdly, if transport money is not offered, there is no way of getting to the group.

A number of practitioners and authors have indicated the particular importance of the nature and role of the context in which dramatherapy is practised. This consists of the complex of social, economic, cultural, religious and political factors which surround and interweave within the clinical encounter, as Meyer's account testifies. Dokter, for example has looked at the ways in which religious differences, ethnicity and cultural diversity relate to each other and feature in practice (Dokter 2000, 2005, 2005/6). The practice Meyer analyses in Chapter 5 (p. 97) deepens the ways in which the relationship between the therapy and the context within which it is practised can be understood. Issues regarding this relationship are considered in a variety of ways within the clinical and theoretical material in this book.

Past and current models of dramatherapy

As Chapters 2 and 3 will show, the way in which drama has been perceived in terms of therapy has changed radically. Courtney has described the current variety of models within the arts therapies as a whole, and says of drama-therapy: 'Even within the one form . . . there are major differences of approach' (1988: 192). The definition of what dramatherapy is and how it is effective can be especially problematic. As Landy has pointed out, 'because both drama and therapy are conceptually complex terms, confusions are inevitable' (1982: 135).

This book defines dramatherapy in its entirety. It does not seek to separate out different aspects into models. Rather, it defines and analyses the key processes which operate within dramatherapy and shows how they can be used in different ways according to the needs of the client group or context. Hence, *the basic processes are constant* and are utilised in different ways according to specific client need. The processes are defined initially in Chapter 5, but the understanding of how they operate underpins the whole book. The research that this book contains concerns the ways in which the field, in its practice and publication, has responded to the idea of core processes. By working in this way I aim to describe these core processes and to examine how, in the decade since their first publication, the field has used and developed them in relation to dramatherapy practice and the theory which supports work with clients.

Part II

2 From amphitheatre to operating theatre?

Drama, theatre and therapy – a history

> The theatre cures the actors. It can also cure the audience.
>
> Evreinov, *The Theatre In Life*

Introduction: three histories

How has dramatherapy come into being? This chapter describes the background to the emergence of the intentional use of drama as a therapy. Chapter 3 describes the evolution of the term, practice and profession of the dramatherapist. There are three kinds of history relating to drama as therapy.

Healing, drama, theatre

The first involves the general, historical uses of theatre and drama in ways that we would now interpret as being to do with healing, or as having a healing function. This history has importance in the examination of the roots of the twentieth-century development of dramatherapy. This chapter outlines a brief history of these ideas and practices.

A twentieth-century context

The second involves the evolution of new attitudes towards therapy and theatre that created the environment which made it possible for dramatherapy to exist. This could be described as the 'immediate prehistory' of the emergence of drama as a specific therapy within twentieth-century Europe and the USA. The increasing awareness of, and contact between, other cultures and different models of health and 'drama' add to this 'new attitude'. It is, therefore, also important to examine the way in which the potentials seen and used in theatre during this period are viewed by non-Western or non-European cultures. This chapter includes the illustration of the history of a hospital theatre as an example of this context. In addition, it features an overview of the work of Iljine, Evreinov and Moreno. Though the influence of Moreno had been acknowledged in dramatherapy literature, the first edition of this book noted that the challenging and innovative work of Iljine and Evreinov had been lost to the field. It is worth acknowledging the subsequent 're-discovering' of these forefathers being placed alongside Moreno in the 'early twentieth century development of drama therapy' (Landy 2001: 6), and further scholarly research into their work in articles such as 'Evreinoff and Moreno: monodrama and psychodrama, parallel developments of Hidden Influences?' (Casson 1999) and in Karkou and Sanderson's account of the emergence of the arts therapies (2005).

The emergence of dramatherapy

The third involves the specific emergence of the term 'dramatherapy' and the practice of dramatherapy which occurs mainly in postwar western Europe and in the USA. This history is discussed in Chapter 3.

Healing, drama, theatre

The earliest documented use of the term 'dramatherapy' in the UK occurs in Peter Slade's 1939 lecture to the British Medical Association (see Chapter 3 for details). In the USA one of the earliest recorded uses of the term in reference to contemporary practice is by Florsheim (1946) in a paper delivered at a meeting of the American Occupational Therapy Association entitled 'Drama Therapy'. However, the notion of the intentional therapeutic use of drama and theatre is much older than this, both within the UK and in western culture as a whole.

Aristotle proposed that the function of tragedy was to induce the emotional and spiritual state of catharsis – a release of deep feelings that originally had a connotation of purification of the senses and the soul. The method by which the emotions of pity and terror are evoked is 'mimesis' – a combination of vicarious participation and suspension of disbelief (Aristotle 1961). His work formally established a theme that recurs throughout the history of writing about theatre and one that is relevant to the relationship which drama as therapy has to theatre.

The theme can be characterised as drama having a unique and direct relationship with human feelings, and as being able to produce change in people's lives. At different times in history different kinds of change have been emphasised – from religious to political change, from an individual's psychological make-up to mass societal change. One contemporary way of understanding the processes that Aristotle discussed is to see this 'change' in terms of healing. Goodman summarises this approach when he says that tragedy is said to have the effect of purging us of pent up and hidden negative emotions, or of 'administering measured doses of the killer virus to prevent or mitigate the ravages of actual attack' (1981: 246).

Traditions such as the medieval Feast of Fools, the Roman Saturnalia and survivals of ancient customs, such as the Padstow Horse or the 'Reign of the

Wild Men' on the eve of St Nicholas' Day in the Bavarian mountains, are often considered within a framework of catharsis – of a healthy psychological and emotional 'release' for individuals, groups and communities (Southern 1962; Turner 1974; Landy 1986; Jennings 1987). The past history of other cultures is often considered within a similar framework – of looking at ritual and rite as a form of drama concerned with healing (Turner 1974: 37). An example of this is Fryrear and Fleshman's consideration of the Seneca Indians and the Iroquois Confederacy's 'False Face Society' curing and carving masks as elements of dramatic processes used therapeutically (1981: 11). One of the key US dramatherapy theorists, Richard Courtney, has analysed the enactment of the ritual myths of Sumer, Babylon, Abydos and Edfu in ways that connect to the central concerns of dramatherapy (1988: 135).

Solomon's description of ancient drama, ritual and rite in relation to contemporary notions of therapy and human psychology sums up the general stance often taken in dramatherapy. He says that although, as an art form, drama has had a varied development, psychologically it has always possessed similar or identical 'inherent qualities and power' (1950: 247). From this viewpoint he says that there is a great similarity between the aims and effects of 'primitive religious rites and rituals' and the uses of drama and theatre in therapy.

This way of interpreting past history or the practices of non-western cultures is difficult, in that it has a tendency to impose inappropriate contemporary notions and concepts upon practices and forms. As Innes (1993) has pointed out, one of the cultural phenomena of the twentieth century was 'primitivism'. This can be summarised as the desire to escape from 'complex' contemporary industrial or post-industrial culture to a notional more 'simple' state. The tendency is to project this need on to other cultures or to project it into the past. A distortion can occur as a tradition or practice is given a false contemporary interpretation. Hence, it can be problematic to describe the forms of other or earlier cultures – forms often thought of as 'ritual' – in terms of being a kind of dramatherapy.

Elsass, for example, routinely runs together psychoanalysis, contemporary theatre and shamanism in one sentence concerning 'shamanistic healing': 'Like the psychoanalyst, the shaman acts as protagonist in the drama' (1992: 338). This type of comparison, frequently made in dramatherapy theory, draws together concepts and cultures in a way that does not adequately justify whether such parallels can be made. There is a danger of attributing motives and concepts which are twentieth and twenty-first century western notions upon systems where they simply are not present.

However, there is a tradition of theatre and drama being directly and overtly linked to healing processes. As Mora (1957) has pointed out, the history of healing and theatre and drama is a long one. He cites as an example Caelius Aurelius who, in his fifth century AD treatise 'On Acute Diseases and on Chronic Diseases', advocates that the 'patient' suffering from madness should see a stage performance. He divides up particular theatrical forms according to the type of illness. If the patient's madness involves 'dejection' then a mime is suitable; if the condition involves 'playful childishness' then a play depicting sadness or tragedy is needed. The mental disturbance must be matched by an opposition in the aesthetics of the play to help attain a 'balanced state of health' (Mora 1957: 267–269). The patient then progresses to delivering speeches according to the same principles.

Both Aristotle and Aurelius saw there to be powerful healing potentials in theatre and in drama. From existing records and documentation, the difference between historical pre-twentieth-century uses of drama and theatre and that of the late twentieth century lies chiefly in the systems in which healing was practised. The twentieth century marks the emergence in Europe and the United States of a form of practice named dramatherapy, which operates within the central health services and provision and within specific notions of health and healing.

The meeting of drama and therapy: a twentieth-century context

In the late nineteenth century and throughout the twentieth, new attitudes towards mental health, theories of the mind and the emotions developed. This was paralleled by attempts to find new ways of approaching the treatment of people who were unwell. In the same period a spirit of experimentation radically altered the ways in which drama and theatre were seen and used. These changes occurred separately. Prior to the twentieth century, in the west it was unusual for the spheres of theatre and health to have a formal connection. In most industrialised countries, for example, the aid of people who were unwell was seen as a medical concern that was usually separated from theatre and drama, which were seen as forms of entertainment. The changes in the fields of health and theatre meant that a connection often assumed to be used in other cultures could be developed, some would say redeveloped, in the west.

Although theatres existed in psychiatric hospitals for centuries, the twentieth century saw an enormous increase in the presence of theatre and drama in hospitals. Another area of development was in the work of three individuals – Iljine, Evreinov and Moreno – in establishing forms of treatment or therapy with drama as a primary means of change. The radical innovations in experimental theatre, educational drama, psychotherapy, the study of play, anthropological study of ritual, cross-cultural contact and the development of the field of dramaturgy in sociology all made important connections between the potentials of drama and direct change in people's lives.

This section documents some of the ways in which this contact between drama and therapy began to emerge; the way a 'twentieth-century context' formed. A series of different contexts will be described: hospital theatre, twentieth-century theatre, early pioneers – Evreinov, Iljine and Moreno – and developments in therapy and education.

Context: hospital theatre

There is evidence that some of the early European asylums had theatre facilities, though this was by no means the norm. In the eighteenth century a move towards reforming attitudes and treatment of people with mental health problems resulted in 'Moral Therapy' which involved occupational and some artistic activity for patients (Fryrear and Fleshman 1981: 13). Many patients were still locked in prisons or workhouses, especially the poor. The majority of asylums in nineteenth-century Britain, for example, were places with very few facilities. There were exceptions. Ticehurst Asylum, founded in eighteenth-century England and 'favoured with the aristocracy', had fortnightly concerts with as many as 36 patients taking part. Also 'an excellent theatre with scenery' was constructed for the use of patients in an environment 'to restore health to diseased minds' (Souall 1981: 207). Coulmier, director of the asylum of Charenton outside Paris, worked with his patients using theatre productions between 1797 and 1811. De Sade was an inmate of Charenton and wrote and directed a number of these productions. By the mid-nineteenth century a number of the large asylums were being built with theatres as part of the main structure. Casson has researched this area in further detail, writing of work such as Goethe's play *Lila* (1775–1777), in which a 'Dr Verazio directs improvised drama in which friends and relatives play the roles of Lila's delusions and hallucinations' as the 'healing through dramatic action of a woman suffering a psychotic grief reaction'(Casson 2004: 55).

Fryrear and Fleshman say that most psychiatric institutions were at best involved in caretaking and this situation was the prevailing one well into the 1940s in many countries. They suggest that the groundwork for the arts therapies lies in the arts and crafts movement in hospitals as part of occupational therapy. These activities were introduced after World War I in parts of Europe and the US. This period also marked the beginnings of 'recreational therapy' (Fryrear and Fleshman 1981: 14).

This emphasis upon the recreational or occupational aspects of drama and theatre activities is evident in much work in hospitals during the mid-twentieth century. Examples include the community theatre which was begun in 1943 by Gibson, the Riggs Theatre at Austen Riggs psychiatric centre, Stockbridge, Massachusetts. Later Brookes produced *The Persecution and Assassination of Jean-Paul Marat as Performed by the Inmates of the Asylum of Charenton Under the Direction of the Marquis de Sade* in Austen Riggs psychiatric centre (Brookes 1975). Chase, working with women in the St Elizabeth's Hospital, in the United States producing *Hotel Saint Elizabeth*, about their lives in the hospital, is another example. However, Mazor (1966) notes that some of those involved in hospital theatre in the 1930s and 1940s saw a more exciting potential for these productions. Reider, Olinger and Lyle (1939), for example, stress amateur dramatics as 'outlets for . . . unconscious strivings', while Price and Nagle note that theatre performance 'unconsciously brings about a socialising effect in both hospital personnel and patients' (1943). Insights such as these mark the beginnings of significant changes in the understanding of the potentials of drama.

A history of a hospital theatre – Julio de Matos, Lisbon

As described above, the tradition of theatres in psychiatric hospitals existed in many parts of Europe. The history of the theatre at Hospital Julio de Matos in Lisbon from the 1930s is not untypical in terms of its structure and usage. Initially built as a part of the recreational services of the hospital, the idea was to create a self-sufficient community according to notions of asylum, whereby the hospital had within its walls a bakery, a tannery and fields in which to grow its own crops. The theatre was part of this process – a centre for entertainment within the life of the hospital.

Later, in 1968, theatre activity involving patients in performances was initiated. A theatre director, João Silva, was invited in by a group of psychiatrists motivated and influenced in part by the writings of Foulkes and Moreno. Initially the director worked with clients with a mainly recreational purpose – staff and patients participating together. The initiative was integrated into a 'cultural group' and club within Julio de Matos. Play scripts were chosen by staff for the group to work with. Fifteen patients took part. Some of these patients were diagnosed as schizophrenic, most were psychotic, though some had depressive illnesses. The performances were internal within the hospital. Both were seen as being mainly recreational in purpose. Hospital psychiatrists worked with the director to support and inform the way he worked.

In 1970, however, a change occurred and the play performed was written by one of the patients – *Caleidocopio* by Eduardo Gama. The play dealt with his own experiences as a patient and the problems he had encountered with his family, the hospital and Portuguese society. The client's play was critical of his experience of the hospital, the professionals there and the military government of the time. The play text was registered with the Portuguese authors' society. It was performed twice and open to the general public.

At this time, however, Portugal was ruled by a military junta and artistic expression, along with many other forms of social and political activity, was governed by censorship and strong repression. There was no formal complaint from the censors. However, communication was sent through the Ministry of Health to the hospital administration indicating that such work should not be allowed. The existence of the group was called into question and the theatre activity threatened with closure. Plays were to be sent to the Censorship Commission for approval prior to performance. In 1971, in response to the threats, the staff chose to confront the censors by choosing Bernardo Santereno's *A Traição do Padre Martinho [The Treason of Father Martinho]* and the censors forbade the performance.

The political climate in Portugal has changed to democracy with an accompanying freedom of expression and the role of drama and theatre has expanded within the hospital. Since the mid-1970s there has been the development of psychodrama, playback theatre and dramatherapy. As well as dramatic productions, patients are regularly involved in psychodrama and the occupational therapy department provides dramatherapy for patients. Individual staff have had contact with Moreno's ideas and practices and with dramatherapy work in England. This contact has helped to encourage ideas and develop the hospital's provision.

In the history of Julio de Matos, then, the initial use of the theatre is for recreational purposes. This is followed by the involvement of patients in performance and writing processes. More recently this had been added to by the uses of drama as a direct therapy in the forms of dramatherapy and psychodrama. Many hospitals and institutions have also seen such a shift: a gradual development in the range of drama and theatre processes involved in work with clients. The range includes the move from drama as recreation alone to drama having a primary role in the therapeutic programme.

The practice of creating performances within health settings is still extant. As the next chapter shows, this area of cultural activity has an important place in the development of dramatherapy. For example, professionals and patients alike were able to discover, in working with this area of theatre and drama, potentials and effects which were wider than those of recreation or artistic expression. These discoveries related to therapeutic change, and would lead to some individuals attempting to find ways to hone the therapeutic possibilities of drama.

Context: twentieth-century theatre and therapy

The tradition of experimentation in theatre and drama during the twentieth century is relevant to the development of drama as a therapy. The most important facet of this tradition is the establishment of certain themes in experimental theatre. This made it possible to view theatre and dramatic processes in a way which helped to open up the possibility that they could be powerfully therapeutic. Another important aspect is the development of certain methodologies, approaches and techniques in theatre training, rehearsal, research and performance out of which the language and techniques of dramatherapy have developed.

The key schools and approaches include the psychological approach to character construction and performance developed by people such as Stanislavski; the emphasis upon political change and representational theatre and *Verfremdungseffekt* of the Brechtian approach to theatre; the theories of Artaud; along with the experiments of Brook and Grotowski.

Later on, the new political theatre born in the 1960s and Boal's work are also important. Their relevance lies in the emphasis they laid upon the role and potential of drama to change society and people's lives as seen by the achievements of feminist, black, lesbian, gay and disability theatre.

This section briefly outlines three themes in experimental theatre relevant to the development of the notion of a form of drama which can result in personal change. It also touches on the development of particular acting techniques related to dramatherapy's way of using drama and theatre.

Memory, the unconscious, empathy and character

The work of Stanislavski at the Moscow Arts Theatre initiated an approach to creating theatrical roles that stressed the ways in which memory, the actor's individual unconscious and the portrayal of feeling could effectively connect. One of the cornerstones of acting described in 'Building a Character' concerns the 'psycho-technique'. The actor creates a physical and emotional state in themselves in order for inner feelings to emerge from the 'subconscious' into the portrayal of the role (Magarschack 1950: 274). The importance lies in a chain of empathy. An actress sees or experiences someone encountering a particular feeling or encounters something in her own life. In creating a role she tries to enter into a state where she can re-create this feeling. The technique involves a series of exercises to create an emotional state whereby an unconscious memory or feeling can enter back into her. In turn the idea is that the accurate re-creation of this feeling will enable the audience to connect through empathy with her, and be involved and moved by the drama. These themes are reflected in dramatherapy's work linking character and life experiences, as Chapter 8 describes.

An important link in Stanislavski's work is formed between the actress or actor's life, the individual's experience of it, the storage of unconscious material, and the creation on stage and in rehearsal of a system by which the actor or actress enters into an emotional state based in their own life experiences. Stanislavski's stress upon rehearsal and the development of character through improvisation was also innovatory and influential.

Transgression and change

Another strand of experimental theatre has concerned itself with different kinds of transgression. Theatre is seen as violating and transforming everyday reality. Theoreticians and practitioners of this form of theatre often claim that they are returning to the origins of drama by rediscovering its religious and mystic roots. Its forms and inspiration are found in carnival, ritual, rite and subversion. This movement can be seen in the late nineteenth century symbolist movement with their attempts to create an unconscious dream world upon the stage; echoed by Artaud in *The Theatre and Its Double* in his search for a 'universal language that unites the total . . . space . . . to the hidden interior life' (Artaud 1958: 65).

This search and approach can be traced through many of the experimental theatre companies and projects in the twentieth century – it is present in Brook's travels in Africa in the 1970s and in both Grotowski's 'Poor Theatre' of the 1960s and his Paratheatrical activities in the 1970s and 1980s. Barrault's practical experiments (1974), performance art and Barba's Odin Theatre (Barba and Savarese 1991) are other notable examples. In these approaches ritual forms of expression and working are stressed. There is a move away from narrative, character and script to an approach that looks at the creation of a situation where 'the stage ceases to be a physical representation of the world and becomes a projection of myth or the . . . inner self' (Innes 1993: 36).

Theatre, distance, disturbance, revolution

Political theatre, in particular the methodologies of Brecht and Boal, has been important in the development of connections between theatre and change. In the 1930s Brecht formulated an approach and a set of theories of performance. These advocate theatre's potential to create direct political change in society and in the life of individuals attending performances. A series of techniques such as *Verfremdungseffekt* and the ideas of Epic Theatre were devised to effect this change. The *Verfremdungseffekt is* central to Brecht's work and can be characterised in the following way: the actor does not enter into an empathic relationship with character and audience, but seeks to remain a reader, making personal political judgements and comments on the action and text of a play. This process also seeks to encourage the audience to remain alert, critical, thoughtful.

These techniques have been widely used in subsequent theatre of the political left. The idea that a political theatre can achieve direct change in the lives of its performers and audience has been taken up by the left in a number of countries, particularly in the 1960s and 1970s. Groups based on this belief include: 7:84 (formed in 1971), Welfare State (1968); feminist theatre such as the Monstrous Regiment (1976) or the Women's Theatre Group (1974); lesbian and gay theatre such as Gay Sweatshop (1975); black theatre such as the Black Theatre of Brixton and Temba; and disabled-led theatre groups such as Graeae. These and other groups have tackled direct political, social and personal issues and thus attempted to create change and social revolution.

Since the 1970s Boal (1979) has developed a political theatre methodology which seeks to assist individuals in changing their lives. Boal's Theatre of the Oppressed and Forum Theatre see drama as a way of achieving direct change in people's lives. Methods are devised to enable this to occur, and performance is used as a tool to work towards personal and social revolution.

Theories of the unconscious and drama, the notions of transformation, areas such as distancing and emotional sincerity in acting have contributed to dramatherapy theory (Landy 1986; Jennings 1987). In addition, during the 1970s and 1980s the development and refinement of specific techniques such as distancing or enrolement have been influenced by the work of Stanislavski, Brecht and Boal. These areas are discussed in more detail in Chapters 8 and 11. Specific ways of working in dramatherapy have been linked to the innovators described above. Jennings *et al* (1994) have written about work related to Artaud; Jones in relation to Grotowski and experimental theatre (1991); and Mitchell on the theatre of Peter Brook as a 'model' for dramatherapy (1990).

Context: early pioneers – Evreinov, Iljine, Moreno

Evreinov and theatrotherapy

In revolutionary Russia a number of new theories and experiments in theatre emerged at the beginning of the twentieth century. Many of these have relevance to dramatherapy in that they helped create ways of understanding and approaching theatre and dramatic practices which reframe the purpose and technique of theatre. One of the innovators working in Soviet theatre at this time articulated a formal connection between theatre and therapy in the modern era with his description of 'Theatrotherapy', as Nazaroff translates it. This innovator was the director and author Nikolai Evreinov (1879–1953) who produced a series of pamphlets and monographs between 1915 and 1924. These included 'The Theatre for Oneself' in St Petersburg (in three parts 1915–1917), 'Theatrical Innovations' (1922) and 'The Theatre in the Animal Kingdom' (1924). A collection of his works was translated and published in the USA in 1927 as *The Theatre In Life* and includes a description of his key concept of 'Monodrama' (1927: 187) and of 'Theatrotherapy' (1927: 122). Golub has described him as 'one of the first and most insistent modern exponents of the will to play as an instinct basic to mankind, and therefore the theatre as not a pastime but a necessity' (1984: 212).

Evreinov's ideas are very similar to most of the current basic tenets of dramatherapy. Unlike most theatre practitioners both before and since his time, he did not put too much emphasis on the creation of theatrical products. Instead he focused upon internal and psychological processes involved in acting. The key ideas outlined in his work in terms of drama as therapy are:

- theatre as a therapy for actors and audience
- theatre as an instinct
- theatre and play linked as necessary to the development of intelligence
- the stage management of life.

Evreinov characterised theatre as entertainment, instruction and aesthetic enjoyment, with the theatre of public spectacles such as military and state functions and even the ritual of the operating theatre as examples of 'a commercial exploitation of my instinctive liking for theatre' (1927: 6). He puts forward the idea that our relationship to theatre is in many important ways 'pre-aesthetic'. By this he means that it 'is something as essentially necessary to man as air, food, and sexual intercourse' (1927: 6). He links the play of the child, acting and the viewing of theatre with the play of animals.

The basic psychological foundation is described by him as a series of instinctual drives:

> The instinct of transformation, the instinct of opposing images received from without to images arbitrarily created from within, the instinct of transforming appearances found in nature into something else, an instinct which clearly reveals its essential character in the conception of what I call theatricality.
>
> (Evreinov 1927: 22)

Theatre is seen as being the desire to imagine and to be different. This is an instinct – not something entered into for its effect or outcome. The experience of transformation is a need. He sees the self as a dramatic dialectic – of the ego and 'another ego'. The second ego 'can leave this world of realities and wander in some other world which it has itself created' (1927: 29). This second ego can be 'theatricality'; in other words it can imagine, it can imitate reality and by imitation master reality. Following on from mastery it can transfigure reality by imagining difference. By this process an individual gives the world 'a new meaning, it becomes his life . . . he has transformed the life that was into a life that is different' (1927: 27). This is to 'imagine himself' different from that which he really is: 'he selects, so to speak, a part for himself. And then he begins to play this part' (1927: 27).

Life is seen as being theatrical. In 'The Stage Management of Life' (1927: 105) he analyses everyday interaction, politics and the military in terms of theatre. Evreinov describes the transgressive elements of life in terms of theatre; the violation of norms set by 'nature, by the state, by the public' is seen as the 'essence' of theatre (1927: 116).

Evreinov's Theatrotherapy is based upon these notions. In his writing about this area he does not propose a specific methodology, but rather seeks to demonstrate a facet of the way in which this instinct can have beneficial effects. Theatrotherapy concerns the ways in which engagement in dramatic or theatrical activity connects to healing, alleviation of illness and the creation of well-being: 'The theatre cures the actors. It can also cure the audience' (1927: 126). He speaks of health on several different levels. On the general level of society he claims that theatre is one of the strongest weapons for safeguarding the health of mankind (1927: 127). On an individual level he considers a number of the ways in which theatre can heal – from clowns working in children's hospitals to the alleviation of toothache.

Evreinov describes theatre as a stimulant: an actor's ailment is overcome by the 'transfigurative energy' of the role he enacts (1927: 125). He cites the example of a performer who is suffering from an illness prior to taking on a role. When on the stage the symptoms may disappear. He says that the actor, when engaged in theatre, enters into an energised state and this helps to alleviate illness – mental or physical. He writes of the reworking and re-forming of unhealthy roles in life and the changing of patterns of living which cause distress or illness through theatre. The actor can create roles anew as a way of engaging with their life differently. Here replaying roles is linked to auto-suggestion and behavioural relearning: 'Play a role well, and you will live up to it' (1927: 125). The ability to utilise the skills of drama is seen to be helpful. The capability to transform the self and the ensuing potential reworking of difficult life situations is enhanced by the development of the abilities to act: 'The theatre "cures" an actor skilful in the art of self transformation' (1927: 125). Theatre can also enable a change in the framework within which someone sees their life. This change can help to alter and reframe difficulties: 'You were induced to leave the place where you had so adapted yourself to things occupying your attention that you could no longer maintain a contemplative attitude to them' (1927: 122).

In formalising these elements of Theatrotherapy, Evreinov anticipated many of the writings and workings on theatre, drama and therapy of the later twentieth century. In revolutionary Russia his ideas were partly realised in theatre events in the early 1920s. He then emigrated to the United States, but his ideas were not to bear direct fruit there. However, the basic concepts of much of his writings are similar to those formulated in Europe and America after World War II which underlie the basic tenets of dramatherapy.

Nilli, in an article referring to Evreinov, 'On the Theatre of the Future' ('O teatre buduscego'), saw theatre as a way of living life; as the connection of fiction and reality. This future theatre extends Evreinov's ideas of theatre in life:

> a group of actors performing a single play and each actor [takes] a single role for an entire season. At the conclusion of the season, the actor would take this role into life and play it among the people, modifying the role according to his observations of the people.
>
> (Nilli, in Golub 1984: 74)

The neglected writings and theories of Evreinov as set out here give an historic example of one of the early experiments in formalising the uses of theatre in relation to personal change. Though his writings had been all but forgotten, 'Theatrotherapy' and its related ideas and notions now receive more acknowledgement in the history of drama, theatre and therapy (Casson 1999, 2004; Landy 2001; Karkou and Sanderson 2005).

Iljine

During the early twentieth century Vladimir Iljine developed a way of working in the Soviet Union called Therapeutic Theatre. Petzold (1973) indicates the main years of this activity to have been between 1908 and 1917. During this time Iljine was developing his techniques through activities with psychiatric patients in hospitals, with students who had emotional problems, and in the theatre. His work brings together theatre and therapy in the form of a particular methodology.

After being made a professor at the University of Kiev, Iljine had to leave Russia for political reasons. He travelled widely, eventually settling in Paris in the late 1920s. His travels took him to Hungary where he came into contact with Sandor Ferenczi and his 'Active Techniques' in psychoanalysis which included role playing.

Iljine describes Therapeutic Theatre as trying to combine sciences such as biology and medicine with the humanities, music and theatre. Like Evreinov, his methods were connected to the turn-of-the-century experiments in theatre taking place in Russia. Three key areas which formed the basis of his methods were improvisation training, instant or impromptu performances and the forming of scenarios around which improvisations could occur. Work could be undertaken with individuals or with groups. A group would usually consist of between 10 and 15 people, though with more therapists a group of 30 could be created. Iljine says that there should be a minimum of 30 sessions, with meetings occurring twice a week. Sessions could last as long as between three and five hours. Within the two weekly meetings one would focus upon improvisation training while, the other would work with Therapeutic Theatre performances. The idea behind this combination was that one area would enhance the clients' work in the other.

Improvisation training

Improvisation training is an essential element of Iljine's methodology. This sought to develop clients' creativity through drama games and exercises. The training encouraged spontaneity, flexibility, expressivity, sensitivity and the ability to communicate. Iljine saw these attributes as qualities which people in general neglected, and said that this phenomenon was especially prevalent in people with emotional or mental health problems. He viewed the loss of these qualities as a distinctive part of their illness. He would analyse clients' presenting problems in terms of 'deficiencies' or 'problems' in these areas. Therapeutic Theatre had as its main aim the bringing about of change for participants so that they could have access to these qualities once more.

Within the improvisation training emphasis was put upon the clients' use of their body and voices. The idea was that the body is essential to the expression and exploration of emotion. By training clients in using their bodies and voices in drama, the aim was to enhance their ability to express and explore emotions in the Therapeutic Theatre sessions and in their lives in general.

To overcome any blocks against playing and creativity, Iljine developed the idea and practice of warm-up techniques such as sensitivity and the ability to communicate. One warm-up used the qualities of animal and bird movements, such as the jumping and falling of cats or the motions of snakes. Iljine observed animals and used them as a basis for exercises concerning self-expression. Clients would express the movements of puppies at play, birds of prey, reptiles, big cats. He used a wide variety of such drama games, developing them over the years. Yoga-based activities were often included within warm-up activities.

Therapeutic Theatre

Therapeutic Theatre consists of a series of stages: theme identification, a reflection on themes, scenario design, scenario realisation and reflection/feedback.

THEME IDENTIFICATION

At the beginning of a piece of work a relevant theme would be established. This theme needed to have the potential for improvisation. In working with an individual it could be identified by consideration of the client's case history, through the recounting of autobiographical details. Diagnostic techniques such as the Rorschach test could be used to assist this process. The aim was that the raw material gathered in these tests and explorations would be developed into dramatic material. In a group context the theme could also arise out of group discussion. Individuals would discuss the details of their lives and situations and from this a theme would be identified. In this way material from clients' lives was gathered together.

A collection of ideas for dramatisation would then be brought together and selected from. Some of the forms for playing out and exploring the theme mentioned by Iljine include fantasy games, the enactment of incidents, folk-tale based performances, specific situations such as problems at work, hospital scenes and political themes. A theme and format would be chosen which the majority of the group felt to be the most relevant to their current needs.

This process of choosing themes was seen as giving diagnostic information to the therapist(s). It concerned the identification of issues which troubled clients, but could also involve the interpersonal dynamics which emerged during the negotiations. The therapists could give interpretations or make interventions which aimed to stimulate the selection process. Iljine says that this would usually take the form of asking questions, or interpreting what was happening within the group or the decision-making process.

REFLECTION ON THEMES

Once the theme had been established it was thoroughly examined and debated. In relation to individual therapy this means that the therapist and client discussed the choice of theme, its relevance, the key areas of conflict contained within it, and the ways in which it might be expressed and explored through drama. Within the group a general discussion of the theme would occur. Therapists and clients alike discussed and explored the key aspects of the theme. Other means of reflection could be used in addition to verbal discussion; for example, group members might paint or draw a picture in relation to the theme.

SCENARIO DESIGN

The next task involved the creation of a scenario, which entails a structure giving a shape to the theme. A scene is established, though this does not involve a specific script. It takes the form of a brief outline to act as a focus and springboard for improvisation. In individual therapy therapist and client would work together to arrive at the scenario. In a group everyone took part in the design. The selection and distribution of roles followed. Within a group this occurred by considering the needs of each role in relation to the needs and potentials of the participants. This process involved a high degree of self and peer assessment and discussion. Within individual therapy both client and therapist would be involved in enactment. In group situations Iljine says that, depending upon the size of the group, there could be four or five staff who can also take an active part. The role of staff is to assist or stimulate the realisation of the enactments.

A scenario design would include: the theme, key words, details about roles and the characteristic behaviours attached to the roles, a short series of basic situations or scenes to be focused upon, and the location or locations.

SCENARIO REALISATION

Within the realisation stage the actual improvisation is practically prepared for and enacted. A stage and materials such as masks and costumes can be used, or the work can take place with a defined space in a room using only some chairs to sit on. If no stage is to be used, Iljine recommends that participants close their eyes and imagine the details of the location. A series of improvisation training exercises could be used prior to the enactment, aiming to warm up the participants to the situations and characters they were to portray. As with Stanislavski's approach to preparation for performance, emphasis is placed upon the use of the five senses in developing an imaginative context for the playing.

The scenario is then enacted. Iljine places emphasis upon the importance of a high level of emotional and imaginative involvement for those taking part.

If a number of basic situations or scenes are included then the group should pause after each one to reflect and discuss it before moving on. The idea was that the discussions deepen the exploration and portrayals in the following scene. A key character might form the centre of a scenario and be at the centre of three or four scenes or situations.

REFLECTION/FEEDBACK

The aim of the reflection section was to help each player discuss their whole emotional experience during the work. Each person said how they felt whilst in role. Particular attention was paid to the levels of emotion and the behaviours manifested by individuals within each scene. The belief was that issues from the life of the player could become connected to the enactment they were making. The reflection time offered the opportunity for clients to make spontaneous connections between the scenario and their own lives. The idea was that memories would emerge and the therapist could assist this process by interpretation and comment.

As reflection periods followed each situation or scene, Iljine intended that the emerging issues and memories could be worked on and resolved through the ongoing alternation of the enactment of the scenes followed by reflection times. Emerging emotions or ideas could be pursued, deepened and resolved. The clients could gain insight into themselves and personal issues through the combination of the enactments, connections to their own lives, their own reflections and the interpretation of the therapists or group members. Emotional material which might be repressed could be expressed and examined during the scenarios and discussions. The scenes within the scenario were seen to be flexible, enabling the emerging material to be followed.

Iljine says that the length of time taken by these different stages varies. As an example he states that the consideration, identification and reflection on a key theme or themes might take between three and five sessions. The scenario design might take a further one or two sessions. The realisation and reflection might take another three to five sessions. These weekly sessions would be running alongside the weekly improvisation training sessions.

Although Iljine's ideas have not been influential in dramatherapy in the UK and US until recently, they have been used in dramatherapy training in Germany and the Netherlands. This difference can largely be accounted for by the unavailability of any English language translation of his ideas and work. As Karkou and Sanderson acknowledge following on from the material presented in the first edition of this book, 'despite its limited application to the British context, Iljine's approach remains a very good example of theatre-based approaches to Dramatherapy that needs to be acknowledged' (2005, 204). Casson, in research similarly following on from the first edition of this book, has written of the possible connections between Evreinov and Iljine: 'It is likely that Iljine and Evreinoff knew each other, if not in Russia, then as émigrés in Paris where they both lived . . . and created theatre' (Casson 2004: 64). He also discovered other interconnections and influences: Moreno knew of Evreinov's *The Theatre in Life* and Iljine translated Moreno's *The Theatre of Spontaneity* into Russian (Casson 2004: 63).

Moreno

Moreno created his first psychodrama theatre at the Beacon, New York in 1936. In the 1920s he had developed the theatre of spontaneity at the Viennese Komedienhaus (Marineau 1989). In 1924 he published *Das Stegreiftheater*, or *The Theatre of Spontaneity* (published in translated form in the US in 1947). This form of theatre aimed 'to bring about a revolution' (Moreno 1983). The theories employed in the Komedienhaus emphasised the elimination of the playwright and written play; everyone was seen to be both actor and audience; improvisation was the main medium of expression. However, these theories met with 'great resistance' (1983: 38) and the Komedienhaus had to close due to lack of public interest and financial problems.

In the 1947 American edition of *The Theatre of Spontaneity*, Moreno divides his ideas into three parts – the spontaneous theatre, the living theatre and 'the therapeutic theatre or theatre of catharsis' (Moreno 1983: 38). The Therapeutic Theatre 'uses the vehicle of the spontaneity theatre for therapeutic ends . . . The fictitious character of the dramatist's world is replaced by the actual structure of the patient's world, real or imaginary' (1983: 38).

Moreno published a plan for a new form of theatre at the International Exhibition of New Theatre Techniques in Vienna in 1921 (Marineau 1989: 83). When he moved to the USA he started working with children at the Hudson School for Girls and also at Sing Sing Prison. Later he began a series of experimental activities, including work with the Living Newspaper – a group improvising and dramatising aspects of current news to an audience. The *New York Morning Telegraph* of 7 April 1931 noted how 'all the members of the impromptu came up on the stage and the doctor told them off for parts' (Moreno 1983). Moreno eventually opened the first psychodrama theatre in 1936 at the Beacon Hill Sanatorium. The first public hospital to build a theatre of psychodrama was in June 1941. This was followed the next year by the first official position for a psychodramatist, Frances Herriott. In 1942 the Sociodramatic and Psychodramatic Institutes were opened by Moreno in New York. In that year he also published a paper on the subject of psychodrama. This paper outlined the principle of three parts to a session: warm-up, action and sharing. It also described the key aspects of the process, such as the protagonist, auxiliary ego, director and audience, doubling and role reversal. Psychodrama training was established by Moreno at the Beacon, New York.

The therapist is termed 'director' and groups meet for between one and a half and two hours. In classic psychodrama a protagonist emerges within each session, and this individual is the focus of the work. Their problems are depicted and worked with using role improvisations. During the enactment of a situation or issue, other clients or staff take on the roles of people relevant to the portrayal of the problem. Specific techniques are used to explore and deal with the protagonist's material. In 'role reversal', for example, players swap the role they are playing to take on a different persona within the action. The psychodrama is divided into different parts. The warm-up stage aims to select a protagonist and help the group to prepare for dramatic activity. The main action consists of role work. In classic psychodrama a catharsis is aimed for. After this a period of reflection, discussion or sharing occurs.

A more detailed discussion of psychodrama in relation to dramatherapy can be found in Chapter 8. Moreno's work has been influential in a number of spheres, from psychotherapy and family therapy (Brown and Pedder 1979), to the study of social organisation in girls' schools (Jennings 1943). In the field of psychiatry many early occurrences involving drama as a therapy took the form of psychodrama. The field of dramatherapy has emerged as separate from psychodrama, as the next chapter will discuss. However, there can be no doubt that the structure of much dramatherapy has been influenced by the warm-up/action/sharing pattern. Specific techniques such as role reversal are used and adapted within dramatherapy. The relationship between the two is lively and papers still explore this relationship (Langley 1989, 1993, 1998; Chesner 1994; Landy 2001).

Context: dramaturgy – doing is being is acting

An important parallel development that influenced thinking in dramatherapy was the emergence of symbolic interactionism and dramaturgy or dramaturgical thinking in social psychology. Dramaturgical social psychology is usually traced to the writings of Kenneth Burke in the 1930s and the development of a dramatistic model of human behaviour. The emphasis was upon interaction as opposed to the analysis of individuals in terms of a 'psychobiological entity consisting of conscious and unconscious elements' (1975: 55). Individuality was understood as a social and not a psychological phenomenon. Within this understanding emphasis was placed upon the ways in which people were subject to external conditioning by their environment.

The writings of Mead (1934), for example, advocate the view that it is only through interaction with others that we learn to identify, recognise and value objects. One of these objects is the 'self' – the 'me' as seen by other people. The individual can have multiple selves resulting from different interactions with others. A 'social self' is developed and defined by interaction:

> Certain interactions will lead us to label ourselves as male or female, mother or daughter, clerk or customer, and will lead us to learn sets of behaviours associated with these and complementary labels.
>
> (Knowles 1982: 6)

Burke put forward the idea that human action and interaction were best described and analysed in terms of drama. This was developed by Peter Berger, Hugh Duncan and Erving Goffman.

Drama is used as a way of understanding the nature of the self. Individuals are termed as actors in everyday life and the way people relate to each other is described dramatistically; that is, in dramatic terms. For example, people in life are said to play different roles, they use props to portray and arrive at their identity. The self is arrived at through interaction with other 'actors'. Society assigns us no permanent identity while at the same time 'exposing us to many alternative universes of discourse' (Travisano 1975: 92).

Life and humankind are seen as inherently theatrical. In a way the approach assumes that living is a form of theatre. For example, Goffman takes the notion of theatrical performance and uses it to understand the way an individual relates to another: 'A "performance" may be defined as all the activity of a given participant on a given occasion which serves to influence in any way any of the other participants' (Goffman 1972: 75).

In *Life as Theatre*, Brissett and Edgeley (1975) describe dramaturgy as the study of meaningful behaviour. A person builds up meaning through day-to-day activities with other people: 'the meaning of the human organism is established by its activity and the activity of others towards it' (1975: 3). Individuals are provided with basic resources that enable them to act meaningfully, not in narrow proscribed ways but in terms of the whole range of human possibilities. The individual is viewed as 'one who creates new meanings' (1975: 3). As Turner (1974) states, roles are not necessarily fixed; Role making is as important as role taking. 'Role making' as a term denotes the way an individual creates and modifies their roles.

Crucial to this area of thought is the notion described by Berger as 'ecstasy'. He uses this not in terms of a heightening of consciousness through trance but as 'the act of standing or stepping outside (literally ekstasis) the taken-for-granted routines of society' (Berger 1975: 14). The player becomes conscious of the play. Rather than being in a state of constant submersion in the roles they take on, the individual enters a state of awareness that roles and role playing involve choices, decisions: 'The actor has established an inner distance between his consciousness and his role-playing' (1975: 14).

Dramaturgy also becomes connected to a way of understanding forms of illness and distress. Illness is seen as an inability to play roles. Change is a consensual affair between actor and audience: 'Change in identity is . . . in the eye of the beholder. But who is the beholder? He is the self-reflexive other, the actor's others, the generalised others, the sociological observer' (Travisano 1975: 91). Problems arise for individuals who cannot follow social ritual rules, the sustenances of the 'social fiction of shared meaning' (Becker 1975: 299).

Dramaturgy creates a way of connecting the worlds of drama and of real life. On one level, by drawing an analogy between theatre and living, a conceptual link is made. On another level the individual is seen to function through the creation and negotiation of roles. This way of functioning assumes a level of consciousness – actors can work and rework their roles.

Hence who they are and who they become is linked to an ability to be effective actors in life. This way of perceiving individuals has been influential in the use of role playing and has affected the way in which a number of dramatherapists see their work. Dramatherapy has been understood as an arena for the client to experience the kind of 'ecstasy' Berger talks about. Roles can be looked at, examined and reworked. The relationship between one's own roles, other roles and society can be examined.

As Chapter 8 discusses, certain forms of role-play work in the social sciences have been strongly influenced by this school of thought. In recent years a number of dramatherapists have also been influenced by dramaturgy. Meldrum has gone so far as to say:

> Although most Dramatherapists use role and characterisation in sessions with their client group, it is the American School of Dramatherapists, led by Robert Landy, who base their theories in role theory as such and on Erving Goffman's dramaturgical model in particular.
>
> (Meldrum 1994: 75)

Context: play and drama in education

The late nineteenth century and twentieth century have seen the emergence of the use of drama and theatre in education. Caldwell Cook's *The Play Way* (1917) developed a method of using drama for learning. A special room was built in Perse School, where he was head of English, called 'The Mummery', and was described as the first purpose-built drama room. Part of this approach asserted that dramatic literature was better understood through enactment rather than formal learning. Drama was also given a wider significance in the education of a child:

> The natural means of study in youth is play . . . A natural education is by practice . . . It would not be wise to send a child innocent into the big world; and talking is of poor avail. But it is possible to hold rehearsals, to try our strength in a make-believe big world. And that is Play.
>
> (Caldwell Cook 1917: 15)

Hornbrook links the development of drama as an acceptable part of the curriculum and of learning with the development of theories of play and playing within the field of psychology. These developments, as described in Chapter 7, in part concerned the ways in which play related to learning processes. He demonstrates how drama was seen to be allied to this new way of seeing play, quoting a Board of Education Report on primary education from 1931 which states:

> Drama . . . for which children . . . display such remarkable gifts, offers further good opportunities of developing that power of expression in

movement which, if psychologists are right, is so closely correlated with the development of perception and feeling.

(Hornbrook 1989: 9)

In the US, John Dewey refocused education by advocating children's natural 'learning by doing'. Neva Boyd founded the Chicago Training School for Playground Workers in 1911 and the Recreational Training School in 1921. The work included drama, games and storytelling to develop creativity in children and adults. In 1945 she wrote that games have therapeutic value for hospitalised children, their efficacy in the treatment of 'mental patients' and in corrective work with the re-education of 'problem youth'.

In the US in 1925 Winifred Ward began a drama department at at North Western University. This included the development of 'creative dramatics' and the move into special education. In 1930 she published *Creative Dramatics*. By 1975 the field of Creative Dramatics was defined by the Children's Theater Association of America (CTAA) as an 'improvizational, non-exhibitional process-centred form of drama in which participants are guided by a leader to imagine, enact and reflect upon human experience . . . the process is appropriate to all ages' (in McCaslin 1981: 7).

The development of the use of dramatics in educational and community settings was widespread, another example being Viola Spolin's work in teaching improvisation for use in community work. Peter Slade (1954) also reflects the shift in the ways in which drama is used. From a perspective of dramatherapy certain significant areas of thought and practice can be highlighted. In *Child Drama*, for example, his aims include the following benefits for the child: emotional and physical control, confidence, ability to observe, tolerate and consider others (1954: 106). Another later example is the way in which Heathcote emphasised drama as a way of enabling the child to develop insight and understanding. In the late 1960s she saw the important potential of drama in 'putting yourself into other people's shoes' and in 'using personal experience to help you understand their point of view'. The emphasis was upon discovery and enabling the child to develop personal capabilities through drama (Heathcote 1989).

The emergence of drama in education involved an increase in the understanding of the ways in which drama could function in personal development. Drama was viewed as a way of helping children to learn about the world and its relationship to them, and as a way of developing empathy, insight and interpersonal skills. As such it can be seen to help the movement towards the connection of drama to personal processes and as a way of apprehending and developing a relationship with the world. As the next chapter will show, this field was to be important in the emergence of dramatherapy.

Summary

This chapter has described the variety of ways in which connections between theatre, drama and therapeutic change began to form. New theories such as those of playing and psychoanalysis, dramaturgy and psychodrama, experiments by people such as Evreinov and Stanislavski and the new uses of the arts in areas such as hospitals and schools all made different but important connections between forms of enactment and the creation of change. Key areas include:

- the development of psychotherapy and uses of playing made by psychoanalysis
- the work of Evreinov, Iljine and Moreno in formalising the connections between therapy, theatre and drama
- the introduction of drama as an educational force
- the experiments of theatre practitioners and theoreticians in developing new insights and methodologies concerning the processes of acting and performance
- the development of theatre in hospitals and of drama as part of the recreational and occupational services in psychiatric hospitals
- the emergence of group therapy and action-based therapies such as Gestalt.

Recognition of the importance of dramatherapy was based on the fact that:

- dramatic processes can be connected to contemporary forms and notions of healing
- drama as a process, rather than as a product, has value
- playing out problems is a natural way in which children deal with difficulties
- working in groups can be therapeutic
- the reworking of experiences in psychotherapy can help change.

As I have described, these processes were already partly utilised in areas such as the recreational use of drama or theatre and in psychodrama's uses of enactment. However, the exciting potential being revealed in all these areas created a context of thought, a background of experimentation and recorded practice and opportunities for individuals and groups to begin to make discoveries as to the depth and breadth of drama's capacity for healing. As the next chapter will show, the emergence of dramatherapy as a discipline and specific area of professional practice and expertise followed on from the wider discoveries, developments and connections described in this chapter.

3 The emergence of dramatherapy

Everything was ripe.

Jennings, *Drama As Therapy*

Introduction

The emergence of dramatherapy as a specific discipline and as a profession has taken place since the 1930s. There is documented evidence of the use of drama as a therapy from a wide range of countries: from Bellevue hospital's work in Jamaica in the 1970s (Hickling 1989) to the development of the Greek Society of Theatre and Therapy in the 1980s (Robertson 1990). The nature of dramatherapy's emergence can be said to be parallel in many countries. This chapter will trace dramatherapy's development thematically, focusing upon material from these three key countries. The emergence is marked by a number of phenomena:

- Dramatherapy's development of a separate identity from other main therapeutic and educational uses of drama and theatre. This includes a separation from psychodrama's use of theatre processes and from the uses of theatre and drama in educational drama, child drama and what was known as 'remedial drama'.
- A movement away from dramatic processes being used as an adjunct to other therapies or treatment processes into dramatherapy being a therapy in its own right.
- Dramatherapy, along with the other arts therapies, achieving an identity distinct from arts in hospital settings or other care settings – such as theatre performances in hospitals or drama projects in day centres.

The process occurs in stages. As discussed in the last chapter, unlike psychodrama or psychoanalysis, there has been no single individual who developed the field in such a way that their name can be uniquely linked with the 'birth' of dramatherapy. The process seems to have involved the gradual evolution of a form, with a number of pioneers contributing to its development in a number of different settings and countries. Dr Alfred Solomon's extensive work 'Drama Therapy', for example, published in the USA in 1950, refers to a wealth of practice already in existence.

From the 1930s onwards, and in the postwar period especially, there is a marked increase in the exploration of the uses of drama in health and special educational settings and the growth of interest in its application. This usually involved individuals with an interest in drama who were employed as occupational therapists, teachers, psychiatrists or drama specialists being brought into care settings from other fields such as theatre. There was little or no co-ordination of this work – it happened in relative isolation.

The next stage is marked by the coming together of these individuals to form groupings of people who developed ideas and ways of working. This is accompanied by the emergence of specific concepts and ways of working concerning drama in therapy or drama as a therapy. Then came the development of specialist trainings, associations and professional negotiations to establish a specific identity and form of practice. During this stage there is an increase in the amount of material documenting dramatherapy practice and theory.

The emergence of dramatherapy: an overview of documented practice from 1939

Work written about in the 1940s, 1950s, 1960s and early 1970s tends to be in three areas. One area concerns dramatic events or activities taking place in health settings. Another concerns the ways in which drama can be an adjunct to other therapeutic or rehabilitative work. The third begins to concern itself primarily with the therapeutic nature and effects of drama and theatre processes – drama as the main agent of change in dramatherapy.

The following sections give examples of the three areas of documented practice described above: drama events or activities taking place in health settings, drama as an 'adjunct' to therapy and drama as the main agent of change in dramatherapy. All contribute to the emergence of dramatherapy from the 1930s to the present day.

Drama and theatre: arts in hospitals

There are many different examples of theatre and drama in health settings from the 1930s to the present day. In the *Nursing Times* (1956), for example, there is a 'Christmas Story Presented by Patients at a Mental Hospital'. Mazor's 'Producing Plays in Psychiatric Settings' (1966) and Green's 'Play Production in a Mental Hospital Setting' (1966) both describe the creation and performance of theatrical productions. Here the emphasis is upon creativity, performance and the special circumstances of a mental health setting.

In the late 1950s Steger and Coggins' work in Tampa General Hospital, Davis Island, Florida is an example of this area of practice considered from the point of view of therapy rather than purely as performance. In an article titled 'Theatre Therapy' they describe the formation of a performance group meeting on a weekly basis. Its primary objective is described as 'entertainment' of patients with an additional byproduct of 'the betterment of personnel relations' (1960: 127). 'Gifted' staff were selected by department heads and invitations sent out to patients on Thursday evenings on their supper trays. An audience of 160 patients is recorded as attending the staff performances. The work is firmly set within the context of rehabilitation processes:

> Attending patients are heartened in many ways, both as individuals and in general. For the long stay patients, from the rehabilitation and con-valescent departments, the show brings welcome relief from the tedium . . . Patients from the psychiatric department . . . discover in being mem-bers of a theatre audience that their return to reality is a smoother path than it might otherwise be.
>
> (Steger and Coggins 1960: 127–128)

This example of 'Theatre Therapy' with its 'gifted staff' performing repre-sents one strand of this area of work. Contemporary attitudes have become more critical of staff being the performers and patients as audience, saying that it reinforces the notion that staff are capable and patients able only to receive. More work has involved patients themselves being included in the creation of productions as writers, directors and performers. In some settings this is clearly part of a therapeutic programme. Others see theatre work in this context purely in terms of its artistic value, with no therapeutic func-tion attached (Pickard 1989). Some work tends to be undertaken for social reasons or to create access to theatre and drama in the special circumstance of a hospital or health setting (Green 1966; Brookes 1975). In this area of practice the emphasis is upon the performative process with therapeutic benefits arising from the creation and showing of the work. Some work con-siders the direct therapeutic value of theatre form and describes it as a part of dramatherapy (Mazor 1966; Read Johnson and Munich 1975; Read Johnson, 1980).

Handmaid and adjunct

In 1947 Lassner writes in the *Journal of Clinical Psychology* of 'Play Writing and Acting as Diagnostic-Therapeutic Techniques with Delinquents'. Dra-matic techniques are used to aid assessment for a verbal therapy programme. Similarly Ellis's 'The Use of Dramatic Play for Diagnosis and Therapy' (1954) and Gunn's 'The Live Presentation of Dramatic Scenes as a Stimulus to Patient Interaction in Group Psychotherapy' (1963) use dramatic tech-niques in assessment and as a way of assisting verbal therapy. These, along with many other examples, form a second common strand of work with drama in therapy. Here the emphasis is upon drama as an adjunct to therapeutic processes, or to other areas of therapy such as assessment prior to treatment, group psychotherapy or rehabilitation and recreation.

This approach is best summed up by Solomon in 'Drama Therapy' (1950) when he says that drama can be used with a therapeutic intent: 'This therapeutic intent, however, cannot be accomplished by the use of drama alone, but drama used in conjunction with the technique of psychiatry and psychoanalysis in a group psychotherapy setting' (Solomon 1950: 247).

Frank Curran's work in 1939 is an example of this phenomenon. Adolescent boys, in therapy due to behavioural problems, write and perform plays such as *Framed* and *How Gangsters Are Formed* (Curran 1939: 215). Costumes, scenery and performance were involved, but this is seen as a way of creating material for smaller verbal group work and individual therapy 'where deeper probing took place' (1939: 269).

In this strand of work drama is seen to be useful in therapy, but it needs the context of another 'accepted' form of therapy to be effective or safe. Drama can be a servant or handmaid to help elicit material to be dealt with elsewhere, or can assist change for clients as part of something else – a brief enactment during ongoing verbal psychotherapy, for example. It is an adjunct or subordinate to an established therapy.

Drama as the therapy?

From the late 1930s to the early 1970s there is an increasing emphasis upon the drama as the primary medium of change and as a therapy in its own right. Usually, though, the concepts, terms and forms are still confused with those of other areas. The phase is typified by the struggle to find clear concepts, working methodologies and languages and to establish whether the use of drama is effective as a therapy. The work is often marked by the attempt to describe a specific piece of work and to extrapolate a method or general set of statements or hypothesis. These characteristics of the work can be explained by the fact that the notion of drama as a therapy is emerging. It is beginning to leave behind the notion of an adjunct or handmaid, but does not yet have a full identity or sense of what it is doing. Much of the work is still taking place in relative isolation. A number of individuals are working in parallel directions, or start to come together into groups from similar backgrounds such as education or occupational therapy.

Examples of the third area include Lefevre's 'A Theoretical Basis for Dramatic Production as a Technique of Psychotherapy' (1948), McMillen's 'Acting the Activity for Chronic Regressed Patients' (1956) or Kors' 'Unstructured Puppet Shows as Group Procedure in Therapy with Children' (1964).

Cerf's practice in 1968 is typical of this phase. He takes a particular way of working based on his approach with one group and starts to generalise about it as a broader methodology. 'Drama therapy' is used as a term and drama is the main means of working. However, it is seen as involving taking methods from education/training into a care setting and not as a special, different type of practice. Cerf was working with young adults in the Children's Treatment Center at Central State Hospital in Louisville, Kentucky. At the time he was director of a children's theatre and ran ongoing workshops. The Department of Mental Health permitted a trial run of six weeks and later funded a regular programme. Cerf describes his work as drama therapy. Sessions were weekly and again ongoing and there is an emphasis on skills learning for the 'students'. He describes his work as follows:

> Drama experiences can enhance personality development in the disturbed young person. Both role playing as well as functional technique exercises can be valuable aids in realization of self and in making contact with others. I use the same exercises with mental patients that I employ in the training of actors.
>
> (Cerf 1972: 112)

He stresses creativity – when discussing objectives they consist of areas such as creative imagination, voice work and the ability to concentrate. The main aims of his drama therapy focus upon process rather than theatre product (1972: 117).

Some very early work places drama at the heart of therapeutic change, and uses the term 'dramatherapy'. Slade's practice, as described later (see pp. 51–52), is one example from the late 1930s. Two excellent examples from the same period are found in the work of Florsheim and Horwitz. In her paper 'Drama Therapy' (1946), Florsheim brings the drama process to the fore in her work. She utilises the enactment of plays as the therapy. Using texts as varied as A.A. Milne's 'A Boy Comes Home' and a marionette show 'Marmaduke and the Red Bananas', she describes the therapeutic value for clients as being in the identification with the played role, the awareness and benefits of being part of a group creative process, and that unconscious, repressed forces (hostility being given as an example) can find needed release and expression in a socially acceptable form.

Vignette: Sylvester's dream

One of the most interesting early examples of this third area of practice is undertaken in the early 1940s by a group working with Selma Horwitz. She describes 'spontaneous drama' in group therapy as a technique to be used with children. Dramas are created by the whole group, incorporating the fantasies and providing the therapist with what she describes as 'a medium of operation' (Horwitz 1945: 252). The aims of this therapeutic drama are summarised by her as follows:

> The implications of the drama for child and group are often far
> reaching and the therapeutic task, as we see it, lies not only in
> bringing about the invention of the drama and the production of
> fantasies, but also in the handling of the material that grows out
> of the drama.
>
> (1945; 252)

In 'The Spontaneous Drama as a Technic in Group Therapy'
Horwitz illustrates how each child communicated their problem to
the group by acting in the group. A specific example describes how
a 'group drama' was employed to bring out 'problems that were
inaccessible to the therapist yet urgently required handling' (1945:
259). Colleagues had made Horwitz aware that four of the boys were
in trouble both at home and in school. Two of the group, Bill and
Danny, were threatened with expulsion from school while another,
Tom, had been told his parents were to divorce and Eddie had
learned he was to be placed in a foster home. The group write a play
together containing 'Sylvester's Dream'. Sylvester, a 'big brother',
has dreams. Each of the boys then contributes a dream within the
drama.

Horwitz uses a variety of drama and theatre processes, including costume, scripting, improvisation, role work and rehearsal with
a clear remit for therapy. There is no notion that drama is a handmaid for other therapies. It is the primary mode of working therapeutically. Horwitz has a laudable clarity about aims, purpose,
the therapeutic value of drama and her role within the dramatic
therapy.

The term 'dramatherapy', then, along with detailed recordings of practice
and the formulation of theories and ideas to analyse and justify the work
undertaken, was created by individuals well before the 1960s. The three areas
described above, and the examples given, show how drama as a therapy was
being explored in a variety of ways by a number of individuals.

From individuals to profession

Three interviews: Slade, Lindkvist, Jennings

Dramatherapy began to cohere and grow as individuals met up and started to
form organisations, societies and trainings. As mentioned at the start of this
chapter, the process is similar in the UK, USA and the Netherlands. I will

focus upon the developments in the UK as an example and describe the process in detail.

Excerpts follow from interviews with Peter Slade, Billy Lindkvist and Sue Jennings. These three individuals have been closely involved with the emergence of dramatherapy as a field and profession in the UK. Their work has spanned a wide period of time, but the following material concentrates on the early stages of dramatherapy's development. Their accounts of this process reflect many of the aspects discussed so far.

Interview with Peter Slade

My relationship with dramatherapy started very much earlier than my discussion of it in *Child Drama* (1954). By the 1950s it was a culmination of a great many things: seeing a lot of children, seeing a lot of schools, my own experiences. I started to use drama as a child at school in the 1920s, because I wasn't happy at school. We would go up into the Downs and dance and improvise. We'd improvise about the masters we hated. The stage, the formal stage, was never enough for me. Later, when I was involved in theatre, looking at children gave me the feeling that a lot of what we were doing as professional actors was different from what children did. In fact they had a drama of their own.

Kraemer would reflect on and try to obtain dream sequences in Jungian therapy. They would come to me in another room and I would do improvised acting of situations and sometimes I would play through the dream with them if they wanted me to.

I remember a man who had some difficulty over getting into trains. He didn't quite know why this was, and in his work with Kraemer this kept on coming up, this business of the train. He came to me and we were doing trains together. We would be sitting here and 'You're in a train and I'm in a train and perhaps we're having breakfast together.' I would say, 'Have you seen the paper today?' or something like that, and that would start him off. Then I would choose something that was in my pretend paper, probably trying to get closer to his mind, and so on and then something would come out of that. This man suddenly said, 'My God! The crash!'

I said, 'No. I don't think we are in a crash. That's something that happened somewhere else.'

'My God, you're bloody right! Yes!' And he remembered the crash and that was why he was afraid to get into trains. It was somebody he had loved very much, they had died in a crash.

You're allowed to be like a child again and you can spit out what you want. At that time I would have said that drama is valuable both in education and in helping people to get better. I must have had the idea in my head for a long time because I wouldn't have used the word 'therapy' otherwise.

I read something by Moreno in the 1930s and wrote to him in New York. We met after the war. I sent him a copy of *Child Drama*. I was interested in a general way. I simply was interested that there was anybody doing psycho-drama, when I was having such a tough time in this country persuading anybody that it was important or that drama would have a contribution to make. I came across Jung which enriched something in me. I'm often asked if I got my ideas about acting from the Russian gentleman, and I hadn't heard anything about Stanislavski and hadn't read anything until years later.

I believed that the inculcation of drama into people's minds in simple ways, and the use of it in a thousand different exercises, would enrich everything in life. Because drama in my sense is the doing of life.

*   *   *

In the 1960s and early 1970s a number of groupings began to form and these initiated training programmes and associations. At first the trainings were short courses in dramatherapy or were part of other courses, such as community theatre, occupational therapy or performance.

Interview with (Marian) Billy Lindkvist

What started me thinking and what motivated me in developing drama in what I thought was a new way was a dream I had. I shall tell you the rationale about why I had this dream – but that's how it was! I had this dream! In a few words the dream was that I saw a hospital ward. Instead of the usual feeling of disintegration in hospital wards, especially psychiatric hospitals, everyone was coming together sharing movement and improvisation. There was an out-of-world feeling – a kind of transcendence – a merging. As I woke I knew what had to be done and I started doing it! So that is how it was – that is how it all started.

As to the rationale for the dream, I had an autistic daughter who was in hospital. I was visiting her all the time and having her home as well. It was about 1964 when I had the dream. I was visiting from 1954 and in 1964 they were still going on. Hospitals were anathema to me, I was terrified. All I could see was people who were not merging at all. I hated the atmosphere and I was terrified as to what I might see and hear while I was there. At that time I was on the council of Radius, the Religious Drama Society. I was seeking a new path for them and the subject was on my mind when I went to bed on the night of the dream. So the dream seemed to be a culmination of the two – my hospital experiences and being involved in Radius. I'd also been training extramurally as part of the City Lit, London, for ten years – studying voice, improvisation, movement and straight play performing.

During the training I was noticing things that were happening to people as well as myself. One time, for example, we wore paper bags with holes in them over our heads and one particular person moved quite differently while she was in the bag. That was interesting to me. We played *The Living Room* and I was Aunt Helen. The role of my sister in the play was played by someone with whom I had absolutely nothing in common. Yet when we were doing this play

I got very close to her because we were sisters in the play. The closeness remained when the production was over. So I was noticing things. I was interested in how I changed according to the play I was in. All this was going on and I was agonising over the hospital situation as well.

I knew nothing at this time of Slade or Moreno. Nothing about any of these things. I knew nothing about music therapy or art therapy. To me it was absolutely fresh.

When I first put my ideas to the Radius council somebody said, 'Well, if the authorities had wanted to do this, don't you think they would have done something about it?' I replied that it was going to happen, going to be! We would run workshops, we would invite people to participate like occupational therapists and nurses, all the people in hospitals who were working with patients. We would teach them about drama and movement and they would take back what we'd taught them and use it with patients. This was a very naive concept. I didn't know about the psychological implications. I hadn't rationalised it or thought about it – I'd just had a dream!

Not long before the dream, I was listening to the radio and Sybil Thorndike and she said 'Drama is psychology', and that really hit me 'Bang!' I thought, 'She's absolutely right!' All these things happened.

I said, 'It's got to be everywhere.' One of the reasons behind my statement was that Radius had performing groups all over the country in the churches and I thought they could take their latest play into places such as elderly people's homes. This was in addition to the training. It was going to be everything! So they were going to go and do plays, staff were going to come and train. I had the bit between my teeth. I was unstoppable!

We have never used the word 'dramatherapy'. It did not come into existence for therapeutic work until the 1970s. We've always called ourselves movement and drama practitioners. We've always considered ourselves to be an adjunct to psychotherapy or part of a treatment team. I'm not sure if that's so much the case now. In the 1970s, this was certainly the case. In 1972 we ran a day-release course at Cassio College, Watford, for one year. In 1974 the Sesame one-year full-time course started.

I suppose we talked about drama and movement in therapy after we met Peter Slade in 1965. It was then that Peter said to a Sesame meeting, 'You know you're going to have to learn much more about psychology'. And we said, 'Stuff and nonsense! We're the artists! The people we're working with know about the psychology. We have the pure art form. This is what we're using and this is what has the effects on people.' By effects we meant the psychological effects. We didn't know what we were talking about because we didn't really know this world and that language – we were artists. However, what Peter said made sense and so we did start to study.

Peter Slade worked with us and we read his books. I always feel he's never had the credit for what he gave to therapy through his philosophy of child drama. Of course it was we who set up the Sesame organisation and it flourished. Individuals may have done things that I don't know about, but bringing about a coherent picture of what drama and movement therapy is, and staying with the same organisation for 30 years, being as well known as we are: it was the dream!

Interview with Sue Jennings

Looking back I don't actually think there's such a thing as 'began' for drama-therapy. Maybe I've used the phrase myself; if I did, I retract it with later knowledge. It's an easy thing to say, 'it began'. What I mean is this particular initiative, an impetus in relation to dramatherapy, began. Maybe it had been fallow for a time and it began in a new way.

For me it goes back to a holiday job when I was 17 and at drama school and the supervisor at the local psychiatric hospital had heard about psycho-drama. He didn't call it that, he'd heard about drama being done with patients. He knew I was at drama school and said would I come and do some drama. I had to put on a nurse's uniform and be called Nurse Jennings. In addition, at some level for me, there was an understanding that in the early part of my theatre career drama was actually healing for me. It was mending me from a lot of early life trauma.

I worked closely with Gordon Wiseman. We were asking how one could take drama to unusual places, i.e. not just schools, but where else, for example, children's homes, psychiatric hospitals, prisons and so on. The two words 'drama therapy' weren't used at all. The origins of the Remedial Drama Group were in the International Theatre Good Will project in the early 1960s. The sole aim was to take a theatre group across the Berlin Wall. Prang was a shorthand term for that project; it means a happening, a ritual, festival or event. As part of the tour we went to this hospital in Germany and none of the group had worked with people with severe learning difficulties before. Because the work there, the project, had gone so well we set up a programme to do that work. The Remedial Drama Group started in 1962 and went on to the end of the 1960s. The Remedial Drama Centre ran from 1967 or 1968 until 1971. In 1971 the Remedial Drama Centre moved to the Drama Centre and we took the plunge and put the two words together: dramatherapy.

I started the Remedial Drama Group with Gordon Wiseman in the early 1960s. I was doing remedial drama in a special school in St Albans before the Remedial Drama Centre and at St George's Hospital, a psychiatric centre there, and also at the Marlborough, as an instructor explicitly to do drama. There was an interest in 'doing drama with special needs'. I was also employed by the London School of Occupational Therapy to teach OT students. I also worked at a Special Nursery in St Albans.

Moreno and psychodrama I didn't know about until the 1970s. Through Gordon Wiseman and his work with the Belgrade Theatre Group in Coventry I was aware of drama in education and Peter Slade. It was suggested that I contact the Religious Drama Society. They said, 'You should ring Sesame and Billy Lindkvist, she's doing similar things.' The Sesame Board and the

Religious Drama Society of Great Britain wanted me to come to meet them, so I went but there wasn't much crossfertilisation.

It was Peter Slade's pamphlet, that was what we all grabbed hold of: *Dramatherapy as an Aid to Becoming a Person* (1959). That was just like a beacon. The minute it came out in the mid-1960s we all got it. I remember the impact of that; the fact that somebody called this something.

I was very aware in the early 1960s of occupational therapy's use of drama for recreation. In a sense, because play reading and drama activities were seen as 'a good thing' in the 1930s and 1940s, it was therefore easier for the likes of us to take it a stage further in the 1950s and 1960s. It wasn't virgin territory.

I hadn't heard of dramaturgy; that came later. I'd heard of Smalinsky's Sociodramatic Play – that influenced me. I found it in a shop. I took it to the Special Nursery in St Albans and the child educational psychologist there said, 'What will they think of next?' I was so excited – so many connections with my own work and how I was beginning to think! It was quite fortuitous.

Everything was ripe. Art therapy started as remedial art. St Albans had a first course in remedial art before it became art therapy. We called our thing remedial drama and it was almost as if one had to make an enormous step to call something therapy. But it was about 1970 that the step from remedial drama to dramatherapy was made. Dramatherapy – one word because psychotherapy was one word. Slade was anyway using the one word. We corresponded but we didn't meet up. He was patron of a lot of what we did. Veronica Sherborne was very formative by her presence, she came and did courses at the Remedial Drama Centre.

The Association for Dramatherapists started in 1976. In the 1970s psychodrama and dramatherapy started to develop more of a relationship. When we launched the association in 1976, Zerka Moreno came along to the first conference. A dialogue was set up between psychodrama and dramatherapy.

Any decade brings people with energy, ideas and perhaps what people do is take the parts of a jigsaw and put them together in a new constellation that isn't unique. I don't think that anything can be unique. I think I've had the energy to move something forward in a postwar time.

*   *   *

These three individuals have described aspects of their experience of the early stages of dramatherapy. Though there was some contact between them, all arrived at their own position and developed their own perspective on dramatherapy. Each person shows in the interviews how a mixture of personal circumstances and experiences, ideas, plans, opportunities and fortuitous events – such as hearing Dame Sybil Thorndyke on the radio, being asked to don a nurse's uniform and run drama activities at an early age or picking up a book by chance – all contributed to create unique combinations. However, the stages of development described earlier in this chapter are clearly demonstrated. Slade, Lindkvist and Jennings all progress from ideas and work as individuals, to coming into contact with others, through to the formation of groupings and organisations. The themes of drama as an adjunct, finding a language to describe drama in relation to therapy, attempts to prove efficacy through experimentation and the increasing emphasis upon drama as a therapy in its own right, all feature in the testimonies. The interviews also illustrate that dramatherapy evolved gradually with a number of starting points which, to an extent, began to converge, rather than being started in one place at one time by one person or group. What can be noted, though, is the importance of Slade in his being a touchstone for both Lindkvist and Jennings and the importance, historically, of his work and use of the term 'dramatherapy'.

Training and associations

In the 1960s and early 1970s a number of groupings and training courses developed. These included the Child Drama Certificate Course, the Remedial Drama Centre, Dramatherapy Centre and Sesame in England, along with a course at Queen Margaret College, Edinburgh, in Scotland.

In the Netherlands the training and identity of arts therapists seems to be closely tied with the development of 'activity leader' training from the late 1940s. For example, in 1947 an educational programme for youth workers to apply art and play in work with war orphans was begun in Amersfoort. In Mikojel at the Middelau Kopsehof, a course trained workers in social welfare and youth care for settings such as community centres, youth psychiatry and residential care. Part of this training concerned therapy, and during the 1950s arts activities began to be included as a part of this course. Drama as part of this approach was strongly influenced by play therapy. In the 1950s Lex Wils produced his book *Bij wijze van spelen* [*By Means of Playing*] and Jan Boomsluiter wrote a number of articles on drama as therapy. Both were influential in the development of drama as a therapy in the Netherlands. In the early 1960s the Nederlandse Vereniging voor Kreatieve Therapie (Netherlands Society for Creative Expressive Therapy) was formed along with the Netherlands Art Therapy Society. From 1974 Middelau offered a four-year Creative Therapy Diploma with specialisms such as drama. By 1978 the Hogeschool Nijmegen offered its four-year arts therapy course with a specialism in dramatherapy; 1981 saw the formation of a branch of the Netherlands Society for Creative Expressive Therapy purely for dramatherapists. The forming of a section needs 100 members.

In 1971, short courses in dramatherapy had begun at Turtle Bay Music School in New York City. Gertrude Schattner was important in the development of these courses and of dramatherapy in the United States. Her work had its origins in working with survivors of Nazi concentration camps. The group was involved in performing plays by the Jewish author Aleichen about life in a small Polish village community. She says that this process enabled the group 'to wake up, to enjoy themselves and to work together' (Schattner and Courtney 1981: xxi). In turn she felt that the theatre work with the group enabled her to see 'drama as an instrument in the healing process' (1981: xxi).

Like other initiators in the field she worked with children, at the Lincoln Square Neighborhood Center, New York and in the early 1970s was involved in the development of the Turtle Bay courses. The United States' National Association for Drama Therapy was established in 1979. This period saw the founding of two Masters programmes in the US: one was an MA in Psychology with a concentration on drama therapy at Antioch University in San Francisco, the other was an MA in Drama Therapy at New York University. In Canada developments were at Concordia, while other programmes followed in countries such as Greece and Ireland.

With the development of training programmes and associations, how did dramatherapy change?

Dramatherapy has established a clearer identity as a specific mode of therapy and as a profession and, as described in this chapter, this is due to a number of factors. These include the increased contact between individuals involved in using drama as a therapy, the creation of professional associations and training programmes, and the increasing publication of dramatherapy case material and theory. This has been accompanied by an increase in the attempts to evaluate the efficacy of the therapy which, in turn, has led to increased confidence in the potency and validity of drama as a therapy, to clear structures and standards in training and the organisation of professional validation.

Dramatherapy has developed within a number of countries during the postwar period, especially in the last quarter of the twentieth century. The work of the European Consortium of Arts Therapies Training and Education (ECARTE), formed in the 1980s, has played an important role within the European Union in developing courses and contact between countries, for example. Training and established practices now exist, or are being developed, in countries such as India, Israel, Greece, Ireland, Jamaica and Norway.

Later developments have included the emergence of training programmes, the creation of professions governed by national associations along with state recognition and registration in some countries. In the UK, for example, independent regulation of dramatherapists, along with other arts therapies, was developed by 1999 through the Health Professions Council. The HPC is an independent regulatory body which oversees areas such as title protection for dramatherapists and 'assures high quality of training and high standards of service provision for most health professionals in the country' (Karkou and Sanderson 2005: 18). This stage – of a coming-together through training, professionalisation and registration – has often produced a desire for a more homogeneous, coherent form or model for dramatherapy.

Orientation and the changing face of health care

Fashions and demands come and go within the different contexts where therapy is practised. In the UK, for example, where a significant proportion of practice occurs within the NHS, funding and government policy-led decisions affect what will be paid for. Dramatherapy research must and does play a part in making the case for evidence of effective practice. However, the nature and form of such 'evidence' is a political and cultural issue, though it is often presented by health authorities as if it is objective and neutral. It is fair to note that in the past 30 years especially, dramatherapy has become increasingly involved in the debate about efficacy and evidence. A lively body of research and practice has been undertaken in dialogue with a range of different attitudes towards evidence and efficacy. This includes practice which responds to the diversity of ideas and approaches, as well as work which creates dialogue with the approaches taken by organisations such as the NICE in the UK or through processes such as state licensure in the USA. The temptation can be to want one monolithic approach, but I would counsel against this – and the evolution of practice has not moved in this direction. There are many approaches, just as there are many individual needs in clients. The emphasis is upon locating and disseminating practice which is alert to effective ways of meeting client needs and to demonstrate effective outcomes. The ways in which the goals and outcomes are formulated varies, and this diversity is a response to the differences between, say, a client with learning difficulties, a group of people dealing with psychosis or a teenager living with HIV. This book includes examples of practice that encompass the very different situations of these disparate life contexts and individuals. It also looks at the different ways in which dramatherapy has created and is creating effective work within these contexts and through dialogue with research from other models of therapy and its own discoveries.

Summary

In the first edition of this book I quoted Mooli Lahad saying: 'We are moving towards that era where we have brilliant ideas, vast experience, and there is a need to conceptualise it into a more theoretical approach' (1994: 182). A number of practitioners have begun to call for work that tries to summarise from a theoretical viewpoint how dramatherapy is effective. As noted in Chapter 1, much dramatherapy writing tends to define dramatherapy either by listing a series of techniques or by what are called 'models'. A number of these are very effectively summarised by Langley (2006: 26–35). However, as Lahad goes on to say, paralleling the comments made in Chapter 1, 'there is a need to move from experience and models to theory' (1994: 182). Chapter 5 considers this problematic area. It attempts to present a theory of dramatherapy that summarises the core processes at work, which explains and accounts for dramatherapy both theoretically and in practice.

4 Dramatherapy and philosophy
Belief and proof

> Neither the action nor the actors can be anticipated, or described in advance. They begin as an unknown adventure in an unknown space . . . Ideas and plans that existed in the mind at the start were simply the doorway through which one left the world in which they occur . . .
>
> Rothko, *The Romantics Were Prompted*

Introduction

This chapter aims to provide a basic overview of some philosophical concerns relating to dramatherapy. It is tempting to think of philosophy as being very distant from everyday clinical encounters: for example, within a regular Wednesday morning in a dramatherapy group in a psychiatric hospital, or in a session for children with learning disabilities, where matters of crisis in living, or vital needs concerning everyday life, need urgent attention. However, the following material will try to keep clinical practice firmly in its sights as it considers philosophical matters in an introductory fashion. Evans and Gilbert have rightly said:

> Without at least a general knowledge of the philosophical bases of a psychotherapy model it is impossible to adequately critique the theory underpinning the model or the values conveyed in the clinical application of the model.
>
> (Evans and Gilbert 2005: 7)

These 'bases' will inform the ways in which therapist and client relate to each other, how they see themselves, the therapy and the world they inhabit. For dramatherapy then, if looked at in this way, the need is to connect practice, theory and philosophy. It is an essential part of understanding what dramatherapists do, why we do it and how we do it. Evans and Gilbert refer to Tanesini's feminist approach to these areas, for example, as they connect them to concerns with values and power:

> It is absurd to assume that a psychotherapist can suspend her values,

which may sometimes be explicit but always implicit in her behaviour and attitudes. Knowledge is instrumental to power and is never politically innocent (Tanesini 1999). So it is highly relevant to ask what power, apparent or implicit in its values, might a psychotherapy method, assuming any particular form of knowledge, convey to a client?

(Evans and Gilbert 2005: 7)

Here, then, shown within this discussion, are the concerns for this chapter: philosophy is vitally connected to values, behaviour and attitude, method, power and politics in therapy. If this connection is accepted, it follows that philosophy can help consider how to view the processes at work within the therapeutic encounter. These areas enable us to examine: how the dramatherapist's and client's values are present in the encounter; how to consider power-based issues within the therapeutic space and relationship; and how to become more aware of what dramatherapists convey to clients.

In the quotation, Tanesini (1999) also draws attention to the way in which philosophy can be both *explicit* and *implicit*. This can help us to consider the relationship between the client's 'philosophy' and that of the therapist. As we will see, no explicit reference to philosophical ideas and positions needs to be made within a session. The need is to include a consideration of the ways in which philosophy, if looked at in the manner described above, is *implicitly* present within and behind attitudes, relationships to the world we live in and to beliefs about living concerning areas such as 'health' and 'fulfilment'. This is important to consider for both client and therapist, and to look at where parallels and differences may lie for both parties.

So, if the perspectives introduced above are accepted and seen as important, it becomes a vital part of any therapeutic work in dramatherapy to ask what philosophical perspectives are relevant to the encounter. For therapists, this importance can be approached by examining and questioning themselves and their work from a philosophical perspective. How, then, to do this? This chapter engages with the following critical questions as a way of introducing and exploring this area:

- What is the relevance of philosophical concerns to dramatherapy?
- How does dramatherapy usefully connect with contemporary philosophical debates?
- How are these areas relevant to the clinical encounter?

The nature and range of philosophical texts and discourse is such that a chapter of this length can only hope to refer to a selection of potential material. The attention could have concerned philosophies purely relating to aesthetics, or to identity politics or to psychological change. I am choosing mainly to consider specific debates within the field of twentieth and twenty-first century European philosophy. I have decided on this focus as material within this area of philosophical debate on identity, change and space has helped me begin to develop my own thinking. I absolutely recognise that, as an initial venture and as a chapter in an introductory book, my discussion will be very partial. The ideal response to this chapter is for the reader to feel informed of some relevant philosophical perspectives, to begin to see connections between some areas of philosophy and dramatherapy, and to go ahead to identify areas which need further, deeper exploration and to discover and identify philosophical schools, writers and concerns which are not yet identified in this writing. The aim is to begin to open philosophical windows on our dramatherapy world.

What is philosophy?

This section gives an introduction to how philosophical debates can be relevant to developing a consideration of therapy. There are two ways of approaching this question. The first method is to look at the ways in which philosophy as a discipline relates to dramatherapy. The second is to ask whether there is such a thing as a 'philosophy of dramatherapy', or whether such a thing could exist. To date, though some have mentioned the second area briefly (Grainger 1995; Read Johnson 1999), no real philosophy of dramatherapy has been explicitly proposed. This chapter undertakes the first method as a way of beginning to approach the second. First, I want to introduce some broad brushstroke definitions of philosophy, and then to focus on outlining two key areas that I consider helpful in beginning to look at how dramatherapy and philosophy relate.

Some have described philosophy as concerning wisdom and knowledge of 'how things are the way they are' (Critchley 2001: 4). For the ancient philosophers, Critchley (2001) says that the central concern was what it might mean to lead a good human life: 'Philosophy is the reflective life, the examined life, the assumption being that the unexamined life is not worth living. Philosophy should form human beings and not just inform them' (Critchley 2001: 1). It is also the reflective practice of examining what passes for 'truth'. Philosophy tries to ask *how* we know what we know, and how such knowledge is *valid*. Dramatherapist Grainger speaks of this area as a part of what dramatherapy offers to or asks of clients: 'What it provides . . . is scope for experiment in personhood, experience in relationships, and the expression of value, meaning and authority in human life, all of them healing events' (Grainger 1995: 6). Though the acts of philosophical enquiry and therapy are different, we can see here that Grainger's summary of what dramatherapy provides connects to areas which are to do with kinds of questioning, 'asking' clients to look indirectly or directly at meaning, value and what he calls 'personhood'. All these echo or connect to themes in Critchley's summary of philosophy's concern with examining, reflecting and the nature of knowledge. But what is the use of this connection?

The following material outlines two debates within contemporary philosophy. I have chosen to include them in this introductory chapter to illustrate how philosophical debates can connect to dramatherapy. The first focuses around the nature of the dramatherapeutic space: what philosophical approaches can help us see what occurs in areas such as change, outcome, or efficacy? The second touches on debates about the nature of the self.

Useful perspectives

Philosophy and the therapeutic space

The therapy space and change

In looking at the connections between philosophy and the therapeutic space, a number of areas emerge that can help us see how we think about what occurs within a dramatherapy session. By therapeutic space I do not refer only to the physical space that the therapy takes place in. The term 'space' here includes the ways that time, physical conditions and the relationship between client, therapist and drama interact and form (Jones 2005). It strikes me that dramatherapists often go into the therapy space with their attention on techniques and relationships but, as we will see, we need also to be aware of the 'building blocks' and basic assumptions that our work is rooted in, which we too often take for granted. This section will begin to show why it is important to be aware of these areas and not to become focused only on the immediate actions between client and therapist.

The dramatherapy space and meaning: harmless bonus or liberation?

Kristeva (1997) has described the redundancy of the purely 'scientific' in contemporary society. She describes the 'scientific imperative' as being founded in methods which she describes as 'the archivistic, archaeological and necrophilic', the process of this methodology being 'the building of arguments on the basis of empirical evidence, a systematizable given, and an observable object . . . [they] are an embarrassment when applied to modern or contemporary phenomena' (Kristeva 1997: 27). This appears in a text on the poetics of language, but clearly the implications of this philosophical analysis of scientism are broader, and connect to phenomena such as the arts and therapy. She goes on to argue that in fields such as linguistics and psychoanalysis the reflections of this approach can be seen in what she calls 'fragmentary attention' – the isolation of experience, the tendency to reflect on moments rather than on 'interdependence or inception' (1997: 28). She contrasts this with both an important contemporary need and the potentials of art. For the arts therapies these ideas may seem both familiar and relevant to developing any philosophical position towards the relationship between art and the therapeutic space.

Kristeva (1997) makes a distinction between the contrasting potentials and nature of both the arts and psychoanalysis. On the one hand they can be *a part of* processes she sets out to challenge in society. These include censure, the creation of oppressive norms, the emphasis on fragmenting experience. Here the arts can become a 'harmless bonus' to living and being, and are part of the norms by which modern bourgeois society exists and isolates and represses difference and connection. Here the arts are a diversion, an amusement, or used as part of capitalist processes such as advertising. On the other hand they can be a part of processes which are *allied to ideologies of 'liberation'*. She uses this term liberation in connection with the arts being seen as at the 'outer boundaries' of the 'subject' and of society. Being at this boundary involves the arts using processes that challenge accepted discourse. They expose what is repressed by society and some of those within it, and oppose the fragmenting of experience and connection.

In 'Reality and its Shadow' Levinas has talked about art as being related to, but separate from, everyday processes of communication and meaning making. He says that 'an artwork prolongs and goes beyond, common perception' (Levinas 2000: 117). Kristeva perceives this connected separateness in a specific way. A key process which Kristeva talks about is art's potential to 'shatter' in order to 'reveal'. By this she is partly advocating the arts' potential to challenge, reveal or comment, to be apart and to be a radical challenge to held norms and accepted 'systems' (1997: 30). She makes reference to areas that many dramatherapists draw on in theorising dramatherapy's efficacy (Grainger 1995; Landy 1995; Jones 1996; Jennings 1997). These include examination of shamanism, ritual and the connections between the arts and religion from a philosophical perspective. The argument at its simplest is that shamanism, magic, the carnival and arts, such as 'incomprehensible poetry', 'all underscore the limits of socially useful discourse and attest to what it represses: the *process* that exceeds the subject and its communicative structures' (Kristeva, 1997: 30; added emphasis).

This, for me, can help us to illuminate a philosophical dilemma for the arts therapies and for dramatherapy. The use of the therapy and arts could be seen to be within the criticism Kristeva makes of the arts as *normative*, of creating contexts for individual participation in the arts as teaching those to fragment their lives, to emphasise a section of their experience and to be part of normalisation and conformity to a bourgeois capitalist 'self-contained isolated island' (1997: 28). Here, the points made from a philosophical perspective can help examine the nature of therapeutic aims and the therapeutic space. For example, care needs to be taken to reflect on aims which *seem* to work to assist a client to participate more successfully within society by *altering themselves* rather than challenging society's attitudes towards difference and exclusion. However, most, I think, would see their experience as more allied to processes that 'reveal', to use Kristeva's term: that stand outside of normal or everyday experience in order to challenge, become lucid or to create connection. Taken further, this position leads to the arts being involved in challenging the forces of repression, or giving voice to those who are oppressed. The arts as created within the therapeutic space could be argued to ally their philosophical position with her ideas of generating challenge and confrontation – the opposite of a 'harmless bonus' (1997: 30).

Vignette: Thomas

Here, such philosophical debate helps ask questions about the nature of the arts in dramatherapy. It assists in examining the nature of the aims of any dramatherapy practice, on the processes which dramatherapy aids and abets in relation to a client. It can help to give a structure to questions about normalisation, about challenge, and how the act of therapy relates to processes of oppression and the management of difference. Dramatherapist Gill, for example, working within UK social services in a community-based dramatherapy service, makes this very explicit: that dramatherapy operates within a political system. The forces of the 'state' are connected by Gill to its 'penal institutions and relief agencies'. Health and social services are some of the main employers of arts therapists and within this framework, he says, 'Dramatherapy can be used for good or ill . . . as a means to facilitate self-discovery and self-expression, or as a means to impose control or prescribe "correct" behaviour' (Gill 1997: 245). Here and in his description of his work with a client we can usefully utilise Kristeva's philosophical debate to illuminate the processes at work and the nature of the dramatherapy space. A client, Thomas, is described by Gill as a man with a learning disability working as a plant pot maker in an adult training centre and attending dramatherapy initially aiming to encourage communication between 'students'. Thomas uses role play and playing to explore different aspects of his life and his identity, his relationship to others and to arenas such as work or education. Masks are made and used with movement – patterns emerge which connect to people in the client's life, others seemed more fantasy orientated. Issues and areas are explored: for example, the client's relationship to his absent father. The roles are, in part, also seen by Gill as developing fantasies of 'escape' from, or of redefining, the more rigid roles that the centre he was in seemed to advocate, with its emphasis on work and being validated by becoming a worker. Gill describes the goals as enabling 'Thomas to move at his own speed to find his outer identity in relation to his emerging personal story, and, perhaps, to construct his own version of manhood and fatherhood in relation to his absent father' (1997: 257). Gill says:

Dramatherapy participants through the construct of make-believe, are offered the possibility for 'reframing' experiences to take place. To open the doors of experiencing others is to redefine the status relation that exists between people: it is in this sense, too, that the 'tacit agreement' of any dominant culture is questioned and worked upon; it is through making such relative mechanisms available that the key to past, present and future doors might be grasped, and validity through self-esteem, status and cultural terms might be achieved.

(Gill 1997: 254–255)

We can see the experiences of Gill and the client as connected to processes that philosophically ally themselves to Kristeva's concept of the arts' potential to 'reveal', to stand outside everyday experience and actions in order to challenge, to be lucid and to create connection. This position on dramatherapy practice can be seen to reflect a philosophical decision made by Gill as a worker in relation to the dichotomy Kristeva outlines. On the one hand is the potential of the arts to be an ally to forces of oppression through normalisation, or through being a 'harmless bonus', while on the other the arts can challenge the forces of repression, or give voice to those who are oppressed.

This issue can rarely be a simple 'either/or', but the identification of such a philosophical debate can help give a structure within which dramatherapy can be looked at; the practice examined and important questions asked for which individual answers within each specific client encounter will need to be formed. These include:

- What is the relationship between the forces at work within society, within groups and within individuals which repress and oppress?
- How is the art form being used within the therapy – is the process emphasising the role of the arts to reveal, to give the oppressed voice, or is the process emphasising normalisation, the suppression of difference?

My experience is that there is never a simple answer to these complex issues, but the philosophical debate here offers an illuminating framework within which such questions need to be asked within any practice undertaken.

The therapy space: scientism and obscurantism

Critchley talks about a key problem facing contemporary philosophy as 'the relation between wisdom and knowledge' (Critchley 2001: ii). He says that there is a gap in much philosophy between theoretical questions of how one knows what one knows, and more practical or existential questions of what it might mean to lead a good or fulfilled human life. This, for me, immediately connects to a number of critical issues within the therapy room. In relation to areas such as *aims forming, evaluation* and *efficacy*, how do we, as therapists, approach what we perceive, what we say we know? For clients, similarly, what are they to make of the encounters and events within the space and how it relates to who and how they are?

What is the position taken by dramatherapy as a discipline, or by individual therapists and clients, on *fulfilment*, on the idea of a 'good' life? Immediately this banishes from our approach to philosophy any notions that it is unconnected to the clinical encounter in the dramatherapy space. The following example is included to illustrate this. It shows how notions about fulfilment, the aims and indeed the form of therapy, have philosophical concerns which underlie the in-the-moment decisions made by therapists about what they say or do in response to a client. It will give a context for a moment in the therapy room, describe an interaction between client and therapist and then indicate how philosophical issues are implicit within the work.

Vignette: Jake

Grimshaw talks about her work with a 14-year-old individual, Jake, within a setting for children designated as having emotional and behavioural difficulties. The referral is described by her as concerning 'yet another and more vicious incident of bullying' (1996: 57). Jake has a history of bullying or bullying 'by proxy', inciting other boys to bully 'smaller, vulnerable children'. Her comments include a perception that staff had no means of 'penetrating the wall' that Jake had built around himself, as well as a question on what Jake sees in the vulnerable children 'that he despised so much, and could tolerate so little, that he needed to destroy them?' (1996: 57). We are also told that Jake's mother left his father and their home when he was seven, and Jake had been 'admitted' into care from the age of eight, though still visiting his father regularly.

Her work focuses on the creation of metaphors, symbols and story after the child informs her in an assessment session that he writes his own stories. In one piece Jake tells a story in the first person about a seven year old witnessing a row between his mother and father. He has run out of the house to avoid the conflict and is wearing a duffle coat with toggles on it, which he has not fastened. The mother asks the boy to come back into the house. She is crying, and shouts at the boy for not fastening up his coat and throws orange juice in his face. His father screams. The boy runs away and sits on the stairs hearing his parents scream, along with banging and crashing. Jake plays the seven year old within the session. Grimshaw describes a moment in the therapeutic process in this way:

> I want to tell her not to go, I don't mind about the orange juice. My dad's crying, I can hear him. He slams the kitchen door. I just sit there holding my toggle thinking, 'If I can keep hold of it, she'll come back.'
>
> After a moment of silent recognition, I ask him if he is able to come out of the scene and stand by me.
>
> 'If you were watching this child sobbing on the stairs, what would you do, Jake?'

She goes on to ask Jake if there is anything he can give to the child 'to comfort him in his suffering' (Grimshaw 1996: 63).

Here is a moment from a therapy session, then, with the therapist having developed a way of working which involves story enactments. Within it she suggests Jake takes a specific role and then invites him to react to the story content and role experiences in certain ways. In the example above she asks Jake to stand outside the role, wondering what he would do if he were observing. She then invites him to 'give', to 'comfort' and respond to what she calls the imaginary seven-year-old child's 'suffering'. Grimshaw frames her practice in the following way: to offer Jake a better understanding of himself and his relationships with others; that the stories represent his inner world; that the story work gives him permission to miss his mother. The stories and enactments express repressed grief and pain in relation to his mother and losing her, and Jake has learned to reject her through his experience of being rejected.

In reflecting generally about dramatherapy work with 'children and young people identified as having emotional and behavioural difficulties', she talks about work in terms of children experiencing inner or internal 'splits' magnified by labelling, and that society's treatment of such children can amplify rather than integrate or resolve such fragmentation. The role of the therapist is described by her as being to help Jake 'pick up those scattered pieces of himself, and to allow that child the space and time to explore and evaluate the pieces; to do what he needs to do in the process of healing himself' (1996: 53). Fulfilment here is seen to be an integration of parts of the self that are denied, an expression and exploration of experiences and roles projected out into others. Hence the initial presentation of bullying is seen by her as a communication and a need to change an aspect of the client's life which is not fulfilled.

Within the moments of such a session, in Grimshaw inviting Jake to do things such as to observe the seven year old sobbing, to stand outside the role and to 'give' a gift, she is making choices. There is not only one way to respond. She has, with Jake and with the treatment setting, created a context for such moments. The therapy is built upon assumptions about the nature of Jake's situation, the context that his 'problem' or needs are seen within, the need to intervene along with the nature of the intervention and the notion of what greater fulfilment for Jake can be. We see here, for example, the notion that Jake has within him different kinds of roles. Grimshaw believes that the story re-enactments are related to himself and that by working together with her, by interventions asking him to see, to give, there will be a resolution of the perceived difficulties. The formulation of long-term goals as well as her in-the-moment responses are rooted in philosophical assumptions about the nature of change and the therapeutic space; the ways in which Jake's life can be fulfilled and the nature of his identity. These are not explicitly explained to Jake, but are inherent within the way Grimshaw responds to the child's situation, the time within the therapy and to the setting which has been involved in his referral.

Such issues and questions are present in every moment of therapy – deeply and importantly so, especially in the formulation and evaluation of goals or aims. Perhaps the problem here is also that these are such huge, complex, even frightening questions, and it can seem easier to carry on either not acknowledging them as the ignored 'elephant in the room'. By assuming or pretending that we all 'know' the answers, without really spelling out what it is we might mean, we can avoid answering them at all.

Many of the contexts in which dramatherapists and clients meet are so dominated by scientism, for example, that no one ever dares to take a moment to step back and question the very nature of the assumptions they assume to be true in areas such as the formulation of goals and the nature of the opportunities and space offered to the client. Many therapists I have worked with, or supervised, at times have a crisis about the relationship between some of the basic tenets of dramatherapy and those of the health service providers. These include tensions around the nature of health, individual identity and conformity, what is perceived to be 'society's' attitude towards individual identity and 'well-being', and the relationship between clinical goals, the way 'efficacy' is seen, and oppression. These, at their heart, are all to do with philosophy.

Grainger has pointed to the partial capacity of any arts therapy approach based in scientism to hold experience: 'The theoretically associated collections of data that we painstakingly arrange in systematic attempts to organise our world can never give life the meaning it craves' (1995: 21). Here he faces us with the philosophical dilemma that many might see beneath the everyday task of dramatherapists working within organisations such as the UK's National Health Service (NHS). If we look at work which is rooted in the need to orientate and communicate within a science-based system, for example, the charting and counting of phenomena as an indicator to clients and the surrounding health system of change, are there areas which are *philosophically unmet*? In addition, contemporary attitudes towards the arts as a field can be argued to lie in an uncomfortable relation to such a philosophical position. The idea that a work of art can have an identifiable or singular meaning or interpretation has been energetically challenged. Blanchot, for example, identifies an essential aspect of art as being that 'it is . . . always at the same time one and the other, the intertwining of the Yes and of the No, the ebb and flow of the essential ambiguity' (2000: 348). Philosophical enquiry connected to deconstructionism has challenged the authenticity of grand narratives and the authority of single meanings: 'Deconstruction mistrusts proper names . . . it will deal . . . with different moments, different applications . . . while trusting no generality and no confuguration that is solid and given . . .' (Derrida 2001: 9). A radical sense of variety, contextual meanings and playfulness replaces the 'univocal definition' (Derrida 1988: 141).

The earlier quotation from Grainger talks about the aspect of dramatherapy that is crucially to do with meaning making, which the position of scientism-based approaches to aim setting and evaluation can only partly satisfy. Is it valid for dramatherapy to philosophically ally itself with an approach to evaluation, for example, that 'relies' solely on observable material and 'quantifiable' phenomena? How does such a dramatherapist respond to the challenges made by Grainger and others who say that crucial areas important to living cannot be acknowledged by such a position, and/or which challenge the idea of linear single meanings? If this is outside the remit of a health provider, what can we do? Are we forcing ourselves and clients into a position that is dominated by a certain philosophical outlook? If we work within a session on different levels – in part counting and collecting data that are observable according to science-based methods, but also acknowledging the spiritual or the intangible – and do not write this up or acknowledge it within the evaluation and account of change presented to a setting such as a hospital, are we lying to ourselves and the client and permitting the organisation to continue to operate a system of philosophical apartheid?

Issues concerning the relationship between therapy space and faith have been much examined. Dramatherapists have written their views and positions relating to belief and therapy (Jennings 1991; Grainger 1995; Landy 2001). In relation to dramatherapy, how does the philosophical debate about scientism and obscurantism relate to the position of those who adopt a theoretical and philosophical position foregrounding faith? Grainger has directly said that dramatherapy is a spiritual therapy. He justifies this by saying that it can become 'a kind of acted mysticism, as its movements take on the form of a meditation, the procession of bodies which are movements of soul, glimpses of personal truth' (Grainger 1995: 21).

McNiff uses similar concepts when he says that 'I believe our work in the arts is more closely allied with the larger continuities of belief and faith. The arts can, in this sense, be viewed as sacramental actions that symbolically represent the mysteries and intensities of inner experience' (McNiff 1998: xxii). At first this would seem to ally the position on the therapeutic space taken by arts therapists such as Grainger and McNiff firmly within the obscurantism arm of Critchley's debate. Language and concepts used by Grainger and McNiff involve mystery, belief and faith. They use the language of the non-measurable to describe a key importance of therapy: talking of therapy's relationship to the 'sacramental', to notions such as 'inner experience' or the 'psyche'. They see efficacy and potency in areas such as the spiritual, or in relation to, 'morality and personal responsibility; ethical awareness . . . an overriding purpose in life involving the transcendence of present experience' (Grainger, 1999, 68), not with measurable, visible outcomes alone. Many working within bodies such as the UK's National Health Service, which are largely philosophically based in the scientific and the material, would find these areas hard to equate with the frameworks, validations and measurable outcomes that are the language of the NHS and its funding of resources. In their report on research into the concepts of psychological health in the factors used within final assessments made by dramatherapists in the UK, Valente and Fontana noted such a rift:

> The ability to pray seems markedly under-represented . . . there is nothing relating to an enhanced awareness of the wonder and mystery of life, or to a developing sense of meaning and purpose behind living.
>
> (1997: 28)

The issue here for me is that, given these apparent divisions in philosophies, is there any possibility of reconciling the different standpoints or providing a method of relating to both to inform practice? Looked at from this perspective, these debates or different positions are reflective of the philosophical divide discussed earlier. Is there any way in which the dramatherapy space can be seen that does not divide in this manner? The next sections on co-construction and phenomenology begin to address this question.

Postmodernism and co-construction

Some have located psychoanalysis and psychotherapy in late nineteenth and early twentieth century modernism and within a liberal humanism that asserted general, overarching applicable theories about identity and change. This is typified by ideas of immutable, generalist assumptions and grand narratives or stories about how all things or all people work. However, in thinking about the therapeutic space and relating it to the contemporary material examined so far from the field of philosophy and from therapists' responses to philosophical questions, we can see that the dramatherapy is not now easily allied to such overarching concepts about change and about how processes such as therapy work. Philosophical engagement with areas such as scientism, obscurantism, phenomenology and meaning help us see that there are complex multiple layers of debate and enquiry when looking at the nature of the therapeutic space, the therapeutic relationship, efficacy and the notion of identity.

Music therapist Pavlicevic (1997) develops this idea. She too refers to the cultural division between the language of science and objectivity and the personal 'idiosyncratically meaningful' (1997: 51), and to Mitchell's writing on themes outlined earlier. With the 'postmodern revolution . . . all knowledge, including scientific knowledge, is regarded as perspectival, not incremental; constructed not discovered; inevitably rooted in a particular historical and cultural setting . . . thoroughly contextual, not universal and absolute' (Mitchell 1993: 20). This is developed by Pavlicevic in thinking about the nature of music therapy in a way that can be useful when considering dramatherapy. She says that this 'new thinking' allows arts therapists to 'revisit' their practice from a position she relates to both art and science. This she describes as 'taking sides' with neither the absolute personal nor the absolute impersonal by drawing on 'both scientific and artistic rather than being either artistic or scientific . . . a part of each of these traditions belongs to a "universal" artistic/scientific tradition of music and therapy, and a part belongs to the highly personal and idiosyncratic . . . both art and science together are necessary to portray and express the life of human beings' (1997: 51).

How then can these issues be drawn into a philosophical stance which informs dramatherapy practice? The following material considers this question as a conclusion to my consideration of philosophy and the dramatherapy space.

A third way? Phenomenology and after

Critchley warns against the dangers of both 'obscurantism' and 'scientism', instead advocating a 'third way'. I want to try to consider this third way as a useful perspective on the nature of the therapy space for those involved in dramatherapy in the twenty-first century. He asserts that we live in a 'scientific world' where we are expected to provide empirical evidence for our claims or find those claims 'rightly rejected' (Critchley 2001: 4). However, life is not reducible to empirical enquiry: 'we need to clip the wings of both scientism and obscurantism . . . to avoid the error of believing that we can resolve through causal or causal-sounding explanation (p. 120). He says that this is 'much easier said than done, but at least we could make a start' (p. 120), and referring to Putnam (1978) advocates the need to acknowledge that the sphere of knowledge is wider than the sphere of 'science' if we are to arrive at a sane and human view of ourselves and of science. This is linked to a phenomenological approach.

Human behaviour, seen from a phenomenological perspective, is determined by personal experience rather than by an external objective reality alone: 'emphasis is put on direct experience and engagement' (Evans and Gilbert 2005: 15). It is often allied with field theory and validates subjective experience as valid knowledge. Phenomenology and the notion of 'clarification' rest on the idea that many important things about ourselves and our world are hidden from us because of their simplicity and familiarity; they are so much in front of us that we find them difficult to see. The task is to make these 'hidden' things more visible, to 'make these phenomena more perspicuous, change the aspect under which they are seen, and give to matters a new and surprising overview. In this sense, phenomenology is a re-ordering of what was tacitly known but went unnoticed; it permits us to relearn how to look at the world' (Critchley 2001: 119). Phenomenology has been described as 'the study of things shown' (Macey 2000: 297). One way of looking at this philosophical approach is that it attempts to 'bracket out' all preconceptions and assumptions that might intervene with the immediate perception of any phenomena. This includes 'scientific assumptions about the nature of the world, and its major appeal is that it promises direct knowledge of the here and now' (Macey 2000: 298).

A phenomenological philosophical approach could be argued to echo through many ways of working in, and thinking about, dramatherapy. One example of this is the emphasis on the authenticity of an individual's experienced reality rather than on abstract given authority. In dramatherapy personal experience is validated through the bringing in and examination of someone's life, for example, through enacted role plays. The primacy of bodily experience and active direct engagement as an important element of being and perceiving and relating to others and the world, rather than by the notion of an 'external objective reality' alone, is a crucial element of such 'enacted' therapeutic practice. Evans and Gilbert's phrase that *'an emphasis is put on direct experience and engagement'* could be a statement of intent for much dramatherapy. Often work with clients can involve the interaction of imagination and physical expression to represent and re-examine aspects of their lives in order to see themselves or experience themselves afresh, in a different way. Again, this could be seen as a natural connection to the philosophical position which, summarised by Garner, says it aims 'to return perception to the fullness of its encounter with its environment' (1994: 2). Phenomenology as a philosophical position has potential uses, then, as a way of creating dialogue between philosophy, theory and practice in dramatherapy. As this summary has shown, areas of emphasis and thought within this philosophical school can help see the ways in which dramatherapy contains certain assumptions and positions about *direct experience* and the importance of *validating individual authority and perception*.

Critchley (2001) also advocates the idea of different philosophical positions for different aspects of experience: 'natural phenomena require causal explanation, while social phenomena require clarification by giving reasons or offering possible motives as to why something is the way it is' (p. 121). Many dramatherapists would recognise both of these perceptions – the notion that science has provided a certain way of validating, knowing and affecting the world, as well as a way of knowing what is effective. On the other hand, many would also acknowledge the sense that there is something else, that this account or philosophical position is partial. The connection between different ways of knowing and working is key to the necessary integration between artistic and scientific approaches:

> The arts therapies need not be seen as either art or science. The arts therapies are a product of a link made in a divide present in cultural concepts and practices. They are a sign of a vital connection between areas often seen as divided.
>
> (Jones 2005: 89)

As Gregory and Garner (2000) have also said of art therapy, it 'has uniquely combined art and science providing a model for interaction between two disciplines often seen as separate' (p. 1). This reflects a similar need to adopt an integrative approach that does not seek to reinforce a cultural division between the areas described above; a philosophical approach that encompasses rather than separates scientism and obscurantism. Phenomenology might provide such a philosophical third way for dramatherapy to pursue.

Identity: selves in relation?

I want to now focus on some specific philosophical concerns that the nature of dramatherapy foregrounds concerning identity. As an arts therapy involving processes researched in Chapter 5, we can see that certain aspects of identity and relationship are emphasised by the very nature of the form of the therapy. These factors include the emphasis on playfulness, on the transformation of identity through drama, on being a witness to oneself and others, the idea of the self as constructed through roles, and that a relationship with the arts and with others can be transformative.

These areas immediately offer connections to some philosophical approaches and debates about identity and selfhood. Here are ideas such as the self as reflexive, on the emphasis of action and physical encounter as vital to identity, and as a part of personal change. Philosophical debates relating to these areas include what being a 'person' involves, the nature of individual identity and the relationship between self, others and the environment. In considering these areas we can deepen our exploration of how dramatherapy can relate to some contemporary understandings of the nature of identity.

Contemporary philosophers such as Jacques have said that new examinations of what it is to be a 'person' have emerged as dominant in present-day philosophical enquiry (1991). Strozier, for example, refers to the centrality of Foucault's (1988) work in relation to philosophy and culture, in particular the shift in Europe from the seventeenth century of 'changing notions of identity: in the earlier period, identity was constituted in terms of relationship (e.g. family or patronage) and in the latest age in terms of the interior self' (Strozier 2002: 14). He examines a series of tensions concerning this shift. The interior self is seen as individual, insular and isolated. However, he refers to more recent debates which challenge this simple construct and 'a new impetus ... given to the premodern deployment of alliance or relational identity, now based on gender, race, ethnicity' (Strozier 2002: 31). Here the idea is that 'identity' is not simply an internally held entity but is to be seen as a combination of 'the interiority of self-experience and self-knowledge' (Strozier 2002: 30), along with a self that is perceived through relations with such groupings as race, by being *in relation.*

Others have raised philosophical questions about such divisions and grouping. Hall (1996) and Schwarz (2002) have spoken of the emergence of a sense of identity that is typified by being 'de-centred' and hybrid rather than individualised and monolithic. This is named as a 'diasporic identity ... it anticipates a politics of identity which is plural in its range of potential identifications, not singular and exclusive; which recognises the imaginative foundations of identity, as opposed by a politics driven by the search for identities ordained by birth (Schwarz 2002: 95).

Action, relation and role

Such philosophical examination relates to, and supports, the work of dramatherapy theory and practice which has sought to establish the nature of identity not just in verbal reflection and self-examination but in the *action* and *relation* of enactment (Jennings 1997; Johnson 1999; Landy 2001; Jones 2005). The self is active though drama and is formed through relationship with others and the society they connect with. The emphasis within much extant dramatherapy theory and clinical account is less on the internal individual, but more on the self as formed in, and through, relation to others and the world around them. Here we can see the way in which form and philosophy entwine each other. Active methods as described elsewhere in this book, from role play to group improvisation to play-based work, could all be said to have an innate connection to philosophies of the self described above. They emphasise connection and interconnectedness as formative and forming to the individual, those around them and the contexts in which they live.

A number of dramatherapy theorists and practitioners have specifically looked towards positions on identity which emphasise the concept of role. These range from the writings of psychodramatists such as Moreno (1947) to social psychologists (Goffman 1959), drama specialists (Courtney 1988), theatre practitioners (Boal 1992) and anthropologists (Turner 1982). An example of this process at work can be seen in the writings of Landy (1994). He draws on a variety of theoretical and philosophical positions on role and selfhood in developing a comment on philosophy and identity. These range from theatre sources to those of psychologists. For example, he cites Maslow (1962) and Rogers (1961) as based within a more phenomenological approach to personality with 'the notion of a primary self as whole and good' and 'psychological life as a movement toward self-actualisation' (Landy 1994: 20). He connects this with a humanistic approach to identity and therapy aimed at uncovering a 'primary self', and contrasts this with approaches to identity rooted in the analytical schools of psychologists such as Freud and Jung which see the self as divided. This he summarises as 'a battlefield between the forces of id and superego, death and life instincts, shadow and godly archetypes', or by a self 'broken down into components such as Mead and James where the self is seen to consist of different components'. Landy, with many other dramatherapists, draws these together to advocate a position where the self is seen in terms of role, as 'multifaceted, derived in part from the social world, and essential in building the human personality' (Landy 1994: 21) and 'the human condition is in part one of living simultaneously within paradoxical realms of mind and body, thought and action, subject and object, actor and observer' (Landy 2001: 380). He draws these into a theoretical and philosophical framework in order to conclude:

> Despite the moral weight of many theologians, philosophers, poets, and humanistic psychologists, the concept of the self as monolithic, monotheistic, and authentic oversimplifies human existence . . . In a culture of multiple choices one needs a way to think about or play out the different parts. One way is through role.
>
> (Landy 1994: 21–22)

Here, then, we have movement between theory, philosophical position and clinical practice. Landy takes philosophical positions regarding identity and debates about the nature of the self and shows how he moves into role as a basis for dramatherapy practice. He sees reality as a complexity of situations and draws on philosophical positions that echo those of the postmodern and humanistic nature of complex identity, role and choice referred to earlier. This is typical of the stance drawn on by a number of dramatherapy theorists who see the self as primarily identified in this way, which relates to a post-modern position. Individual identity is seen as multifaceted, responding to complex multiple situations, and as reflexive, in that one part of the self can look at and change another part of the self.

The embodied self: a connected world?

The embodied self is another key philosophical perspective that relates to aspects of dramatherapy theory and practice referred to by a number of authors (Dokter 1996; Jennings 1997; Jones 2005). Merleau-Ponty has argued that consciousness is always *embodied* consciousness and gives much import-ance to the physical body. He links a phenomenological approach to clinical and gestalt psychology. The emphasis is on rejecting dualisms that separate subject and object, advocating a continuum of existence where 'I' exists *alongside* 'others'. Perception does not involve the registration of objective data, rather, as Macey summarises, it involves an individual perceiving some-thing by 'constructing a bodily schema out of memories and perceptions. The body is a way of having the world' (Macey 2000: 248). This is of value to dramatherapy as it proposes a particular kind of connected identity. Here the perceived world is seen as being deeply involved in a self which is not a disembodied intellect, but one in which the world is a part of bodily memor-ies, feelings, perceptions and impressions – a connected world. This philo-sophical position of a connected world can be seen to reflect some of the core processes described in Chapter 5 of this book as at the heart of drama-therapy. These include the dramatic body and embodiment where the self is seen as being intrinsically connected to the world it perceives through participation in arts processes.

Vignette: clients with eating disorders

Dokter (1996) describes an example of her work with female clients diagnosed with eating disorders. The work took place in a psychi-atric unit offering a variety of therapies, with her dramatherapy work orientated in what she describes as a psychodynamic orientation:

> The psychodynamic input can focus on underlying conflicts and emotions. In this approach the difficulties around food are seen as a symptom . . . the arts therapies usually form one of the psychodynamic forms of treatment following or accompanying weight restoration.
>
> (1996: 184)

The example below is from a six-month intervention focusing on 'difficulties in interpersonal relationships', with the art medium being seen as enabling exploration and the cited aim to 'address and adjust' fixed obsessional thought and behaviour patterns' (1996: 184). The extract shows the ways in which some of the philosophical ideas about the embodied self can be used to look at the philosophy implicit in the way the dramatherapy is practised:

> A client with anorexia, for example, in an open dramatherapy group . . . always chose a solid piece of rock to represent herself. She described the rock as unwanted, ugly and unmovable. Working with other clients and their objects meant that the identity of her rock changed with other people's perceptions; they saw its solidity, its hidden attractive veins, its smooth shape. Staying purely within the story metaphor, alternatives to her perception were offered. She would not easily accept these other perceptions but recognised their possible validity.
>
> (Dokter 1996: 184)

Within this work certain assumptions about self, other and change are implicit. These can be seen to reflect the philosophical concerns in work such as Merleau-Ponty on embodied consciousness. The client's situation as described by Dokter connects with ideas that the self is embodied. The self is seen in the physicality of the body, but also through objects – the rock. This could be seen to exemplify the notion that 'rejects dualisms that separate subject and object', and the idea of connection between the world around and the self. In addition, the way in which the client, the rock and the perceptions of other clients interact to help the client re-evaluate her identity and situation could be seen to reflect Merleau-Ponty's notion of a continuum of existence, involving self, objects, other clients and the idea that 'I exists alongside others'. We can also see at work here the practical reflections of a philosophical position cited above, in which people construct 'a bodily schema out of memories and perceptions. The body is a way of having the world' (Macey 2000: 248), in that the client's relationship with her self, body, bodily image and the perceptions of those around her are intimately bonded. Here, by bringing the philosophical debate reflected in Merleau-Ponty into contact with dramatherapy in a clinical situation, we can see the ways in which philosophical assumptions are present within the work and the way it can deepen and illuminate how the practice is analysed.

Conclusion

These positions and debates are important to consider in relation to a number of areas concerning the dramatherapy. Philosophy can be seen as something which is needed to help negotiate and inform many aspects of clinical practice. In this chapter I have shown how philosophical debates and positions concerning the therapy space, meaning or the goals of life, what 'health' is, the nature of the therapeutic space and identity can relate to dramatherapy. In an introductory manner I have touched on issues concerning the ways in which self and identity are seen within some contemporary philosophical schools of thought, whilst examining some of the ways in which dramatherapy theory and practice relate to philosophies of identity.

As Valente and Fontana (1997) have pointed out, therapy should never be solely therapist driven and the philosophical meaning and nature of psychological health must be core concerns for therapist and client alike. They say that the 'good therapist' is:

> always functioning in the role of a researcher, observing and learning from client responses, and from his or her own application of therapeutic techniques ... [with] the ability to formulate research questions that probe deeply into the effectiveness of what one is doing, and to identify perceptive and appropriate responses to these questions.
>
> (Valente and Fontana 1997: 29)

This chapter has shown that such questions must include those that are philosophical in nature and which ask and demand thought and enquiry about the nature of the space itself and the notions of self, identity and personhood that we engage in within that space and in life outside it.

Part III

5 Dramatherapy: therapeutic core processes

> The challenge . . . is to keep the discourse open and allow the richness of voices to be heard.
>
> Landy, *New Essays in Drama Therapy*

Introduction

Why should change happen in dramatherapy?

This chapter defines how dramatherapy is effective. It does so by identifying a number of different elements which combine in dramatherapy work. These elements, or core processes, describe the ways in which drama and theatre forms and processes can be therapeutic. The factors or elements do not consist of specific techniques or methods. They concern fundamental processes within all dramatherapy. The processes will be defined and then clinical vignettes drawing on research into the experience of dramatherapists will be included. These examples from clinical work will analyse the ways in which dramatherapists have responded and contributed to the idea of the core processes originally proposed in the first edition of this book (Jones 1996). The core processes are:

- dramatic projection
- dramatherapeutic empathy and distancing
- role playing and personification
- interactive audience and witnessing
- embodiment: dramatising the body
- playing
- life–drama connection
- transformation.

Each area is defined in turn. Then a piece of practice is analysed in relation to the processes. This is intended to give a specific illustration of how the theory of the processes can be used to understand how specific pieces of dramatherapy practice are effective. Karkou and Sanderson used the original core processes (Jones 1996) to create a table form denoting the nature of change in dramatherapy (2005: 203) and refer to them as 'elaborations on Yalom's (1970) curative factors . . . installation of hope, universality . . . imitative behaviour . . . adapted . . . for different arts therapies practices (Karkou and Sanderson 2005: 76). This was my original intention: to try to distil and describe what might be at work within any dramatherapy. They go on to add that:

> According to Jones (1996) most of the so-called 'models' do not constitute comprehensive theoretical frameworks. Instead, they stress a particular idea and area of work over another. Alternatively, he attempts to define what is common across different approaches using primarily the language of drama and theatre. He suggests nine core processes, otherwise known as 'therapeutic factors', that are relevant to all Dramatherapy approaches.
>
> (Karkou and Sanderson 2005: 201)

Langley analyses them as a way of foregrounding process over method in understanding the nature of change, and sees the 'core processes . . . as [a] guide for dramatherapy' (2006: 22). Her commentary contrasts with Karkou and Sanderson's linking them with Yalom's *therapeutic* curative factors in her emphasis on their approach to dramatherapy as being derived primarily from *drama and theatre*. She analyses their value as lying precisely in this focus on the healing potentials of the art form:

> Jones' view is particularly appropriate because dramatherapists agree that it is involvement in the process of drama, enabling self-realisation that creates the potential for change in dramatherapy. These nine core processes are present in theatre and Jones shows how they apply to dramatherapy.
>
> (Langley 2006: 24)

Here are examples, then, of the core processes as defined in the first edition of this book being used in the literature within the field to create a table to describe the nature of change in dramatherapy; the notion that they are a 'guide'; their involvement in writing about debates concerning method and process, and the relationship between theatre and therapy. I decided to conduct research into how *clinicians* and their experience of working with clients relate to the processes I had originally tried to develop from my own practice into general principles. This chapter shows how the 'tide returns', as I described in the introduction to this second edition; how the original ideas have been developed by clients and therapists in therapy together.

The following sections combine the original ideas of the core processes with the findings of research into the ways they are seen by dramatherapists in their work with clients (see Appendix pp. 321–327). Clinicians were offered the opportunity to contribute vignettes which illuminated how they saw core processes in dramatherapy. The vignettes are a way to identify how drama-therapists describe and account for efficacy, how they depict why change can occur for clients in dramatherapy.

The processes are not neat categories, rather they are a language to try to describe aspects of a whole: dramatherapy. The chapter is organised into the different 'parts' or processes. Each vignette foregrounds a particular process such as 'witnessing', though it is easy to see as you read them that others naturally combine and enter the descriptions. The final vignette (pp. 126–133) is deliberately discussed in a way that shows the 'whole picture' of the processes together, after the individual concentration on the different elements within the other vignettes in the chapter. I include research conversations between the dramatherapist and myself after each vignette (see Appendix pp. 323–329), to help elicit the therapist's way of seeing what is occurring in the practice they have chosen to illustrate how drama-therapy works.

Dramatic projection

How do clients' lives become intimately involved and changed through drama? What are the effects of life experiences being connected to drama?

In dramatherapy individuals can take on a fictional character or role, play with small objects, create scenery or enact myths. As this happens, they project aspects of themselves into the dramatic material. A theatre in miniature is created within the group and within the self.

The classic Freudian position sees processes such as projection and identi-fication as primarily defensive. For dramatherapy, though, the importance lies in the way in which this phenomenon of dramatic projection creates a vital relationship between inner emotional states and external forms and presences. Dramatic forms and processes, whether playing with objects or playing roles, connect outer expression in drama with inwardly held feelings or life experiences. One of the clients in Casson's dramatherapy group described a part of this process beautifully when she said:

> *Shiela*: I found that was quite good because it made you realize what the other person was seeing in their mind's eye.
>
> (Casson 2004: 172)

She goes on to say:

> One week John brought some little trinkets and asked us what they were and what they represented to us . . . I think [I chose] a little jewellery box . . . at the time I didn't realize it but afterwards I thought, 'Ooh it's like secrets being locked up and you're opening the box and your secrets

coming out. That's what I've done in the group. I've opened up . . . Before I went to the group I wouldn't open up to anyone, I wouldn't tell anyone how I was feeling.

(Casson 2004: 173)

Dramatic projection within dramatherapy is the process by which clients project aspects of themselves or their experience into theatrical or dramatic materials or into enactment, and thereby externalise inner conflicts. A relationship between the inner state of the client and the external dramatic form is established and developed through action. The dramatic expression enables change through the creation of perspective, along with the opportunity for exploration and insight through the enactment of the projected material.

The following vignette reflects these processes, as a client finds a way to communicate and find form for their feelings and experiences through drama. The story provided by dramatherapist Jo Van Den Bosch creates a way first to express and then to change the client's relationship to difficult personal material. Van Den Bosch describes the client in this way:

> Brenda came to her first dramatherapy session on an acute assessment unit for older adults. She had been irritable on the ward and staff and other patients found communication with her difficult. She had been depressed for a while, in fact ever since she had a mastectomy at 62 years of age. She had been treated with several different classes of antidepressants with little success. By the age of 70 the cancer had returned and spread to her bones and she had become even more depressed with suicidal ideation. Unfortunately, events earlier in her life had caused her to become distanced from her family. She had divorced her husband and was not close to her sons. She felt isolated. She was admitted for ECT but this only produced a transient improvement in mood. The group Brenda was joining was a slow, open group on an inpatient assessment unit. The other members of the group had been given many different diagnoses including depressive illnesses, psychotic illness and alcohol dependency. Before she came to the group Brenda refused to speak about her cancer, and to believe it had anything to do with her low mood. The staff and other patients on the ward experienced her as difficult and irascible.

Research vignette: Brenda

Brenda joined the ward dramatherapy group. The third session she attended began with an opening ritual with the group throwing a ball as a way of introducing each other to the space including both their names and anything they wanted to say about how they were feeling. Brenda spoke about feeling lonely and unhappy. The group went on to explore the story of the two wolves, from Gersie and King's *Storymaking in Education and Therapy* (1990). The story, called 'A Storm Coming', told of an Uncle and Nephew Wolf who lived together. The Nephew ran a farm and the Uncle was lazy and left him to do all the work. The Uncle only wanted to eat the produce. The Nephew went away for a few days and the Uncle just ate his way through the manioc crops which had been grown for winter. When the Nephew came back he said nothing but started making a rope. The Uncle was curious and wanted to know what he was doing. The Nephew told him there was a storm coming and if he didn't tie himself to the tree he would be swept away. The Uncle persuaded the Nephew to tie him to the tree first. The story ends with the line 'The bones of Uncle Wolf are still there.'

After the story was told the group discussed their reactions. Brenda was angry. She strongly identified with the elderly Uncle Wolf, even though the others in the group felt the Uncle had behaved appallingly. The elderly Uncle was tricked and left to die as a result of lying, cheating and stealing from his nephew. Brenda empathised with the older wolf saying, 'Why didn't anyone ask him about his behavior?' She then said very angrily, 'He was old. Perhaps he was ill and couldn't do things for himself, perhaps he had terminal cancer!'

Interestingly the rest of the group felt very differently about the story. The sympathies of this particular group lay with Nephew. I didn't respond to Brenda at this time wanting to leave her feelings with her in order for her to make her own connections. In later sessions she was able to acknowledge her identification with Uncle Wolf. She was able to tell the group about her cancer and speak about how because of her fear of it she had pushed her family away. In the group at this point we did not work dramatically with her story as Brenda verbally made the connections. However, as result of her disclosures in the group the rest of the team decided not to try further ECT to lift her mood but to refer her for individual dramatherapy sessions.

Brenda became very committed to the dramatherapy group and after discharge from the inpatient ward she began individual sessions. She wasn't immediately happy with this referral as part of her was still looking for a magic 'cure-all' pill. However, when she engaged in the therapeutic process she began to regain control of her life, contain her anxiety about dying and worked in drama-therapy to mend the relationships with her sons as she realised that, like Uncle Wolf, she had never told them about her illness or explained the behaviour which led to the breakdown of the relationships

We were able to use role reversal and placing members of her family in an 'empty chair' in order to think through her relationships with them. Eventually, she was able to accept her admission to the local hospice and died shortly afterwards reunited with her family.

Jo Van Den Bosch

Research conversation with Jo Van Den Bosch

Jones: What processes do you see at work in the vignette?

Van Den Bosch: Dramatic projection, witnessing, empathy and distancing. I was interested in the group projecting issues into the story and witnessing each other listening to the story and then responding. I felt that by sitting in the therapeutic circle they were able to listen and watch each other's reactions. For example, what were other people thinking – were they bored, interested, surprised? The whole group was in fact, engaged with the story. The rest of the group had a more or less unanimous reaction to the story. They mostly connected with the Nephew. Brenda's reaction was very different and she would have been aware of this in the group, not just because of what she said but also by witnessing the group. I believe it was this startling difference which helped her to examine her reaction and make the life–drama connection.

Jones: Jo, what do you mean by the life–drama connection in this vignette and how do you see it working therapeutically in this context for Brenda?

Van Den Bosch: I think the life–drama connection is Brenda projecting her own situation into Uncle Wolf and his behaviour. She was so upset by the Nephew's treatment of him and the way he appeared not to care about what was going on for Uncle Wolf. When she said to the group that Uncle Wolf might have been terminally ill, I'm sure she knew she was speaking about herself.

Jones: You say you developed the work with Brenda taking the themes the story work evoked, and developing it from metaphoric material with the wolf to more direct work with

	her playing roles from people in her life? Is that right, did it progress in that way?
Van Den Bosch:	The shift was from the group having a story read to them and examining their reactions to becoming the identities in order to think about familial and other important relationships.
Jones:	So, was part of what you were doing using different aspects of drama to help evoke things in different ways – seeing things from different angles, if you like?
Van Den Bosch:	Yes, and for Brenda it gave her space to acknowledge the presence of her sons, as up to this point she had never really spoken about family. I think this was like the idea of a play space, which apart from trying things out without consequences gives distance between the client and the material and enables both therapist and client to explore the material.
Jones:	I was very moved by the idea of bringing people/situations from her life and you put it beautifully in the vignette – 'to think through her relationships' – and then this seemed to have an effect on her life outside the therapy space, is that right?
Van Den Bosch:	Yes, she was able to use the therapy to practise talking to her sons and to explore what they might have felt by what seemed her rejection of them. I think what made it possible for Brenda was hearing the story and being 'witnessed' in her reaction to it. She was a bright woman and made the connection easily at the time and seemed to feel safe enough in the therapy space to express her opinions. I think the reactions of other people were very important. In our one to one sessions we did a fair bit of role reversal, which allowed Brenda to hear and think about how people around her might be thinking. So her usual thoughts were challenged. She also spoke about her fear of the cancer and the dying and these thoughts had felt unspeakable before which is why she'd tried to keep them locked up inside.

Dramatic projection, then, enables access to dramatic processes as a means to explore the issues which the client has brought to therapy. The dramatic expression creates a new representation of the client's material. The projection enables a dramatic dialogue to take place between the client's internally held situation or material and the external expression of that situation or material. Both through the expression and the exploration a new relationship to the material can be achieved by the client. From this, the reintegration of the material can occur, within the new relationship.

Further research on this core process can be found in the following research vignettes:

Sarah, Chapter 6 (p. 146); Jilly, Chapter 6 (p. 148); John, Chapter 12 (p. 302).

Playing

How can playing be therapeutic?
What is the relationship between life and play in dramatherapy?

In her research conversation, Jo Van Den Bosch refers to the idea of a 'play space' and this is central to much dramatherapy practice. Play in drama-therapy refers to processes that involve both children and adults. A state of playfulness is created whereby the client can enter into a *playing state*. The dramatherapy session is a space which has a playful relationship with reality. This does not necessarily refer to a humorous response to real life. Playfulness in dramatherapy concerns the way a client can enter a state which has a special relationship to time, space and everyday rules and boundaries. This relationship is characterised by a more creative, flexible attitude towards events, consequences and held ideas. As Van Den Bosch mentioned in her research interview about the previous vignette, this space enables the client to adopt a playful, experimenting attitude towards themselves and their life experiences.

Playfulness also refers to the ways in which playing can often involve the representation of events or feelings which a child, for example, is trying to assimilate, come to terms with or master. This can sometimes involve the playing out of an event or situation, and at other times the play taking on the theme or issue which reflects the material the child is concerned with, or troubled by.

Within dramatherapy play is seen as part of an expressive continuum – as a part of drama. As such, it is a specific language (e.g. object play, toys, games) that can be a part of the way in which a client explores or expresses material in dramatherapy. In Chapter 7 this is described well by Clare Powis in terms of the benefits it can bring to clients p. 189. Play content in dramatherapy usually includes play with objects and symbolic toys, projective work with objects in the creation of small worlds, rough-and-tumble play or make-believe or dramatic play involving taking on characters and games.

Playing can be seen within a developmental continuum of different stages such as sensorimotor play or symbolic play. This continuum is often con-nected to cognitive, emotional or interpersonal development. For some clients in dramatherapy, the therapy will consist of moving to a new devel-opmental level through play. For example, with a client with severe learning difficulties the therapeutic work might involve engaging in a shift from one level to another. This might be a change from playing in a solitary fashion to co-operative play. This change would entail a therapeutic shift in the way the client can interact with people and with their environment. They begin to be aware of others through playing, for example, and to use objects in inter-actions with others rather than remaining involved in solitary play activity (see Chapter 7).

A developmental perspective can also involve interpreting a client's prob-lem as concerning a blockage or difficulty at some stage in their life. Cattanach describes this as 'a stage in our journey where we got stopped and got stuck' (1994: 29). Dramatherapy's use of play can involve the re-creation of a state where such a block occurs, and the reworking of that stage in a more satisfactory way. The playing process within the dramatherapy session would aim to revisit that aspect of the client and their life and to assist them in renegotiating the developmental stage.

The following example shows a 13 year old developing a relationship with the therapeutic space and the dramatherapist, Jay Vaughan, in a way that relates to a number of these core processes. Within the vignette it is possible to see the therapeutic potentials of play language, the revisiting of a devel-opmental stage and time along with the notion of the play space giving permission for Colette to try different way of expressing, communicating and assimilating her experiences. Vaughan contextualises a part of the work with Colette by noting that 'Colette was five when she and her siblings were removed from their birth family for physical and sexual abuse and placed in foster care'.

Colette was 13 years old when she was referred to Family Futures for an assessment because of absconding and school refusal. The referral had been triggered by an incident when the police picked up Colette late one night in a local park with a large group of older boys who were taking drugs. Colette was already known to social services and to the education welfare officer as a difficult and troubled young person who often refused to talk when they interviewed her. Vaughan says, 'Everyone agreed that Colette needed help, the only problem to date had been getting Colette to engage with anyone to think about the choices she was making and why.'

In this initial assessment session, which was part of a whole assessment day involving the rest of her family, an individual arts therapist specialising in working with adolescents sees Colette. The aim of the session was 'to see whether or not Colette could be helped to engage with the therapist and begin to consider the reasons for her troubled behaviour'.

Research vignette: Colette

Colette was very wary. She spent the first 45 minutes of the indi-vidual session eyeing me and picking at her fingers. After a long silence she suddenly said, 'I never feel happy you know, never. Why is that?' I said that lots of young people find it hard to enjoy life when they have had difficult things happen to them when they are little. Colette breathed out, relaxing her shoulders, and looked curiously at me. I asked her what was the main feeling she had most of the time: angry, sad or scared? Colette explained that most of the time she felt scared. I explained that when scary things happen all human beings have a sort of animal response to try to save themselves from whatever is scary. This animal response is either to fight, or take flight or freeze. I asked Colette what she thought she did when she was scared. Colette sat bolt upright and widened her eyes. She said, 'Well I run as fast as I can and I just keep running.'

Up until this point the conversation had largely been one sided with me doing most of the talking. I suggested that perhaps using a sandtray might help Colette think about her need to run and keep running. Colette looked at the sandtray in the corner of the room allowing her eyes to linger. She said that she did not want to use the sandtray but after talking for some time about Colette's problems I saw her look once more to the sandtray. I said gently, 'Why don't you give it a go, it might help.' I brought the sandtray closer to Colette, who said it was silly, but with a sort of question in her voice. Colette's hand drifted to the sand and she stroked it lovingly. I put my own hand in the sand and joined with Colette in the touching the sand. I said how many young people find it helpful to express themselves using such things as sandtrays, not just little children. Colette ran the sand through her fingers enjoying the sensation and sprinkled the sand over my hand very gently. I then asked Colette to choose ten objects from three boxes of toys and arrange them in the sand.

She slowly gathered all the babies together from the boxes of toys and put them in one corner of the sandtray. She worked intently, stroking the babies as she gently placed them in the sand. At one point she brought a baby up to her lips and kissed it. She then built a wall of wooden blocks with no door cornering the babies in one end of the sandtray. On the other side of the wall Colette put two large monsters that towered over it and the babies on the other side. Colette then rearranged the monsters so that they were nose to nose and facing one another and, to all intents and purposes, seemed to be fighting. Colette sat back and looked at the scene. She sighed and began to run her hands up and down her legs in an agitated way. I asked her to describe what was happening in her body. Colette said she felt cold and could feel tingling all up and down her legs. She went on to say that looking at the sandtray with its picture of the trapped babies made her feel like running away.

Colette then began to talk as if she would never stop, tears slowly trickling down her face, which she kept brushing angrily away. Colette said she had tried to run away from her birth family but always felt bad about leaving the babies. Every time she ran away somehow she ended up back there and eventually she gave up running away and tried to barricade herself and her baby sisters in the bedroom. It did not work. They still got in. Sometimes she took the beatings and hoped that they wouldn't hurt her baby sisters. But sometimes she let them take the babies and hurt them, and she didn't try to protect them. She said, through convulsed sobs, that she had covered her ears trying not to listen when her sisters cried. She said she felt so bad that she had let that happen and often thought about it. Colette looked up at me and whispered, 'I still want to run away but all the pictures in my head of what happened to me come as well.'

Jay Vaughan

Research conversation with Jay Vaughan

Vaughan: Developmentally, though Colette is 13 years old, due to her early experiences she would not have had many opportunities to play. Even more strongly than is usual, adolescence in traumatised children brings up all the earlier childhood stages. It is not unusual for adolescents that come to Family Futures to really need to rework the developmental stages that they have missed. In fact Colette is more of a scared toddler than a 13-year-old girl and, as such, needs working with in a way that respects both these parts of her.

Colette was struggling to engage in playing in the sand and yet she was fascinated by it. I think that she needed to feel joined in the sand, as if the therapist was prepared to play, too. I followed her lead and joined in the invitation from Colette to play. In my view my willingness to join with her and play enabled her to engage with the sandtray. My engagement enabled Colette still further to share a haunting memory in the sandtray.

Jones: I was thinking about how it seems that so many things were happening at the same time! Colette seemed to building an appetite, or an interest, or an ease to allow herself permission to project into the dramatic materials. She seemed to be building a relationship with you through them, as well as testing herself, the capacity of the materials to 'hold' her and your new relationship. Do you see it that way or do you see the process working differently?

Vaughan: I would absolutely agree that whilst at one level a simple unfolding of the story of running away is told there are many levels of different things happening at the same time. Colette is absolutely learning in this small way to trust the therapist as well as to trust the process of working with the art. As the sandtray facilitates Colette to tell part of her story the feelings come with the story. It feels like it is a first time for Colette. Whilst lots of children are able to tell their story, and Colette may well have told hers before, what is significant is that she allows the feelings to emerge and the therapist to witness them.

I am also very aware that for many of these young people and children they have not had the opportunity to work in this way ever before, and it is a tremendous relief to work with a therapist who knows about the sort of things they may well have experienced, who uses the arts to help them express what is inexpressible in words, and who is able to pick up their non-verbal cues that they are actually still a scared small child. It is often unhelpful to listen just to what is said because so much is held within the non-verbal communications that often contradicts the verbal communication. I believe that if a therapist can attune to the child's non-verbal messages, as well as respecting their verbal messages, then the whole story that they need to tell can be heard.

Jones: What difference do you see your playing as making (compared to if you'd just watched)?

Vaughan: Whilst there is a time and a place for watching the process, there are also times when it is helpful to play alongside (parallel play) with children and young people in order to work with them. One crucial part of an assessment of a child is to assess what developmental stage they are at, whether or not it is possible to get close to them in some way and join with them in play. I suppose our work is ultimately about the relationship between the child/ young person and the adults around them. In order to think about how the child makes, or does not make, relationships and attachments the therapist has to think about how to form a relationship with the child.

Jones: I was interested in the reading of Colette's physical movement and then your comment about legs and running – what processes do you see at work there?

Vaughan: I would view Colette's tingling in her legs to be a healthy response to a terrible situation and one that she is bringing to the session, even though at first she does not know the significance of this response. By just thinking about the horror of what happened, her body responds in its usual way with her wish to take flight. In other words her unconscious old brain mechanism of responding to trauma is taking over. I would hypothesise that the smallest trigger at home or at school means that Colette's body is activated to take flight.

I am very aware of how the trauma response of fight, flight or freeze needs to be considered in these very traumatised children and young people. Understanding how this instinctive response is triggered in the body, when the trauma is revisited, is an important part of working with these children. This relates once more to the idea that one needs as a therapist to observe the non-verbal body cues and, as I would put it, 'micro track' (Pesso 1997) what is happen to the child's body. Body therapists would think about working with the trauma response in the body and helping the client understand when the sympathetic and para-sympathetic nervous system is being activated to enable them to put on the brakes (Rothschild 2000, 2006). It is crucial in a therapy session when a child has disclosed a traumatic memory to be aware of what is happening in their body. Rather than perhaps focusing firstly on the sandtray, the first thing in my view is to focus on the bodily response and heighten awareness of this. On the one hand, this allows the child or young person to be aware of what is happening in their body and feel in control of their trauma responses. On the other hand, as in this case, it allows them to see the connection between their bodily response and the story.

The creation of a play space in dramatherapy, then, involves the creation of an area set apart from, but connected to, the everyday world and which has specific rules and ways of being. It enables the client in dramatherapy to create within the sessions a playful relationship with reality. Dramatherapist Vaughan, in her research conversation analysis of the vignettes within this book, describes the work of Family Futures and play in a way that summarises how playing is a core process in dramatherapy:

'The play space offers the family an opportunity to step out of the daily life and try something different with enough distance to allow them to feel safe. In the play they can explore all the possibilities of what can happen and a range of different endings, the beauty of it being that it is safely contained within the play space. In this way, the family can rehearse different ways of being so that they can begin to bear to think about how to change the sometimes extremely challenging reality of their lives.'

Further research on this core process can be found in the following research vignettes:

Two weeks left, Chapter 7 (p. 170); Joe, Chapter 7 (p. 185); Patrick, Chapter 8 (p. 209).

Role playing and personification

1   How is someone's identity represented in dramatherapy?
2   How can playing a role be therapeutic?

The client in dramatherapy has a variety of expressive forms to choose from to represent the material they are bringing to therapy. There are two particular aspects which are common within practice: one might be best described as role playing, the other as personification.

Role is one aspect of the range of representative forms which an enactment within dramatherapy can use. Role taking or role playing refers to processes such as someone playing themselves, or an imaginary character or a person taken from life experience within a role play or improvisation. Landy has defined impersonation as the ability 'to fashion a personality' through taking on and playing out various personae or roles (1994: 30). For the client in dramatherapy this would mainly involve the mimetic expressions produced by their own body, face and voice along with the use of space and interaction with others to play a role, but could also include the use of make-up, mask, costume, objects and props.

Personification is the act of representing something or some personal quality or aspect of a person using objects dramatically. The literary definition of personification states that 'an inanimate object or abstract object is spoken of as though it were endowed with life or with human attributes or feelings' (Abrams 1981: 65). So, for example, in Shakespeare's *The Two Gentlemen of Verona* the clown Launce could almost be using personification to begin a family sculpt:

> Nay, I'll show you the manner of it. This shoe is my father: no, this left shoe is my father: no, no, this left shoe is my mother: nay that cannot be so neither: yes, it is so, it is so, it hath the worser sole. This shoe, with the hole in it, is my mother, and this my father . . . this staff is my sister, for, look you, she is as white as a lily and as small as a wand.
>
> (II, iii, 1511)

In dramatherapy, then, a client can represent a feeling, issue or person, themselves or aspect of themselves within a dramatic framework. They often do this by role taking – depicting something or playing a part themselves, or by personification – using objects (e.g. toys or puppets) to represent the material.

Role taking and personification can enable the client to experience what it is like to be someone else, or to play themselves within a dramatic representation of an aspect of their own lives. This connects to the process of creating empathy and can help in developing the ways in which a client relates to others. It can also assist in the process of seeing a problematic situation from the point of view of another.

The involvement of fictional or imaginative material through the role taking or personification can create opportunities to transform and explore the issue in a new fashion. The fictional world created can give permissions and allow explorations which the client might censor or deny in their everyday life.

The research vignette in the next section on empathy and distancing includes role playing within its focus and analysis. Further research on this core process can be found in the following research vignettes:

Island, Chapter 8 (p. 198); Grace, Chapter 8 (p. 217); Suraya, Chapter 12 (p. 229).

Dramatherapeutic empathy and distancing

1   How can empathy and dramatic involvement bring about change?
2   How can reflection and distancing be useful in dramatherapy?

Empathy encourages emotional resonance, identification and high emotional involvement within any dramatic work. The development of an empathic response to role, object or dramatic situations or dramatic activities may be an important part of the therapeutic work in itself. For example, some clients may have problems in developing relationships or dealing with others, due to a lack of understanding or capability to empathise with another. The development of an empathic response during dramatic work can help to encourage empathy towards others in life outside the dramatherapy group. Empathy often plays an important part in warming up clients to engage with the material to be worked with. This is the case both for clients who are working on their own material, or for people who will act as doubles in a role play.

Distancing encourages an involvement which is more orientated towards thought, reflection and perspective. In Brecht's terminology, the client functions more as a 'reader' to the material presented. This is not to say that the client becomes completely disengaged, but that they are involved with material from a different perspective. In some situations, the use of a distancing approach can help a client create perspective on themselves or an issue – the capability to develop such a response may be the therapeutic work in itself. For example, clients who feel emotionally overwhelmed may, within the therapy, try to develop a more distanced perspective on a life situation or ways of dealing with their feelings.

Both processes can refer to clients whether in an active engagement with the dramatic material or as witness/audience to the material. The functions of empathy and distancing within dramatherapy are related but different for 'actor' and for 'audience' member.

In the following vignette the issue of distance is key. Working with a group of teenagers, Kirsten Meyer describes how the taking on of roles gave the clients enough distance to allow their HIV status to be voiced with peers for the first time, at the same time permitting the articulation of the issue of secrecy and disclosure within the group, as well as in their lives outside the therapy space. The work took place in a project in South Africa. Meyer notes that recent statistics show that if someone is under the age of 20 years there is a 50 per cent chance of contracting HIV:

> Statistics South Africa produced a report on death registration data showing that deaths among people 15 years of age and older increased by 62% from 1997–2003 due to Aids related conditions. Craig Higson-Smith in his evaluation report on work done by my NGO says that 'the potential impacts of HIV/AIDS on childhood are enormous and complex. To begin to explore this question it is essential to move beyond thinking about children as an homogenous group but to think about the impact of HIV/AIDS on children at different developmental stages in different social, economic and cultural contexts.'
>
> (Higson-Smith et al. 2006: 6).

Meyer also places her work in the context of the ways that the stigmatization of HIV does 'not allow expression amongst the "normal" peer group (at school or at home), so a psychosocial support group of adolescents living with HIV provides a space for the "unspeakable" (HIV).'

The group formed part of a project that was set up between Zakheni Arts Therapy Foundation, which Meyer founded with an art therapist, a UK-based funder, HopeHIV and a perinatal HIV research unit at a hospital in South Africa. The doctors are mainly pediatricians who see the children on the clinical trials once every three months or so. The project was set up to run groups with positive children (ages 7–11), initially for psychosocial support, and to see if adherence to medication improved.

Meyer says, 'My non-government organisation, funded by HopeHIV, set up four groups. Two art therapy groups with children were run for a year. I ran one dramatherapy children's group for six months and, after that, one adolescent group for 12 sessions.' The specific goals of the group were:

- to develop self-esteem
- to develop a containing environment in which to explore feelings around living with a chronic illness
- to encourage different ways of expressing feelings.

The short-term therapy was for 12 weeks, sessions lasting one and a half hours, and referral was from medical doctors within the unit. Meyer described the group as being composed of five adolescents (one male and four females) ranging from 12 to 15 years of age. They had all been disclosed to (advertently or inadvertently). Two had contracted HIV through sexual abuse and three had contracted it at birth through mother to child transmission. She notes: 'Some of the group members had also suffered earlier bereavements and traumas such as the loss of parents, rape, physical and sexual abuse. None of them had disclosed their status to anyone but their families, and they were living with the "weight" of their secret and the "unspeakable", also the fear of rejection if they disclosed.'

Research vignette: Zandile and Nomsa

Group members were aware of their status, but had not disclosed to anyone outside of their families. During the pre-group assessment and interviews, all participants were informed that the group was for adolescents like themselves, living with HIV. They all expressed both to their referring doctors and me how much they would appreciate a group like this, in which they could explore and talk about their feelings around living with HIV. Until this point no one had mentioned the word 'HIV' in the group; it was still the 'unspeakable'.

In the session prior to the vignette below, a very confident and open group member, Zandile, disclosed to the group that she had been raped. The group was supportive and expressed their concern for her. When asked what it felt like to tell the group, she answered that she was scared to tell us in case we laughed at her. The discussion then led into feelings around disclosing very personal information to others. Zandile said she wanted us to know this fact as it is the reason she comes to the clinic (*the reason she contracted HIV*).

I was reminded that in our society having HIV is perceived as very shameful, as if having the virus were confirmation of having done something really bad or sinful. Zandile had never had the space to explore her feelings around being raped, and appeared to be emotionally stuck. Her relief in telling the group was not about working through her feelings of being raped, but having an opportunity to explain her HIV status. I understood her and the group to be saying it is okay to be raped but not to have HIV.

Zandile was not able to attend the following session when Nomsa and Busisiwe disclosed their status to the group.

At the beginning of Session Four one of the girls, Nomsa, was speaking about how her teacher had told her she has got 'adolescence'. 'I've got adolescence,' she said, like it was some kind of affliction or disease. (I was struck by how much easier this was to talk about.) The group then went on to explore what it meant to have 'adolescence'. They spoke of romance, bodily changes and mood swings. Nomsa said the thing she missed most about being ten years old was that you could 'play and get dirty', now, she said, things were different.

I was struck by the poignancy of her comment and wondered about interpretations of play and dirt: i.e. contamination; and who is contaminated; and what it must feel like to live with HIV in a society that views it as dirty. Also, at a time in her life when it is vital for her to 'play' with her identity, what it meant to be living with HIV? I was struck too by the fact that at the time when she should have just been playing (eight years old), her father had begun to continuously sexually abuse her.

I responded by saying that I wondered what felt different for them now. The group went quiet for a long time. Then I said, 'Well maybe some things are difficult speak about?' They nodded. I invited them to think about secrets and we threw a ball around the group, free associating around secrets. After this, there was a brief discussion of different types of secrets, feelings around trust and what it meant to keep others' secrets. This led into a role play around secrets. In the previous sessions the group had engaged well with role play and seemed to enjoy the process.

Nomsa suggested they do a role play and the rest of the group said they would like this very much, and then the session moved very quickly. Nomsa wanted to 'act' first and asked Miriam to join her. Miriam accepted.

After a warm-up, I invited the audience group members to say what the two girls' relationship could be. Busisiwe suggested they were 'best friends'. I then asked for suggestions as to where they might be. Busisiwe also suggested they were in the playground during break. With this in mind I suggested that one of them had something to tell the other that is important. Nomsa said she would like to be that person and commenced the role play. (They chose to keep their names.) It was a very brief role play. Both were sitting on chairs. Nomsa turned to Miriam.

Nomsa: 'Can I trust you?'
Miriam: 'Yes.'
Nomsa: 'I am HIV positive.'
Miriam: [giggles with hand over her mouth]
Nomsa: 'Did you hear me?'
Miriam: 'Yes.'

Nomsa: 'Well?'
Miriam: 'Just don't tell anybody else.'

After this we de-roled, during which Nomsa said she felt 'relieved' and that that was the first time she had ever told anyone she was HIV. I felt relief too; holding this 'secret' had been difficult and intense.

We were grouped on our cushions in a circle and I invited the group to reflect on what had happened. This led to a very intense silence. Nomsa then said it felt so good to say it out loud. We spoke about the difficulties of disclosure and other people's perceptions. Nomsa also said she would like to set up a support group at her school at some stage. There were long periods of silence and I reflected on how difficult it was to talk about HIV. Then very quietly Busisiwe said, 'I have something to say. I am HIV.' The group fell quiet again.

In reflecting on the group afterwards, I wondered about the significance of saying out loud (naming), 'I am HIV.' They all knew their status, and they were aware that the others were positive as well. It felt as though a process had been necessary in which they could begin to name it for themselves. Through embodiment and distance (lack thereof), they were able to summon the courage needed.

Kirsten Meyer

Research conversation with Kirsten Meyer

Meyer: I think the process of empathy was core. The witnessing of each other's processes and words was very moving and powerful from my perspective as therapist; and I think for them too, the very many quiet moments as they looked at each other, and the tone of their voices. I think that having a space made for this group of teenagers was very meaningful to them. In my view, it somehow represented the possibility of the idea that space could be made internally to contemplate the illness. Creating the safety of the space was very important for them and I think they only really began to trust it towards the end. So in the vignette it felt as if they were 'testing the waters'.

Jones: I'm just wondering about your thoughts/ways of looking at that space: the space of the group/the individual's internal space. In the next sentences you use the word 'play' twice: something being 'played out' and 'play out telling'. In a profound way, do you think the space was linked to ideas about a play space? I am just wondering about your thoughts about your use of the term there. I'd be interested to hear your reflections about why you used it/what it might mean?

Meyer: Something was being played out in the sessions around 'telling' and 'trusting' between and within them. I had a sense that if they could play out 'telling' in dramatherapy, an internal shift may occur around acknowledgement, and the very beginnings of the process of integrating the 'unwanted' aspects/'sick' parts of themselves. In my view, this is what needed to happen long before they could even contemplate speaking about it outside the therapy space.

Jones: The way you talked about what was happening was almost as if you saw them trying to touch and name their status, as if the distancing wasn't so much a process of achieving distance from overwhelming feelings so much as a way in – to respect the tentativeness but at the same time, through saying 'it's a role', to allow their status to enter the room and be named?

Meyer: Absolutely. They were hungry to say it and the roles gave them the space to say it and say it, and say it again.

Jones: I was very interested in the way the young women acted as 'best friends' so in role not just playing themselves, and yet chose to keep their names. What did you make of that when you were in the session?

Meyer: For them it made no sense to change their names (as they told me). I think it relates to the 'me and not me' process in role play. They needed to say 'I've got HIV' as themselves, but needed a context to say it in, and the context of best friends allowed this.

Here the two group members seemed to need to create a degree of distance from themselves by creating roles in which they are talking as 'friends', yet they keep their own identities, in that they choose not to play other people or invented characters. The dramatising creates a combination of distancing and empathy within the group. For Nomsa, the distance of dramatising herself provides a way of expressing the secret. For Busisiwe, witnessing the dramatised roles creates empathy with the scenario, and with Nomsa's disclosure, and she is able to talk for the first time also. This shows how the processes of distancing and empathy can work in a number of ways within the therapeutic process.

Often empathy and distancing are presented as oppositional forces, two opposing processes within theatre and within dramatherapy. I would argue that it is more profitable to see both as part of any reaction we have to a dramatic phenomenon whether in a theatre or a therapy group. One may be foregrounded more strongly than the other, but it would be inaccurate to describe a response as being completely distanced or completely empathised. These processes have been linked to mediation and the ways in which an individual relates to others and events in life: 'Healthy functioning requires a balance of feeling and thought' (Landy 1994: 111). Within any one reaction or engagement, the client is likely to experience aspects of both processes and this can be used to fuel development and movement within the dramatherapy session. The tension, or movement, between the two can create the dynamic of change which is essential to the work being undertaken. For example, moving under the skin of a role by playing the part and then looking at the role during de-roling can engender insight, and a changed perspective upon the role and the situation the role has encountered during the enactment.

The dramatherapist needs to consider the specific context: the client's needs at any particular point in an enactment and the relationship of an exercise or activity to the empathy/distancing phenomenon.

Further research on this core process can be found in the following research vignettes:

Children and the tsunami, Chapter 7 (p. 157); Kia, Chapter 10 (p. 261); Bilal, Chapter 10 (p. 257).

Active witnessing

Can being an audience member be therapeutic?
What does witnessing in dramatherapy involve?

Witnessing is the act of being an audience to others or to oneself within dramatherapy. In dramatherapy the therapeutic possibilities of witnessing others and being given the opportunity to be a witness to oneself are of equal importance.

Within much theatre work there is a shift from the rehearsal phase to the performance phase. In the first phase the actors and director act as an audience to their own work, the future audience being present as an anticipation. In the performance stage there is a shift whereby the main response is that of the audience present at the performance. Within dramatherapy work this shift does not occur in such a marked fashion, except in cases where a performed piece is part of the therapy. In ongoing dramatherapy work, it is unusual for there to be an audience called in to witness the work. The audience in dramatherapy is interactive and has little of the formal demarcation of place and continuity of role of traditional western European theatre. Within one session the client can experience both audience and performer roles and functions.

In dramatherapy the audience phenomenon is present in a series of possible interactions between group members, and between group members and facilitator. Both aspects as outlined above – that of the rehearsal phase and of the performance phase – are paralleled within these interactions, but their form and effect shift. For the client within dramatherapy:

- the client can function as a witness or audience to others' work

- the client can become a witness to themselves: for example, by the use of doubling or role reversal, or by use of objects to represent aspects of themselves
- the client can develop the 'audience' aspect of themselves towards their experience, enhancing the capability to engage differently with themselves and life events
- the experience of being witnessed within a dramatherapy session can be experienced as being acknowledged or supported
- the projection of aspects of themselves or aspects of their experience on to others who are in an audience role (e.g. other group members or the dramatherapist) can help the therapeutic process by enabling the client to express problematic material (Jones 1993: 48).

Witnessing in dramatherapy can take place briefly, as one person observes an improvisation of another or others; as the group witnesses the improvisation of a small sub-group or pair; or in a more sustained way as during an individual's work, when group members and the therapist become audience to the role play or enactment which emerges. Often a key part of the dramatherapist's role can be as a witness to the clients' expressions.

The degree of consciousness of the role of audience can vary greatly. It does not have the formality of many theatres where the audience area is clearly demarcated, separated off with curtains, seated in rows, etc. It may change from moment to moment. The client in dramatherapy is a participant observer to himself or herself and to others. At one moment the client working on material may be at the centre of an enactment, the next he or she may be in an audience role, or doubling. Similarly, someone as an audience member can find themselves shifting as they are suddenly asked to double or to play a role in someone else's enactment. The client is called upon to act and at the same time to witness.

The audience–performer relationship can be slight, with no areas being clearly demarcated or no clearly defined roles. Alternatively, the role of audience member can be clearly delineated within dramatherapy, with the area in which the clients who are to engage in enactment being clearly marked and roles clearly differentiated. This creates a different relationship between those who are engaged as actors in drama, and those who are in an audience position. In such a situation more distance is created between one state and the other, and the act of witnessing is made more visible. This can serve a number of purposes: the creation of safety; the enhancement of boundaries concerning being in and out of role or the enactment; the heightening of focus and concentration and the heightening of the theatricality of a piece of work. The shift from audience to actor can act as a pivot for change, enabling perspective and insight.

The audience's presence can be used or experienced in a number of ways: as support; as confronter; as guide; as companion; as a pool for individuals to take part in enactment. This is as true when clients are the audience as it is when the therapist is the main or only witness. For example, as a recipient of projection the witness can be seen as punitive, as judgemental, as all-understanding, as competitor.

The idea of the witness in dramatherapy, proposed in the first edition of this book has been responded to and developed by practitioners and authors alike. In conversation about role work contained in the vignette Patrick in Chapter 8, dramatherapist Nancy Secchi offered another angle on the witnessing process in dramatherapy.

Excerpt from research conversation with Nancy Secchi

Secchi: I use my feelings as a guide to deciding what choice I make in the session and how to respond. My feelings take the role of witness but should not become 'infected' by the emotion too much (as may a witness). Witnesses by their nature may be over-distanced or under-distanced by the event they experience, the therapist has to try to remain aesthetically distanced.

Jones: Lovely ideas about witnessing here that stretch the ideas I put forward in the first edition. . . . I want to learn from your experience and thoughts . . . this intriguing idea about 'infection' and under-over distance . . . would be very interested to have your thoughts about how these notions connect with what was happening in the vignette?

Secchi: Due to my strong countertransference to Patrick (maternal if you like), I was at risk of becoming despairing (infected) on behalf of Patrick. I therefore had to let my emotions witness not only Patrick but myself as well, and process that simultaneously within my responses. I expect my responses were crude in shape, as I was trying hard to balance my distancing, while allowing him to have as much of an opportunity as possible to take something meaningful away from the brief interaction that he permitted himself on this occasion. When I say 'distancing' I mean that we as therapists are trying to let clients reach the most optimum congruence of emotion, which should lead towards improved emotional repertoire. This gives us insight into ourselves and others, and allows for better affective regulation.

Here Secchi looks at the way she operates as a witness to the client's work in the dramatherapy. She uses the concept of witness, along with that of distance, to describe the ways she monitored her own feelings and uses them to alert her to processes at work in the session. The role of therapist as witness as seen here is also to gain insight from emotional reactions to the client's participation and expressions.

Heymann-Krenge (2006) has said that 'Jones' concept of the "active witness" (1993, 1996) points to the present spectator acting within the dramatic space. I want to suggest that dramatherapy uses and stimulates two active states' (2006: 17). Here the original idea of active witness is refined to the 'retroactive spectator' and the 'present inner spectator'. The retroactive spectator describes the witnessing that occurs when the client steps out of the dramatic space and is therapeutically useful 'in the processing, sharing, self observation which appears after the dramatic enactment'. The present inner spectator describes the witnessing that occurs during the active engagement in the drama 'within the dramatic enactment' (2006: 16). Heymann-Krenge takes this even further and talks about the 'engendered spectator' connected to the ways in which dramatherapy witnessing can involve processes such as being observer and participant at the same time. One of Heymann-Krenge's clients from the research describes the process succinctly as I 'take myself outside to observe' (2006: 20), with another noting how the creation of perspective – the witnessing within the dramatherapy – took them to 'a different dimension. The context became clear to me' (2006: 19). The research into witnessing notes themes in clients' responses to its therapeutic possibilities. These include the involvement in the drama, feeling bodily engaged, a strong identification with the dramatic action taking place and at the same time a process of being a spectator, emphasising 'the spectator' to their lives and to the drama. Several clients in Heymann-Krenge's work commented on 'surprise' as a key part of the therapeutic process of witnessing, typified by them as the 'strength to choose and create . . . courage to act, understanding and strength' (2006: 21).

The audience–performer relationship in dramatherapy, then, can consist of a series of possible interactions: being witnessed by other group members or by the facilitator, witnessing others or in clients witnessing themselves (e.g. through video, role reversal or being represented by objects). The audience can play an important part in the processes of dramatic projection, the dynamics of the group and in the creation of perspective and support. Drama therapist Jan Stirling Twist points out a number of aspects of witnessing which develop the original ideas represented in the first edition of this book. Her ideas show how witnessing can enable particular kinds of empathic relationships between group members and that 'witnessing' skills and qualities can be developed within the process of group work. These aspects of the process have an emotional and psychological impact. Her research vignette also shows the ways in which the process of being an active witness can create relationship across difference – in this incidence across the divide of age and culture. In addition, she illuminates how witnessing within a facilitated environment can offer healing properties relating to the situation of people who cannot have, or have not had, their experiences witnessed in life outside the opportunities offered within the creative space.

The following vignette is from an arts project facilitated by Jan Stirling Twist. As she noted within her research conversation: 'There are themes, dynamics, interactions and processes that are akin to those we might find in dramatherapy.' The context is described by her as 'an intergenerational arts project facilitated by an organisation called Magic Me that brought together eight frail older people living in a residential nursing home with eight Year Five children from a neighbouring school'. Initially Stirling Twist and a co-facilitator prepared the children and elders separately to meet and work together; then the children visited the nursing home for nine weekly sessions. The session is described by her as follows:

> This vignette focuses on an experience between two ten-year-old boys, an older man living with dementia and myself. Each elder had been paired with a younger partner(s) in order to share a story about an important celebration in their lives. It was the task of the young partners to ask questions, tease out details and make a drawing that could be shown later when they told their elder partner's story to the whole group.

Research vignette: Bill, Ahad and Ileem

In the rest of the group, celebration events such as weddings, winning bicycle races, seeing the Queen's Coronation were emerging from the elders. As I walked around the room helping to facilitate the process, I noticed that two boys were engaging more with each other than their older partner. Ahad and Ileem were sitting on footstools at Bill's feet with paper, pens and clipboards but were talking to each other not to Bill. Bill looked a little lost and confused. I stopped to help them along and learned that the memory that had been triggered by the exercise was from a period in Bill's life when he had been a prisoner of war in a Japanese prison camp. The liberation was his celebration.

I joined the little group as I felt the emerging material could be quite sensitive and the process needed some support. I wanted to assist the boys to become more involved in helping Bill's story to emerge. I also wanted to ensure that Bill and his story were contained in helpful ways. I initially supported the process by modelling asking questions to elicit some detail and the boys soon joined in. We asked who had come to liberate Bill, what they were like, had they brought food and medical help? Bill spoke about starving, about rice, and a nurse who had come with the liberating soldiers. The boys drew images of prison bars, guns, a soldier, trees, a bowl of rice, a nurse's hat and of Bill smiling, happy to be liberated. I said how glad I was that Bill had survived such a difficult experience and that he had lived to tell us his story.

Back in the larger group pairs of older and younger partners shared stories of celebration, each child narrating the image they had made of their partner's memory. Using their pictures, Ahad and Ileem related Bill's story, witnessed by Bill, the group of elders, the other children, the support workers and my co-facilitator and me. There was a sense of real attentiveness in the room. People listened with care. Later the activities organiser, who had been present in the session and had accompanied Bill back to his room, commented that Bill had remarked on the event, saying how kind the children had been.

Jan Stirling Twist

Research conversation with Jan Stirling Twist

Stirling Twist: A key process we try to enable is witnessing. The importance of being witnessed as a young person (especially by a genuinely interested adult), or as an elder whose life story may never otherwise be told at this point in their lives, cannot be overstated. To have one's story heard and retold with care, to be able to tell one's story into receptive, compassionate ears – these are things that all too rarely happen for the people we work with. The process of getting to that level of witnessing needs to be deliberate, sensitive and responsive, with much reflection in peer groups and between generations.

Jones: Looking at your description, what about the experience would you see as valuable for Bill, and how was it valuable?

Stirling Twist: The evidence of value for me was in Bill's statement about the children being kind. He had recalled an experience of cruelty and ultimate liberation. That his story was listened to with kindness – that he experienced kindness was meaningful and remarkable. That there might be parallels between the kindness he experienced as a young man, a vulnerable prisoner, and the kindness he felt as a frail elder in a nursing home is interesting to me.

Jones: So, are you saying that the witnessing in the group re-enacts or represents previous acts of being witnessed – or, maybe, can even repair previous experiences of someone's not being witnessed or witnessed in a way they found harmful or inappropriate?

Stirling Twist: I think witnessing in a group can go either way. It can re-enact previous acts of being witnessed in helpful or unhelpful ways. If it's focused and benign it can redress or

	repair difficult witnessing experiences. I also think the story and the storyteller can find unexpected nuances and previously unacknowledged truths as they speak into the listening space around them. This can be healing too.
Jones:	I'm interested in your points about unexpected nuances and unacknowledged truths. Do you think a part of that involves changing role/perspective maybe?
Stirling Twist:	I think that listening to someone else tell your story can lead to discoveries, yes. A detail, or an embellishment or the tone of voice, even one's own impulse to make a correction or add a detail during the retelling (among many other things) might offer a new perspective. But I was talking mostly about telling one's own story and feeling it move into the space between you and the listener in new ways. This is most affecting when the listener(s) are present. I don't think you can speak about witnessing without also speaking about presence. When the listener listens with their whole body, the teller's body responds too, spaces open inside in response to a receptive containing spaciousness outside. The teller becomes more present in this instance, more present to the story, more open to the places where the story has been held. And this enables the story to become more present as well.
Jones:	I'm also very curious about your words about being witnessed in 'unhelpful ways'. Can you say more about that? When I originally wrote about the active witness it was as a helpful or healing process, so am very interested to hear about this to change and develop the original ideas. . . .
Stirling Twist:	Being witnessed in unhelpful ways is tantamount to not being witnessed at all, I think. If the story has never been told because of a lack of trust in the available audience, or has been told and not heard and reflected back with care, then there is no repair, but maybe there is more hurt. The listener isn't present. And when the listener isn't present the presence of the teller is impaired or even denied.

Stirling Twist talks here of the potential for a negative or harmful experience of witnessing. The following vignette touches on this, along with a number of other concerns regarding the dangers and potentials of witnessing as a therapeutic factor.

Mario Guarnieri and Emma Ramsden describe a moment within an intensive series of dramatherapy sessions that form part of an 18-month structured group programme, facilitated by multidisciplinary team members, for mentally ill adult male offenders in a high secure UK NHS hospital. Pre-group risk assessments and forensic histories are carried out with each patient (group member). Within this excerpt they describe the group as 'working with the concept of "victim empathy".' A patient, aged 23, is dramatically contained within the re-creation of a scene of his offence. This offence resulted in the loss of life at the hands of the patient. The personal enactment is witnessed by the group.

Research vignette: Witnessing

The patient describes the scene of the offence, where it takes place and who is in it. He is asked to briefly embody each role in the form of a sculpt. The group witnesses each image. The patient is then asked to return to the role of the victim, who he earlier depicted lying on the floor on his back. A member of the group is sculpted by the facilitators into the role of the perpetrator standing over the victim (making use of the physical space and representing, through mirroring, the authenticity of the action and the powerlessness/ ruthlessness evoked by this situation). In these positions, the patient (in the role of victim) starts to cry. He maintains eye contact with the person in role of perpetrator throughout the enactment. Both remain in role. A long silence follows, lasting between three and four minutes. Staying with the pain seems important for him. The enactment comes to a natural end, as the patient turns to look at one of the facilitators who is standing close by.

Intuitively the second facilitator, who has been a witness to this enactment, invites the patient to de-role. De-roling is used to disengage the patient from the active role and enactment he has participated in. During this de-roling exercise, the patient is asked to push against two patients who acted as audience witnesses as hard as he can, whilst verbalising any thoughts and feelings which have been building inside him in the silence of the role embodiment. He lets out a strained scream, yet pushes with all his might, almost overpowering his fellow group members.

Throughout the enactment all other group members are sitting on chairs, some distance apart, in the role of silent witnesses (i.e. watching the enactment without any verbal input). All the patients who are witnessing the enactment have themselves committed violent offences. During the enactment all group members seem engaged and focused on the enactment. All eyes are fixed on the scene in front of them. An emotionally charged atmosphere is noted. When the enactment comes to an end, the silence continues. Some non-verbal acknowledgements expressing support are made towards those who have been in the enactment. The group as a whole is invited to gather in a circle, ready for reflection and group de-roling.

This reflective period lasts between 30 and 45 minutes. There is no direction to this part of the work other than everyone being encouraged to provide some feedback. Direct connections and empathic responses are evoked and articulated as a result of the internal narratives of both those involved in the enactment and the witnesses. Both conscious and unconscious parallels with their own offending histories are made.

During the group reflection, the patient whose offence has been explored acknowledges a connection with the responsibility of his actions and his unexpressed and unresolved grief. He states that the impact of seeing himself through the eyes of another has put him in touch with the feelings of both the victim and himself. Participating in the enactment enabled this patient to begin the long and painful journey of coming to terms with his own capacity to destroy whilst in a position of aesthetic distance.

Having carried out work of this nature a number of times over the past several years in forensic settings, we chose this particular moment as it embodies for us one of the many important elements of this work: the ability to allow destructive and vulnerable aspects of the self to be seen and explored creatively by the group, supporting each other and allowing themselves to enter into the safe and trusting environment which is enabled for them by the facilitators.

Mario Guarnieri and Emma Ramsden

Research conversation with Mario Guarnieri and Emma Ramsden

Jones: What key processes do you see at work in the vignette?

Guarnieri and Ramsden: Witnessing, dramatic projection, embodiment and role.

Guarnieri: The empathic possibilities of witnessing an 'other', imagining being in their shoes. The benefits of witnessing relate to empathic qualities such as sensing – listening, seeing, identifying and differentiating, generally heightening of awareness in every way.

Jones: This being in someone else's shoes, I was interested in you saying that the witnesses to the vignette had been in similar circumstances to those playing roles. All the patients who are witnessing the enactment have themselves committed violent offences. Do you think this made a difference to the audience and to those playing?

Guarnieri: I definitely think it does help them to relate. You see, in my experience of working in forensic settings, patients have, in general, a particular feature: they consciously and unconsciously avoid thinking. They avoid linking thoughts with emotionality. They prefer not to acknowledge the impact that they have on others and others have on them. One way of doing this is to be destructive in therapy. One way of being destructive in drama-therapy is by an 'incapacity' to relate to what is happening in a given enactment. Hamlet employs a group of players to perform a play in which certain events of the play relate directly to the circumstances of his father's killing. Claudius and Gertrude watch the play, the mirror is held up to them, they simply could not turn round and say, 'It's a good play but it has nothing to do with me!'

This patient population can be very concrete in their thinking and if one works solely in metaphoric and/or symbolic forms of the dramatherapy then one might run into problems. This way of working does not shy away from the fact that we are focusing upon, and exploring, specific problem areas that have got the patients where they are now. It's much more direct, and they cannot help but identify.

Ramsden: Group members embody literal moments of past events, which they often only talk about in treatment. Whilst we never re-enact the actual moment of the offence (i.e. the death, or the stabbing or the penetration), we go up to, and immediately after, in a series of sculpts. In this way, the feelings in the physiological and psychological body are brought forward in different way.

Guarnieri: Patients talk about their offence and offending history endlessly to everyone who goes to interview them – they learn the script. Eventually there's no affect with these narratives, and they never expect to be 'exposed' by telling. In fact, its meaning is reduced . . . so embodiment surprises them.

Jones: In what way 'surprise', and how do you see this as therapeutic?

Guarnieri: They are surprised by the effect that working physically, dramat-ically, with their bodies, has on them as they often try to dampen their own affect or have it dampened for them by medication. I see this as therapeutic because of potential for reconnecting emotions with thoughts and behaviour.

Ramsden: The connection within, for example, eye contact is almost beyond words. I was in the position of seeing both roles during this enactment and the experience that was in the constant gaze (the patient was asked to keep his gaze constant and not look away) was a profound moment of human connection. Eye contact connects us directly to ideas of empathic exchanges. If I look into the eyes of another, I am making a non-verbal connection which can be read. This begins the process of making a person seen as inanimate into an animated being, with life and will and thoughts. This connection with eye contact whilst being in role, it keeps the past in the present, if that's possible. The feelings are brought into the here and now and are experienced in the room.

Guarnieri: The past becomes more 'alive' in the present, and 'off the script'. It then makes it possible to work through the 'stuckness' of the trauma that resulted in the perpetration of the offence. The patient is encouraged to make links with the victim and the way they, the patient, might have felt about themselves at that time. The whole process is about evoking empathy for themselves and for the victim; to understand the victim in the perpetrator. If they don't have empathy towards themselves they won't do towards another either. And yes, it is also about the patient taking us to 'see' that.

Ramsden: Often the offences were committed in chaos, in states of great mental distress, in great fear and with little or no thinking space (reflective space – as, with it, some of the offences would not have been committed). It's as if some of the patients have wiped out these memories for years and tried to sublimate them or just disassociate with them.

Jones: Very interested in what you're saying about stopping time within the re-enactment – specially when you talked earlier about it being common for clients to be bringing very 'chaotic' experiences of their past. I am wondering if part of the process in dramatherapy is to do with you helping them create a different relationship to what was happening than in the original real life context? Maybe their becoming 'readers' rather than 'victims' of their experience?

Guarnieri: Exactly right, Phil. The moment-by-moment freeze-frames bring some clarity to chaotic thoughts and feelings. The thoughts and feelings can then be explored further in some detail – the patient's associations to the thoughts and feelings, bringing to the fore earlier memories. This untanglement is part of the working through of the knots, the stuckness, the repetitions of defence mechanisms, particularly projection, that is, blaming others.

Ramsden: I like this idea of being a reader as it suggests a need to consciously *think*, which is of course part of this work, in trying see where the choices have been made. Often we can easily see many choices which have been made from the thought to the action of the crime – which is where slow motion work, such as sculpts and frozen images comes to the fore. In this way it is, as you suggest, to enable the reading of the events. Hopefully, this education could lead to knowledge in future and change the way of being for the patient if faced with another situation. It is a positive reframing as it is in a therapeutic environment where we as facilitators are holding the boundaries of safety for the group and in turn, as the work progresses, asking them to take hold of that responsibility for themselves in the group and with others through empathy. Many of the patients have played and replayed the incidents in their minds and in their previous environments which have themselves been chaotic. In the therapy thought and feeling enable positive action – where perhaps feeling and no thought for these patients has led to negative action.

In this vignette there are different layers of witnessing. Through playing out the incident the client is *witnessing* their own life – being a witness to themselves, a reader of their own life as well as a participant. Through playing the role of victim they are also witnessing someone playing themselves and, as the therapists note, inhabiting a dramatic version of the 'other' within a violent incident ending in the death of the person they play. The piece is witnessed by the person playing the role of the patient, by the group and by the therapists. In this way other people are, as audience and players, being allowed by the client to share a moment of their life. Perhaps sharing this moment with others can change the client's relationship to the incident. Ramsden, Guarnieri and Heymann-Krenge all talk about 'surprise' as a key element of this. This witnessing might open up an experience that they have felt silent and stuck with to exploration and reflection. In addition, the process of involving others by letting them see such an incident can be a key moment in developing the client's relationship to the group – whether the sharing leads to a deepening trust due to opening up, or to challenge through group members' comments. Ramsden and Guarnieri identify the importance of developing the group as a holding and containing environment to enable witnessing. The vignette demonstrates how the involvement of others in being with the intense experience of a dramatised life event is a powerful factor in change.

Further research on this core process can be found in the following research vignettes:

Patrick, Chapter 8 (p. 209); Grace, Chapter 8 (p. 217); Desert journey, Chapter 10 (p. 311).

Embodiment: the dramatic body

How does someone's body relate to their identity?
What does the active use of their body in therapy offer to clients?

In theatre the body expresses an actor's imagination, and helps actors to discover and express their imaginary ideas. The audience is engaged by an actor's bodily expressions through movement, sound and interaction with others. For most forms of theatre and drama, in all cultures, the body is the main means of communication. The actor discovers and expresses roles, ideas and relationship through face, hands, movement, voice – the body. The audience will experience theatre primarily as these bodily expressions in the stage space.

In dramatherapy the dramatising of the body is of similar importance. This concerns the way in which an individual relates to their body, and develops through their body, when involved in dramatic activities within dramatherapy. Embodiment in dramatherapy involves the way the self is realised by and through the body. The body is often described as the primary means by which communication occurs between self and other. This is through gesture, expression and voice (Elam 1991). Attention is given to the ways in which the body communicates on an unconscious, as well as conscious, level.

The way the body relates to an individual's identity is, then, an important element in dramatherapy work. On a general level embodiment concerns the way a client physically expresses and encounters material in the 'here and now' of a dramatic presentation. This participation results in a deepened encountering of the material the client brings to therapy. Hence the use of the body in dramatherapy is crucial to the intensity and nature of a client's involvement. There are specific ways in which this process relates to change in dramatherapy:

- The first area involves clients in developing the potential of their own body. Here the body is focused upon in terms of dramatic skill. Dramatic work aims to aid the client to inhabit or use their body more effectively. This might, for example, concern communicating with others more efficiently. This is related to the area described by Jennings concerning people who have 'difficulty in using their bodies in positive, effective and creative ways' (1975: 27).
- The second area has as its main focus the therapeutic potentials and benefits of the client taking on a different identity within the dramatherapy. Within this area the self is transformed by taking on a different bodily identity. This transformation can result in insight, new perspective and release, which can bring about changes in the client's life outside the created identity. For example, the client might grant themselves new permissions in terms of their relationship to their body.
- The third area concerns work that explores the personal, social and political forces and influences which affect the body. Here dramatherapy offers the opportunity to work on areas such as body image or emotional traumas related to the body.

Sociologists have considered how identity is connected to the ways in which the body is presented in social space. Some consider that the self presents selected personae in different situations and arrives at a sense of identity through bodily expression and behaviour in relationship to others.

Courtney (1981) has stressed the importance of the connection between the body, action, change and drama. He argues that in drama the body plays a particular role in the way we know ourselves and respond to the world. When an individual is involved in drama, knowledge is gained primarily by and through the body in action: 'Dramatic knowledge is gained not through detachment, but through an actual, practical and bodily involvement' (Courtney 1988d: 144).

By physically participating in a dramatic activity the body and mind are engaged together in discovery. Issues are encountered and realised through physical embodiment – they are made, and encountered through, the body. In dramatherapy this physicalised knowing and being within a dramatic representation of a problem or issue makes a crucial difference to the verbal recounting or description of a client's material.

As Courtney says, the acted out embodiment of an issue involves a bodily experiencing of the material *in the present*. It means that through embodiment the client presents and encounters their issues in the 'here and now'. The client, in physically portraying material in acting, explores something through immediate bodily experience. In addition, the client can reflect upon the material. Embodiment in dramatherapy is the client's physical encountering of material through enactment, and combines the knowledge to be gained through sensory and emotional feeling with the knowledge to be taken from more abstract reflection.

The following vignette from Taiwan illustrates the ways in which the taking on of different identities and images for the self can enable a client to explore their relationship with their body. A client who self-harms uses dolls and bags to express what previously has been communicated through self-injury. By creating a space and dramatic language, she expresses and then explores her feelings about herself in a way that permits communication and creates images that 'tell', that become focused into the therapeutic space and relationship. It also shows the ways in which drama can examine personal and social forces that affect someone's relationship with their body.

Maya is a 16-year-old girl transferred from ECPAT (a network of organisations and individuals working together to eliminate the commercial sexual exploitation of children). Dramatherapist Shu Ling Lin says, 'She attended this dramatherapy group because her social worker was concerned that Maya lacked confidence and self-expression'. Maya often self-harmed, creating knife cutting marks on her arm, for example, or screaming and self-injuring in her bathroom. Lin adds that as part of the treatment team she was told that Maya would also 'sometimes . . . present herself as seriously physically unwell and needing to be sent to hospital. When there, or on examination by a doctor, no physical problems could be found. Variations on this "script" were replayed again and again'. Lin was informed that both family and social workers all saw these behaviours as Maya not really intending to hurt herself, but as expressions of how much she needed attention, and her not being able to express it in any other way, or to allow people to talk with her.

Research vignette: Maya

At the beginning of sessions, Maya often lies down on the floor even when other participants are vividly playing around. For example, in some improvisation and role-play activities she often sits and watches rather than participating like the others, and she rarely expresses her own opinion to the group. However, it didn't seem to me that this meant she had no interest in this group, as she often tries to discuss the content with me after the sessions, so I considered that perhaps this is a reflection that she hasn't found a comfortable way to let out her own feelings within the dramatherapy.

In one session the girls talk about their one outdoor trip together as part of the project and Maya quietly smiles during the others' sharing. I wonder whether this could be an opportunity for her. Therefore I offer the group the chance to playback their happy time to me as witness. In the playback they would play each other. Within this Maya naturally takes one of the other group member's roles and they played it out straightaway after telling me what had happened on that day. While they talk about how they had fun on the beach, I take one more step forward. I suggest they start free associating with other happy times in their lives, including seeing shooting stars.

Because they all see this weekend trip as the first happy time since they came to this organisation, I invited them to talk about other happy times in life in order to break through reality life into the inner world. That's the moment Maya shared her memory. As everybody knows that when you see a shooting star you could make a wish, I used this metaphor as a key to reach their desire. Normally they would act tough and rejected concern and anything to do with feelings. Maya shares that she had been happy in her childhood. There was a period of time when she and her mom and dad often strolled on the beach and that was the most happy time she had with her own family. However, she also associated her mother's death with the beach, because her last memory of her mother is that she was walking towards the sea and she also went 'missing' on the beach. Maya didn't say in the group that her mother had drowned or committed suicide. Therefore, after her mother's death, every time she felt lonely she would go to the beach and wished she could finally get her mother back.

Maya says she has an image that her mother was walking back to her and comforting her loneliness by patting her head and whispering, just like talking to a baby. We enact a conversation between them. Maya is full of anger in that she wonders why her mother left without saying goodbye. She also shows how massively she misses her mother. She has a long cry and says, 'I miss her very much. If it's possible, I would do anything to have her back.'

In the next session, I observe Maya comes in earlier (normally she would be late), and makes a lively request for us to start our 'play'. In the session, we play with objects. She places a small weak ugly doll in the right hand of a big strong pretty doll. She says to the group that this image represents her physical pain and the worry that she can never grow up if there is no big person's protection. After her sharing, the group give her feedback. They say the big doll could be her social workers, the group facilitator (me), other group members. The two dolls she used were mainly the same body structure and characters. However, the big one has a very clean body and a smiling face but the small one has been marked with lots of scars on the body especially hands and face. I, and other members, ask her about the choice of doll. Maya quickly says, 'Maybe this is me as well?' She starts to use the doll to express those hard feelings. She described the small doll as a patient who suffered with lots of pain from scars and headache, and she even said that the doll had tried to commit suicide, because it lacks the ability to protect itself. She mentioned about sadness, depression, weakness, hopelessness and helplessness.

With this group we would have a long break in the summer, so before the vacation came I developed a symbolic closure activity. Each member could create an autobiographical video. This would be a way to reflect on the group and they could plan their video script according to how different exercises affected them. Maya planned her script in a very organised way and she chose a very specific way to show her evaluation of the work. It seemed important for her to show that the 'game' she made for the video is a way to let other people know her. In her video she talked very directly about her whole reflection on this group, including feelings of hate and love. Maya also showed us an image for a 'new' way she tries to deal with negative emotions. She takes a plastic bag representing when she feels 'bad' and she writes down those words and throws them into the bag.

Shu Ling Lin

Research conversation with Shu Ling Lin

Jones: What impact did Maya embodying herself through the scarred doll have on the group?

Lin: This emotional statement also stimulated other group members. From then on, the participants not only made jokes, they also started to talk about their loss and emotions regarding their families. Maya not only openly made her first expression directly to the group, but she also ritually opened a door for the group to start to talk about loss and emotions.

Jones: How would you describe the effect of Maya witnessing her own body in the doll?

Lin: Actually when we witnessed the scars on the small doll, we all could recognize the similarity. She described the big doll as an ideal character she is looking forward to being. When I asked the participants to change the image as they wish, instead of destroying the small doll she wiped away the scars and placed the small doll within the big doll's arms. She made two dolls look like holding together. She described that before the small doll could grow strong enough it would need to have enough support and protection. And when I asked her about the doll's pain, she answered in a very soft voice, 'She is getting better and better.'

Jones: How do you see the use of the bag and the video?

Lin: Showing that she can be powerful enough to take control rather than feel overpowered. During the video making and playing to the group, I was very touched by her confidence before the camera and her self-expression. This witnessing made all group participants amazed that the small doll has grown up and could be strong enough to express herself directly, to communicate directly and externalise her feelings.

Further research on this core process can be found in the following research vignettes:

What the thunder said, Chapter 9 (p. 230); Potential body in action, Chapter 9 (p. 233); Biomechanics workshop, Chapter 9 (p. 235).

Life–drama connection

How does the therapy space relate to the world outside in dramatherapy? Can something occur in drama that directly affects real life?

In some performances or enactments there is a clear split between the theatre world and real life – in traditional western plays, for example. In others drama and life might be said to intermingle for some or all of the time; an example of this might be certain types of festival or carnival. In yet others drama and theatre are given the function of reflecting on society or life; political theatre, certain forms of ritual expression or puppet shows in some cultures have this function. Courtney (1983) has described actors as being in a liminal state – 'betwixt and between'. They move into a fictional world to perform and yet they come from, and return to, 'ordinary' life.

In dramatherapy there is an intimate connection between life and drama. This is intentional and essential to the process of change in dramatherapy. If the connection did not exist, then the client might be able to create and maintain a separate dramatherapy world. This could be counter-therapeutic. Any change, any new way of being, insights, new relationships or discoveries might be contained discretely within the dramatherapy space. The client would not be able to bring life experiences into the dramatherapy, nor would they be able to take the experiences within the dramatherapy into their life outside the session or group. A number of authors have likened the dramatic state in therapy to Winnicott's notion of a 'transitional space' (1974) – a realm which occurs between subjective and objective worlds. Blatner and Blatner, in making this comparison, refer to a 'fluid dimension' in psychodrama, where reality becomes malleable and hence safer, enabling 'creative risk taking' (Blatner and Blatner 1988a: 78).

The notion of a life–drama connection acknowledges the therapeutic potentials of bringing life into contact with drama within a framework of intentional personal change. At times within dramatherapy the work involves a direct dramatic representation of reality: for example, in a role play of a specific life event, or the improvisation of an experience. At other times, the actual dramatic work will have an apparently indirect relationship with specific life events. Examples of this might include the re-enactment of mythic material, or performance-art-based work which uses abstract or non-specific movement and singing.

Many activities make a number of different kinds of connection simultaneously. A realistic role play of an interaction between a client and her mother exploring an unresolved problem might have a number of significances. To the client presenting the material, to the other actors and to the audience, the interaction might symbolise a struggle between two aspects of the self, personified by the mother and daughter, for example.

At times the life–drama contact will be conscious and overt for the client. They might decide on an issue from their life and proceed to create a dramatic expression deliberately linked to it. However, the client might proceed into a piece of work without knowing what the contact with themselves or their life might be or become. They might, for example, spontaneously create a story which is enacted. Only during or after the enactment might the connections with themselves be made. A client might be working in someone else's drama, for example. They might have been asked to play a role or to improvise with another client's material. During this involvement in another's work, issues might arise spontaneously which connect to their own life. For some clients, the experience of the drama, rather than a cognitive acknowledgement, is the connection between the enactment in the dramatherapy and their life outside the group. An activity might involve a change in the way they respond to a situation, or the way they feel about an issue. This change might not be made overt within the session, or even be conscious.

The fact that the dramatherapy space is connected to, but not part of, everyday life is important to some clients. Artaud has spoken of the need for 'true action' in theatre. By this he means that, in some theatre, the freedom can be taken to act 'without practical consequences' (Sontag 1977: 177). Solomon has spoken of dramatherapy in a similar way. It must be 'sufficiently removed from reality so that unconscious motivations can find gratification without the anxiety and hazard attendant upon actual gratification' (Solomon 1950: 267).

In some work the life–drama connection will be constantly acknowledged. This would be important for clients whose relationship with reality might be confused or tenacious. For others, as in the vignette, 'The prince in the tower' (pp. 242–249), it might be important to work in a way which has little direct acknowledgement of the life–drama connection.

Further research on this core process can be found in the following research vignettes:

Joe, Chapter 7 (p. 185); Island, Chapter 8 (p. 198); Beth, Chapter 10 (p. 267).

Transformation

What difference does it make to bring your life into drama?
How can life be transformed by drama?

A number of authors and practitioners point to transformation as central to any theatre or drama event. Transformation can be seen within a great many aspects of dramatic and theatrical processes. It can refer to the transformation of human being to player/performer, or to audience member, of objects or props into representations of other things, for example. Schechner (1988: 110) identifies two kinds of theatrical transformation. One involves the displacement of antisocial/injurious behaviours by ritual gestures and displays. The other is the transformation of events into fictional representations acted out by invented characters. Evreinov goes so far as to place it at the centre of all theatre:

> Transformation . . . is the essence of all theatrical art, [it] is more primitive and more easily attainable than formation, which is the essence of aesthetic arts.
>
> (Evreinov 1927: 25)

Read Johnson, in discussing dramatherapy, says that human consciousness is always transforming 'as the stream of inner life shifts, ebbs and flows' (1991: 285). He parallels this with a dramaturgical model of the self. An individual should not be seen as 'a character in a play, but an improvisation . . . an active constructing of experience that is taking place all the time, a becoming, not a being' (1991: 286).

Within dramatherapy dramatic processes facilitate this 'becoming', this development of the client through transformation. Transformation refers to the changes in state which the client experiences through the enactments in dramatherapy. These changes in state are therapeutic.

Read Johnson depicts this as a dynamic relationship that is created between the internal feelings and images of the client and the characters, activities and relationships within the dramatherapy (1991: 291). He describes a transformative series of stages within the dramatherapy where the client:

- expresses the material
- confronts and remembers unhelpful or unresolved issues
- works with them.

Read Johnson analyses this in terms of:

- owning the experiences
- actively engaging with them in dramatic form
- resolving and integrating the material.

Dramatic representation and exploration in dramatherapy can be described as a reorganising, a rearranging of material. Often this transformation can be experienced as destructive. Anderson says that growth is the 'disintegration of one way of experiencing' something (1977: x). Koestler echoes this, saying that creative development involves a temporary disintegration of the traditional forms of reasoning and perception: 'A de-differentiation of thought matrices, a dismantling of its axioms, a new innocence of the eye, followed by liberation from restraints . . . and a re-integration in a new synthesis' (Koestler 1977: 5). Looked at in this way, a number of transformations help change to occur in dramatherapy:

- Life events are transformed into enacted representations of those events.
- People encountered in everyday life are transformed into roles or characters.
- Objects are transformed into representations of something, or are transformed by being given significances which are additional to their concrete properties.

Experiences and process which occur within dramatherapy can be understood to assist change by offering transformation through bringing drama and life into contact with each other. Everyday life experiences and ways of being are brought into contact with dramatic ways of perceiving and dealing with experiences. The life experience can be transformed by this different dramatic reality.

The everyday, usual ways of experiencing the self and events are altered by the use of dramatic language. The self can be described through an enacted story or through a puppet. An event can be improvised rather than lived, for example. This means that the life event takes on the improvisatory qualities of enactment. It can be experimented with, and altered through, the playing and replaying of the experience. The dramatic language and process can transform the experience as it opens up new possibilities of expression, feeling and association.

The process of being involved in making drama, the potential creative satisfaction of enactment, can be transformative. In part this is due to a transformation of *identity* – the artist in the client is foregrounded within dramatherapy. The creation of dramatic products, the involvement in dramatic process, can bring together a combination of thinking, feeling and creativity. This combination has a transformative potential as the different aspects of a client's way of apprehending and responding to themselves and the world – thought, emotions, creativity – are brought together. Often these aspects can become separated, fragmented. In dramatherapy the client is often called upon to bring these elements together; they can become more creative, active within their own lives. Jacques (2006) describes how this idea of 'transformation' is a key part of the way active methods can empower the client: to assist them in 'user involvement and user empowerment'. He emphasises the ways in which drama within therapy can encourage the exploration of what it is to be a user of health services. Here the participants become active as users, rather than passive receivers of treatment. He describes this as an element of transformation in dramatherapy: 'the potential for personal transformation as well as social transformation as a result of the creative experience' (Jacques 2006: 11).

The relationships that the client forms with the dramatherapist or with other group members can be experienced as transformative. Past relationships, past events and past ways of responding can be brought into the present of the dramatherapy group. Here they can be reworked within the drama and the relationships within the group.

Dramatherapist Christine Novy gives an illustration of the life–drama connection along with the process of transformation in work with women who have come into conflict with the law. The setting was an organisation in Canada that intervenes at various stages in the detention process to assist women determined to change their lives but who are unable to do so on their own. The Narratives of Change project was designed for women in situations of transition and combined two methodologies: dramatherapy and narrative therapy. Novy describes her role: 'My focus, as project facilitator, was to provide the participants with dramatic and narrative means to explore alternative and preferred stories about their lives and identities and, in so doing, to give a shape and history to their progress.' She outlines the origins of the idea for the work in the following way:

> There were two principal ideas underpinning the project methodology. The first was an idea shared by both dramatherapy and narrative therapy, that people's lives and identities can be represented in different ways and from varying perspectives; that the stories we, or others, tell about us are creations and, as such, they can be created or constructed differently. Participants in the project were invited to step out of their everyday lives and into a play space where they might creatively explore personal life stories. The process concurred with Jones' ideas about transformation in dramatherapy: 'The everyday, usual ways of experiencing the self and events are altered by the use of dramatic language . . . The dramatic language can transform the experience as it opens up new possibilities of expression, feeling and association' (Jones 1996: 121).
>
> The second idea influencing the project, an idea from narrative therapy, is that the stories we, or others, tell about us have real effects on the way we live our lives. While some stories generate possibilities, others have limiting unhelpful effects. During my research for the 'Narratives of Change' project I was struck by the frequent gender-blind treatment of women within the criminal justice system and forensic literature. Women's voices, their experiences and their preferences were barely represented. This inspired me to design a project that would privilege the participants' own special knowledge and understanding about their lives and identities. Throughout the project the participants were invited to distinguish between stories, preferred stories that inspired hope and problem stories that they experienced as unhelpful and limiting. I found that the dramatic languages from dramatherapy brought this narrative idea to life, offering not only different points of view, but, through the creation of characters, different voices who had different stories to tell.
>
> The idea that the stories we or others tell about us have real effects on the way we live our lives also seemed to contribute an entirely new dimension to dramatherapy's 'life–drama connection' (Jones 1996: 121).

Research vignette: Lynne

To prepare for the project I interviewed each of the five participants about their life, the changes they were making and any themes they might wish to explore. Lynne shared that she had never really chosen her path in life and that currently she was in a lot of pain due to an inflamed knee. Physical pain, she explained, coloured every aspect of her experience and she was curious about its link to her emotions and the part it had played in motivating her offence. She chose 'rejection' as her theme for the project.

During the initial meetings, as the participants explored different dramatic tellings of their themes, associations with their bodies' experience became apparent. The women were interested to explore these associations and so I began our third meeting with some relaxation exercises that would assist them to tune in to their bodies. I then asked them to localise their theme within their bodies and to tune in more specifically to any sensations or images arising from this connection. In pairs the participants then worked to express these sensations or images non-verbally, firstly with their hands, and then extending the movements into a body sculpt, which I asked them to name. The following week they created characters based on their sculpts and I guided them to interview each other in-role about their characters' preferences and hopes, as well as some of the obstacles they faced and how they had or planned to overcome these. Lynne named her character Fragility. In role as Fragility she explained that Lynne frequently ignored her. She suspected that Lynne judged her as a weakness and explained that this intolerance caused her physical pain. She also shared a hope that in future Lynne might 'let her out' more and take a protective role towards her. Lynne later described this process of 'welcoming this part of me' as a turning point in her understanding.

At the project's completion I was asked by the host co-ordinator to write a report documenting any changes that the participants had made or seen in their lives during and since participating in the project. I decided to involve the participants themselves in measuring the outcome and in two follow-up meetings I interviewed them as a group about whether their experience had inspired new options for action in their lives. The interviews provided a valued opportunity for the women to identify and share detailed accounts of their progress. Among these Lynne explained that she had lowered her expectations and was now softer towards and more accepting of herself. She linked the changes she had made to the character interviews in which she understood 'It's okay that Lynne, who is perhaps stronger and less sensitive than Fragility, should take care of the other side of myself'. She explained, for example, that rather than seeking approval from her mother, who was always quick to find fault, she was now finding other sources of affirmation.

The group's feedback revealed that the invitation to distinguish between stories had sparked a greater awareness of personal autonomy, and that this resulted in several of the women making preferred choices in their lives outside the project. One participant explained it this way:

'For me the most helpful method that we learned was writing in a journal. You realise things, but what do you do with them? That's when you can write in your journal. You don't have to write it all. Because before I wrote about everything I did and that was discouraging. And it's good because you can go back over it and say "okay . . . that's when I had that realisation, and that's when that happened".'

Another explained it this way: 'Before I let any thought come into my head. I discovered that some thoughts don't make sense.' Lynne explained it this way: 'There are other means that I can use to help me feel okay about myself, like coming here, classes, taking responsibility for myself.' In other words: 'I don't see things in the same way'; I am beginning to 'take my life back in hand', and 'to make choices that suit me'.

Jones writes: 'The notion of a life–drama connection acknow-ledges the therapeutic potentials of bringing life into contact with drama within a framework of intentional personal change' (1996: 118). Their detailed testimonies in the group interviews also revealed how the participants were bringing the drama, or in this case their preferred story, into contact with their lives.

Christine Novy

Research conversation with Christine Novy

Novy: The processes I see in the vignette include transformation and the life–drama connection. Lynne was able to use the dramatic language of body sculpting to transform her understanding of herself.

Jones: I was very interested in the ways you linked sculpting with the body and role. How would you see that as therapeutic for someone like Lynne?

Novy: I think because she is a person who has been judged a lot by people in positions of power and so body sculpting and the role work pro-vided her with a language to share her own perspective. She described it as providing her with an emotional language.

Jones: So is part of what you're saying that the body work for Lynne was connected with reclaiming herself, and with issues concerning power relations?

Novy: Yes, my understanding is that the transformative quality of dramatic language provided her with a language to tell her story on her own terms and so reclaim her identity from those in positions of judgement.

Jones: Can you say a bit about what you understand by 'emotional language' as you put it earlier and how it relates to drama. I'm fascinated by that idea.

Novy: Well, Lynne described the non-verbal processes as providing her with an emotional language, a way 'to speak from inside'. She said that verbal language was like a mask that she had used to hide behind to avoid judgement and being rejected. She felt that it was the spontaneous quality of the non-verbal processes that helped her see behind the mask.

Jones: I guess I'm thinking about the way the body can 'mask' feelings and experiences, or it can become open to express and explore the things it has been 'holding' but not expressing? Is that maybe a part of how you saw transformation for Lynne?

Novy: I would say that the body/movement processes assisted Lynne to explore some things that she had been holding but not expressing, but which were surfacing in physical conditions. So it seemed to create room for another point of view, in the voice of Fragility.

Jones: I really wanted to ask you how you look at clients' understanding of what was happening, say in the embodiment work, and how it 'connected' to their lives outside the group – how they made connections?

Novy: My hope was that the transformative quality of the embodiment work would provide a sense that the stories we, or others, tell about us are creations and so can be created differently. This ties in with what you write about transformation of identity. But I especially wanted to highlight the artist's privileged position as an interpreter of life experience and to privilege the women's own special knowledge and understanding by encouraging them to differentiate between stories, both within the project itself and in their lives outside.

Here the process of transformation occurs as the clients' lives are connected to drama. The relationship between the client and the way they see or inhabit their lives is altered. In the vignette, and in the client reflections, the process can be summarised as their becoming readers and scripters of their lives rather than feeling as if they are passive actors living a script for which there is no alternative. The contact with the drama space, with playing, for example, transforms the way they see themselves and their relationship with their life.

Novy talks about this as a move into a separate space – 'stepping out' of their lives. The area they move into is typified as being a 'play space'. As described earlier in this chapter, it is accompanied by a playful state. This new arena enables them to be creative, and to allow creativity contact with the way they see their lives. It's interesting in the feedback that this is allied with feeling empowered, feeling more of the scripter and author. The clients use words like 'taking responsibility for myself' or 'making choices that suit me'. The transformation here is in the way in which exploration in the drama-therapy space allows the clients to experience new ways of being, thinking and relating to their lives. In this way, a relationship between life and drama is made whereby life and living is taken into the space. Drama processes such as playfulness, creating stories and experimenting with different ways of inhabit-ing long-held roles are opened up, examined, re-created. In turn, this is taken into the client's life outside the dramatherapy space. This is the life–drama connection and Novy's use of a journal helps to emphasise this process by asking clients to reflect and note what is happening. As the client evaluations of the journal writing testify, becoming a reader, scripter and reviewer of their lives aids the process of change and the acknowledgement of that change.

Further research on this core process can be/ond in the following research vignettes:

Kia, Chapter 10 (p. 261); Suraya, Chapter 12 (p. 299); Desert journey, Chapter 12 (p. 311).

The vignettes in this chapter so far have been reflected on in a way that helps to see a specific core therapeutic process at work. As I stated at the start of the chapter, within any client's experience of dramatherapy a number of processes are occurring at any one time. The next vignette gives a lengthier description of a client's experience in dramatherapy and is reflected on in a way that helps to demonstrate how the core therapeutic processes are present together.

Dramatherapist Roya Dooman's work with Abui took place in an edu-cational context in the UK. Abui is a ten-year-old boy who had fled from Sierra Leone and lived in a refugee camp for two years. He had become separated from his mother and all that was known of his father was that he was 'missing'. This was all that the school knew of his background. Referral occurred through the Emag teacher. Dooman notes:

> There was difficulty accepting and integrating difference both for Abui and the class. The class teacher and the head were concerned that Abui was being bullied by his peers for being different. The students in the class were ethnically and socioeconomically mixed, but had had no new African children recently come into their class. For these Year Six stu-dents 'status' in the group was important and Abui could not compete. What also annoyed the students was that the new boy wanted so much to be like them. They criticised his broken English, his clothes, his smell and

especially the way he played football! Even though the teacher had spoken to the class, there was no empathy for Abui. The 'difference' seemed overwhelming on both sides, so how to get them to meet in a shared reality and to empathise (Jones 1996: 106)?

When his mother saw me on her own she could express her anxieties for her son but when they saw me together there were obvious difficulties in sharing the same space. Abui looked to his mother for approval and she subconsciously rebuffed him. I was struck by her continual attempts to push him away. (She said 'He's so ugly, he's the ugly one, looks like his uncle.' [laughs] 'I don't know why he doesn't do more homework.')

Huge for this mother–son relationship were obvious attachment and separation issues being enacted through the fear of empathising one for the other. Seeing the limits of time imposed on us, I was led by Abui's needs for acceptance and assimilation in his peer group, and the need for integration prior to the next transition on to secondary school. Abui also expressed a wish to come on his own for dramatherapy.

I looked at this in terms of the fact that 'dramatic expression creates a new representation of the client's material' (Jones 1996: 27): a new relationship with an overpowering traumatic past can be created allowing one to function more competently in the present. Dramatherapy was offering a safe place for Abui to come to in school where he could begin to express his story in his own way and be witnessed by somebody outside of the family. The headmaster and teacher agreed to continue liaising about the class problems.

Research vignette: Abui

Abui's attention in the first session was drawn by an African wooden statue of a man that I had placed on the story mat. We entered into the dramatic space by playing a game of touching, smelling, tasting the object and saying only one word. Eventually this triggered a safe physical memory of the feel of wood before. Eventually a rich sensory memory was created, and Abui began to tell me a story of how wood was prepared for carving and the different types of wood used in his part of Africa. How the people cut the trees in the rainy season and left them to dry out . . . Perhaps he was now beginning to project unconscious or repressed parts of himself slowly onto his story.

The next session we began again with a statue of a wooden giraffe. Abui began to go into detail about how the wood was cut and carved, then gently glued together, but only very few could do this properly and it took many years of skilled practice. Was this his externalised feeling that perhaps healing was possible? And it would be important to stay with where Abui felt safe to go with his projections, as the interpretation of the unconscious material could make the glue become unstuck.

Slowly, as Abui began exploring the object, another memory surfaced, re-created as a new story of a man, an old man, carving the wood and being watched by Abui. So we have the first moving image of the young boy in the camp. He was now able to access internal material and dramatise it in story form to myself as his witness. Abui told me he had carved many objects. He told me how he and the old man had made a horse to sit on. As his empathetic witness I responded with pleasure and amazement that he could create something so beautiful, when life there was so hard.

It was at this stage he began to recognise his helplessness. The school's anti-bullying strategy of speaking directly to the children appeared to have little impact on the relationship between Abui and his class. Insults continued to haunt him daily. The slow move into metaphor.

'He looks like a slave', he said of one of the statues. He began to talk about the lack of freedom and cruelty that those Africans felt at the time. Almost finding a way for me to bear witness to his own tragedy. The part he had played having had no autonomy, being a victim of war.

He began to play with the idea of trains. Abui built a model train:

Me: Where is the train going?
Abui: Across the border into Bo.

Time to think and just be with the sensory pulling of the toy train slowly over the tracks, mastering its course simultaneously holding onto painful memories. Me just being there quietly with him.

Abui then used some wooden bricks to make a ship. He began his story: 'I sat on a ship once; it was going to Guinea . . . There was a big ship and another smaller ship, the sea was rough, very rough . . . People were vomiting, no water to drink, they drank sea water . . . People don't know what to do . . . Later small boat rescued us.'

We went up to the art table so he could re-create his story and we agreed that I would write his words down on paper and he drew the two ships and stuck them in his book.

I invited Abui to use the art materials; he wanted to make a hat. He presented me with a large Captain's hat and said I was to try it on. Each week when he came he asked me to wear it. Was I his chosen Captain maybe to find a way to rescue him again?

Having placed the therapist in role of steering his ship for the present, could he now explore more sinister roles?

The next session Abui wanted to make a mask. He cut out a large head, stuck on wild hair and called it 'evil'. He talked quite a lot this session, decorating the mask, then trying it on himself, as if freed from the fear that this evil could harm him now. Abui spoke of a man with powers to do harm to people in the villages, the man people feared most back home. Using the name of 'holy spirit' or 'The Dr': the man who decided who would die, and left people to burn on rubber tyres. This was the man who shot his brother in front of the whole family.

I was a witness to part of the horror Abui had experienced. How could I reflect back to him anything that didn't overwhelm us both with the enormity of what he was telling me? I needed to be an anchor in a rough sea, a safe sandbank; I couldn't let the tidal wave drown us both. The best 'witness' to me is an honest one, offering truth of feeling but allowing the act of telling to be done as it must.

The next week he worked on some clay, needing to return to his place of sensory calm. Gradually, features of a face appeared from the smooth wet texture, as he projected feelings of love and pride onto the clay through his hands. He began to talk about a very different sort of man, an important man possibly a chief: a 'good, kind man, with a nice face'. He liked this clay portrait. I surmised on the possible likeness to his yet unmentioned father. Abui was now able to acknowledge to me the absence of this type of man from his life.

Jones has stressed the importance of the connection between the body, action, change and drama. Embodiment play is intrinsic to change in the clients' perceptions of themselves.

One week Abui was interested in a large picture book sticking out of the bookcase, *The Three Little Wolves and the Big Bad Pig*. He asked me to read the story. He became quite excited, and so I asked if he would like to play it with me. Putting structures in place was very important even at this level. Because the book had been one container for his anxiety now could he cope with the role as another? We decided which materials we could use for each house and what we could use as the pigs' weapons to destroy them. We set the room up. Then I told the story and he played the Big Bad Pig. Then we role reversed. We both embodied the houses exploding, making loud sounds and large movements on the floor together. This was the first time I had seen Abui laugh. I had underestimated his need for release of adrenalin that was caught up inside with the terror.

Abui was able to acknowledge how good it felt to laugh with me now, but how angry he felt at the explosions back in Sierra Leone. At the end of the session he said, 'I would like to do this with my class.'

'What would you like to do?'

'Act explosions and guns shooting!' The excitement of the physical play had opened other pathways for Abui to explore, which he now wanted to share. Could embodiment play and dramatic enactment help Abui and his class to reach empathic understanding?

I introduced a story from African folklore, *The People Could Fly*. Abui was interested in this story of redemption of slaves who could suffer no more pain from their masters, one amongst them saved them by giving them the magic to fly away above the fields leaving their suffering behind. Abui became angry, 'Why could they all not be free? Why did the others get left behind?' He looked at me to answer him, and I echoed his anger at a situation where the characters seemed unable to act. This anger energised Abui, and he spoke very quickly, his words flowing from somewhere deep giving clarity to his thoughts. Allowing me to witness a new part of himself, I could barely write 'his-story' fast enough.

'Who could hear this story?' I asked, 'Your mother?'

'No. My class. I want to share it with my class.' This was a clear and brave statement of need, and I couldn't dilute its intention to engage with those who had rebuffed him, and its possibilities for change.

Could we come out of the therapy room and allow his class to be his witnesses? I discussed the possibilities of a class drama with the teacher and head of the school. The head could see that pupils needed to be given a chance to engage emotively (empathise) with a condition other than their own.

Abui became empowered by his own script, as his eyes shone for the first time describing to me how he could imagine playing out 'The War on Tinder Hill' with his class. I saw this as a possibility to also create shared meaning through the drama.

The head gave the class some background to wars in Africa and we located Sierra Leone on a map. The teacher gave the class rules for the session and together we created group boundaries of respect and confidentiality.

The performance began with warm-ups which used movements to a drum, heightening body awareness and awareness of others in the space. As a group we blew ourselves into a balloon and bursting; heightening our senses, preparing ourselves to embody the explosions later on in the enactment.

The children energetically shared in the building of a refugee camp with tables and blankets. There was anticipation of play and make believe. The children were excited. Abui had chosen two boys to support his role as a 'brother' in the drama. Everyone wore badges 'Brother', 'Sister', 'Auntie', 'Mother', etc. The teacher's role as a Red Cross worker gave the group a place of safety, externalised through her 'white coat' and 'medical kit'.

The group replayed the story of the refugee camp. I could see Abui observing his fellow actors from the safety of his 'tent' with his brothers, till he too felt confident to join the tirade with them. Bombs were falling and notices were put up that they had to leave their homes and must move on. The group began to move excitedly in different directions, laughing as they jokingly bumped into each other and fearful as a 'guerrilla' was threateningly behind them. Abui was laughing and trying to stay close with his role 'brothers'.

We 'froze' in role and each fed back how they felt in their character at that very moment. So many said frightened, scared, angry, upset, distressed – an echo for Abui of another reality.

'I hated it when I couldn't find my family group', said one girl.

'Yeah that was horrible! I thought they'd been killed', replied a boy.

Abui was witnessing others playing out his roles. As we de-roled our characters sitting in our circle, passing the drum, children shared how they had felt playing their role. Abui said how he had felt supported by the two boys he was with. This was a new relationship for him in this class. The class were now accepting their need of each other in the group. Then Abui spoke with the drum. 'I enjoyed it,' he said. I felt this to be a really poignant moment, for this was the first time he had experienced 'joy' and a bonding with his class. We gathered together at the end for the group to now bear witness, not as participant and fellow actor but in the hearing of Abui's story.

I read it for Abui as he sat still by my side, his audience silent as tears unashamedly fell down their cheeks.

I asked the group to make a statement of what they heard without posing any questions to Abui, but what they felt able to tell him from themselves. The witnessing of Abui's story was honest. The children were expressing their own deep emotions of sadness and shock for what Abui had to endure, and their awe that Abui could survive and be living a life with them in the UK! One girl spoke for the class when she said, 'I'm so sorry we treated you badly.' Abui thanked the class for listening to his story and then said to me, 'And I liked playing with the class'.

Postscript

The bullying stopped and Abui was included by his classmates in the playground. Dramatherapy had served its purpose for Abui. Three years later in secondary school he tells me that sometimes when he needs good friends he will be with the two ex-pupils from his class who went to the same school.

Roya Dooman

Research conversation with Roya Dooman

Jones: How do you see the initial contact between Abui and the dramatherapy space?

Dooman: I had hoped it may provide a dramatic link to something familiar but 'distanced' enough, from the painful memories back home. An example of this is the early connection with the wooden statue of a man. It was, of course, easier to talk about the wood itself than the story of the man, imaginary thinking being stunted by his trauma. It is always developmentally better to start from the sensory level than the metaphorical, for what could this statue stand for – man, male, father, missing, maimed, killings, atrocities?

Jones: You talk about the therapist as a witness at this early stage of the work. How do you see that?

Dooman: Abui had not been able to share his memories with his mother as the trauma of their separation had made communicating about his time in the refugee camp difficult and uncomfortable for both of them. Dramatherapy could provide emotional 'distancing', enabling dramatic projection to create a vital relationship between inner emotional states and external forms and presences.

Jones: You talk here about memories finding a form of expression in the play space. Do you see the work with the train in this way?

Dooman: Playing with the trains had allowed him to project his feelings of fear outside of himself and then integrate them into a story of survival as the drawing of the smaller boat coming to help the larger boat took on a bigger significance on the paper, visible and concrete, allowing him to distance himself, yet read own his story simultaneously as he looked at it again.

Jones: You talk about the need for release within Abui's use of the space. Can you say more about that?

Dooman: Dramatherapy could offer a safe place to allow Abui to feel his emotions again, including joy in the moment releasing serotonin in the brain. More than this, I would add laughter and its importance, particularly in the release of the 'stress' adrenalin that remains on high alert long after it is needed in a state of fight or flight.

Jones: Unusual to move out of the therapy room, to present a separate but related drama to others. How do you look at that aspect of the vignette?

Dooman: On reflection, breaking out of the therapy room could be seen on a parallel to breaking out of the refugee camp. It had to be done for Abui to be acknowledged, to have his peers bear witness to his traumatic story and to reaffirm the value of his existence. I would argue that the therapist was the first witness to his hidden story, but then only acted as the mariner to help transport him to his real audience – those he would ask to become witnesses and in so becoming take part themselves in the role play on a very deep level often undervalued in school drama. This was therapeutic drama or drama as therapy at its best, because the boundaries were made very clear and the school community pulled together from the head through to the teachers, pupils and therapist.

In this extended vignette Dooman shows in her reflection how she sees the processes interconnecting, taking on different importances as the work progresses. Here we see dramatic projection moving from statues to trains to enactment. Witnessing develops between Abui and therapist in the early stages of the work to a much more profound holding of deep and traumatic experiences as they become seen and shown. The process acquires another layer of meaning as the work is taken out of the therapy room and aspects of it are linked to the life–drama connection, as Abui presents a drama to be witnessed and shared by people in his daily life. Dooman also illustrates in her description and her analysis in conversation how she uses the core processes to help her make sense of phenomena as they occur, and to assist in the way she tries to engage Abui and move the work forward with him.

Summary

The research into the core processes described in this chapter illustrates how they are being used to serve as a framework within which we can understand and examine dramatherapy practice. Though by no means exhaustive, the research vignettes and the conversation analysis of the practice demonstrate how they are drawn on by dramatherapists to provide a language, a way of seeing how drama and theatre processes are at the heart of dramatherapy.

As Landy has said, dramatherapy, though an 'interdisciplinary art and science', is primarily an art (1986: 229). The core processes are rooted within drama and theatre, yet they show how the inherent healing potential of the art form is marshalled and developed within dramatherapy.

Part IV

6 Dramatic projection

It is characteristic of theatrical fictions that they are, curiously, acknowledged both as real and not-real.

Courtney, 'Aristotle's Legacy'

Introduction

Projection involves the placing of aspects of ourselves or our feelings into other people or things. Usually it is an unconscious process. Aspects of projection are present in our everyday life. Main describes it as a 'normal mental activity' (1975: 64). It is a part of the way we relate to and understand the world. One manifestation of this is the way we imbue other people or things with our own feelings. As psychotherapist Theilgard has pointed out, a child might unconsciously project their own sadness into the sight of trees in autumn as they describe the falling leaves as a 'tree's tears' (Cox 1992: 164).

Projection is often the inspiration for creative activity. Edvard Munch, in recalling the experience that led to the creation of his painting *The Scream* in 1893, describes a moment on a walk by a fjord when a sunset felt to him as if it were 'a loud, unending scream piercing nature' (Dunlop 1977). One way of understanding this experience is to say that Munch is projecting his own feelings of anxiety and despair into the sunset. The act of creating this painting is, in part, a way of reproducing the projection and exploring it.

Shakespeare's Antony, as he senses his own declining fortunes, also looks into the sky, seeing in clouds the constantly shifting and dissolving forms of dragons, bears, towering citadels or mountains. As he describes the cloud forms to his fellow soldier, Eros, he realises that he is projecting a part of his sense of personal confusion and dissolution into them:

My good knave Eros, now thy captain is
Even such a body: here I am Antony:
Yet cannot hold this visible shape, my knave.

(*Antony and Cleopatra,* IV, xiv, 12–14)

Antony is projecting his inner feelings into external forms. As he unconsciously projects his feelings, he is able to make a connection and to gain insight into his situation – he realises that he too is unable to hold his shape. This process of unconscious projection followed by insight has parallels with dramatherapy's use of projection. Shakespeare's words in Antony's mouth are paralleled within one of the vignettes in this chapter where therapist Van Den Bosch observes a client dealing with hearing voices. After play work with objects of a miniature lion and lamb, the client 'spoke about her voices as being like the anger of the lion which smothers her. She said she saw herself as the sacrificial lamb.'

Dramatherapy encourages the projection of an inner emotional trauma or problem into a dramatic representation. It builds upon, and uses, the everyday and creative aspects of this process to therapeutic ends. For dramatherapy, the importance lies in the way in which projection creates a vital and special kind of relationship between inner emotional states and external dramatic form or presences. At times the projection of material that has been held within, unexpressed, can be releasing in the sheer act of expression and communication. One client reflected this when describing the experience of dramatherapy as 'effective in helping me express and release difficult emotions and concepts' (Barry 2006: 8). However, for many, the expression or release is only a part, or a beginning of the therapeutic process of dramatic projection. The projected material is explored during the ongoing dramatherapy sessions and is engaged with as part of the therapeutic work. Dooman described aspects of this in the vignette Abui in the previous chapter where a wooden giraffe is worked with:

> Slowly, as Abui began exploring the object, another memory surfaced, re-created as a new story of a man, an old man, carving the wood and being watched by Abui. So we have the first moving image of the young boy in the camp. He was now able to access internal material and dramatise it in story form to the therapist as his witness.

Here Abui begins to project aspects of himself and his life experience into the object and finds a way of expressing and communicating internally held feelings and experiences. As Dooman observes, this is the spark which can be developed into further dramatic exploration and development within the dramatherapy space.

This chapter explores the ways that such dramatic projection occurs in dramatherapy and details the therapeutic potential of this phenomenon. As an illustration of dramatic projection in dramatherapy I want to draw a parallel between Shakespeare's clouds and a moment in an ongoing dramatherapy group. It occurred in the fifth weekly session in a UK special school for children with emotional and behavioural difficulties. A boy of 13, Peter, stands under a spotlight. He is dressed in a cloak and is covered by a mask in the form of a shiny, totally black helmet, twice the height of his head. In appearance it is not unlike those worn by medieval jousting knights. The previous week he had spent over 30 minutes colouring the helmet's card in several layers of vigorously applied black wax crayon. No part of his face is visible. There is only a small slit for an eyehole. A flap is hinged over the hole and this is attached to a string which the boy can pull down to cover his eyes completely. As he turns round slowly to the group he says, voice muffled, 'No one can be seen unless they kneel down first in front of me.'

This black helmet is linked to Antony's seeing himself through cloud forms, in that they are both examples of dramatic projection. Like Antony, the boy is interpreting an aspect of himself, though through the form of the created helmet rather than through clouds. However, whilst Antony's words to Eros might be seen to be part of an everyday process, for the boy in the special school the act is more complex.

Antony's projection into the clouds gives him a momentary insight as he connects it to his own life situation. For Peter, though, the projection into the helmet is part of a process rather like Munch's in painting *The Scream*. In creating and using the helmet within a dramatherapy group Peter is being encouraged to explore and develop the projection. A theme was given to the group: 'Difficult feelings and relationships'. Masks and costumes were made with the aim of looking at personal issues for group members within this area. As a therapist I was trying to help him find a form to articulate and examine a problematic aspect of himself. This connection between inner problems and dramatic expression lies at the heart of dramatherapy's use of projection.

Projection: a psychological perspective

In *The Theory and Practice of Group Psychotherapy* Yalom (1985) describes projection as an unconscious process which consists of 'projecting some of one's own (but disowned) attributes onto another, toward whom one subsequently feels an uncanny attraction/repulsion' (1985: 117). It is possible to identify a series of key stages which describe projection as understood within psychotherapy. First, the 'projector' or client experiences unmanageable feelings. Second, there is an unconscious fantasy of putting this unmanageable feeling/state into another person in order to dispose of it or to make it manageable. Third, there is an interactional pressure, with the unconscious aim of making another person have these feelings instead of the client. The emphasis here is upon projection as a defence mechanism within therapy. It is seen as a way of denying feelings by putting them outside oneself. The aim of the psychotherapy might be to enable the client to achieve insight into this process and to re-engage with the disowned parts or feelings through discussion and analysis.

Dramatherapy's relationship to projection differs from this. Whilst the area Yalom describes forms a part of the way the process is utilised within dramatherapy work, the description of projection needs to be broader. Landy points out that, from the classic Freudian position, concepts such as identification and projection are primarily defensive processes. He adds that for the dramatherapist they can be utilised differently in the creation of a 'balanced form of therapeutic dramatisation' (1985: 74).

Dramatherapy emphasises the ways in which projection can be linked to dramatic form to enable a client to create, discover and engage with external representations of inner conflicts. This is the 'therapeutic dramatisation' identified by Landy. In dramatherapy, projection becomes expressive rather than being primarily defensive. The fantasy of professionals and clients alike is often that the client's projection into a role will merely be an amplification; that it will aggravate or encourage a problem rather then help to alleviate it. Brookes describes this situation in her production of *Marat/Sade* in a Massachusetts psychiatric hospital:

> One nurse asked, 'What kind of part does Jack have?' He had a leading role and I described what his character was like. 'Oh no!' she protested. 'That's how he is around here!'
>
> (Brookes 1975: 433)

I would argue that this is more a problem for theatre than for dramatherapy. In the research vignette Kia (Chapter 10, p. 261), Mann-Shaw talks about the capacity of dramatic projection in dramatherapy to enable clients to express, explore and contain material: "I felt that overall the move into the creation of a landscape, a dramatic set, would enable containment and dramatic projection of Kia's internal process on and into an external space. I was hopeful that this would enable Kia to engage with exploring the issues which had brought her into therapy with a level of dramatic distance."

Theatre form enables the expression of projection, but does not necessarily allow for the experience to be explicit, to be worked with or resolved. In dramatherapy dramatic projection connects personal material with the therapeutic process and space, as this chapter will show.

Vignette: Peter and the helmet

Peter attended a special school for children with emotional and behavioural difficulties. One of the behavioural problems he was presenting with was a way of relating to others which was chiefly characterised by violence and withdrawal; he refused most contact with adults and peers. His relationships with his peers mainly involved aggression and violence, both verbal and physical. Verbal interactions would be mainly kept to commands or orders. He had a history of truanting from schools and of absenting himself from rooms. His interactions with others were characterised by silence and avoidance of eye contact. Any attempt to discuss or explore these areas would be met by Peter's flat denial of the behaviour. He had, however, participated in a series of drama classes offered by one of the teachers at the school. His teacher and educational psychologist agreed to his participation in a dramatherapy group. The main aim of the work was to explore relationships through the creation of costumes and performance art.

By the fifth session the group had made masks and costumes, and had engaged with a number of activities which explored the theme of 'difficult feelings and relationships' as mentioned earlier (see p. 139).

The mask material and cloth used to make costumes acted as a way for Peter to create forms reflecting the theme. He was able to make his own design or interpretation, developing from the activities we had introduced to the group which had initially explored the theme. The mask and costume aimed to reflect his inner emotional preoccupations rather than any brief given to him by staff or other group members.

Peter was able to project the aspects of himself he verbally denied into the forms. He made a cloak which was decorated by the repeated screen-printed image of a clenched fist. The helmet described earlier was also designed by him to go with the cloak. After costumes had been created, the group were encouraged to improvise a series of interactions using abstract movement as well as stories which explored aspects of their costume's qualities. Characters were created based on the costumes and masks. Short improvisations developed from this.

The character he developed was an increasingly exaggerated persona based on some of the attributes mentioned earlier: aggression, silence, the rigid controlling of interactions. An example of this was that the eye flap would be shut down suddenly to end conversations; another was that the cloak had magical controlling powers. As described above, he would not express his problems by talking about himself with the staff. This work gave him the opportunity to express the aspects of himself which were problematic, which seemed to restrict his ability to relate to people. The improvisations helped him to project these parts of himself into the helmet and cloak. Each improvisation was completed by a clear time when the pupils left the characters they had been playing. This was followed by a space to talk about the characters and what it had been like to play them.

Two main outcomes were achieved by Peter. One was that the sessions enabled him to de-role and to discuss the character of the dark helmet. He was later able to talk about the relationship of the dark helmet character to himself in his everyday life. Hence, the previously censored aspect of his life and behaviour had been made accessible to reflection.

The improvisations led to the creation of different, alternative ways of behaving with the helmet. The improvised stories witnessed a change in the role of the helmet, becoming less extreme. Following the discussions about the dark helmet, Peter began to give the character alternative ways of behaving. It became more involved in the action and began to act together with other characters in

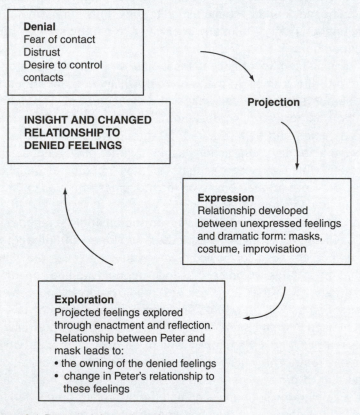

Figure 6.1 Peter and dramatic projection.

planning plots and co-operating in ventures. Again we were able to discuss these different ways of relating with Peter in terms of the relationship between the helmet and his life outside the session.

The second main outcome was that Peter was given the space to work beyond his stuck modes of relating. The projection of inner fears and fantasies into outer dramatic material gave an opportunity to gain access to locked, fixed behaviours. It also provided the means to create a distance to look at the material and an avenue to experiment in order to alter and change the problematic area. This new access also led to discussion within Peter's work with the school's educational psychologist.

A significant part of Peter's difficulty seemed to be a verbal denial of any problem in his life. Whilst he manifested complete distrust and fear of others and excluded contact with them unless on his terms, he rigorously denied this. This created a 'stuck' situation. In the dramatherapy group Peter could project aspects of himself into the dramatic form. He explored and developed this projection by taking roles, creating masks and costumes and improvising. Through de-roling and separating from the projection he was able to talk about aspects of himself. Through experience and exploration he was able to change his awareness and understanding of that part of himself.

CORE PROCESS BOX

Dramatic projection

In the making and use of the helmet Peter is able to express aspects of the ways he sees himself, and relates to others. The improvisations enable him to explore this projection, opening up his self-image and ways of relating.

Role

Through creating a role around the mask, Peter is able to express a dramatic identity that is both himself, but also distanced enough from his own identity to allow him to discuss and reflect personal material which he has otherwise refused to refer to.

It is possible to formulate a basic description for the way in which the process of projection is utilised in dramatherapy. Peter's work illustrates many aspects of this. Box 6.1 is a summary of the basic stages in the process of dramatic projection in dramatherapy.

Dramatherapy – projective techniques

Dramatic projection in dramatherapy can occur in a number of ways. The dramatic vehicles include play work with objects, sculpting, improvisation in movement and character, puppetry, script and mask. For the purposes of this chapter, I intend to concentrate on the ways in which the various activities can be considered within the process of dramatic projection.

Small worlds

The creation of miniature dramatic worlds or play worlds has a long history within therapy and analysis. Melanie Klein, in her psychoanalytic work with children, used spontaneous play and projective play. Miller (1973: 226) says that spontaneous play was used by her as a direct substitute for the verbal free association used by Freud in his treatment of adults. Klein assumed that what the child does in free play symbolises the wishes, fears, pleasures, conflicts and preoccupations of which they are not aware. The therapist is given roles by

---

Box 6.1 **Dramatic projection in dramatherapy**

- Dramatic projection within dramatherapy is the process by which clients project aspects of themselves, or their experience, into theatrical or dramatic materials or into enactment, and thereby externalise inner conflicts. A relationship between the inner state of the client and the external dramatic form is established and developed through action.
- Dramatic projection enables access to dramatic processes as a means to explore the client's material.
- The dramatic expression creates a new representation of the client's material.
- The projection enables a dramatic dialogue to take place between the client's internally held situation or material, and the external expression of that situation or material.
- The dramatic expression enables change through the creation of perspective, along with the opportunity for exploration and insight through the enactment of the projected material. Both through the expression and the exploration a new relationship to the material can be achieved by the client.
- From this, the reintegration of the client's projected material can occur, within the new relationship.

the child that reflect other people/feelings towards them. These are linked to the problems the child is encountering. The therapist's function is to make the child aware of this by interpreting the play for them. The process consists of the stages outlined in Box 6.2.

Lowenfeld's World Technique is a particularly precise way of working with this concept. It utilises similar notions relating to therapy and play within a structured format. The projective material here consists of miniature replicas of people, animals, fences, means of transport, houses and 'unstructured materials' such as plasticine, paper and string. Water and sandtrays are made available and the child is told to play as they would like. The child is then asked to explain the world built to the therapist and to say what will happen next. Lowenfeld (1970) refers to her tools as a multidimensional language requiring no special skills. The World Technique can be divided into the phases outlined in Box 6.3.

I would argue that the dramatherapist can use the approaches described above. The area can be included within the remit of dramatherapy in the same way as dramatic play can (see Chapter 7). The dramatherapist, however,

---

Box 6.2 **Dramatic projection and small worlds**

- Client experiences problem, or is encountering unconscious material which is problematic.
- This is projected into play material or into the relationship with the therapist during play.
- Therapist makes interpretations of the client's play or the relationship which is emerging between client and therapist.
- Client becomes aware and conscious of the material and is able to effect change.

Box 6.3 **Dramatic projection and World Technique**

- Introduction: client's use leading to familiarity, repetition and exploration through activity, a relationship is established with the materials.
- The client becomes deeply engaged in the projection of a revived expression of earlier life processes.
- The client works out unconscious processes. The materials are used to express and explore the problem and to change the client's relationship to the problem.
- The fantasy experience tapers and the materials become less and less absorbing for the client.

has the additional possibility to develop this work with small play worlds into additional dramatic expressions. This area of work within dramatherapy creates a theatre space in miniature. Within the therapeutic space client and therapist work with dramatic representations using objects as the main medium. The technique has a more complex relation to projection than the earlier comparison with free association made by Miller (see p. 144). Bowyer (1970) rightly contradicts Miller's description of Klein's play work being analogous with free association, saying that this is an understatement. The area of work, including Lowenfeld's World Technique, creates 'a world in which the child lives through its stresses again sometimes over and over in a long drawn out process of working through' (p. 109).

Dramatherapist Nancy Secchi draws on this process of dramatic projection in her work with Sarah and small animal objects. Secchi described Sarah as 'a woman in her late twenties who was presenting as borderline body dysmorphic. She found it awkward talking, as if she would say too much and expose herself. She always wore a floor-length black PVC coat even in 70 degree heat.'

Research vignette: Sarah

I had a large bag of animals, every type imaginable, some in family groups, big, small, with and without limbs, golden, gruesome and minute. I invited Sarah to choose an animal that represented herself. She chose a pig. I asked her to describe it and she said it was fat, ugly, dirty and smelly. I added that pigs are highly intelligent, sociable and provide valuable resources, and that many people believe they are adorable. I then invited Sarah to choose an animal that represented the self she wished she could be. She chose a cat. I asked her to describe a cat and she said it was sleek, agile, loveable, soft but independent. I added that cats had useful claws that could defend them when they needed protection.

I then asked Sarah what it would take for Pig to become Cig or Pat (a combination of the two animals). Sarah wanted Pig to disappear and for Cat to become the prominent self. In order for this to happen she felt that past events and present experiences needed exploring and addressing. We spent the next few weeks talking through the metaphor much more freely and explored many aspects of Pig, Cat and Pat. When Sarah spoke of her abuse and her attempts to establish non-abusive relationships, I would query what part of her was making a judgement, who was speaking right now, Cat, Pig or Pat. I would query what would the other animals (part of her self) think or do in the situation that would help her gain insight and build resilience. This way we flicked between the different aspects of self through the metaphor without having to role play (as we did not have any space to expand into or move in).

Sarah believed that she had probably had the potential to become Cat early in her life but that her abuse had caused her to become Pig. I wanted to enable Sarah to appreciate all that Pig had to offer her as opposed to her rejecting Pig out of hand. This had to be done gradually, in case I started to impose my own wishful fantasy of Sarah learning to love herself (as I wanted her to do), and thereby not allowing her to really rubbish Pig as she probably needed to, in order to move on.

My clinical intention was to refine the technique of flicking between internal roles as a daily coping mechanism that would give Sarah options and choices. Six weeks after our initial animal selection Sarah arrived in a floral short-sleeved top, trousers, some make-up and nothing else. It was the first time I had seen Sarah in any clothing other than the coat. Sarah announced that she thought she had reached Cat.

Nancy Secchi

CORE PROCESS BOX

Dramatic projection

Sarah draws on a selection of objects and creates a relationship with them whereby aspects of the object, such as the pig being fat, ugly and smelly, enable her to express issues she is bringing to therapy. In this way she is able to take material into the therapy space and to open up her difficulties to dramatic processes within the therapeutic space and relationship. By seeing them in front of her, as they are smaller and as they suggest play, she is able to create a playfulness with the help of the therapist so they become flexible, open to new combinations, to comment and change. Initially, the therapist models this process, suggesting alternative ways of viewing the objects. Then, gradually, the client herself opens up the objects to difference rather than their being fixed as only dirty or fully independent, the split between the 'pig' and the 'cat' parts of herself.

Role

Though the client does not physically take on roles, she is able to project aspects of her role identity into the animals, and to role play through objects.

Life–drama connection

Sarah develops, with the therapist, a flexibility in looking at herself within the sessions. This is transferred into the way she sees herself and functions in her life outside the sessions. Hence, ways of being are experimented with inside the safety of the dramatherapy space and then transferred into her life outside, bringing this into the session through expressions such as her clothing.

The following vignette illustrates parallel processes at work within an entirely different context. Jo Van Den Bosch describes work with Jilly, an older adult diagnosed with schizophrenia. Jilly was a member of a Hearing Voices group, which specialized in working with older adults who have psychotic experiences. The Hearing Voices group was run in a UK day hospital setting but includes inpatient, day patient and outpatient referrals. Jilly was a member of the day hospital. Van Den Bosch orientates this dramatherapy work within the theories of Romme and Esher (1996, 2000) and says it is, 'less concerned with trying to cure members of their voices and other psychotic experiences than helping them feel in control of them'. She uses animals, as did the previous vignette, and observes: 'Jilly was able to use objects in dramatherapy to make the unspeakable, and even what appears unthinkable, able to be talked about'. Jilly is a 72-year-old woman with a long history of schizophrenia. She is described by Van Den Bosch as often saying that she feels 'quite low and her appetite and sleep patterns are poor. She lives on her own and comes to the day hospital twice a week. After an operation for a hysterectomy where, she believes, her ovaries were removed without her consent, she remains very angry.'

Research vignette: Jilly

After a few sessions of the group I brought in a collection of my plastic wild animals. I asked the group to pick something to represent their voices. She chose a roaring lion and placed it among all the other animals. She said she wanted it 'where it could see everyone else and was ready to pounce'. After a while she laid a lamb at its feet.

She spoke about the symbolism. She spoke about her voices as being like the anger of the lion which smothers her. She said she saw herself as the sacrificial lamb. She told the group that her voices constantly swear at her and tell her she is responsible for all the world's disasters. She said she identified with the lamb. She said she felt very vulnerable and as if her life had been sacrificed to her voices. She was also able to make a connection with her own anger which she had split off and was perhaps placed in the voices/lion.

As she spoke she began to talk about the anger of the lion and to be able to articulate her own anger about the way the hysterectomy had been carried out without her full consent. She made a connection between her anger, the anger of the voices and the way she felt about her hysterectomy. We spoke about how powerful and frightening her anger was. She had after all chosen a lion, the king of the jungle. I wondered how frightened of her anger she was, for example. We thought about how frightened the lamb must have been of the lion. Did she think she could harm someone with her anger? She admitted she did. She spoke about her guilt as she became very angry with the nurse in hospital after the hysterectomy and she had made her cry. She believed that was unforgivable. In the group we were able to explore this further. The explorations of these thoughts were helped by focusing more on the voices by using playdough to make a shape about how the voices felt. Jilly made what looked like a beautiful piece of coral with extremely sharp edges, and through this she was able to articulate the pain her voices caused her. We were able to think about how Jilly split off her anger into her voices. The anger was the lion. She was the lamb. The anger was painful. Jilly found this very difficult to think about.

The work with the plastic animals had given Jilly some distance from the voices, and she was able to feel stronger in relationship to them and even practise asking them to go away. This was an idea which she had previously ridiculed, but now she was able to feel more in control of the voices than they were of her.

Jilly now works in individual therapy with me and often uses an artist mannequin to speak about her relationship to her illness. Once again, this allows her not only to focus on the issues but also provides distance and clarity which helps both Jilly and myself as therapist to think.

CORE PROCESS BOX

Dramatic projection

Jilly makes immediate and powerful connection with the animals. Whilst this is crucial to the therapy, equally important is the fact that the client can feel they can *control* the dramatic material, the animals.

They can become witness and director to the animals and their voices, rather than feeling directed by internal voices.

Play

Jilly can use the space to try out and experiment with new possibilities and relationships.

Empathy and distancing

The client can feel connection, empathy with the animals, but can also achieve distance, space from the animals and their voices – an important shift in her relationship to the voices.

Research conversation with Jo Van Den Bosch

Jones:	I was amazed at the way Jilly just seemed to pick up the lion, then the lamb and make what seemed like very direct life–drama connections. Was it like that, very quick, very strong? How do you see what happened in that 'connecting' up?
Van Den Bosch:	It was a very powerful connection and quite immediate. Jilly is able to use dramatic projection very easily, perhaps because in her psychosis she is used to splitting things off. The problem for Jilly is often in putting it all back together again.
Jones:	Do you think there was the possibility of the connection with play, with fantasy and externalising inner material, might be problematic or even countertherapeutic for Jilly? I'm thinking about that maybe in terms of attachment or being almost over whelded to the things she projects into. Sorry – my typing mistake! 'Over whelded' – interesting typo – mixture of overwhelmed and welded!
Van Den Bosch:	I think this is a fascinating word as she has become over 'whelded' to objects at times: at times she could find it frightening. Jilly would come out with some powerful connections and interpretations, but then become scared by her disclosure. I also think it challenged her whole way of life. If she could understand these voices and feel in control of them, perhaps she didn't need to have them. I think Jilly's ability to distance herself from over-identification was key in this work. She seemed to function better when she had more of a chance to control the pace, and I think the feeling of externally projecting into objects, of being in control, has been very important.

The use of small representational work creates a parallel but different relationship between the fictive created world and the client than do 'larger' enactments in which the client uses their own body in a physical representation, or conceptualises on a 'life-size' scale. The following summarises the main four differences between small world work such as that undertaken with Sarah and Jilly and 'larger' enactment in dramatherapy:

1   The client's relationship to the events or issues can be affected by the fact that the play world is a miniature representation of a much larger reality. The play world materials such as Jilly's lion are small and can be easily moved around by the client. The client can feel more powerful, more able to physically change the materials than the life events or issues they represent. This in turn, through analogy, makes the client more able to feel empowered to make change in terms of the real events or issues. As Van den Bosch comments in the vignette concerning Jilly's work with objects: 'This was an idea which she had previously ridiculed, but now she was able to feel more in control of the voices than they were of her.'

2   The objects chosen affect the client's awareness of the issue represented. For example, if objects already existing as a specific form (small dolls, farm animals) are deliberately chosen to represent an important other, or if they were chosen 'at random' and the significance is realised during the action/play, then the object's form will add an additional factor of awareness, another level of possible meaning to the work. Aspects such as its texture (e.g. soft, hard, furry), identity (e.g. cow, bulldozer, baby) or memory associations (e.g. a fond childhood memory attached to a particular kind of object, a dislike of sand or water linked to a particular experience) will affect the client's relationship to the issue. Sarah, for example, says the cat is 'sleek, agile, loveable, soft but independent' and that the pig is 'fat, ugly, dirty and smelly', but combines both to develop and explore aspects of herself within the projection into the small objects.

     The different shape, physical properties and position of the object in relation to other play objects may all give information. If a client chooses a furry elephant to represent a father, then different aspects of their relationship will be highlighted than if a hard, cold object such as a stone had been chosen. Jilly's choice of lion and lamb or Sarah's choice of pig and cat are used by client and therapist to create a dialogue. An internal drama is externalised and can be opened up to working with drama. This can enable internally held 'stuck' material to become open to exploration and to change.

3   The cultural associations of clients concerning playing with objects will frame the experience. A common association is that object play is the domain of children, therefore associations for the client may be linked to this area – with their own childhood, or children with whom they have some current or previous connection.

4   The relationship between therapist and client shifts as the object world

becomes a key part of the language of the work. Objects may represent the client's perception of aspects of the relationship between therapist and client.

In dramatherapy it is also possible to work with this notion of the small world as part of the dramatic continuum. The work with objects can be developed into role play, improvisation and movement activities. This can be used to amplify, extend, initiate and develop the small world work.

Puppetry

Puppetry in dramatherapy can be considered as an extension of this kind of object work. Within dramatherapy the puppet can become a vehicle for projection in much the same way that an object can. As described in Chapter 7 (see p. 177), the puppet may be seen as a progression from the symbolic use of objects in play. So in projective use, the puppet can be seen as a progression from object usage, rather than a completely different area of practice (see Chapter 10 research vignette, Kia)

Masks

Ensor, the Belgian painter, acknowledged as the inventor/precursor of Expressionism, has described the mask as an empty shell for a soft creature to hide in. There are parallels between this process and the use of masks in dramatherapy. In terms of its relation to dramatic projection there are three main points to consider. The first is that, as in object work, the form of the mask affects the nature of the material projected by the client into the form. Hence a blank mask will enable the client to project one kind of experience, whereas a mask of a clown might bring out a different kind, and a client's own decorated mask might bring out yet another.

The second concerns the paradox which Brook (1988) speaks of that the 'mask is the expression of somebody unmasked' (p. 219). The creation of a second skin, as it were, means that the client can present a part of themselves through the mask. The presence of the mask creates a sense that this is not really themselves, but rather the mask that is speaking or moving. This enables the client to project into the mask feelings or ways of behaving specifically to do with the part of them which is highlighted by the personality of the mask. The mask creates a freedom to express material that would be repressed within the client's usual presentation of their identity. Hence the mask can enable a client to project aspects of themselves usually denied or hidden: the mask unmasks.

The third relates to the way in which the mask encourages a projection of a focused aspect of the client's personality or experience. The selective quality of the mask – its fixed form – means that the one frame is presented, rather than the continuous moving and shifting of the natural face. The effect of this is that one aspect or facet of the client is highlighted to the exclusion of others. This means that the client is invited to present a concentrated, heightened part of themselves. The mask, then, encourages a concentration upon a particular aspect of the self, along with an emphasis on the expression of parts of the self usually denied expression.

Script and story

In dramatherapy clients can use an existing text or create their own script to work from. These are worked with so that the client can find their own associations, meaning or interpretation. This might develop into improvisation or work on the text which further explores the association. The emphasis becomes less on the intention of the author or therapist and much more upon the themes or meanings which the client feels to be significant. Images, interactions, characters and reactions to the text can all be part of this. As detailed in Chapter 10, the text or story can take on personal meaning for a client. As Gersie has said: 'The potential for positive, projective identification between a story-character and oneself does inspire new ways of being' (Gersie 1991: 242).

Theatrical play production includes the notion of interpretation of a text. As Esslin points out in *An Anatomy of Drama* (1978: 88), audiences are drawn to plays in part to see the particular interpretation an actor or director brings to a given text. So in dramatherapy interest in projective work with a text relies on a process akin to the interpretive work undertaken by director or actor. The interest lies in the ways that the client can use the text as material in which to project their inner preoccupations, in order to use it as a means of self-exploration.

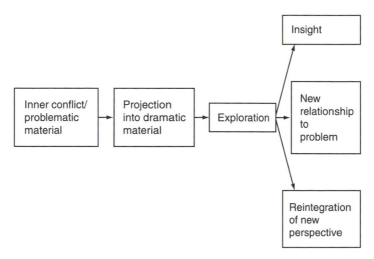

Figure 6.2 Dramatic projection in dramatherapy.

Summary

All the above areas – the creation of small worlds, mask work, improvisation, story and script – have a basic process in common. Figure 6.2 shows the four key stages that are at the core of the way dramatherapy relates to the process of projection. Despite the individual differences outlined above, at its simplest dramatic projection can be described as a process which lies at the heart of all dramatherapy. It enables the client to project inner conflicts into dramatic material and this allows the problematic area to be connected to the healing possibilities of drama. This chapter has illustrated some of the ways in which dramatic projection relates to the exploration of problematic material. It is this process that enables the client to see and feel themselves in the drama which is created in the dramatherapy group. Without this seeing and feeling there would be no potential for involvement or for change.

7 Play and playing

> What the child likes most is the theatre, that is to say, the transformation of actuality as given from without, into something that he himself creates.
>
> Evreinov, *The Theatre in Life*

Vignette: The falling man

Brown, Curry and Tittnich (1971) describe how a group of school-children witnessed an accident – a man, working on lights, fell 20 feet and was killed. The incident occurred only a few feet away from where a dozen children were playing. Their teachers recorded the play of the children, aged between three and six, for a number of months after the incident and studied the play and the children's feelings.

They found that for months afterwards the children's play reflected the incident. Children played falling and jumping, referring to falling on their heads, asking questions such as 'Where's the body? We have to go to hospital and take the body', giving instructions such as 'Fall like that man' (1971: 29). In their play they used details of the accident such as bleeding eyes, nose and mouth, wearing hard hats and hospitals. A variety of dangerous situations concerning falling and death were created: for example, a cat was shot dead and fell out of a tree; a group of boys played out an incident repeatedly for many months in which one of them fell and died, was taken to hospital and examined with stethoscopes.

The staff described the play as being a way for the children to accommodate the experience, to deal with the stress and shock, to adjust to and accept the death they had witnessed and the fears it caused in them. Play is a natural way of exploring and resolving the experience. Simply to talk about the experience would not have allowed the depth of participation and the working through of feelings and fantasies in enactment.

Here is a parallel illustration of play processes at work, this time within a dramatherapy session rather than in the naturally occurring play of children. Debra Colkett was working with children who had recently survived the tsunami in 2005. The following vignette was part of a raft of programmes and initiatives in Sri Lanka offering ongoing support for children. The dramatherapy was part of the 'Psycho-Social Program' headed up by Unicef for the whole of Sri Lanka and was within an initiative funded by the Ministry of Education 'arts in schools' and Funforlife who support work with children in countries experiencing war and natural disasters. This dramatherapy work began three weeks after the tsunami. The practice also connected with a local organisation, The Foundation of Goodness, who provided resources such as resident psychologists and translators. Colkett as a dramatherapist worked with the children on an ongoing basis with additional support and aftercare being provided by the foundation:

> The circumstances we were going into were unclear. Only that we would be working in villages and camps with children, many of whom had been orphaned by the tsunami. Buildings were at a premium so we asked the head monk of the village if we could use the temple (the only structure still standing solid). For this I took a deputation of children of all ages and got the teenagers involved to help organise/advertise/draw posters for the dramatherapy program ... the temple was open for everybody, Buddha didn't turn anyone away. It had been their sanctuary from tsunami and it represented safety, which is why I thought it would be a good space for us. *Everybody* did turn up on the first day. Parents, villagers, press, Americans taking photos ... The head monk, after much explanation and scrutiny, waved an arm dismissively and said, 'Go dance!'
>
> The group ran every day for one month initially. It was an open group so children of all ages could attend. Some people were sleeping in the temple; they had nowhere to go. Finally they were allocated a tent. As the curiosity subsided the group settled down to between 12 and 24 children per day. Not all came every day. Around 50 children were in regular attendance on different days.

Colkett describes the aims of the work as being:

- to provide a safe space
- to provide some relief from post traumatic stress disorder
- to offer containment
- to offer support.

The following research vignette is from one of the first groups.

Research vignette: Children and the tsunami

We began by holding hands in a circle – me, a co-worker, a translator and some children who had come to join us. I had placed a blue
cloth in the centre and waited to see what would emerge. The children began to move their arms up and down and we all began to
sway spontaneously. The energy began to build and a section of the
circle lunged into the centre and then another section. There was a
lot of laughter, the lunging became more intense and I requested
that the translator ask, 'What is the sound to this movement?' Then
it came: 'Whoosh!' Others joined in. We were running in and out
of the circle, hands linked: 'Whoosh!' The energy and the noise
built further, bouncing off the temple walls, a sort of contained
chaos. 'What's happening?' I shouted above the din. They told my
translator, 'It's tsunami! Tsunami coming!'

'What can you see?' I yelled. The children were laughing, playing
with the movement and replying, 'House!', 'My house!', 'My grand-
father!', My grandmother!', 'My sister!', 'Mango tree!', 'Gone tsunami!' The noise became more intense. We were in the thick of it.
Then the howling, ear-piercing, soul-wrenching howling. I tried to
ask, 'What is the howling sound?' No one heard. It was almost
unbearable.

One of the children caught my eye. The other children were still in
the 'play' of the enactment. His face had changed. He had broken
off from the circle. Everywhere else it remained intact. The movement and sound built to a crescendo and died down and we were
back to stillness, panting and smiling with the effort. B sat just outside the circle. His eyes were downcast and his face sad. I checked
the rest of the children. They seemed to be having fun.

My attention was drawn back to B. I asked the children to sit. He
was now sitting with his head bowed and he had isolated himself
slightly. I felt that he was back there with the full horror of the tsunami. How could I bring B back into the present? I desperately
searched my intuition to somehow reach out to him. The right intervention was important. I asked my translator to ask him what he
was feeling. He looked up, fear and sadness in his eyes. He said
nothing. It was unspeakable.

After a long moment I shuffled a little closer to B, still unsure of what to do, and the other children followed. In an inspired moment they picked up the blue cloth, gathered around him so that he was encased in the circle, and sensitively placed the cloth over him like a shroud. Aware that we were all watching him, I spoke to the children; I knew they had the answer.

'How can we make B feel better? I can see that playing the tsunami has upset him.'

'We can sing to him,' they replied.

'Would you like that?' I asked B.

He nodded. My connection with him and the loss he was feeling was palpable. We carefully edged closer. The distance seemed important; not too close as to overwhelm him and not too distant to isolate him. After a count of three, the song 'Iren Handen' echoed around the temple and everyone was focused on B. ('Iren Handen' is a popular Sri Lankan song meaning 'Sun and Moon'. It is the theme tune to a film about two boys who go through many struggles together, but their friendship, faith and spiritual bond keep them strong.)

> *Iren Handen*
>
> Iren Handen elija aran
> Gahen velen suwanda aran
> Elen dolen sisila aran
> Apata sebuna ape lokaye
> Sathuta wenna enne galuwe.

Translation:

> *Sun and Moon*
>
> Getting light from the Sun and Moon
> Getting cool from the rivers and waterfalls
> Fresh smells from the trees and bushes
> This world is for us.

He looked into all our faces and eyes. We were clapping, smiling and singing to him. Soon he began to smile and the tsunami no longer had him in its cruel grip. B was back with us.

B continued to come to the group and presented as a playful, shy, sensitive nine-year-old boy. As far as I could tell he showed no signs of flashbacks as intense as that first day. He was one of the group of children who asked me to take them to the ocean because they feared the sea since the tsunami. Together we took 'the first steps to the sea'.

Debra Colkett

CORE PROCESS BOX

Embodiment

The individuals in the group create the thing that has terrified and traumatised them. They embody it and play with it. Here embodiment – their physical expression of the wave through movement and cloth – enables them to represent together a trauma and to start to express responses towards it. Something that has been held in is allowed expression through physical means. Rather like the children in the 'Falling man' play episode embodying an experience that they are trying to assimilate, here the physical making of the tsunami wave together represents a similar way for the child to encounter the wave as a means of trying to accommodate their experience. Play enables this to be done safely – a state they can enter into and leave, images they can make and stop. A thing they can physically embody and share together may make this less frightening than the isolating experience of terror with the wave taking away their family and becoming alone, for example.

Playing

In this vignette the language and atmosphere is reminiscent of play and games. As with the 'Falling man' example which starts this chapter, the vignette also reflects how playing can involve the representation of events or feelings which a child is trying to assimilate, come to terms with or master. Here, the activities which Colkett seems to develop from the children's cues balance game-related work that captures the image of the tsunami, alongside the creation of moments which involve the playing out of specific experiences of the event or situation. In addition, the work exemplifies how the therapist and space create safety, a holding in which the conditions for play are reproduced and where an individual's distress is expressed, responded to and held. The play state offers opportunities for expression in a way which combines safety and spontaneity.

Research conversation with Debra Colkett

Jones: I was very moved by the work you and the children did with the tsunami in the temple. Looking back how did you make that space for them? How did you prepare, for example?

Colkett: Safe buildings were at a premium after the tsunami. It was very difficult to find a safe enclosed space. After a week or so it was suggested we use the temple. I got children of all ages involved in the task of finding a place for us. We finally ended up with a deputation of some 20 kids. We found the head monk and he agreed that we could use the temple. I can't tell you how happy I was! In terms of preparing the therapy space in the vignette, we stood in a circle. We said our names and made a movement to match it. The name was the music and the movement the dance. Then we all mirrored the movement and the name of the person creating their personalised 'dance'. My translator Rajhita spoke in Singhalese to the children. Their English was limited, as was my Singhalese, so the universal language of movement and mime was very useful.

Jones: The words you used at one point to describe the session talked about the 'whoosh' 'bouncing off the temple walls'. That image stayed in my head and I thought about it from reading the vignette . . . I had the feeling it was almost like the temple walls were echoing not just the sound but the holding experience of bringing in (some other words you use) the 'chaos' – that for this particular horrendous event you needed a very secure space – is that how it felt? That the temple as refuge paralleled your group as refuge – a safe place amidst all the chaos? I'm wondering if the circle and the movement work acted as a mirror for that – a shape to contain?

Colkett: The majority of the temples, certainly in the Southern Province, remained intact and survived the tsunami. The surviving villagers ran to the temples for safety and remained there for several days until the government said they had to go back to what was left of the villages. So the temple was a symbolic safe space – some people lived there until their tents arrived. I thought it would be perfect for the dramatherapy work. The dramatherapy sessions provided a vehicle for expressing the children's life drama of the tsunami. Many people witnessed the work and some 600 villagers came to the final show. In this way the transformation of the trauma with the children rippled out into the direct community and finally the surrounding villages. It appeared to have a healing benefit for all.

Jones: From the vignette it sounded like you managed to hold the processes that the children naturally reached out to in their play – almost like you were taking cues and holding the way they were going – the reaching for the cloth, the shrouding. Is that how it felt or was it different?

Colkett: Yes, I completely followed their lead. I had preconceptions about post traumatic stress disorder and how this might manifest itself. During the therapeutic process they didn't get angry. They experienced emotions and got on with it. It was a lesson to be learnt for them. I was in a very feeling, intuitive state. I had to trust my solid training and my instincts.

This vignette illustrates how dramatherapy utilises the natural process of play as a means of dealing with trauma or life problems. However, play relates to dramatherapy in three particular ways.

- The first concerns the way in which *playfulness* and the general process of playing can be the vehicle of therapeutic change within dramatherapy.
- The second relates specifically to the notion of *developmental play* and drama. Here both are seen as parts of a continuum of different developmental stages. The continuum relates both to assessment and to the way change occurs for clients in dramatherapy.
- The third focuses upon *content*. Play involves particular areas of content and has a particular way of articulating that content. For example, in many cultures play usually involves certain subjects, certain recognised forms of expression, along with rules regarding that expression. Play also has a special relationship with reality. In dramatherapy this content, form and relationship with reality become particular ways for the client to express and explore experiences.

Play in dramatherapy

Play is a close relative to drama and is a source for both content and process within dramatherapy. Evreinov speaks of this close relationship between play and drama in his discussion of the Soviet Malachie-Mirovich's work on the educational value of toys: 'All children have the ability to create a new reality out of the facts of life' (1927: 36). The child plays naturally, without instruction, creating their 'own theatre', proving that 'nature herself has planted in the human being a sort of "will to theatre" ' (1927: 36).

It is interesting to note how many key figures within the development of dramatherapy began their initial thinking and work in the areas of play and dramatic playing with children. From Moreno's work with children in Viennese parks in 1908 to Slade's work with child drama and initial use of the term 'dramatherapy', the inspiration for the use of drama as therapy has been found in play. Play has a great deal of relevance to the therapeutic use of drama. Blatner and Blatner have spoken of the 'common basis of drama, psychodrama and the play of children' (1988a: 51).

For the dramatherapist and for the client in dramatherapy play is a part of the expressive range which can be drawn on in creating meaning, exploring difficulties and achieving therapeutic change. Crucial to this relationship is the way in which the client finds meaning in play processes. Play has been seen to have a healing quality. In dramatherapy individuals and groups can reflect upon and deal with encountered problems by playing.

Meaning and play

Vignette: Girls' play in Silwa

A study of Egyptian children in Silwa describes how girls often engage in play representations of adult women's activities and ceremonies. The play involves making straw figures, bedecked in bits of cloth as men and women and children, and with the help of stones, building a house. All the details of an event or ritual 'are played out in a make-believe way, thus marriage, circumcision, cooking and social meetings are all imitated' (Ammar 1954: 119).

This process can be described as the child playing out events they have witnessed in order to master and learn how to come to terms with them. The child's experience is seen as an essential part of assimilating and accommodating reality – what things *mean* to the child.

Shaw (1981) describes a key connection between play, the development of intelligence and the creation of meaning. The kind of experience described above is grounded in a form of 'symbolic transformation' of 'experiential data (overt enactment of the "as if")' (Shaw 1981: 72), which she says is essential to the development of human intelligence and a fundamental way by which children make and find meanings in the world they encounter.

A similar position is taken by Bolton (1981). Early play is typified by an individual finding meaning in the world about them in solitary or parallel play. Bolton describes the development of more complex forms of play into drama as focusing around a shift concerning the *communication* of discovery and the mutual finding of meaning. In dramatic play children not only involve themselves in a solitary discovery but also in a mutual one which involves the sharing of meaning discovered through an enactment. Bolton stresses the importance of interaction and acknowledgement of meaning in dramatic play, indicating a self-consciousness and desire to articulate. There must be 'some significance related to the concrete action that all participants can share' (Bolton 1981: 185).

Blatner and Blatner also emphasise the meaning-finding process in play and drama. From a psychodramatic viewpoint they equate the notion of play activity as an arena to sort, solve and resolve, with the space later taken by drama. The dramatic mode is seen as an adult equivalent of child's play. Play is marked by the child's struggle with understanding and emotionally apprehending the world, a clarification of problems and testing of new approaches. Blatner and Blatner describe make-believe play as an arena in which children test out their experiences and abilities. They go on to say that 'in adulthood this becomes the activity of drama' (1988a: 50). The aspect of play whereby a child reproduces experiences of reality symbolically, mentioned by Shaw and Bolton, is developed by Blatner and Blatner in terms of its potentials for healing and therapy: 'Drama is a more mature extension of the natural phenomenon of play, and this capacity for symbolic manipulation of experience is . . . important . . . in psychosocial healing' (1988a: 75).

Winnicott describes play as an area of 'potential space', essential for the infant to establish relationships between the inner world and outer experience: 'Play is, in fact, neither a matter of inner psychic reality nor a matter of external reality' (Winnicott 1966: 368). This space is one in which a negotiation between personal identity and surrounding world takes place in terms of meaning and relationship.

This creation of a special state that has a symbolic framing relationship with reality is part of the way in which the client finds meaning in dramatherapy. The areas of communication, the manipulation, mastery and coming to terms with reality and the notion of testing and assimilating that typify the state of playing are all relevant to the way in which play manifests itself in therapy.

The creation of meaning in play is crucial to all three areas of dramatherapy identified at the start of this chapter: to playfulness and the general process of playing; the developmental framework; and play content. The main aspects of meaning finding through play relevant to these three areas are:

- the symbolic transformation of experience
- finding meaning in the world
- sorting, solving and resolving
- mastering and learning
- negotiating a relationship between inner and outer reality.

Cultural factors in play

Cultural and socio-economic factors relating to play are important for the dramatherapist to consider. A degree of research has been undertaken into the different cultural forms, processes and societal significances given to play; similarly into the different ways children and adults relate to play given their social and economic position (Sutton-Smith 1972: 8) The conclusions drawn from the research vary widely. Some researchers have explored cultural and socio-economic differences according to notions of 'deficit'. This considers the ways in which specific processes such as dramatic play or play with objects are inhibited within certain cultures or within socio-economic status. For example, children in some cultures are considered as an 'economic asset' and

participate in work which depletes playing. Adult attitudes in actively pre-
venting children from playing are considered in some studies such as Levine
and Levine's exploration of Gusü childhood in Kenya (Levine and Levine
1963: 9). In other cultures play is described as being essentially absent
(Ebbek 1973).

The methodological approach of some of these studies has, however, been
questioned. Fein and Stork (1981) and McLoyd (1982) have criticised the
stance taken by researchers as inadequate: 'If lower-class pre-schoolers and
children from non-Western societies have not been observed to engage in rich
fantasy play, it is only because we have not used the right methods or techniques to discern their play' (Johnson, Christie and Yawkey 1987: 145). They
advocate an approach to research orientated to considering difference rather
than deficit.

For the dramatherapist it is crucial to contextualise play within cultural
difference. The use of dolls, objects, space relationship differs between cultures. Feitelson (1977) has discussed the different roles of toys and objects
in some Middle Eastern and African societies and in North African and
European immigrants in Jerusalem. A child originating in a home or culture
where objects do not have a primary role in playing, for example, will need to
be worked with in a different way to one who does not come from such a
background.

Play and dramatherapy

Play in dramatherapy refers to processes which involve both children and
adults. Playing has a part in all dramatherapy work in that it is usual to
involve clients in forms of playing as part of the dramatherapy. This occurs
on a *practical* level in that many warm-ups involve forms of playing such as
games. The dramatherapy work might use play activities and processes as
a mode of therapeutic intervention. It also occurs on a *conceptual* level:
dramatherapy can be said to involve clients in a playful relationship with
themselves, other group members and reality.

However, it can be argued that play in dramatherapy is clearly not the play
that a child engages with in the spontaneous circumstances of natural play
within their usual environment. In dramatherapy aspects of our understanding of the way play functions are separated and emphasised. The notion that
a natural play state is totally re-created within dramatherapy is an incorrect
assumption. Play in dramatherapy occurs within specific boundaries and
frameworks that differ from those in which the child will usually play. The
condition aimed for is related to but different from a child's usual play. This
chapter aims to identify this difference, to describe how dramatherapy connects with and uses play and play processes, and to examine technique in this
area of practice.

Overview: key concepts

The area of play has come to have considerable influence within drama-therapy, both in terms of the understanding of the general processes at work and in the development of specific methods linked to playing. The key conceptual areas in the relationship between play and dramatherapy include playing and playfulness, play content and the 'play shift', and developmental issues.

Playing and playfulness

In dramatherapy the creation of access to 'playfulness' is often central to the therapeutic work. Access to playing can form a way of engaging in spontaneity, a route to becoming creative. This process can be seen as therapeutic in itself. The access to playing may be the main aim of the therapy, in that the creation of spontaneity can be therapeutic. Playfulness in dramatherapy can enable the client to engage with self, others and life in a spontaneous way. This allows the group or individual to engage creatively and playfully with problematic material where before they have only been able to remain stuck and uncreative in response to problems.

> When I watch children absorbed in dramatic play, I marvel not only at their dual level of consciousness, at all that is communicated and revealed, and at the growth and healing that takes place, but also at the delight and pleasure the players indisputably experience . . . dramatic play in therapy results in a process that is most often pleasurable.
>
> (Emunah 1994: 5)

Play content and the 'play shift'

For children and adult clients play is important as an area of content and in discovering meaning within dramatherapy work. Play is characterised by specific activities and by particular kinds of relationships between individuals and the way they deal with the world around them. These activities and relationships form one key area of the way play features in dramatherapy.

In 'Play Behaviour in Higher Primates: A Review,' Loizos (1969) tries to define the function of play within primate play. She says that it is a 'behaviour' which borrows or adopts patterns that appear in other contexts. In their usual place these patterns appear to have immediate and obvious ends or goals. She states:

> When these patterns appear in play they seem to be divorced from their original motivation and are qualitatively distinct from the same patterns appearing in their originally motivated contexts.
>
> (Loizos 1969: 228–229)

Here, then, emphasis is placed upon a shift in meaning – a 'play shift'. Whilst many of the forms or structures of real life are retained in playing, the intention is different. Piaget (1962) has said that in play the individual's interest is transferred from the goal to the activity itself – to enjoyment of the pleasure of play itself.

Read Johnson has allied the play space with the dramatherapy group. Both are 'an interpersonal field in an imaginary realm, consciously set off from the real world by the participants' (1981: 21). Schechner (1988) echoes this, paralleling the workshop experience with play. He says that the workshop is a way of playing around with reality, a means of examining behaviour by 're-ordering, exaggerating, fragmenting, recombining, and adumbrating it'. The workshop is a protected time and space where 'intergroup relationships may thrive without being threatened by intergroup aggression' (Schechner 1988: 103–104). Pitruzzella's description of improvisation, and the state it creates, echoes many of these qualities, depicting the ways in which processes in play and drama are closely connected: 'improvisation aims at the group creation of a spontaneous and unpredictable artistic event', and stressing qualities of 'inventiveness, spontaneity and imagination . . . attention, intuition and empathy' (Pitruzzella 2004: 4).

In dramatherapy this paralleling of reality within a playing state is important. The notion of a 'play shift' is the fulcrum of dramatherapy's use of play. As described by Loizos (1969) and Piaget (1967), in play elements of real life are retained but they are subjected to different motivations – enjoyment, exploration, assimilation. The play shift involves reality being taken into the play space and treated in a way that encourages experimentation and digestion. In dramatherapy the mode of play is used to enable a further development of this 'play shift'. This process is directed towards intentional change.

Developmental approach

The twentieth century saw a great deal of study into the developmental processes that are marked by play and are aided by play activities. These concern the cognitive and psychological development of an individual. The psychological, cognitive and emotional developments that are enabled by play (or which accompany playing) form the third area of importance of play's relation to dramatherapy.

Play is seen as the precursor to the development of drama. As Figures 7.2–7.7 (pp. 177–183) indicate, a clear connection can be made between activities described as 'play' and 'drama'. They form a continuum of increasing complexity and richness of meaning. The dramatherapist works with a dramatic continuum. The detail and processes involved in this continuum are important for the dramatherapist to understand and utilise in their work. I will now examine the notion of dramatic development and its main uses in dramatherapy.

Dramatherapy practice and play

The general process of play as a vehicle in dramatherapy

At the start of any work in dramatherapy it is important to discover the play language of the group. This involves seeing whether a group plays or not. If it does, how does the playing occur? If it does not, how does the absence of play manifest itself? From a diagnostic perspective, the issues that are presenting as problems may be manifested through play language.

This is followed by the consideration of whether play processes can be utilised as part of the therapeutic work to be undertaken.

The next aspect involves the position of play within the therapeutic work. This usually entails either the introduction of play processes and languages or the group's spontaneous use of play and playing. This approach can be codified as a series of stages that are summarised in Box 7.1.

Box 7.1 outlines the ways in which the general process of play features within dramatherapy's efficacy. As described, there are specific areas of play and play process that are pertinent to dramatherapy.

Box 7.1 **Dramatherapy guide – discovering play language**

1   Learning the language of play within a group: what is happening here and now?
2   What is not happening or has not happened in terms of play? Are there elements of play content or process not occurring or seemingly unavailable to this group?
3   In what ways can the play language be of therapeutic use to this group:

  •   Are there ways in which playing can be therapeutically effective for the group?
  •   Can the developmental aspects of play/elements of play missing in the group be involved in the therapeutic work?
  •   Can the client use play as a way of communicating and exploring the problems they are encountering?

4   How can the dramatherapist provide the conditions for effective play processes to be created within the dramatherapy setting?
5   How can the assessments concerning play connect with the aims of the dramatherapy group and developing a potential play space and play activities within the group?
6   How can connections be made between the actual play within the dramatherapy session and the client's life outside the play?

Play content in dramatherapy

Landy (1986: 52) gives play as one of the key areas of the 'media of the dramatic arts' that inform the practice of dramatherapy. He includes child play, especially dramatic play and the ability to play as an adult (p. 56). Activities used within dramatherapy include:

- sensorimotor/body play
- imitation activities
- play with objects
- play with symbolic toys
- projective work with toys in the creation of small worlds
- rough and tumble play
- make-believe play involving taking on characters
- games.

Dramatherapy tends to echo Peter Slade's approach in seeing play as a beginning and as a part of dramatic activity (Slade 1954). In some work the activity is mainly focused in play activities, while in others there can be a mixture of play and more developed dramatic activities such as role play.

The use of play space in dramatherapy

Creation of play worlds

In dramatherapy one of the important aspects of play is the notion that entry into play means an entry into a specific 'special' state and space. Most authors dealing with play concern themselves with this phenomenon, though stressing different aspects.

Feitelson and Landau (1976) have commented upon cultural differences regarding play space, writing about Kurdish immigrants in Israel. Authors such as Cohen (1969) and Ammar (1954) have also considered cross-cultural issues in the use and creation of spaces to play in. Sutton-Smith (1979) notes that cultural attitudes to play space differ, which affects the way space is used in play. Some cultures discourage play and adults are observed to actively disrupt the play space. In others, social patterns concerning work mean that children are involved in work from an early age (Levine and Levine 1963). Sutton-Smith (1979) has argued that in such cultures physical space and time to play are minimised: 'The adults know what must be done to survive and they cannot afford the wasted time of child play' (Sutton-Smith 1979: 6). However, this view is challenged by Schwartzman (1978: 192) who, in referring to a variety of cross-cultural studies of play, says that in virtually all cases where children contribute to the economy they devise ways to combine playing and work.

Play work in dramatherapy echoes Griffing's four areas of preparation for activity. Griffing (1983) considers that in preparing for play an adult needs to provide four things: time; safe space; appropriate materials; preparatory experiences. Singer (1973) has said that physical space and privacy are pre-requisites for imaginative play skills to develop. Some theorists say that children must have an 'as if' stance towards reality modelled or encouraged (Smilansky 1968; Singer 1973).

In a therapy situation the qualities of play can be produced, but though there are similarities there are also differences which are crucial to under-standing the shift. Within dramatherapy play processes are part of a deliber-ate therapeutic programme for working with the client. In addition an adult therapist will be constantly present within the play area. The dramatherapy session will produce the conditions necessary for play to occur. Much of the content will be identical in form and structure. However, they will occur and be contained within a therapeutic framework.

Stage one of the shift is the reproduction in play form of activities from or related to reality, which are played in a special time and place. The activities do not have the same context – they are out of their usual framework.

Stage two in dramatherapy involves the reorientating of this activity within a framework which hopes both to keep the qualities of play and enable it to have new goals. These goals are to offer personal therapeutic change for the client.

The following research vignette illustrates these aspects of the creation of the play world within therapy. The dramatherapy sessions took place as part of a course within a mainstream college in the UK. The course was intended for young people between the ages of 16 and 20 who had moderate to severe learning disabilities, all of whom had attended special schools throughout their primary and secondary education. Dramatherapist Jo Rogers says:

> The work is different from the therapeutic work normally described in therapeutic literature where the clients have been identified as having emotional problems and where the therapeutic aims focus upon those problems. The setting believed that the young people needed a space apart, within the course, where they could 'get things off their chests'. In particular they recognise the 'load' the young people carry in managing the demands of the college, family and their identity as teenagers. They recognise the impact that moving to a 'mainstream' from a 'special' environment has on a young person with learning difficulties. Some rec-ognise that this group – which moves through the college, and they do just that for the most part, move visibly as a group – carries something for the college. This block of students carries the disability for the college.

Rogers describes the way she created a context and framework for the 'playful space' to develop. It is interesting to note here, and in the following research vignette, how she and the group handle the difference I noted earlier – that she as a therapist is present with and within the play and how the relationship between play, improvisation and drama naturally emerges and they merge and interchange within the work.

> We used a large room with a clear space in the middle. I provided masks, dressing up clothes, small world toys, art materials, musical instruments and props in boxes around the room. I saw these as a stimulus and encouragement to work symbolically and as a visible sign of the sort of work which could take place. I had an expectation that drama would take place and that what the eight group members would say or do could be part of a dramatic communication: a communication which spoke from their inner and outer worlds. In order to convey that drama was being used as a means of expressing feelings and exploring ways of being and relating, I created a circle of chairs at the beginning and end of sessions and sat in the circle myself at these times, and often for large parts of the sessions.

The research vignette is from a session which took place at the end of two years of work together. The young people are about to leave college.

Research vignette: Two weeks left

This is what happened. It starts just as I think, 'Maybe this will be the shape of it: a sort of formless, noisy partying?' Sheila picks up the ribbons dropped by Alan, Peter and Amit. They have been using the ribbons, which are on sticks, as if they are sparklers. There is a celebratory, festival-like mood. This changes as Sheila starts to tie one, and then a second ribbon across the length of the room. The circle of chairs is still intact but is getting pushed back as Sheila sets about her task. I remain seated. I suggest, in the running commentary to the group, in the running commentary style I usually use, that these are obstacles, barriers, maybe the two weeks left, when suddenly Alan jumps over one and rapidly over the other.

I then suggest, 'A sort of tripwire? No sooner over the one than you have to jump the other?'

Sheila continues to tie ribbons from table to chair, whilst Alan and Mehul tell us, 'Fire fire, bomb, bomb – you have to get out!' They have made the far side of the ribbons the bombed area by laying some of the ribbons on the floor in a heap. Amit has taken a sheet of paper and written 'BOMB'. They say they need us to clear out.

Sonal, meanwhile, has taken two baby dolls from the box and gives one to me to hold and sits next to me holding hers. Lilly has been taking items of clothing from the box and sits behind us, dressed in shirt and cap and flowery trousers with a hole near the crotch. Amit and Peter are sat in the bombed area by the ribbons and are the first to be moved.

For the second week running I feel I am needed to play, as Sheila comes and takes my hand. It is interesting that I have not been called to work in role since the early weeks of this group. I ask, in role, 'We have to get out?'

Alan says earnestly, 'It's for the best we have to move out there's no more time.'

'Why?' I ask.

'Why?' says Sonal, 'I don't want to go.'

Alan now says, 'It's the council. They are building a road through you have to go, hurry up you can take your babies.'

Lilly giggles and says, 'Go, go.'

Alan says, 'Over there.'

'No,' says Sonal, 'I don't like it over there. I want to stay here.'

'Sonal doesn't want to move on. She's not sure where she's going?' I offer.

Alan says, 'We've got you bed and breakfast.'

Peter has sat himself near the area we are being sent to and is knotting up a couple of ribbons. Amit is sat a little away from him on the edge of a chair.

'What choice do we have?' I ask.

Alan says, 'You can live on the streets like him.' He points at Peter.

Sonal starts to scream at him, 'I don't want to leave the old one! I don't like the new one!' He takes her by the shoulder, and Sheila helps him for a while and they physically lead her to the tables behind Dan and Sheila tells her, 'This is the bed.'

Alan says, 'It will be a bit bumpy at first, but you'll get used to it.'

Sonal sits down, and she holds out her hand to me. Lilly follows behind, and we three sit on the table.

Alan and Mehul are now busy moving all the tables at the other end of the room. Mehul and Alan keep bringing us news of the moves. Alan says at one point, 'We have built a new kitchen.' Mehul makes enthusiastic noises in agreement. He takes Sonal across to see. He clearly wants to impress her.

She says, 'I don't like the new kitchen.'

Alan keeps asking, 'Sonal are you all right?' There is an edge to his voice which indicates to me that he fears this might be all too real for Sonal, but perhaps for everyone.

She says, 'I'm okay,' as if shrugging off the idea that she cannot manage. She insists however, 'I want to go back.'

Alan says, 'Sorry, there is no going back now.'

Sheila has virtually cordoned off all the areas and it looks like a building/demolition site. She then sets up another table in front of Dan's table and has a large sheet of paper. Sheila wants everyone to go and sign it, saying, 'This is all going to cost a lot of money.'

Alan then comes and says, 'There's good news and there's bad news.' Mehul and Sheila stand solemnly beside him. Alan says, 'The good news is you are going to fly to Spain and the bad news is there is definitely no going back.' Mehul and Sheila nod seriously.

Lilly drops her head and I add in commentary style, 'The news has come as a shock to Lilly.'

Sonal says, 'Why are we going to Spain? Why why why?'

The three news bearers look at each other for an answer.

I suggest, 'To take your mind off the bad news?' [The group is indeed being taken on a week's residential soon as a way of ending the course.]

'Yeah,' says Sheila as if this makes some sort of sense. She adds, 'Dan play us another song.'

I ask, 'Why does he sing us songs?'

Sheila says, 'It's about how we feel and he tries to cheer us up.'

Dan puts on the song 'Daniel' and Lilly drops her head down towards me.

I announce to the group, 'Oh dear, something's happened to Lilly. She isn't taking this change well.'

'What matter?' asks Mehul.

She whispers to me, 'I dead.' I sense she wants this shared.

'She's dead,' I announce. 'The news has been too much. She cannot bear it.' I notice tears running down her cheeks. 'She's dying of a broken heart she is so sad to be leaving.'

Mehul rushes to get a cover and Sheila fetches tissues. They take her to be 'dead' in the cordoned off area.

Sonal looks at me and says, 'I love you.'

I say, 'It's our last session together.' She looks at me and bursts into tears.

It is time for us to pack away and re-form the circle. I say to the group as I usually do, 'It is nearly time to finish. Time to pack the drama away.' I sit and watch as they help each other to put back the clothes and props and chairs and they re-form the circle.

There are not many words as we sit in the circle afterwards. Sheila voices that it was good today. Dan asks if they liked his music. There is much praise for his music and he looks pleased. Lilly is the person who looks most pleased with herself. I have not known her take on such a visible role in the group. What I am most struck by is their ability to take a hold of this medium called drama and make it their own. Within the drama they are eloquent.

Jo Rogers

Rogers describes the impact of the work on one of the young people in the following way:

Alan thanks me as he leaves and I am struck by the changes in this young man. Alan began the course by saying that he wanted nothing to do with this dramatherapy. It seems to me that his fear early on was that there was something exposing and revealing in dramatherapy. But he has been able to use the sessions to make connections between the drama and his life. In term three Alan starts to name one of the functions of the group. He leaves some dressing up trousers at the end of a session and says he is putting them into the 'dry cleaners'. He collects them from the bag in the next session and is pleased to see that they are 'clean'. He then goes on to do his own 'laundry' in the session before half term of term four. The function of the group then is to empty out unmanageable feelings and to receive them back in a more manageable form. Through repeated encounters of this nature it becomes possible to learn to perform this process for oneself. The drama, it seems, has enabled Alan both to make use of the process and to explore it as a process.

CORE PROCESS BOX

Dramatic projection

The clients create a world of barriers, death and carrying babies, of relationships of looking after, dying, injury. Through the content of the images they develop and in the fictional identities and relationships the group project internally held but unvoiced anxieties and issues. The group process and the drama hold them and allows them to be explored as the playing and improvisation develops.

Empathy and distancing

The therapist offers commentary and occasionally articulates possible meanings in the work. Potentially this could be problematic. Difficulties in developing the processes at work might occur if the group felt exposed by her readings. They might lose their involvement through becoming too distanced, or the power of her readings in position of therapist might hinder their own meaning emerging. Members might become too self-conscious and the analysis might stop the development of the playing. However, given that therapist and group have been working together for a long time, the relationship seems mutual and the therapist's comments seem to be a recognition between her and the group that she can perceive and receive the different layers of meaning occurring. The group, in reflecting on the play, become witnesses or readers of their own expressions. Within the same session they have been immersed within the play and also coming out and reflecting on it, giving it a meaning through words in reflection as well as through the action.

Research conversation with Jo Rogers

Jones: What do you see as important about dramatherapy for the clients?

Rogers: I guess there are hundreds of possible benefits but with this particular client group it is something about them being able to communicate with parts of themselves that have been shut off or never fully brought to life.

Jones: How do you see your role within that?

Rogers: I feel my main role as first and foremost to accept whatever they bring, and whoever they are, without judgement. I feel that there has been a real obstacle against playing for many of them; that experiences in society can lead to people with a severe disability looking to see what they have got wrong. So, yes, first and foremost I model that every sound, movement, gesture, feeling is 'right'.

Jones: Am interested in the idea of modelling and what you say about 'fully bringing something to life' in play. Also, how you see your role in this coming to life. Say, when Lilly dropped her head down, you mentioned it to the group – 'something's happened' – and then, after she whispers to you, you say, 'She's dead.' The group responded and fetched tissues, took her over to the cordoned off area. How did you see your role there? And how do you see what was happening for the group, for Lilly?

Rogers: I guess most of the time I see my role as giving a running commentary; providing a function or role which 'notices' and also begins to wonder. . . . At the same time I am always looking to help the drama to hold. Obviously, this all relies on me taking risks, and I would not have been risking so many interpretations when I first started with the group. My running commentary at that stage was at a very literal level I think as far as Lilly is concerned I also act as a support, an intervener to assist her to . . .

Jones: So what effect do you see that having for her?

Rogers: First, she is helped, because I feel she experiences being understood. Speech is not her strength, the words she has are too few, so I think she feels empowered when what I say might connect with her potentially intended meaning. Also she is able to make her contribution to this group play in a very powerful way

Jones: Would you say you are there as an improvising player yourself? Is that how you see it?

Rogers: Yes, up to a point. I enter momentarily into the world of 'as if' as a participant, rather than just a commentator, and I guess I also model that ability to move in and out of role as player. Mind you, I guess I feel I improvise in whichever role.

Jones: A tricky but important question this. Do you work 'off the hip' improvising your comments, or would you say you are thinking – reflecting and analysing before offering a response?

Rogers: I am constantly feeling first and foremost, responding to what is taking place in the room, and reflecting upon that. I'm trying to make connections with, and sense of, the information I am receiving through the projections coming at me, and the words and actions I see literally in front of my eyes. All the time I am linking back, and imagining forward. I try to think, before I speak, what the impact of what I say or do will have on the various group members, or what the impact of me acting or speaking will have on the group process. I try to receive, hold, make sense of the group's conscious and unconscious communications and hand them back in a way that will help the drama and world of 'as if' stay intact and keep doing its job.

Jones: I'm curious about the ways you and the group work within the metaphors and symbols. I wondered if you and the group felt that elements – such as the council building a road and making them move, or the bad news about no going back from Spain – are a mirror to the world outside – but by not referring to it directly, it gives certain kinds of permissions. What do you think of that?

Rogers: Yes, I certainly agree. An example of this would be Sonal, who lets me know most clearly that the divide between the drama, the world of 'as if' and the real world, is a fine one. I believe that we all know that the 'move' we are talking of is the one from the college.

The group's participation in this research vignette shows many of the facets of dramatic play. However, the playing activity takes place within a therapeutic framework. The goals of the play activity concern personal change. The therapist, in line with Griffing's (1983) four areas, has provided clear time, a safe space, materials and preparatory experiences. The clients connect the play work to personal material. They use the playing to reflect a range of issues and difficulties and to try out expressing and finding some resolution in the play world within the dramatherapy.

In the work of the group the playing that is facilitated occurs within a therapeutic framework. The processes that the clients are engaged in enable play to become a way for the group to express their fears, anger, distress at the group's ending and the changes in their lives, and to voice things within the play that they could not express in their 'non-play' relations with each other and the therapist.

Play occurs within a special created, facilitative context within dramatherapy. In both research vignettes the activities aim to explore problematic issues through playing within a therapeutic framework. Clients and therapist together create play in order to express, explore and work towards a resolution of problems.

A developmental approach and the play–drama continuum

As described earlier, there is a great variety of models of play development. Many include the notion of a continuum. Within dramatherapy the consideration of play within a continuum is of use as an assessment tool, as a means of finding an appropriate developmental level of play to work with clients, and as a means of understanding therapeutic change. As also noted earlier, play can be seen as a part of a continuum of development leading to drama. The continuum can be considered in terms of creative development, psychological development and skills development.

The play–drama continuum

Specific developmental stages have different implications for dramatherapy practice, and are associated with different methods. It is important to discover an appropriate developmental level for a group concerning their use of play and drama. Until the dramatherapist has established the level at which the group appears to work, or might be able to work, or chooses to work, then communication will be marred. The therapist needs to understand which areas of play and drama the group can best use to find meaning in. Schwartzman (1978) has pointed out that developmental notions concerning play are often culture specific; she compares a number of different studies of play in different settings in her book *Transformations*. Authors such as Fortes present specific developmental studies of play. He considers the developmental stages of the play of Talinese children (1938). Irwin has pointed out that it is useful for the therapist to be aware of developmental levels to determine how an individual uses drama and play. During the course of treatment, many clients and children 'experience regression and/or fixation in both the form and content of their play' (Irwin 1983: 105). Awareness of the developmental continuum from play to drama 'can help the therapist be sensitive to shifts in functioning and to deal with them . . . via appropriate media and materials' (Irwin 1983: 150). The following section gives a general overview of this process.

Summary of the play–drama continuum

First, an individual discovers their body and is involved in a relationship with an important other such as a parent. At this level play involves the discovery of body parts and the body, along with contact with the important other. Later play develops to include forming relationships with concrete objects and the physical qualities which they possess – rolling, holding, dropping. This is followed by the development of symbolic play with objects, either as representative toys or as symbols with personal meaning. At first this is in solitary play or play with an important adult. Solitary play is usually followed by parallel play where a child plays with toys in a way which is similar to other children who are near, but individuals do not play together. The next phase involves playing together. This involves object play or brief sociodramatic play – activities which engage with playing other identities for a short while. The next phase involves the shift from dramatic play to drama. This concerns more sustained activities that involve taking on an identity in relationship with others, accompanied by more consciousness of showing activities to others and communicating the meaning of what is happening. This outline is presented as a general summary and is not intended to be seen as the only avenue of development for all individuals.

The following pages focus on the key aspects of this developmental process as it relates to dramatherapy. First, the main aspects of development along the play–drama continuum are summarised (Figures 7.2–7.7). Second, two specific areas are focused upon: character and object usage. The stages are set out in Box 7.2.

Figures 7.3–7.7 indicate important aspects of each stage. For example, the stage of 'imitative play' is summarised by five areas (or stages) of capability, which usually follow on from each other. For the dramatherapist each stage should not be seen only to be appropriately worked with by the listed activities or areas, but rather as opening up additional areas of expression and meaning for the client. As the vignettes show, the developmental stages summary is appropriate to groups irrespective of age. For people with learn-

---

Box 7.2 **Key aspects of the play–drama continuum**

- Sensorimotor play
- Imitative play
- Pretend play
- Dramatic play
- Drama

ing difficulties the developmental levels are important as sequential steps, similarly for other groups for whom developmental progression is an issue within the dramatherapy work.

Figures 7.3–7.7 are used not only to aid understanding of the development of drama but also to ascertain which activities can be undertaken by a group able to work at a certain developmental level. They do not aim to summarise development for all groups but to provide general guidelines.

A summary of the key developmental stages in terms of play, dramatic play and drama follows. Each area is given a title that indicates the main quality of the developmental stage and key characteristics are indicated.

Sensorimotor play

Context

Jernberg typifies the sensorimotor stage as being concerned with 'movements through space and [the] handling of objects in the outside world' (Jernberg, 1983: 128). (See Figure 7.3.) The following vignette illustrates how this sensorimotor stage can be present and important in the range of dramatic expression of adults within dramatherapy work.

Sound and movement
explores own body and
own body parts

Contact with and
physical exploration
of **OBJECTS**

Locomotion
rolling, crawling,
standing, walking

Physical relationship
with another

Figure 7.3 Sensorimotor play: motor play and use of physical properties of objects.

Vignette: Ellen

At one point Ellen brings her hands over her eyes as in a game of peek-a-boo. It is a playful gesture that makes us both laugh. I begin to relax, and forget some of my own fear as I feel . . . contact and exchange taking place between Ellen and myself.

> I cannot say for certain, but I believe she is experiencing similar feelings.
>
> (Schattner and Courtney 1981: 72)

Here the expression primarily concerns 'sound and movement' and 'physical relationship with another', as noted in Figure 7.3. The sensorimotor play helps to establish relationship between the two and to indicate that playful relationships and expression are possible in the dramatherapy group.

Certain types of solitary play are also contained within this expressive range. This can happen in individual client work in dramatherapy, or when an individual is engaged in individual play within a group. The following vignette is from work with a group of adults with severe learning disabilities. Assessment had established that they could not engage in symbolic usage of objects, nor could take on identity. However, they were interested in objects and concrete properties of the things around them. They did not relate to others at all within the setting, and the group had been set up with an aim of helping to create more contact between the individuals.

Vignette: Objects

Clients in a dramatherapy group were working with objects, pushing and pulling them, rolling them over one another. For the first weeks the clients mainly kept the objects to themselves. I began to initiate relationship through objects – offering them, playing in parallel to clients with the objects. Eventually clients began to offer objects back to me, and began to play with objects I was using. Later in the work clients began to play with each other using the objects. All the activities concerned the concrete qualities of the objects – rolling, pushing, banging.

This is an example of sensorimotor based work in dramatherapy where the use of objects remains concrete, non-symbolic. In working with client groups who are not able to relate to objects symbolically the work with the concrete properties of objects can:

- develop the client's ability to relate to their environment
- develop their repertoire of responses to the concrete qualities of the object, e.g. to move from pushing to rolling, throwing, catching
- develop their relationship to, and with, others as expressed through the use of the object.

Imitative play

Context

In this area of dramatherapy work the emphasis is upon the therapeutic possibilities of the developmental range of dramatic imitation. This includes facial and bodily imitation and the imitation of object usage. (See Figure 7.4.)

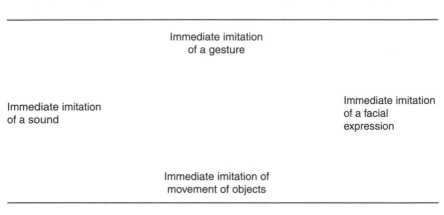

Figure 7.4 Imitation: the brief repetition of phenomenon.

> **Vignette: Facial/bodily imitation**
>
> In working with a group of people with severe learning difficulties, the work started with imitation of gesture, facial expression and movement. This established a relationship between group members and marked the early stages of contact and of playing. The work built up into playing with facial expressions – stretching the mouth, yawning in unison, opening the eyes wide. From this we worked with the development of an expressive range using the face and the body. Group members began to parallel each other's facial and physical expressions. The imitation of physical gestures and facial expressions was a way of developing a relation between group members and establishing language and a structure of interpersonal contact.

> **Vignette: Imitation of gesture**
>
> With an autistic young man a series of 15 sessions were devoted to the establishment of relation through a play language based on

imitation and parallel movement. In all his contacts the young man would push people away if they came into close proximity. The dramatherapy sessions were given the brief to try to help establish a form of communication which would help him to sustain proximity and contact. Developmentally the client could not engage in symbolic use of objects, nor could he take on characters. He did not use verbal language but could produce some sign language representing concepts such as 'biscuit' and 'toilet'. He could reproduce gesture. My work with him involved establishing contact through my paralleling or imitating some of his gestures. Eventually he began to imitate gestures initiated by me. Through this medium we were able to establish contact and to develop conversation.

Pretend play

Context

In the vignette Irwin describes the responses of five-year-old Theresa to the death of her mother.

Vignette: Theresa

> She made a line of animals in the sandbox, led by the baby giraffe. The 'mommy giraffe' had gotten killed by the 'bad monsters' and the baby giraffe was leading 'all her friends' into the forest to find the mommy and unearth her, to bring her back to life.
>
> (Irwin 1983: 27)

Irwin interprets this as the child dealing with her pain, a denial in fantasy, and her own wish to bring the mother back. The child is revealing inner conflicts – between the reality of her mother's death and the desire to deny that reality. Here pretend play involves combining objects, using them to depict simple events and the imaginative use of the giraffes. The expression of the child's feelings around the mother's death through the play materials gives both a means to express the feelings and a language to begin to work through them. (See Figure 7.5.)

Use of combination of objects
to represent other objects
(e.g. pebbles to represent cakes)

Acting single pretend events
*(e.g. imitating drinking or
digging, not in a sequence)*

Functional use of
symbolic toys
(e.g. using toy phone)

Brief wearing of other's
clothes to signify imitation
of another person
*(e.g. father's hat to
indicate father)*

Use of body to evoke/
mime objects when not
actually present
*(e.g. hand to mime
an apple)*

Figure 7.5 Pretend play: the representational use of objects and beginnings of make believe play.

Dramatic play

Vignette: Amy

A child, Amy, used a doll's house to play out problematic issues concerning her mother. She would lock herself in the house, as the 'Mummy', saying that she couldn't possibly come out to the other children. Another time she locked all the children in the house to 'keep them safe from the slimy monster'. In another activity she insisted that another child should play mother and lead the children for a walk, single file, returning them safe to the house for tea.

Amy had been placed in care, her mother having frequently left her alone and locked in the house and finally abandoning her totally. The dramatherapy sessions provided her with an opportunity to play through these feelings with the other children. Issues about caring and uncaring were prevalent in the group. The children were able to hold characters for a brief period of time, to participate in an imagined reality and to work together in a scenario. The situations and identities were only held for a short period of time before they switched to a different situation. However, this amount of expression allowed the children to briefly play characters and to experience a different perspective. It also enabled them to pretend to be in situations which they experienced as anxiety provoking, and enabled us to play out and discuss their troubles. Through playing the mother Amy was able to explain her upset to us and to play through the traumatic events in her life. (See Figure 7.5.)

	Continuous portrayal of others – people, animals *(e.g. sustaining a series of activities as a fox)*	Complex play with objects *(recognising, acknowledging and interacting with others' use of objects)*
Mastery of gross and fine motor skills in evoking and using objects		Ability to use the body to pretend to be in a different, imagined reality
Acting out make-believe situations (a short sequence of events) playing self or other briefly		Ability to use objects as part of situations– props in make-believe play
	Simple games involving play identities *(e.g. farmer and his wife)*	Appropriate response and co-operation with others during play

Figure 7.6 Dramatic play: sustained fantasy and enacted portrayal of others.

Drama

At this level clients are able to sustain the kinds of enactment described in Chapter 8 on role. Here complex engagements with dramatic representation of the self can be sustained. (See Figure 7.7.)

	Acting out make-believe situations (A sequence of events) playing self or other for sustained periods	
Can keep in role and deal with interactions of others		Can develop a sequence of imaginary events with others being connected to roles being played
Consciousness and use of audience performer space and relationship		Can devise themes and prepare plot for enactment
Ability to use script		Division of roles in making drama *(e.g. director/actor roles)*
	Consciousness of communication to others of dramatic product	

Figure 7.7 Drama: sustained enactment with consciousness of audience.

Vignette: Developmental play

Sandberg describes a client, aged 13. He was anxious about drama, and his expressive range was unable to sustain concentrated dramatic enactment. For two months she works with short games, non-verbal transformation, short mimes, 'young tree, old tree, various animals' (Sandberg 1981: 41). She describes the first long interaction in the second month, lasting virtually a whole session: 'He took on the role of a kangaroo ... He developed an unembellished plot of two kangaroos fighting for their lives against white hunters' (1981: 41).

Here Sandberg uses the understanding of developmental progression in her dramatherapy work. The client initially works at a pretend play level – the use of the body to evoke/mime objects when not actually present, acting single, pretend events. This is the level at which he can find meaning. As he gains confidence and skill, the client develops on to dramatic play – sustaining portrayal of the kangaroo and involving a simple sequence of events.

The client or group often parallel the stages of this developmental notion, needing to work through various phases before reaching a state where they can begin to use dramatic form fully. This may be learning or relearning skills or a way of approaching being with others, or it may be linked with regression occurring within the group (e.g. refusal to work with any objects as symbolic reflecting rejection or refusal to participate).

Alternatively, clients can use different aspects of the continuum at different times, following their own needs – moving from dramatic play to full drama to object or sensorimotor play. The knowledge of the different properties and qualities of the different stages can help the therapist to respond to the client's play in an informed and appropriate way. For example, if they can see the client is engaging with object play they can respond with insight into that aspect of play language and process.

The following research vignette contrasts with the way Sandberg and her client discover meaning through moving from pretend play to sustained dramatic portrayal over time. Here dramatherapist Clare Powis focuses on the importance of the therapist holding the boundary and availability of play. The vignette illustrates the way a dramatherapist tries to stay alert to the different play processes which the client is engaged in. Here we will see the client moving not in a developmental line from simple to complex, but engaging in different kinds of play form and language. The focus becomes not the kind of play itself, but on the relationship between Joe and Powis which the kind of play creates and reflects. Indeed, the therapeutic outcome of the work is seen in terms of the changes in relationship within the playing.

Due to an increase in anxiety resulting in self-injurious behaviour Joe, a teenager with autism, had been referred for dramatherapy by staff at his residential home. Following an assessment period of six sessions, Powis began seeing Joe for a total of 29 once-weekly sessions of individual dramatherapy.

Research vignette: Joe

Joe began his dramatherapy sessions by pacing up and down one side of the dramatherapy room, vocalising sounds and repeating phrases of speech from cartoons: 'I don't like the look of that.' 'This is the sentence: Death!' 'And then there was an almighty crash!'

In order to establish a therapeutic relationship I would attempt to interact with Joe. Initially, I might invite him to describe what was happening in the scene from which these phrases came, thereby placing them, along with any associated feelings in a context. I wanted to get a sense of images, characters, situations and themes that were significant to Joe. To me, this approach made sense: I was familiar with the concept and structure of a dramatic scene. And, of course, it was crucial to assess how – and indeed whether – Joe would relate to me at this beginning stage of his therapy.

However, at the start of Joe's therapy I felt that my playfulness was ignored, blanked, or even unwelcomed by Joe. On one occasion I had joined in with the pitch and volume of his vocalisations. He stopped pacing and placed his hands over his ears. This felt like a clear message to me: too much, too soon. I realised that perhaps I was being presumptuous by asking Joe to share his world and play with me so early in the therapy. I came to appreciate – and respect – that at this stage in Joe's therapy each of our experiences of the world around us was so different. What was familiar to me may well have been strange to him, and vice versa. It felt like we were both learning a new language. I wondered if in dramatherapy we could find a connection.

And so I took up a position in a chair on the opposite side of the room, where I could see and hear Joe. This is where I remained for the next few sessions.

The scene was set: Joe had defined an area of the room as his 'stage' and I, by default, had defined an area for the audience. It is usually the case that I introduce the clients to the possibilities of a defined 'stage' and 'offstage' area in the room, if it looks like we're going to engage with 'as if' or enactment. I was somewhat in awe that this 'theatre' had been created – without conscious intention on my part – in order, I believe, to give order and containment to Joe's therapeutic process that was about to unravel between us. It seemed to me, then, that the context of theatre was a *natural therapeutic space*; and that Joe unconsciously *knew* this.

What I'm saying here is that I have a sense that Joe's unconscious process recognised the inherent therapeutic nature of theatre. I noted that Joe had engaged with the *creative space* before feeling ready to engage with me. I suspect that he engaged with the context of theatre so readily partly because he probably found it less threatening than engaging with me in the beginning.

Therefore, Joe began his therapy by seeking out where he felt most comfortable and secure. At this stage I realised that my role was to recognise the value of the theatre space he created; respect his need to create, and moderate, a degree of distance between us; and be a witness to what I saw, heard and felt within that space.

Sessions took on a regular pattern: Joe 'performed' a sequence of pacing the 'stage' area whilst speaking lines from the cartoons. Sometimes I would comment on what I saw, heard and felt during his 'performance'. 'Who's there?' 'What happened next?' 'Is he [the character] all right?' 'I wonder if he's hurt?' 'Does he [the character] need a torch [to go into that cave]?' Joe might then stop and look at me, seemingly startled that I had spoken. And it had *felt like* he had forgotten about me.

I continued to attend to the content of Joe's speech which had, at first, seemed to me to be made up of random, repetitive phrases. I had even considered that their quickfire, urgent delivery might have been intended – consciously or otherwise – to set up a barrier between us. However, I began to realise that these words contained intent, emphasis and emotion. I started to recognise recurring themes and images in the words. Even though I felt Joe was not engaging in creative interaction with me, I continued to make observations and comments arising from his 'performance'.

After a period of pacing, vocalising, maybe trying on costume, he could become more animated, even anxious at times. I was aware that staff at his residential home might view this as a point to intervene with 'deflection' in order to prevent an escalation of Joe's anxiety. At this point he would leave the 'stage' and go to another area of the room where a sandtray was placed. Again, he seemed content to play on his own. He lifted the sand in his hands and watched it fall through his fingers. Soothing, flowing, easy movement. Once more, I felt he was *discovering* what he needed to ease any anxiety that had been let loose in his 'performance'. Although I showed him the jug of water and toys that were available for sand play, I held back from joining in. I sensed that immediately after his 'performance' Joe may have needed some space to process the meaning of those words and feelings.

I came to understand that when he initiated eye contact with me he was choosing to make a connection. And so I decided to wait for him to invite me to interact with him when – or if – he was ready. And sure enough, once Joe's 'performance and reflection' pattern had become established after a few sessions he was able to tolerate – in progressive stages – more interaction with me.

In the middle of a 'speech' Joe would seek eye contact with me, as though making sure I was there. Occasionally, he even began to come over to me, and stand still in front of me for a few moments before resuming his place 'onstage'.

I became aware of the development of dramatic content in Joe's expressive phase. At first, it was the intensity and duration of his eye contact. He might then place a hat on my head. A week or two later he was accepting my presence 'onstage' alongside him. He began responding to my wonderings, word play or improvisation around his phrases. For example, after:

Joe   . . . And the King lost his Kingdom in a storm . . .
Powis   . . . [reciting] . . . It was a dark and stormy night . . .

Joe went to fetch a crown from the costume rail and then began to march on a route *away from the path he had routinely marked*. What felt so significant here was how Joe had *shared* a creative idea with me, and it had led him to *try out* a different path, a different possibility.

This development was, I suspect, a response to the reflective phase of the session.

At first, when he looked over at me from the sandtray, I moved my chair closer. That was okay. Then, he gestured for me to refill the water bottle. Fine. The next step was being asked to hand him some sand-play toys. And then . . .

I rested my hands, palms upturned, on the edge of the sandtray, on the edge of his play world. How would he respond to this action? As an invasion? As another sand-play toy? As a nuisance? As a request to join in and share his (play) world? Joe responded by filling my hands with sand. We played around with this: giving and receiving, pouring and holding, lifting and falling, catching and letting go. Most of this play was in silence, maybe with some vocalising of sounds that complemented the quality of the play.

One day, I was jolted out of what had seemed restful and comfortable play. Joe spoke a phrase that I realised was related to a comment I had made earlier in the session, whilst 'onstage'. As Joe lifted a plastic mould from the sand, revealing a sandcastle, he announced 'King of the Castle!' I understood this possibly to be a reference to the King who had lost his kingdom in the storm.

Until now, I had been thinking that my comments had passed unnoticed by Joe. But here he was, *responding* to my wonderings and reflections – *with me*. I began to feel more certain that *Joe was creating and using this sand play to process the emotive material in his dramatic 'performance'*.

Clare Powis

CORE PROCESS BOX

Witnessing

Powis takes on different role functions within the work, but a key one is the role of witness to Joe's play. Part of her reflection considers what function she holds for Joe within his playing. She talks about holding the space in terms of giving Joe's play her attention: She feeds back what she sees and hears to support that attention, and views this as part of developing trust. By creating 'onstage' and 'offstage' Powis also enables the client to move from the taking part or active space to a non-taking part or resting area. In this way the client who finds the building of relationships with people, rather than objects, challenging can establish his own play space which he can then, at his own pace, invite Powis into. She becomes an active witness.

Playing

Powis makes use of the notion of the play space, the play drama continuum and the play shift. The idea of a play space is used: an arena that has particular properties which can allow experiment and permissions in areas such as the formation of relationships. Powis uses her knowledge of the play–drama continuum to inform the way she understands Joe's expressions, and gives her insight into how to respond appropriately to his language in play.

Transformation

Powis and Joe show how the very process of being involved in making drama, the potential creative satisfaction of dramatic playing, can be transformative. Powis emphasises the centrality of providing the therapeutic space and relationship and following the client's leads as carefully as she could. The involvement in dramatic process brought together a combination of exploring, thinking, feeling and creativity. This combination for Joe has a transformative potential as the different aspects of a client's way of apprehending and responding to themselves and the world – thought, emotions, creativity – are brought together in new combinations. For Joe they transform the way he relates to another by allowing him to experiment and explore, taking initiative in relating to another.

Research conversation with Clare Powis

Jones: I was interested in the way you talked about yourself as a witness but also you said a 'presence' and that you talked about 'my playfulness'. What did you mean by your 'playfulness'?

Powis: It was important to be a witness. More so in the beginning. My 'presence' was as a witness and also, in this case, in sharing play and being there. I think a client – not just Joe – wants to know their therapist can be playful. I'm also using presence in the sense of feeling I was being accepted by Joe as another *person* – player, if you like – as opposed to an object, which is how I had felt in the early stages, that is, like a non-person whose function was to hang up his coat/tie his shoelaces/hand him a prop. I want to stress how, by being playful, therapist and client can make a connection; and experience a shared pleasure. There's a recognition of our sameness as human beings. I find it a very powerful and bonding experience when in a brief moment, maybe, there is a shared experience. It's through moments like these that the client's therapeutic process can shift.

Jones: I'm just thinking about your comments about bonding and sharing and pleasure, which in my experience can be the case for many individuals, though play can also be tough, excluding, frustrating and isolating. For some individuals (maybe for Joe in your descriptions?), the spontaneity and personal relationship common in many people's play can only be developed with an experience of distance and through the presence of a . . . guide? . . . Was that part of your role maybe? So were you, do you think, in your role, making good use of your ability to be an active witness, first in maintaining a respectful distance and witnessing his play, and then testing out possibilities, becoming active, a player?

Powis: Of course! Somehow I'd managed to forget the darker side of 'play' – as is experienced by some. Certainly many of the people I see as clients would be familiar with that. Memories of being excluded or not 'chosen' are still around for me too. This being the case, it does seem that the positive benefits of play can be introduced and experienced in dramatherapy, with the therapist not only as a guide but as someone who *wants* to engage with you, the client. 'Yes' to all your points about witnessing, waiting, offering, testing out opportunities to play together – these responses are judged according to how the client might seem at the time.

Jones: In a way, the core process could be seen not just to be about a playful state, but the dramatherapist – you – bringing your experience and self in play? What do you think? Was Joe responding not just to the opportunity of the play but to you as a presence – holding the possibility of play for him – and responding to him when he did play?

Powis: Yes, it was like Joe was being allowed to play. It was like the significance of his play was acknowledged in his dramatherapy. I trust that Joe sensed his play was valued. Dramatherapy offered a space and a therapeutic relationship within which his *difficult* feelings could be heard, allowed, acknowledged, explored and given meaning to. Play had significance as a means of his creative and therapeutic movement.

Jones: I was interested in the ways you used drama in relation to his work. It's almost as if your practical knowledge of the play–drama continuum – the ways in which different processes can link together or one can emerge from another – helped you keep aware of 'creative possibilities', if you like, potential avenues to go along with Joe?

Powis: It's great that you identified a sense of the fluidity of the play–drama continuum in this vignette. It feels an important aspect of the dramatherapy process. I think this fluidity in the continuum lends itself to the path of a client's therapeutic process. Sometimes the client will go one step forward and in the next session she or he will be two or three steps back. Confronting a difficult, hitherto unbearable feeling may result in a self-protective withdrawal or regression. And often it may be comforting to return to an early stage of sensorimotor play where there's a familiarity, and where strength can be gathered in order to face the next challenge or process this one. Hence access to the full continuum helps to inform the therapist where the client is in his or her process. The therapist can then respond accordingly. I guess the continuum becomes a barometer of the client's therapeutic process. And, sure, it's possible to mark developmental progression. Useful in evaluation. So yes, part of having open access to the continuum means being open to the communication and to the creative possibilities within and across the stages.

Summary

Drama and play are part of a developmental continuum. As a part of this continuum play is included in the expressive language, which the client uses to create meaning and explore material in dramatherapy. For clients in drama-therapy, playing is a way of discovering or creating access to their own spon-taneity. For some clients this process forms the main therapeutic benefit within dramatherapy.

Dramatherapy creates a playful relationship with reality. The drama-therapy space enables clients to play with elements of their life – to rework issues, to try out new configurations or possibilities. This can be described as a 'play shift'. This playful exploration can produce changes, which can be integrated into the client's life outside the dramatherapy.

The understanding of a developmental continuum from play to drama can assist in assessment and evaluation work. It can also help to find an appropri-ate expressive level for clients to work with in dramatherapy.

Cognitive, emotional and social development can be worked with using a developmental understanding of the play–drama continuum. Changes in the dramatic developmental level that a client is able to use in dramatherapy, for example, can be accompanied by cognitive or social changes for clients.

8　Role

Rain-stopping magic is made by pouring water on red hot stones . . . : the rain is not just represented, but is felt to be really present in each drop of water.

Cassirer, *Language and Myth*

The enacted self

Any work with role in dramatherapy makes the assumption that the self can assume different, fictional identities. The development of this notion in dramatherapy is that the fictional self can be enacted. A relationship is set up between the enacted fictional self and the client's usual identity, and this dynamic, active relationship is seen as the basis of therapeutic change in role-based work within dramatherapy.

Many people assume that role play is primarily a 'one-off' event. A person plays out a situation once and this 'solves' or resolves an issue. This is rarely the case in my experience. Role play in dramatherapy is a much more complex affair. There are many ways to adapt the idea of playing a role to suit the needs of clients whether in individual or group therapy. Roles can be played to rehearse life situations, to practise or develop skills or personal qualities such as confidence or communication. They can be used to explore events that have happened recently, in the long past or yet to occur. They can be reality based or formed in fantasy worlds. The process within the role work may be playful and improvisational – trying out, not really developing along a particular story; working towards a release, or insight or feeling of resolution – some people use the word 'catharsis' to represent these areas; or the role play may need to be repeated a number of times. As Secchi's research vignette shows us (pp. 209–210), role play in dramatherapy need not even involve the client playing a role themselves. Role can surround work in the way the therapist and client experience other processes such as drawing pictures of roles as dustbins and playing roles through objects. Often clinical practice uses a combination of these ways of playing with role. The creativity of therapist and client is to find together the most appropriate form to meet the client's needs and abilities.

Landy (2001) has said that role work in dramatherapy usually concerns a situation where a role that a client needs to play in life is either unavailable, poorly developed or inappropriately aligned with other roles, or people in their roles. In my experience these variables often have at their heart three main ways of taking role within dramatherapy. It can help the therapist to see which direction might be most effectively pursued within the work depending on the kind of role the client seems most to need.

1 The client assumes a fictional identity which is not their own. In this way, as we'll see in the research vignettes in this chapter, they might find themselves playing another person, or an animal from a dream, a broad role such as 'teacher' or 'cheat', or an abstract quality such as 'doubt'.
2 The client stays themselves but role plays a situation from their life outside the session from the past, present, future or in a fantasy situation. So the client might play themselves at the age of ten, at the present time enacting a relationship problem, or confronting their employer next week.
3 The client deliberately isolates a specific aspect of themselves or their identity. The highlighted aspect or characteristic forms the basis of a created role but linked to their life (e.g. a role function such as 'daughter' or 'leader', or a characteristic such as 'the part of me that wants to sabotage my life' or 'the part of me that wants to leave hospital').

Langley offers a fascinating perspective on this division into three ways of looking at role taking. She links it to the efficacy of role work being seen in terms of a tension being developed:

> Jones (1996: 197–9) goes on to point out that, in dramatherapy, there are three ways in which a dynamic tension may be set up between an enacted fictional self and a client's identity. It is this dynamic tension that is the basis for therapeutic change in role work.
>
> (Langley 2006: 85)

In the research conversation about 'Grace' (pp. 220–221), Lili Levy sees this tension in the different kinds of relationship her client experiences as she takes on roles:

> On one hand, Grace is at a distance from herself when she embodies the characters physically and as such increases her fantasy: she becomes someone else's identity. On the other hand, this distance allows her to experience herself in a different way. She starts observing herself and being emphatic with her pain and hurt.
>
> (p. 220)

Clare Hubbard, in her research conversation about the 'Island' vignette (pp. 198–199) echoes an important element of this as she talks about the useful tension which playing and reflecting on role can offer to clients: 'They thought about themselves from a distance.'

The following vignettes each reflect examples of these ways of taking role and illustrate and research this 'tension':

The client assumes a fictional identity which is not their own

> #### Vignette: Ballet dress
>
> In a dramatherapy group a young woman, Popi, had selected an important object which she was attached to. From her childhood she selected a ballet dress which her parents bought her. It was too small and she never wore it, but kept it. Even after leaving her parental home she still had it with her. She said she didn't know why that was. In the group Popi took on the role of the dress. She first indicated its shape by mime, and then mimed placing the dress in the centre of the group. Popi then stepped into the space where the dress had been put and, as she did so, took on the role of the dress. Speaking in the first person she began by describing her texture, where she was in Popi's flat and what Popi felt about her. The group helped her to improvise and explore the role by asking her questions. The direction of the role work began to turn towards the dress's feelings about being too small, never having been worn, and eventually towards the parents who bought the undersized dress for Popi. The reason it was never taken back to the shop emerged and the needs of the parents to keep their daughter smaller than she really was began to be voiced.

CORE PROCESS BOX

Dramatic projection

Popi chooses something from her past, indicating by her choice that it must have some significance she wishes to explore. She begins to use the dress as a focus to reflect internally held issues – it starts to express them in an outer form, enabling her to project issues and concerns into the image.

Role

By embodying the dress Popi increases her involvement – rather than speaking about it she physically becomes it. This increases her engagement with the image, both imaginatively and personally. By taking on and speaking as the role spontaneously she starts to say 'I' as the dress, beginning to explore what parts of herself the dress might represent.

The client plays the role of themselves in the past, present or future or in a fantasy situation

The second vignette is taken from a long-term closed group for people under the secondary mental health services, mainly with depression and/or anxiety. The group had been together for a year, working with Clare Hubbard. The vignette describes the six group members playing themselves, but in the fantasy scenario of an island. Hubbard says that she introduced the activity to 'help the group think about their roles, both in the group and in their life, in response to thoughts about the group dynamic which had developed from anxiety expressed about a new member joining'.

Research vignette: Island

I asked the group to imagine they were stranded together on a desert island. Together they made a drawing of the island, negotiating how they thought it should look, and then drew themselves on it. Everyone camped separately but close enough to meet and to hear if anyone was in distress. Jack camped high up in a cave at the top of the river where he could see the others, which helped him feel safe. Shannon and Liz were on the shore in view of each other. They both expressed some anxiety about being on the island. Cath placed herself quite separately (but in view of others). I asked the group to choose five items from home they could have with them. Mark took his computer (he used solar power), Liz had a teepee and her duvet, both Jack and Cath brought their dogs for security and company. Jack also brought a first aid kit for the group. Mike had a knife and string and made himself a hut from coconut trees and a fishing device. Shannon brought cigarettes and cans of beer, which she hid. Her anxiety about running out of these surprised Shannon, and led to the group also thinking about their medication and whether they would still need it in this environment. They decided on a meeting point and that if anyone wanted to call the group together they could bang on a drum. Cath isolated herself. Others decided they would regularly check on her. It soon emerged that she felt she couldn't join the group until she had something to offer.

Exploration, using the drawing, was over three sessions. The group returned to it a few weeks later after the new member, Brian, had joined. They invited him to find his place on the island. He found this a little difficult as he wasn't yet sure of his role in the group. The group transformed the therapy space into the island and set up their individual camps. I invited people to say where they were and what they were doing and feeling. They then enacted a single day a few weeks into arriving. I watched the action from the side, every so often asking the actors to freeze and say what they were thinking, or feeling, about what was happening or being said. Shannon called a meeting, which was a big step for her in taking a lead. They agreed on plans for catching/collecting food and cooking. Cath came to the meeting with encouragement and found she could contribute her skill in knitting by making blankets for everyone. The islanders talked about a part of the island they hadn't discovered and were divided on whether to explore. Some worried about what might be 'out there', or were content to stay where they felt safe and had all they needed, while others thought there could be helpful things outside. Jack was bursting to explore, whilst Liz and Shannon were curious but also fearful. I asked the islanders if there was a compromise they could reach. They decided that some of the group would explore initially but they would stick to the coastline, stay in each other's sight and only be gone for two hours.

The exploration waited to the following session. Two of the men went, Mike and Jack (Mark was absent). Cath asked them if they had any instructions for Brian while they were gone. This led to a debate about gender roles. Cath saw Brian's role as taking care of the women which Shannon objected to. Brian said he thought the women were all strong and capable. Those at the camp waited anxiously while the explorers enjoyed their journey. Brian took on the role of cook, and tried to keep the others' spirits up. At this point the action was divided into two simultaneous parts: the camp, set up in the familiar therapy space, and the unknown part of the island in the less familiar storage area of the room. At intervals I asked the camp to freeze while we watched the explorers and vice versa. I monitored the time, counting down how long the explorers had left. Mike had to discourage Jack from venturing too far off the track. They returned safely and talked about a beautiful waterfall they had seen where you could shower. They added this now familiar territory to their map of the island. On their next trip (the following session) they took Shannon with them. Liz and Mark were ill and Cath said she wanted to be alone. Cath later shared that she did really want company as she was feeling low, but didn't want to ask.

The group reflected on the island experience. They thought about why they did, or didn't, want to explore and how it felt when they did. Cath reflected on her need to feel worthy of being part of a group. Realisation of what was important to each of them was powerful. They were also surprised at how they could adapt to change. For some, the idea of the island, being away from home, feeling vulnerable, not having 'essentials' like cigarettes, alcohol and medication, had been terrifying at the start of the work. But they now felt quite attached to the island.

The island was referred to in future sessions as a place individuals got comfort from thinking of when they were feeling anxious or low. Reflecting again some months later, the group felt things had changed. Cath, for example, felt she would be more confident of her place in the group and therefore more involved. Shannon was surprised at how important alcohol had been then and wouldn't take it with her now.

Clare Hubbard

CORE PROCESS BOX

Role taking

Group members stay themselves, but are placed in a symbolic fantasy scenario. This enables them to explore and experiment with their ways of being and relating to others. The island becomes an open symbol for clients to create meanings. It can, for example, be a stage to reflect the roles they take within the group, and also the roles they take in life outside the group.

Play

By suggesting a scenario familiar from dramatic play, as a child or from the media, 'the desert island', and by inviting an imaginary situation of being 'stranded together', Hubbard encourages the group's creation of a playful state where normal rules and ways of being become more flexible and people can experiment with new combinations.

Life–drama connection

By returning week after week to the island scenario, group members can make connections between their island roles and the ways they handle roles outside the group, reflect on the experience with other players and experiment with new ways of relating or being.

Research conversation with Clare Hubbard

Jones: Interested in you saying that there was a 'move' from drawing to physically embodying roles. Clare, how do you see the significance of this 'move'?

Hubbard: It was a progression from thinking to experiencing: feeling in their bodies and spontaneously reacting to the situation and each other. With the drawing they were setting the scene and background to the drama. I think for some who had been apprehensive, drawing first and checking out how they might be helped them feel safe.

Jones: In the embodiment – playing themselves in the island fantasy situation – how do you look at that in terms of the 'therapeutic value' for the clients?

Hubbard: They were exploring how they relate to and work with each other as a group, but in a fantasy situation it is removed from the real situation, and enabled them to explore in a less self-conscious way. They were also exploring how they cope with unknown situations in their lives.

Jones: I was very interested in the way themes like illness and medication came up in the island. How do you see that?

Hubbard: I think because they were very much feeling that they were on the island they thought about how it would really be, and what was essential to them, and so illness, medication, etc. came up as very real concerns for them. So, yes, the drama enabled them to bring these up. For Shannon the idea of being without alcohol and cigarettes was very real and very frightening.

Jones: I am struck here by the way you've twice said 'very real' about the content and process of the island – and that the drama (almost paradoxically?) enabled the real to come out? How do you see what it was about the processes at work that enabled these very 'real' concerns to emerge?

Hubbard: I think this relates to empathy and distancing. They thought about themselves from a distance. By working at a distance from their real life situation, with the extreme situation of being stranded on an island, it was perhaps safer to think about their needs and difficulties and coping because it isn't likely to really happen to them.

Jones: A great phrase – 'They thought about themselves from a distance'. What do you see that 'place' where they are looking from, the distance, as being for them in the vignette? How would you describe what this distance was?

Hubbard: Outside of their box (that's safe but confining). I'm not sure why but I am imagining them watching themselves on television, on a reality programme like 'Survivor'. Group members did refer to this television programme when I introduced the exercise.

The client deliberately isolates a specific aspect of themselves or their identity

The following vignette illustrates the way in which role playing an aspect of identity can occur within dramatherapy, whilst also showing the ways in which different types of role experiences can occur within one session. It also asks interesting questions about the nature of the role of witness, or audience, within role-based work, and how this can feature as a very active part of the therapy.

The dramatherapy takes place on a UK residential locked ward for women with bipolar disorder (BPD) and who self-harm. The approach taken generally within the setting is described by Debra Colkett as 'dialectical behavioural therapy (DBT) with some psychodynamic interventions. The dramatherapy group I was asked to set up was a new group which was to run alongside the behavioural care plan already in place.' Colkett is conscious of the value of interdisciplinary awareness, liaising with and involving staff: 'I have encouraged them to co-work the group and we debrief together after, where we share insights and observations about the group process. A mutual support and appreciation has grown over time.' The group was ongoing and the following aims had been agreed with the women:

- to offer a safe, supportive and contained space for expression
- to look at different perspectives
- to express difficult emotions
- to have fun.

The following vignette occurs six months into the work. Colkett describes the context of the session as being within a time when 'the issues of boundaries, trust, power and control were emerging. All of these women had been abused either emotionally, physically or sexually, in most cases they had experienced all three.'

Research vignette: Women with BPD who self-harm

In the early stages the ten clients would display a lot of resistance. One week they all – except one client – sat in the 'time out' space – and laughed at me, saying they were going to analyse me. The activities I introduced were met with varying degrees of engagement. They would quickly disengage and attack me if they felt threatened. Rebecca, for example, advised me that I should do a course because I didn't understand a person who had been abused. This was a tightrope act for me and I had to choose my words and interventions very carefully. Most of the time I felt anxious, drained and as if I was being strangled.

The following week I decided to go with the idea of asking the clients to play the analysts. It seemed they needed to experience some of the power they identified as never experiencing as a patient within the mental health system. If they didn't trust me then perhaps they could trust each other. I asked them to get into pairs and gave each pair a small soft ball. I asked one of them to explore the ball, run it over your body. 'That's perverted.' 'I don't like my body!' 'The anti-psychotics have made me so fat [deep breath]. Okay, I understand.' I asked them to label themselves A and B. I whispered to A to play with the ball in any way she wanted. I whispered to B, 'You be the therapist and observe, offering encouragement when necessary.' Suddenly the room was buzzing with play and laughter. They like the secrecy aspect of the game. Once focused most of the women immersed themselves completely, a kind of all-or-nothing approach.

Rebecca continued to complain and disrupt, but the others did not collude with her on this occasion. She often competed with me for control of the group. She joined in superficially, I could see her defences dropping and she looked vulnerable. As she played with the ball and watched the others she began to look sad. I could see this exercise was a big struggle for her. Alice, always one to push the boundaries, was throwing her ball at the clock (the only breakable object in the room). 'Alice, please don't break the clock,' I called. She smiled and ignored me, she had my attention. 'Alice I can see that you are throwing the ball at the clock, you can stop now!' She smiled and continued throwing the ball harder. 'What are you trying to tell us?' I said gently. 'Is it something about time? Not enough time for you?' Then in a more authoritative tone, 'If you break the clock we have to stop having fun with the balls.' She stopped after throwing a gentle defiant last ball at the clock, looked at me and smiled. She seemed satisfied with our interaction.

The group had continued with their play and had changed over so they all got the chance to play therapist. Suddenly Sharon had got the ball. Sharon is a big woman, very direct in manner, likes things organised – constantly criticises me if I'm late, appear unprepared, or make what she perceives as a wrong comment. She's very concrete in her thinking. She is – in her own opinion – limited in her creativity and imagination. When interacting with Sharon I feel that she reels me in with positive stroking comments and then makes a judgement. It feels like a slap in the face, and slightly sadistic. This may be indicative of her own early experience with mother, I wondered, and perhaps she is testing me in some way? Perhaps it's a re-enactment? Sharon gets to play the controlling mother and for once gets to feel what it's like to have the power? But now Sharon has the ball and this child bursts out of her. She was bouncing it with glee. It was as if she had become a five year old making a magical discovery for the first time. The whole group stopped and watched her. We were all amazed. She giggled and bounced the ball as hard as she could. I was delighted; I saw this as a breakthrough. I praised Sharon and her ability to play, and I said that is exactly what this group was about. The smiles fell from the faces of the other group members. Sharon, and to a lesser extent I, suffered in the sessions after that. I had underestimated the amount of envy present in this group.

The feedback at the end of the session was that it had been enjoyable. Rebecca thanked me, saying that this 'lesson' had made her think about trust and being gentle and how this was very difficult for her because she had never had it. She was tearful and apologetic about her 'bad behaviour'. Simone said I had done very well this week and that I should do more trust exercises, and although she and her partner made an unlikely pairing, she had seen her in a different light and learnt things about herself – she wouldn't say what. Sharon said that she didn't know what came over her but she had really enjoyed it and she never lets herself go like that. I asked Alice about the business with the clock. She shrugged and said nothing. I asked her how she felt and why she did it. She replied, 'I don't know', and I believed her.

CORE PROCESS BOX

Embodiment

Through game-based work the therapist allows group members to physicalise and express issues through the interaction between the ball game, their bodies and each other. The game creates an opportunity to physically acknowledge and verbally comment on issues relating to their experiences of their bodies. As the vignette description shows, clients were able to see the activities in relation to issues concerning trust and gentleness and being allowed, and allowing, different permissions and experiences.

Play

Play features in different ways within the session. A playful space is created where normal roles can be left and new ones attempted and experienced: for example, playing the 'analyst' or being a 'child'. The play activities enable clients to revisit and rediscover playfulness: for example, a child-like quality in the way Sharon plays with the ball and she explores and connects this with issues of control and fears of 'letting go'.

Role

There are different layers of role work taking place within this vignette. On the one hand the group challenge the role of the therapist by taking on the 'out' role, moving out of the drama space, while at the same time they 'enrole' themselves within the 'time out' space saying that they are the analysts, leaving the therapist on her own under the gaze of this group of analysts. This both challenges roles and the boundaries of the session – not just 'who is who' but also challenging the time out space by making it dramatic by putting themselves into role. The therapist follows this by offering them a containing experience using role and role reversal. They can play this role with permission and the session can 'hold' their challenge. This enables them to explore and experience this role relationship with each other and within themselves along with themes of power, the critical gaze of the 'analyst' and themselves, for example. They can safely express and explore different aspects of themselves and their life experiences.

Research conversation with Debra Colkett

Jones: What processes do you see at work here?

Colkett: Dramatherapeutic empathy and distancing. Sharon's engagement with the ball created an empathic pathway to her unexpresssed inner child. She presented as a 'good girl' who arrived on time and liked everything under control. She took on the role of critical 'mother' in the group when we all 'played' together in a childlike way.

Jones: How do you see the connection between the work and client's lives outside the group?

Colkett: Alice, for example, may have been playing out her life's drama –

she as a regressed child and me as the neglectful mother who she felt she would test by pushing boundaries to check out if I cared enough to prevent her from damaging herself or her environment. The clock may have represented 'stopping time'. She had stopped at a time in her development where she needed 'mother' to take responsibility for her. In subsequent sessions she often returned to this kind of unspoken dialogue with me through dramatic play.

Here we see the way in which the processes of role imbue the dramatherapy space on different levels. It provides a technique or method to allow the clients and therapist to explore material. However, Colkett also uses it as a way of looking at the processes at work within the session, a dramatic way of analysing processes and dynamics within the dramatherapy.

Why should the dramatising of the self or aspects of the self in this way be therapeutic? Schechner (1988) sums up our role-taking capability in a way that indicates a part of the answer: 'Unique among animals humans carry and express multiple and ambivalent identities simultaneously.' Part of the therapeutic possibilities of enacting the self concerns the quality that Schechner indicates: we are *conscious* of having *potential identities*, and we relate to these in an 'ambivalent' way – we *reflect upon* these identities and *express ourselves* through them.

In all three examples we see clients expressing potential identities: as dresses, island dwellers, analysts and small children. These are all ways of expressing and exploring life experiences and problems, along with ways of changing, developing and meeting the needs which the therapy connects to. Dramatherapy's approach to role, illustrated in these vignettes, has been strongly influenced by theatre, psychology, psychodrama, dramaturgy and anthropology. In creating a context for further discussion of dramatherapy practice and role, the next section will illustrate these influences.

Contexts for role in dramatherapy

An enacted role is a dramatic persona assumed by an individual within theatre. The term 'role' has also become used as a way of describing and analysing identity in life, not in theatre alone. Moreno (1960), for example, identifies three main types of roles – somatic, social and psychodramatic – which cover all possible aspects of an individual's identity. Somatic roles include activities such as sleeping and eating, social roles include family, economic and occupational spheres, whilst psychodramatic roles are those of fantasy and internal life. Landy has described the role as a container of the thoughts and feelings we have about ourselves and each other, as a basic 'unit' of personality. An individual's self consists of a number of roles or units. Any role has specific qualities providing uniqueness and coherence to each of these units (Landy 1994: 7).

The work of Mead (1934) and Goffman (1959) has become influential in dramatherapy's approach to role. Mead's notion of the self is that it is developed through social interaction. An individual's identity is seen as constructed through the roles they perform in various contexts. Goffman's work describes individuals, groups and society using theatre as a metaphor to help understand how self, role and other relate. These writers, along with others such as Sarbin and Allen (1968) Sarbin (1986), and Hampson (1988), have helped dramatherapists to discuss the nature of the self and identity, the relationship between role and personality, between theatre and life (Read Johnson 1988; Landy 1994; Meldrum 1994; Jennings 1997).

Within fields such as psychodrama and social psychology, the role in therapy is usually allied with dramatised role functions. Within dramatherapy, role is not confined to dramatic ways of working with role functions. It is used in its wider sense, describing a fictional identity or persona which someone can assume, and is also a concept used to understand the different aspects of a client's identity in their life as a whole. Both therapist and client can take on fictional roles during a dramatherapy session.

Breach, disturbance, change

The capability to assume a different persona is often linked to disturbance or breach. Identity has been defined as being reliant upon an interconnected system of roles (Argyle 1969). The coherence of the individual social role and its connection with other roles is crucial to the functioning of societies and to the individual's well-being (Brissett and Edgeley 1975). From this point of view, the health of any society and the effective functioning of an individual in terms of their sense of identity are interdependent. Argyle, a major proponent of this view, asserts that social organisations consist of a number of individuals interacting in a regular manner. The description of this regular pattern is made possible 'by means of the concept of role which [is] . . . defined . . . as the modal behaviour of occupants in a position' (Argyle 1969: 277).

The enacted self is linked to breach and disturbance by a number of authors. Within this approach to examining role, the shifting in identity in taking on a role is seen as a way of responding to crisis. A special set of circumstances exists in reality and the recourse to an enacted identity is a response to this. The shift is seen as redressive and this pattern is often present, for example, in Shakespearean disguise. Becker describes the performance of Wayang, a traditional form of shadow puppetry, as a way of society dealing with political or spiritual crisis: 'a way of subduing or at least calming down dangerous power' (1979: 34). Turner describes a process of 'social drama' in certain cultures, which is used when 'the peaceful tenor of a regular norm-governed social life is interrupted by the breach of a rule controlling one of its salient relationships' (1974: 37). Here a drama is used to deal with and manage the disturbance.

In terms of dramatherapy this connection of the enacted self to disturbance and to change is important. It is usually due to some disturbance in their lives that individuals attend dramatherapy. The way that taking on role functions in dramatherapy can be seen within the chain of connections made above is as follows:

Disturbance/crisis – role entry and exploration – alternatives sought – change

There are two additional elements that are especially important within this way of looking at role and dramatherapy. The first involves noting that entry into role can often be experienced as socially and individually disturbing. It marks an experience outside the usual framework by which an individual is known to others and by which individuals know themselves. The second is that entry into an enacted self, a dramatic role, is, within certain disciplines, seen as connected to creating a space which is separate from usual reality to redress problems or difficulties.

The temporary change of identity gives permission and alters the experience of self and others in a way which is seen to help bring about difference and change. The experience of being in character can also allow the client to discover things or allow access to repressed issues. Guarnieri and Ramsden, for example, in Chapter 5 (p. 110) observe:

Guarnieri: They are surprised by the effect that working physically, dramatically, with their bodies, has on them . . .
Ramsden: The feelings are brought into the here and now and are experienced in the room.
Guarnieri: The past becomes more 'alive' in the present, and 'off the script'. It then makes it possible to work through the 'stuckness' of the trauma that resulted in the perpetration of the offence.

Here, the experience of clients representing themselves in the past can lead to new experiences and insights into their life. A number of therapists in the research carried out for this book identified the importance of physical experience within role as key to the work. As in Ramsden and Guarnieri's account, whilst the client's body is engaged in role it is in a state of heightened awareness where processes are deepened within the drama.

Self, learning and exploration

As discussed in Chapter 7, the taking on of roles can be seen as a capability which marks the development of certain social and psychological processes. These include the ability to develop relationships with another, along with the ability to identify with others and their emotional perspective. It can mark the development of social skills, cognitive perspective taking and moral reasoning:

The act of consciously transforming their own identities into a variety of make-believe identities may hasten the decentration process, thereby promoting perspective taking and a number of other cognitive skills.

(Johnson, Christie and Yawkey 1987: 102)

Wilshire (1982) has echoed Evreinov's (1927) ideas concerning the essential nature of drama in human development. He places role taking and imitation in a context of learning: 'bodies biologically human learn to become human persons by learning to do what persons around them are already doing. The learning body mimetically incorporates the model' (1982: 116).

Blatner and Blatner place role taking and playing in the context of learning to creatively explore reality and to deal with problems encountered in the world. They see this, in terms of Winnicott's ideas concerning the individual's creation of 'transitional space', as an important developmental stage. Role playing takes place within a realm between what they call 'subjective' and 'objective' worlds: 'the relatively fluid dimension where people can utilise the potentialities of their imaginations. It is more explicity expressed in drama, which allows it to be more consciously manipulated . . . safer', and enabling 'creative risk taking' (Blatner and Blatner 1988b: 78).

Ecstasy and rationality

Wilshire (1982) discusses role by analysing its function in theatre. He considers the involvement of audience and actor in creating enacted roles as reflecting a basic human trait. When acting or watching theatre he describes those involved as being in a trance-like 'primal mimetic absorption in types of being and doing' (Wilshire 1982: 23). Within the area of role this issue of 'primal absorption' is a focus of much debate. The discussion of this area concerns:

- the level of our emotional involvement when we play or witness roles in theatre
- the relationship between the usual, everyday self and the enacted self; the degree to which the usual self becomes lost or submerged in the enacted role
- the nature and qualities of the way the usual self reflects upon the enacted self.

Often this issue is debated in terms of 'ecstasy' and 'rationality' (see Chapter 11; Scheff 1979; Jennings 1987). Ecstasy refers to a sense of being 'taken over' by a role or dramatic experience – of being 'lost' within it. Schechner refers to both Balinese trance and Stanislavski's approach as being linked by this ecstatic approach to enactment, 'performing by becoming or being possessed by another' (1988: 177). Rationality refers to the analytic, thought-orientated aspects of role taking and playing. In this way of seeing role taking, emphasis is placed upon the degree to which the role taker stays aware, reflective and analytical of the role playing during and after enactment.

These two notions of ecstasy and rationality are often used as oppositional criteria in the analysis of the processes involved in playing a role. To what extent is the role taker immersed in the role? What levels of contact do they have with their everyday, usual identity? To what extent do audience members become emotionally involved or rationally engaged?

Theatre theorists and practitioners discuss role within this dialectic. In certain types of theatre, absorption is so total that the actor claims to have lost a sense of any identity outside of the role. A drama student in Mast's study of acting described this process: 'You're no longer yourself . . . You are the medium of the character you're playing . . . you're no longer yourself so you shouldn't be looking at yourself' (Mast 1986: 158).

Brechtian-influenced theatre aims for a more rational approach and experience for actors and audience. The actor constantly thinks and tries to stay outside the role, reacting to the role. In the creation of an enacted role the actor must remain intellectually aware and a minimum of the experience of ecstatic merging with the role must occur. This relationship is seen to lead to political, social and personal change.

Johnson and Johnson (1987) define the taking on of a role in 'role play' within a strictly rational process. The role taker stays fully aware of the reason for the activity and is open to cognitive learning processes. The work is skills orientated and role playing is a tool for 'bringing a specific skill and its consequences into focus, and this is vital for experiential learning'. It is 'intended to give . . . experience in practising skills and in discussing and identifying effective and ineffective behaviour' (1987: 24).

In *Games for Actors and Non-Actors* Boal (1992) aims for a more balanced relationship between immersion and disengagement: 'The rationalisation of emotion does not take place solely after the emotion has disappeared . . . it also takes place in the emotion. There is a simultaneity of feeling and think-ing' (p. 47).

Within role work the two states are seen by some to coexist. This is reflected in Garvey (1977) and others' observational work on children tak-ing roles in play. Garvey describes two kinds of communication: one within the played role – the role, as it were, talking; the other outside the role. Exchanges occur about the play activity – comments on what to do next, how to deal with problems in the play. This is referred to as 'metacom-munication'. Though these observations concern play and not theatre, the existence of this metacommunication could be seen to indicate that there is a natural coexistence between immersion and disengagement in playing a role.

In dramatherapy a balance is sought. Immersion and rationality together affect an outcome where feeling and thought are united. During a session, however, the balance of ecstasy and rationality in terms of role work might vary enormously. In Hubbard's research vignette 'Island' (pp. 195–197) this balance can be seen. The clients engage emotionally and empathically with the characters they create and with each other. At the same time, they are readers of their experience, reflecting, as Hubbard succinctly says in her research conversation: 'They thought about themselves from a distance.' Some techniques used by dramatherapists emphasise a distance from a role, while others encourage a high level of immersion. For dramatherapy it is important to note the centrality of the 'ecstasy/rationality' issue. Of equal interest to dramatherapy is the connection outlined above between intention, levels of involvement and technique. The relationship of these areas to dramatherapy is returned to later in this chapter.

Dramatherapy and role

In contrast to theatre's relationship to role, dramatherapy does not usually have performance or creative expression as a primary focus. Even when a performance occurs within dramatherapy it is not the main goal. The focus of dramatherapy would lie in the therapeutic benefits to be gained by the creative process of role taking and the performance. A performance in dramatherapy is a means to a therapeutic end. Exercises and techniques may seem the same on the surface. However, when seen in terms of context, intention and effect, the experience of theatre is different from that of dramatherapy. (See Figure 8.1.)

For psychodrama and for the social sciences' use of role, an individual or group problem is identified primarily in terms of role, and techniques and structures which focus upon role are used to redress the problem. This is not the case with dramatherapy. A problem may present itself in role terms, but the dramatherapist would consider the spectrum of dramatic processes and expressive languages to find a way to explore and work with the problem or issue. Looked at in one way, a theme or issue can be investigated and developed by a client over weeks and may be experienced using different

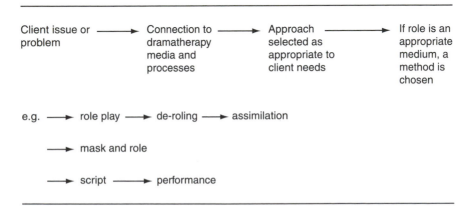

Figure 8.1 Dramatherapy and role.

dramatic forms – through object work one week, using story making another week, to being shaped in role form yet another week. Each different medium may have different things to offer the client in the way it engages and works with the issues the client brings to therapy. So in dramatherapy role play can be seen as one element within the expressive canon of drama and theatre media. For example, the presenting issue might be explored first through play-orientated activity and then move into role play. This in turn might lead to the creation of a piece of work based in performance art.

The following research vignette illustrates the flexibility between role and play, for example. Patrick is a 13-year-old boy who spent most of his week absconding from school during open hours and climbing into school during closed hours. Nancy Secchi notes: 'He usually tried his best to disrupt the dramatherapy group by challenging everyone to a fight or argument.' Secchi described how she uses the distance object-based work can offer along with the concepts of role. Roles played are imagined and imaged, but the roles are not directly taken on through enacted role playing.

Research vignette: Patrick

Patrick selected the old-fashioned purse from the objects laid out in front of the group. I reflected he had chosen a 'container' and that valuable goods were usually to be found inside. He stared at me, and I decided to seize the moment and suggest that the group draw a 'container' of their choice. This was the first moment of 'meaning' he had permitted himself.

Patrick drew 'a dustbin' and looked at me again. I asked the group the significance of their container and Patrick (usually the joker) said, 'Well it's me isn't it? People dump all their rubbish in till it's overflowing and there's nowhere else for it to go.' Patrick looked at me and I tried to convey my appreciation of his situation and pain in my eyes. I said perhaps the group could act as a container for the bin and it could be emptied here bit by bit.

Patrick then returned to his 'masked self' in the session as joker/disrupter. The tiny permission he had given himself to expose his vulnerability was too much to bear, yet the group was able to perform its role of 'witness' and thereby container to that moment. I realised that although there were no further obvious 'moments' for Patrick in future sessions perhaps the *group* had become the purse of valuable things. Patrick's impulsive behaviour was to an extent tolerated by his peers and they all at some point shared their 'valuables'.

The group that consisted of ten adolescent males was a stark arena for the playing out of roles that were anything other than 'masked selves'. Patrick's exposure was not noted by the other members and I chose not to expose him further by drawing attention to his moment, as his stare indicated I was to tread carefully if I was not to 'lose' him from the group.

CORE PROCESS BOX

Role taking

Here roles are worked with, but objects are used rather than playing the roles themselves. In this incident the object play seems to be a response to a need for distance. In a sense, the roles are kept 'manageable' by not being embodied.

Dramatic Projection

The group project aspects of themselves and the way they relate to others in groups into objects and images. This enables them to express issues and to work dramatically with them – exploring material. In this instance the meaning is not immediately made overt as this might be too much for the clients to acknowledge to each other. Hence dramatic projection enables expression without exposure. Secchi in a sense, holds meaning for the group and allows herself to structure activities in a way that stays sensitive to possible meanings, whilst allowing clients to make connections and acknowledge them verbally at a pace that fits them – the brief analytical comment by Patrick being an example of this. Too early acknowledgement might lead to exposure and the closing of exploration, hence halting the work.

Research conversation with Nancy Secchi

Secchi: I think that Patrick was initially drawn to the purse as he was from a family of criminals and his instinct was to check out an opportunity. I believe Patrick would have attempted or at least considered whether to attempt to steal some of the money if that is what he had found inside. Nonetheless, once he had found it to be full of 'junk' I then moved the opportunity on and asked the group to each draw a container in order to take the spotlight off Patrick to avoid exposing his vulnerability. Clearly, the core process was one of dramatic projection. There was his projection or fantasy of what the purse held, my fantasy of why he selected it and then the second symbol of the dustbin emerged. I expect the image of the dustbin was triggered by Patrick's disappointment in finding nothing of value in the purse and this reminded him of how he felt about himself, that is, to be also full of junk.

Jones: When you talk about Patrick's disappointment re the purse, and then the dustbin image and about him feeling 'nothing of value', do you see him being aware of that, or as something that was unconscious, or a meaning given by you that he may not have had?

Secchi: Patrick made his own connection at the point at which he chose the dustbin, hence his comment about how 'everyone dumps their rubbish in till it's overflowing'. I would have made my own personal interpretation at this stage, but remained within the metaphor and tried to move the therapeutic process on by asking the group to change their image in some way to 'improve' it. I would have been able to assess Patrick's ability to self-heal, or his need for an alternative form of intervention. It could have gone a number of ways at this point. What made this whole activity rare is that Patrick did make the symbol explicit. In my experience, not many people choose to do this for whatever reason. I like the safety of remaining in the metaphor and rarely invite people to make explicit connections. Re dramatic projection, if I thought that Patrick's ego could stand the group focusing on him, I would have liked to have the group embody a container, and for him to be inside having the junk thrown in on top of him, but enabling him to vocalise something about the experience and to physicalise it in some way. The others could have taken turns being inside it and trying out various ways of 'managing' that feeling. We could have had an audience observing from the outside, and acting as a further container to the experience. They all could have opted to take turns in this and add ideas, but at the time the 'moments' of resonance in the group were so fleeting that it was hard to grasp much of substance. I assume this reflected many of the group members' daily experiences.

It is hard to know what play is about in a group like the one Patrick was part of. The creative links from individual to individual were tentative and fleeting. My role was often mediator or mother/mediator, mediating between conflicts, both physical and internal as well as difficult uncontainable emotions. The boys were all referred to the group due to their challenging behaviour in class. The boundaries were endlessly being pushed. I think that the dramatist is a role that acts as a filter to the drama, and thereby a 'reconstituter' of the drama. It becomes distilled and refined before becoming 'useful' drama as opposed to just activity.

Here we are taken into a dramatherapist's reflection on role work. We see Secchi debating how to meet Patrick and the group's needs both from a therapeutic and creative perspective. We see her considering dramatic possibilities: whether to ask the group to change their image or not? Whether to have Patrick inhabit the dustbin? She is trying to find an appropriate dramatic form for the therapeutic work. Secchi analyses aspects of her work in terms of her being given a role of 'mother mediator' and she also uses role as a way of reflecting on her process as facilitator. Some dramatherapists enter into an explicit dramatic role within the therapeutic work (see Rogers, pp. 170–173 and Levy, pp. 217–219). This might be in order to take part in a role play – to assist in the exploration of the material which the client is bringing. The entry into role by the therapist might also concern the exploration of transference issues which the client is experiencing. Landy has given a detailed account of a therapist in role in his 'One on One' essay, where he plays the role of an elephant in relation to the client taking on the part of a mouse (Landy 1989).

So role in dramatherapy is part of the expressive canon that the client and therapist can utilise. It might be used as the main way of working or in combination with other methodologies. In addition, dramatherapy does not necessarily frame the presenting problem in role terms. An example of this might be the way that issues are considered within a developmental framework, as described in Chapter 12. Andersen-Warren and Grainger contrast an approach which is rooted in role to one rooted in theatre, an interesting contrast to Landy's approach which sees human nature as role centred and role based:

> Human awareness is not simply a matter of playing roles in inter- and intra-personal dramas, but of constructing our own personal theatres, theatre being most accurately described as the human ability to look at oneself, acting in the world. The first organised theatres in western Europe, those of classical Greece, developed out of a cast of two actors – plus an audience.
>
> (Andersen-Warren and Grainger 2000: 20)

The process of the work would not need to have the structure of the classic psychodrama or the role play. These structures might be used. However, the client's need is considered in the light of a variety of dramatic processes. For example, the client might only need to *create* a role for the therapeutic work to be completed. No role playing with others, or catharsis, may be needed. A role might be developed over a number of weeks through a variety of media until the client has worked with the issue or problem sufficiently.

Dramatherapy practice and role

Within dramatherapy there are different approaches that emphasise particular aspects of role taking and playing. For example, Landy (1994, 2001) stresses the importance of distancing and the notion of a role inventory or taxonomy as a framework for dramatherapy. Jennings (1987) examines the importance of developing the client's role repertoire, whilst Grainger (1990) considers the more absorbed, ecstatic, ritualistic aspects of engagement with role. Read Johnson (1999) looks at the nature of role in terms of the therapeutic potentials of transformation. Emunah and Read Johnson (1983), Jennings (1997) and Mitchell (1992) regard role within a performance and paratheatrical context in dramatherapy. Meldrum has discussed dramatherapy's approach to the relationship between self and role (1994).

Landy (1994, 2001) sees role as the primary component of healing in dramatherapy and has developed an approach rooted in this area. The form of the work takes an approach that initially involves the naming of a role, taken from a taxonomy of roles created by Landy. Each individual has a system of roles. The work involves 'reaching in' to the system and extracting a role, 'a single aspect of personality' (1994: 46). This develops into the playing, working through and exploring of the role followed by reflection and the eventual integration of any change into the client's life. The presence of the taxonomy of roles aims to underpin role work, providing a systematic presentation of the role choices it is possible to make. There is a basic pattern to all role taking in dramatherapy that is summarised in Figure 8.2.

Figure 8.2 Pattern of role taking in dramatherapy.

Enrolement

Enrolement is the process through which a client enters role (Box 8.1). This may happen spontaneously: a client may simply begin to play a role. In a similar fashion the dramatherapist may invite the client or clients to 'show' or to act rather than to describe something verbally. If this happens it is usually within a group that has experience and skills in drama or dramatherapy. In

---

Box 8.1 **Enrolement factors**

- the concentration span of the clients
- the developmental level of the clients' use of drama
- the level of engagement and emotional investment
- the quality of creative involvement and skill
- the cultural background of clients in relation to theatre/drama traditions of role taking and playing
- the history of the group, previous experience of rote work.

some situations an individual might begin to act out a situation in this way but have insufficient impetus to sustain the role.

This lack of impetus would usually be due to some, or one, of the following: a lack of interest; a lack of emotional engagement; too much emotional engagement; confusion or disorientation concerning the direction of the enactment; lack of concentration or skill; a psychological issue present as a resistance to entering into or remaining with a role.

Enrolement seeks to help clients move into role and to sustain the impetus of the role they are playing. Before engaging in enrolement the group or individual's relationship to role work would be assessed (see Chapter 12). This would concern areas such as the developmental level of the client's ability to use drama and roles or the way in which they find meaning in dramatic expression in dramatherapy. For example, an enrolement for an individual or for groups who are well versed in role playing who can sustain roles and create sophisticated dramatic interactions with each other would be run differently than for a group that is easily confused, has short attention spans with little role playing skills or experience. Box 8.2 helps to focus upon these skills and capabilities. It can be used in pre-role-taking work to help establish whether individuals or groups might be ready to move into role work.

Enrolement activities need not have a clear goal in terms of aiming to create an 'end product' of a specific role. An enrolement can be completely exploratory with the roles developing out of the work.

Cultural differences are an important factor to consider with regard to role work. With some forms and traditions the emotional absorption and engagement of the player in the role is high. For others the emphasis is upon a

---

Box 8.2 **Pre-role checklist**   *Tick appropriate boxes*

A client can be considered ready to undertake role work if they display a high proportion of the capacities listed below:

	A	B	C
• can pretend an action	❑	❑	❑
• can imagine what someone else might say	❑	❑	❑
• can imagine what someone else might feel	❑	❑	❑
• can imagine how someone else might respond to something	❑	❑	❑
• can respond to others' imaginative ideas	❑	❑	❑
• can communicate effectively with others	❑	❑	❑
• can use objects as substitutes for other objects with an imaginative intention	❑	❑	❑

A = Yes   B = Some evidence   C = No

more distanced relationship between player and role. The cultural background of a client may mean that their assumptions or approach to role may reflect a particular relationship to engagement and distance. Within much dramatherapy a balanced state of engagement is aimed for, where 'the emotional and rational parts of the self are in balance' and the client is 'capable of feeling without fear of being overwhelmed by the emotion, and thinking, without fear of losing the ability to respond passionately' (Landy 1986: 8).

An additional factor in enrolement lies in de-roling and the assimilating phase. Many structures for enroling are used again or used in reverse for de-roling.

The role of the dramatherapist is to try to ascertain the emotional and creative/artistic needs of the group at the start of any role-based work. If necessary they need to help to provide a structure to enter into role.

Role activity

At the end of enrolement the individual is engaged and involved in the role. The 'role activity' is any structure that enables the individual or group to explore and develop the role. It will engage with the material presented by the client or clients that the role activity aims to address. The role activity may have a single focus, a particular role or a series of roles interacting together. It may move from a scripted role to improvisation to mask. Within dramatherapy, role activity can usually include the following:

- role sculpts
- role play
- improvisation
- work based on existing scripts
- enactment of scripts created by clients
- performance of a play
- role activity using media (masks, puppets)
- dramatic play.

Processes such as doubling, the soliloquy and role reversal can be used within this expressive range. The role of the dramatherapist is to work with the individual or group to find an appropriate dramatic vehicle and process to meet the therapeutic needs of the client or clients.

The above material creates a structure for assisting the therapist and client to see how best the necessary skills or aspects of role play might meet the client's needs and abilities in terms of the media of drama. Landy succinctly provides a clear description of the second component of any assessment process within dramatherapy concerning role:

When a client begins drama therapy, the drama therapist working from the point of view of role theory often assumes that at least one role the client needs to play in life is either unavailable, poorly developed or inappropriately aligned with other roles or other people in their roles. The initial task of therapy, then, is to help the client access that role and identify it.

(Landy 2001: 32–33)

De-roling and assimilation

De-roling – the leaving of a role – is as important to the effectiveness of role work as enrolement and even the role play itself. In some circumstances the leaving of the role can be the most significant part of the process for the client. Generally de-roling involves not so much a routine separation or severance of the role from the player, but a time to establish relationship. This has a function to assist the player to leave the role and return to their normal identity, but also to create perspective. A part of this might be to underpin the process of leaving the role – saying what is different, what is the same. It might involve physically emphasising the shift. This might be to create a kind of dialogue with the role through messages, comments, dialogue or the writing of a letter. In some situations the client will discuss and reflect on their experience with the therapist or other players or audience. Depending on the situation, de-roling often combines different elements of these processes. The research vignette 'Grace' (p. 217) demonstrates a mixture of physical work, message giving and reflecting with the therapist.

It is usual for a structure used within role activity to have a clear ending. At this point the client or clients will usually leave the roles that have been played. If work has been in a group, this involves individuals both leaving the role they have played and acknowledging that others have also left their roles.

Activities often aim to affirm this fact. As noted earlier (p. 204), the taking on of roles is culturally associated with disturbance. The usual ways in which people consider their own and others' identities have been shifted during the role activity. The notion of disturbance is important to remember in the de-roling process. It is not only a time for people to leave their enacted roles, but also a time for relocating and readjusting to people's usual identities. The actors also de-role for the audience. If audience members, those who have witnessed the playing, have strongly identified with roles, emotions or issues, they might need to de-role as audience members, and to witness the return of those involved as players as they move back into their usual selves as group members.

For individuals who have been in emotional states, for people who are vulnerable or who can become confused, or who are not used to dramatic role taking, clear de-roling is seen as important. It is an act of reorientation. As in enrolement, it is important to understand the individual's or group's specific needs in this area. The length, quality and depth of the de-roling will depend upon the specific group and the preceding role activity.

Assimilation involves the establishing of relationship between self and enacted self as represented in the played role. As discussed earlier (p. 207) there is a variety of opinions concerning this aspect of dramatherapy practice. Assimilation might take the form of further dramatic activity or verbal discussion within the session. Alternatively, assimilation might be left to occur outside the session, or might be considered to be happening adequately during the enactment and de-roling and therefore not needing specific attention within the session.

The dramatherapist's role is to offer a procedure to disengage from the role activity and to consider and act upon the way of dealing with how the group or individual assimilates the material which has arisen from the role work.

Lili Levy shows how a number of role-related processes interconnect to enable a client to enter into, develop, leave and reflect on role. Levy describes the client Grace, in her mid-fifties, as a married woman with one child, Peter, in his twenties, who suffers from psychotic episodes. From an early age, Levy notes that Grace had cared for her mother who had suffered from Alzheimer's disease and her father who had cancer. Her parents had both died. At the time of the therapy she was carer for her son. She was referred to dramatherapy sessions by UK social services, after her son had been hospitalised for the second time. Grace started showing symptoms of depression and disturbed sleep. Levy says she was 'feeling that she was unable to cope with everyday life and overwhelmed by the situation'.

Grace had two dramatherapy assessment sessions of one hour each. Levy described the aims of those meetings as:

> to assess her emotional state, how she related to others and her willingness to work within the creative media. I assessed that Grace was emotionally overwhelmed and needed at that moment to be within a one-to-one therapeutic relationship. She was enthusiastic about expressing herself through drama, stories and movement. We then agreed to have eight one-to-one sessions and following this to re-evaluate the possibility of referring her to an ongoing dramatherapy carers group.

The following vignette is a part of the sixth one-to-one session.

Research vignette: Grace

Grace appears tired and weepy and has talked without pausing since entering the room, expressing that there were no boundaries between the outside and inside world.

She describes her feeling towards her son. I ask her if she could think of an image which represents what she is saying. Grace responds with an anxious laugh, 'The first image that comes to my mind is a lump, a burden that sits or stands there, and waits.' The other image is of an old English poem, 'The Albatross and the Sailor'. The sailor is in a small boat in the middle of the ocean. 'The albatross has a disability, it cannot fly away. Although one of its wings is broken, it has a lot of power; it embraces the sailor very tightly not leaving the sailor space to move or breath. The sailor feels suffocated unable to liberate himself from the albatross's wings.'

I suggest embodying the characters that she has created. She accepts and we move from our chairs to the creative drama space and start a warm-up together, mirroring each other. First I start a movement by stretching my arms up, down and to the sides and emitting sounds which she copies. Grace then begins to lead the movements and I follow her lead. I then ask Grace to try to become the embodiment of the albatross through her movements, and to repeat the action as the sailor.

I take two steps backward to give her physical and psychological space and it is here that I stand and witness.

Grace represents the two characters: the albatross and the sailor, with a moving sculpture. She continues moving her arms representing the albatross's wings, first in a playful manner and gradually starts flapping in panic showing despair and helplessness. Immediately, without a pause Grace tries to move from representing the albatross to the sailor, as if the two characters were enmeshed, and I, as a witness, couldn't differentiate between the two. I ask her first to find a way to let go of the albatross's role. She breathes deeply for a couple of minutes, walks around the room, calms herself down, looks at me with a smile and says, 'I am not an albatross, I am Grace.'

At this point she seems to feel ready to embody the role of the sailor, as if engulfed by the wings of the albatross.

'What I really would like to do is to shoot the albatross.' Grace laughs in a manic manner, showing signs of joy and triumph expressing her fantasy, 'The sailor is free.' Soon afterwards she breaks into tears and covers her face with her hands ('I am a bad mother').

I ask her to stay in the metaphor, and offer the possibility of giving a voice to the characters, saying what they feel and what they need from each other. I come closer to her and briefly lay my hand on her back. It takes her some minutes to recuperate. She moves her hands from her face and opens her arms representing the wings of the albatross, she then begins to talk. In the albatross's role Grace says, 'I feel miserable, helpless and frightened. I need to be loved and understood.'

In the sailor's role she says, 'I feel so many things: trapped, suffocated, guilty, sad, angry. . . . I need to be free, but also I would like someone to care for me as well, I am so lonely and tired. I need you to give me space, do not embrace me so tightly.'

Grace de-roles from her characters, rubbing both arms from her shoulder to her hands, as if cleansing her body of the roles she had taken on. She then proclaims, 'I am not an albatross or a sailor, I am Grace and these are my arms.' We both go back to our chairs and she reflects on the whole experience. She identifies her son as the albatross who suffocates her and doesn't allow her to live, 'He is unpredictable, abusive and self-centred', and the sailor as herself, a lost soul in the ocean, not knowing what to do or where to go. She recognises her isolation as the sailor, totally alone in the middle of the ocean. She talks about her need to be cared for, to be loved by her husband, to be seen by others not only as Peter's mother but also as herself.

In the enactment, Grace experiences in her body not only the albatross's suffocation but also his vulnerability. The broken wing reminds her of her own exposure and weakness.

She finds in the albatross qualities of herself, her own vulnerabilities and her difficulties to detach from her son.

The fantasy of shooting the albatross brings Grace feelings of exaltation, relief and guilt at the same time. Grace is able to explore through the metaphor her complex and enmeshed relationship with her son Peter, where the boundaries are blurred and distorted. The metaphor/enactment allows Grace to express openly her love/hate relationship with her son, but she also discovers her profound feeling of sadness and empathy towards him and herself. Her compassion permits her to separate from the rage that invades her. In this process Grace starts to see other aspects of herself and to have a better understanding of her situation.

CORE PROCESS BOX

Embodiment

By physicalising the images Grace deepens her involvement. The non-verbal exploration sees her move from playful flapping to 'despair and helplessness' as the bodily exploration enables emotional expression and discovery. Levy talks about the embodiment enabling Grace to physically experience the 'suffocation' and 'vulnerability' as a way of deepening the experience of the metaphor.

The therapist accompanies her by physically moving inside the imagery Grace creates. In this way embodiment is also a means for the therapist to enable the client to begin work, and a bodily demonstration of her accompanying the client into her fantasy world – physically expressing that she is with Grace.

Witnessing

Levy refers to herself as witness several times within the vignette. By entering into the dramatic world Levy seems to gain insight from being in the drama, and then giving herself an additional perspective by 'witnessing' the drama. She combines the roles of participant and witness. This deepens her perspective as therapist. Within the work the client is also invited to witness herself, reflecting on the fantasy roles. This process assists her in developing a sense of perspective and insight missing at the start of the work: where there seemed to be no boundaries 'between the outside and inside world'.

Role taking

The client's creation of fantasy roles enables her to create a distance to allow her to explore a life situation. Within the images she is able both to express her perceptions and felt experience, whilst also gaining insight, which the roles help her to see.

Research conversation with Lili Levy

Jones: How do you see the difference between Grace, for example, talking about her situation using images, and her actually embodying them with you?

Levy: I see that, by talking, she *tells* me how she feels, but by embodying the characters she has the experience and *feels* it in the 'here and now'. Embodying allows her to get in touch with her emotions and to express her wildest fantasy: 'What I really would like to do is to shoot the albatross.'

Jones: So are you saying that embodying, physically becoming involved in the fantasy, increases the emotional intensity or significance of the images?

Levy: This is a paradoxical process. On one hand, Grace is at a distance from herself when she embodies the characters physically and as such increases her fantasy – she becomes someone else's identity. On the other hand, this distance allows her to experience herself in a different way. She starts observing herself and being emphathetic with her pain and hurt. She gets more involved with her emotions. She is more able to feel and think in a more integrated manner.

Jones: Lovely answer. So, for example, when Grace laughs when she says as the sailor she is free, and then cries and says she is a 'bad mother', you're saying that the depth of exploration is because she is physically 'in' the roles?

Levy: Yes, yes, yes, I think that when she is physically 'in' the roles she gives herself permission to express freely her denied feelings, what is not socially accepted, her desire to 'shoot the albatross', metaphorically her son. Probably she got surprised and frightened by her revelation, as she was discovering an unknown territory. I think that by embodying the roles she frees herself, and as such allows herself that depth of exploration.

Jones: If that's so, why do you think that mattered in the therapy being *effective* for Grace, this being in 'touch with her emotions' that the embodiment enabled?

Levy: I think that only after she got in touch with her emotions, she starts changing her relationship with those parts of herself that had been denied (her need of being cared for and loved).

Jones: I'm interested in how you see Grace's relationship with de-roling. Why do you think that was important in the vignette?

Levy: She has identity problems due her enmeshed relationship with her son. I think the de-roling is fundamental. It prevents the possibility of role confusion. By role confusion I mean the role of someone who doesn't know who he/she is, who cannot differentiate between fantasy and reality. In dramatherapy we work in the connection between fantasy and reality, so it is fundamental after the client finishes exploring and enacting their fantasies to de-role. That means to find a way to leave behind and separate themselves from the role he or she has played, in order to prepare herself or himself to face the reality or outside world.

Jones: So are you saying that de-roling is an important part of the client establishing boundaries and relationship between life and drama? How do you see this separation/preparation operating in the vignette?

Levy: I see de-roling in this situation as a two-pronged process. On the one hand she is separating herself from the dramatic roles she plays (albatross and sailor), a separation from fantasy to life. On the other, the completion of this process allows her to differentiate and separate herself from her son, leading to reflection.

This vignette demonstrates the ways in which a variety of roles can be taken on by the client, and that the process of entering and leaving the roles is a crucial part of the dramatherapy. Here we see Levy in role within the drama and emphasising her function as a witness. Her response to Grace's material contains a rhythm common in much role work within dramatherapy: enrolement, role playing, role reversal and de-roling (see Figure 8.2).

This research vignette and conversation illustrate the ways in which a client can explore a variety of different roles and aspects of role taking within a session. They can become different aspects of themselves, play real or imaginary others and witness themselves, other group members or their therapist in role.

Summary

1   In dramatherapy a role involves the creation of a dramatic identity. This may be entirely different from the client's usual identity, or may be the dramatic representation of this usual identity. All work with role involves the development of a dramatic identity, the enactment of that identity and the separation from that identity.

2   In certain instances 'role' in dramatherapy can refer to a focusing upon a particular role function. For example, the dramatherapy work might focus upon a family role, a social role or a group dynamic role (e.g. daughter, friend, saboteur).

3   Dramatherapy can involve a client in creating a role, but this is only one possible option or element of enactment within the therapy.

4   A role enactment might be connected to other dramatic modes or processes within a session, or over a number of sessions.

5   The length and nature of engagement with role can vary according to the context and to clients' needs. The therapeutic work might involve only the creation of a role with no extended enactment, it might involve a role played within a traditional role play or a role might be taken up over a number of sessions.

6   Within a session the engagement with the created role can involve different degrees of absorption. A client might be highly emotionally involved or highly distanced. There might be a great deal of cognitive analysis and discussion in relation to a role or there may be none at all.

7   Engagement with the role might be momentary or prolonged. There is no emphasis put upon catharsis as in Greek tragedy and psychodrama, or the notion of climax. Nor is there emphasis upon the completion of a learning process as in the social sciences' use of role play. The dramatic contact is adapted to fit the therapeutic goals and needs of the client in terms of depth of involvement, length of time spent in role and degree of analytic reflection.

9   The dramatic body

> The history of the theatre is the history of the transfiguration of the human form.
>
> Schlemmer in Gropius, *The Theatre of the Bauhaus*

Introduction

The early twentieth-century Bauhaus movement in Germany is primarily known for its work in art and architecture. However, its attempt to revolutionise culture extended to theatre in a way that provides a useful starting point from which to consider the body within drama and therapy. Oskar Schlemmer began work in the Bauhaus community as head of the scripting workshop, but he gradually transformed it into the Bauhaus 'Stage Shop', as the leader of the movement, Walter Gropius, describes it. The remains of the output of the Shop are with us in the form of writings, photographs and diagrams. The recorded images contain many of the costumes and productions of the Bauhaus, but all return to Gropius' central theatrical aim: to experience stage space through the body.

The photographs show strange creatures, part metal, part flesh, humans with limbs connected to spirals, captured by multiple exposure camera work. Gropius and Schlemmer produced a series of diagrams that attempt to illustrate the 'transformation of the body as it exists in theatrical space' (Gropius 1979: 5). Schlemmer's acting forms depict figures from which emanate lines of power. Geometric waves emerge from the actor's chest and stomach (see Plates 9.1 and 9.2). The statue and the audience arena become a receptacle to be filled by 'the actor whose body and movements make him the player' (Gropius 1979: 20). As the quotation at the start of this chapter states, theatre is seen by Schlemmer and Gropius as the transfiguration of the human form.

According to the Bauhaus approach, the body changes when it enters dramatic space. The human figure and its expressions automatically change on stage so that 'each gesture or motion is translated in meaningful terms into a unique sphere of activity' (Gropius 1979: 92). Even someone from the audience, if removed from their 'sphere' and placed on the stage, would be clothed

Plate 9.1 Schlemmer's body transformations in theatrical space (from Gropius 1979), © 1961, Wesleyan University.

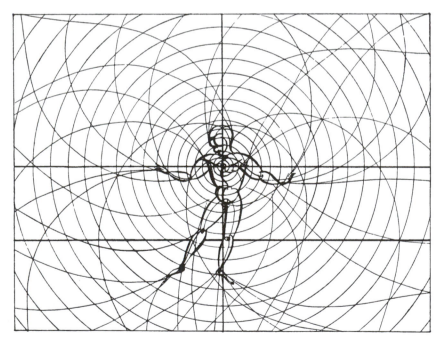

Plate 9.2 Schlemmer's body transformations in theatrical space (from Gropius 1979), © 1961, Wesleyan University.

in a 'magic nimbus'. The same change can happen if someone simply moves back a step in front of two or more curious spectators to act something out for them.

The building of the 'Total Theatre', which was to be the culmination of the Bauhaus ideas, was abandoned after 'Black Friday' which brought Hitler and the Nazis to power. The vision of the Total Theatre was not realised, though their work continued elsewhere (Jones 2005: 67). However, the Bauhaus experiments usefully introduced an approach to the body in dramatic and theatrical space that helps in the discussion of the 'dramatic body' in drama-therapy. The Bauhaus concern with the changes which occur in the body, and the way in which forces meet and emanate from the body when someone is engaged in theatre bring me to the key questions of this chapter:

- What changes occur in someone when they enter into enactment within dramatherapy?
- What role does the body have within theatre, drama and dramatherapy?
- What is the relationship between an individual's identity and their performing body?

The term 'dramatic body' refers to the body when it is involved in a theatrical or dramatic act. The dramatic body is a place where imagination and reality meet.

Actors' bodies express their imagination. Their bodies help them to dis-cover and express their imaginary ideas. The audience's imagination is engaged by an actor's bodily expressions through movement, sound and interaction with others. For most forms of theatre and drama, in all cultures, the body is the main means of communication. As the artist might work with brushes, paint and canvas, so the body is the chief means of theatrical expres-sion. The actor discovers and expresses roles, ideas and relationship through face, hands, movement – the body. The audience will experience theatre primarily as these bodily expressions in the stage space.

In dramatherapy the body of a client is of similar importance. As will be explored later, in a dramatherapy session an individual might find their body wearing a mask, its shape disguised by cloth, represented by a painted body map image, covered in paint, or entering a different bodily identity through taking on the character or role of another. A disguised client, after an impro-visation, summed up many of the issues concerning the body in drama-therapy when she observed, 'It felt like me, but it wasn't me.' She felt herself to be a part of the disguise, but also recognised some kind of difference. Courtney (1983) argues that the body is important in exploration and discovery within drama. As dramatherapist Lili Levy within the research conversation in Chapter 9 comments: 'I see that, by talking, she *tells* me how she feels, but by embodying the characters she has the experience and *feels* it in the "here and now". Embodying allows her to get in touch with her emotions and to express her wildest fantasy.' Many dramatherapists within this book's research emphasise that the bodily engagement with drama is crucial to the core processes at work within dramatherapy.

This chapter explores the theoretical and practical issues concerning the body, identity and enactment. The dramatic body will be defined and its relationship to dramatherapy practice described. In this way the chapter intends to detail the reasons why the body can be a primary focus of therapeutic change in dramatherapy.

Background to the dramatic body

The body and identity: an overview

The body and its relationship to the self and to society has been the focus of discussion and debate in a number of disciplines – from theology to medical science, psychoanalysis to anthropology. Four main aspects of this debate are especially important in the consideration of the dramatic body in dramatherapy:

- the relationship between the body and an individual's identity
- society's regulation of the body
- bodily expression and communication
- the role of the body in the construction of a social persona.

Psychoanalysis (James 1932; Deutsch 1947, 1952; Lowen 1958) and object relations theory (Krenger 1989) have suggested a relationship that connects body, emotion and identity. Rossberg-Gempton and Poole (1991) summarise the psychoanalytic approach as follows: the mind and body is seen as a functional unit. Unconscious material can be physicalised through bodily expressions that are orchestrated by the ego. They add, however, that, though bodily movements were considered to be important, 'therapeutic improvement could not be realised until the client could verbalise feelings associated with those movements and the accompanying bodily sensations' (1991: 40).

This position is echoed by some dance movement therapists. Siegal (1984) states that 'because a person lives with, in and through the body, their total being is affected by life's bodily experience'. The self is often seen to be realised by and through the body. This is usually presented as a relationship that involves duality or tension. The Christian tradition, for example, is permeated by the individual's battle between body and soul (Marcuse 1969). Freudian consideration of the body in works such as *Totem and Taboo* (1950) emphasises the tension within individuals between gratification and social regulation. Nietzsche (1967) and Walter Benjamin (1955) both point to a division in bodily expression within societies – between the Apollonian and the Dionysian. Apollonian expression emphasises the rational, discursive and analytic. Dionysian expression is characterised by rapture, sexual ecstasy and the frenzy of the body in dance. They discuss the tendency of societies to emphasise one of these modes of bodily expression at the expense of the other.

Turner (1982) reflects upon the history of this duality, concluding that in western philosophy and theory the body/self relationship is one in which the body appears simultaneously as constraint and potential (Turner 1982: 4). The potential refers to the body as a means to express, discover and develop the self. Constraint can be understood as the ways in which the body is regulated and restrained by self and society. This constraint is often allied to a perceived set of limitations or regulations put upon the individual (Scheflen 1972). Feminist social theory (Mitchell and Rose 1982) and the writings of Foucault (1988), for example, point to the ways in which society constrains and uses the expressions of the body. Sexual activity, public and private expression, family, social and economic behaviour are all analysed in terms which ally suppression of the individual with suppression of bodily actions and expressions.

Within western culture then, the relationship between an individual's identity and their body can be characterised by a tradition of duality. In all the material described above there is a tension indicated between identity, body and society.

The body is often described as the primary means by which communication occurs between self and other. This is through gesture, expression and voice (Elam 1991). Attention is given to the ways in which the body communicates on an unconscious as well as conscious level (Lorenz 1966; Argyle 1972). Douglas, in works such as *Purity and Danger* (1966), has indicated how the body communicates in a metaphoric way. The body is also seen as a surface which is used to mark identity in terms of social status, age, gender and religion through marking and clothing (Benthall and Polhemus 1975). This approach focuses upon the body as both the key to communication and as a primary aspect of an individual arriving at a sense of identity. The body communicates the individual's identity to others. It is also seen as a means by which the individual arrives at a sense of their own identity and as an expressive medium through which society and the individual connect.

Sociologists have considered how identity is connected to the ways in which the body is presented in social space. In particular, Goffman has analysed the role of the body in the construction of a social persona (Goffman 1972). In his work the self presents selected personae in different situations and arrives at a sense of identity through bodily expression and behaviour to others.

Constructing the dramatic body

Certain traditions contain a rigorous training for the body. Kathakali, for example, has numerous exercises for the eyes and face. Boys begin training for six years between the ages of 8 and 16 and their bodies are 'literally massaged and danced into shapes suited to Kathakali' (Schechner 1988: 270). The training is seen as an important way of enabling an individual to enter into a dramatised self. In *Poetics of the Oppressed: Experiments with the People's Theatre in Brazil*, Boal (1974) gives a rather different perspective on the relationship between self, dramatic body and training. He too speaks of the necessity of training the body, which is done within a context of control. However, he seeks to enable the spectator to become the actor, seeing it as a journey from the passive reception of a product to the state of becoming the producer of that product: 'To control the means of production, man must, first of all, control his own body, know his body, in order to be capable of making it more expressive' (Boal 1974: 125).

Boal sees the body in drama as the key to meaning, understanding and power. The first three of Boal's four stages of transforming the spectator to actor concern training the body. He calls these 'knowing the body', 'making the body expressive' and 'the theatre as language' (1974: 127). Through this work he aims to enable participants to become aware of their own bodies. This involves finding the possibilities for positive expression and the 'deformities' (1974: 128) which society and the individual's work impose on the use they make of their bodies.

So, here, two aspects of the trained body in theatre and drama are highlighted. The first concerns the way training is often connected to the creation of a special theatre language and theatre identity for an individual – a separate dramatic body. The second is that training can alter the expressive possibilities of someone's body for performance purposes. In turn, this can lead to a greater awareness of the body for an individual.

The dramatic body in dramatherapy practice

In its work with the body dramatherapy uses a variety of approaches and techniques. It is fair to say that in most dramatherapy sessions the therapist tries to be aware not only of verbal communication, but also the ways in which the client and therapist communicate to each other non-verbally. These are not two distinct categories, but naturally combine and interrelate. Whether in or out of the drama space, the client's and therapist's bodies are in communication all the time. In Chapter 5 Jay Vaughan captures a part of this when she says:

> On the one hand, this allows the child or young person to be aware of what is happening in their body and feel in control of their trauma responses. On the other hand, as in this case, it allows them to see the connection between their bodily response and the story. (p. 93)

Here the therapist shows herself to be aware of the different connections between body and thought, word and physical expression.

Dramatherapy's relationship with the dramatic body can be divided into three main areas. Each area is not totally separate from the others, but should be seen as an aid to help describe different aspects of practice. The first area involves clients in developing the potential of their own body. The second area has as its main focus the therapeutic potentials and benefits of the client taking on a different bodily identity within the dramatherapy. The third area concerns work that explores the personal, social and political forces and influences which affect the body.

Developing the potential body

In the first area the emphasis is often upon the client inhabiting, or using, their own body more effectively. This might be the main therapeutic aim. In other situations, however, this 'inhabitation' might be preparatory work. For example, until a client can inhabit their own body they will find it difficult or impossible to develop their body's capability to represent another identity through the key processes of personification or impersonation. Whether as preparation or as the main focus with the therapy, this work usually concerns the areas listed in Box 9.1.

Box 9.1 **Main areas of concern – the potential body**

- the developmental level of the client's relationship with their body
- the range and quality of communication a client can achieve using their body within dramatic activity
- the range and quality of the client's physical relationships with others within dramatic activity.

Presenting problems here include clients who are experiencing difficulties owning or relating to their body. This might happen, for example, after a stroke or as a result of trauma. Clients might be experiencing difficulties around the physical use of their body in terms of motor skills. Issues might concern the use of their body in everyday relationships with others. This might include, for example, people who have been in long-term hospital care who are moving into the community, and whose social skills have not had the opportunity to develop due to institutionalisation.

In general this area of dramatherapy is appropriate for people who experience difficulties because they have not developed their body's range of relationships and possibilities. A developmental issue may be present as a problem. (For further details on developmental levels concerning the body in dramatherapy, see Chapter 7.) With some clients this area might remain the chief focus of the work. For example, an issue might be located in the way a client uses their body in communication. The dramatherapy work might be to aim to enhance the individual's ability to communicate with their body.

In this way of working, then, the dramatic body is being used to effect change in the way someone relates to their body in everyday life. The dramatherapy space and dramatic activity allow the individual to discover potentials and ways of using their body. The drama activities can also have a training aspect, as the improvisation helps new skills in voice or gesture to develop. Through dramatic projection clients become personally involved in the impersonations or personifications they create. The client can develop a new relationship to their body and to the way they relate to other people through their body. The client's dramatic body is given different permissions than their everyday body. The client's relationship to their own body is transformed by the enactment in dramatherapy. Through the life–drama connection, the work in the dramatherapy group can affect the client's life. The client can begin to assimilate aspects of the new relationship they are making with their body in dramatherapy into their everyday life.

Body transformation

Body transformation in dramatherapy refers to an aspect of the adoption through a dramatic act of a change or alteration in identity. This adoption is shown to others and experienced by the client through their body, through embodiment. The client may take on a different character through impersonation, or may alter their usual identity in some way or may play themselves in the past. This may involve the use of the body to represent a thing or quality – the client's body might depict water moving, or personify 'temptation', for example.

The following research vignette illustrates the ways in which this transformation of the body through embodying an imagined role can be used within dramatherapy. The vignette is a moment from a text-based training group facilitated by Madeline Andersen-Warren during a joint conference of the British Association of Dramatherapists and the Association for Dance and Movement Therapists.

Research vignette: What the thunder said

The participants were female dance movement therapists and dramatherapists. The text that informed the work was a short section from 'What the thunder said' in T.S. Eliot's poem *The Waste Land*. The narrator questions another about the third person wrapped in a brown mantle and hooded whom she or he sees on the white road ahead. It is unclear whether the three characters are male or female.

The structure of the workshop followed Jennings's paradigm of embodiment, projection and role. The road and the thunder were embodied and became important aspects of the structure both as participating characters and as commentators on the actions of the three travellers.

Each participant created all of the characters and shaped their own dramas. My roles were director, scene setter, facilitator, prompter and side coach. My antennae were attuned both to the aesthetic and structure of the drama itself as well as the level of therapeutic involvement and engagement the participants were experiencing. As a facilitator it was important to allow short periods for sharing the experience of translating the text into dramatic action.

My dilemma arose during the sharing following the creation of the hooded character. It was clear that the participants were all unsure whether the characters they had created were safe and honourable.

My previous experience of working with this verse had been that this figure had been interpreted and embodied as kindly and trustworthy. My workshop plan was for the hooded figure to act as a wise person to impart knowledge and wisdom to the travellers to assist them during the long journey.

While the text can be concurrently a container, a structure, a metaphor and a source of dramatic imagery open to interpretation within dramatherapy practice, it is not intended to be constraining. However, the enabling device needs to be sourced from the text.

Madeline Anderson-Warren

Research conversation with Madeline Andersen-Warren

Jones: How do you see embodiment as a process within the vignette?

Andersen-Warren: As the observer of the stages of embodiment in the group, I recalled the relaxed and sprightly movements that were inspired by walking on the road as the narrator. I therefore asked if the road might have a guardian. This was agreed and our closing drama incorporated a wise guardian who offered words of wisdom and a gift. All of the group were involved in each scene and were both the actors, script adaptors and the directors of their plays. Each person played each character so they were both the givers and receivers of wisdom.

Jones: How do you see this embodiment of the different roles within the group process?

Andersen-Warren: An integration of the narrator, the commentator, the companion, the terrain, the unknown figure and the guardian took place. Although this was a training workshop and our contract was not for therapy, participants commented that the enactment of the metaphor of the text and the metaphors in the text were an inspiration for gaining an altered perspective on some obstacles they were encountering during their journey through life.

Here each participant explores different feelings, qualities and experiences through physically embodying different identities and elements of the text. Such transformation of the body into being able to take on other qualities, or those of other personae, can be used in dramatherapy in a number of ways. By taking on other personae through impersonation or personification, permissions concerning the client's relationship with their body can occur. The distance achieved by taking on a different identity can enable them to experiment with alternative ways of using their body.

Bodily memory and the two bodies

Within dramatherapy the client can explore the relationship with their body in terms of the problematic memories and experiences with which their physical self connects. On occasion a particular exercise can evoke a particular strong or difficult feeling or response. This might be to do with an experience which occurs in the present for the client or it may be one rooted in the past or a combination of contemporary and historic issues. Social and political forces at work in the client's experience of their body might also be important to consider.

This might be worked with in a number of ways. The basic task in this area of work is to find the appropriate dramatic vehicle which enables the client to explore their experience of their body. The work of the group might concern people's relationships with their bodies in terms of body image. The focus would be upon the exploration of the forces which have shaped the problem. The aim would be to enable the client to achieve a different relationship with their bodily selves through the dramatic work. This kind of work is often undertaken with people who have body-related issues such as eating disorders, or those who are experiencing physical symptoms that might be linked to emotional trauma or difficulties.

Dramatherapist and dance movement therapist Ditty Dokter reflects upon a piece of group work practice using the idea of embodiment and the potential body as a way of seeing therapeutic change. The practice takes place in a group therapy context. The group consists of eight young people in a day-patient therapeutic community and is co-facilitated by a dramatherapist and a dance movement therapist. The group is a slow open therapy group with the emphasis on movement and embodiment. The community has a psycho-dynamic/group analytic orientation in a psychiatric context. Dokter describes the group in the following way:

The young people are 18 to 30 years old and have mixed diagnostic backgrounds. The psychiatric diagnoses are depression, (borderline) personality disorder, addiction, self-harm, bipolar affective disorder, adjustment disorder, and anxiety/panic disorder. The clients are often diagnosed with two or three of the categories combined. The psychodynamic stressors identified are sexual/physical/emotional abuse, parental separation and being bullied at school. The group focuses on developing the potential body (Jones 1996: 156). The clients are asked to engage in sensorimotor play with the aim of inhabiting their body more effectively. Most of the clients are experiencing difficulties owning or relating to their bodies, due to their experiences and presenting problems. Many of them have been in inpatient and/ or child and adolescent psychiatric treatment, so have been living with these problems for a large part of their lives.

The following vignette is from the stage in the groups's life where one client has been there for ten months, three clients for six months and three new members have recently joined the group.

Research vignette: The potential body in action

Today four clients are absent in the group: two clients had walked out after the early morning community meeting, two had not turned up. The group started with a discussion about the absent members and their possible reasons for absence. Al was quite vocal in the discussion, Hattie sat quiet with her arms folded in front of her chest, Ted occasionally contributed, but was becoming more physically agitated as the discussion progressed, rocking front and back on his chair, crouching on top of his chair, he seemed agitated but unable to talk about this. Al and Sam in particular talked about their fear of giving offence to those clients who kept creating crises, taking up a lot of group time and then were absent. Sam had come in with the cassette recorder and some CDs of his own at the beginning of the group. He said he tried to be in the background. One of the therapists joked that that might be difficult given his multicoloured clothing. Sam said he had different selves, and was not sure which was the one he brought to the group today. He hated how a bully at school had said he walked very humbly and associated that with trying not to be noticed.

I asked if the group wanted to start moving and Ted and Sam said, 'Yes.' Sam requested a breathing exercise as a transition, however he was the only one taking part. I suggested a warm-up to music. Sam said he had brought some music but Al and Ted requested a different CD. The group really struggled to get moving, even Ted who had been hopping on his chair now held very still. When I asked what made it hard to move, Sam said it did not connect to how he was feeling. He started with throwing a punch as a movement to be changed (I suggested passing a movement round the circle and transforming it between one person and the next). However, this dwindled into non-existence. Group members again said it did not connect to how they felt and suggested using a physioball to facilitate the movement and express some of the frustration. The ball was bounced from one to another. Even Hattie joined in and there was laughter and increased energy. However, when the energy went up further, Hattie moved to stand next to the door. I checked whether that space felt safe enough, and she nodded. Al took off his glasses and the three young men bounced and threw the ball hard round the room, at each other, the therapists and the furniture until a lamp was broken.

The end of the group consisted of clearing up and reflecting with Hattie smiling at the damage, but not saying what had amused her. Sam had become very quiet and said the movement had disconnected him from his feeling. Al said he felt he had been able to play and have a go, while Ted said it was a good release to have a ball.

The body language during the initial discussion seemed to indicate some of what the clients were feeling, Hattie's crossed arms indicating 'leave me out of it' and 'I do not want to join in'. She did find a moment of engagement with the others in the movement, before withdrawing again. Ted's movement showed frustration and restlessness. Initially he became self-conscious about showing this directly and being witnessed in this embodiment. With the use of a ball he was able to express and embody his feelings directly, finding some release. Sam voiced the group's difficulty in connecting the movement to how he was feeling. He also needed the ball as a distancing device to enable the group to join together in movement. The movement with the ball fairly soon became more embodied aggression, at which point Hattie removed herself from the action, while the three young men continued with the therapists. Al and Ted were able to own their aggression in the reflective time, but Sam remained disconnected. The psychodynamic understanding of his fearing his own potential for aggression but also hating his own 'humility' for him remained stuck between the 'different selves'. Having his music rejected may have contributed to his sense of being rejected by the group and not being allowed to assert himself.

The conflict within the group, embodied by the absent members through their non-presence, was embodied by the present members in their difficulty connecting their feelings to their bodies and connecting to each other. The anger and frustration evoked can be expressed by two of the (longer standing) group members. However, at this point in the group the destructiveness cannot yet be transformed. As a first step it can be acknowledged and given form. The ambivalence and fear of aggression are held by the other two clients (who recently joined the group).

Ditty Dokter

The following vignette is based on Anna Seymour's experience of conducting a biomechanics workshop with trainee dramatherapists. The approach was based in Meyerhold's system of actor training called 'biomechanics', which was used to enact a story. Seymour describes the background to her approach in this way:

Meyerhold's gestural code of movement looks at the construction of the theatrical *mise en scène* – what goes into the theatrical picture – and questions the economy of each action with choices made about the 'rakus' or surface of the body that is shown to the audience. Each movement goes through a cycle involving the creation of a dynamic starting point or stoika, the gathering of resources through a backward movement, in the opposite direction to the intended action, known as the refusal, the otkaz, which produces the energy for the posil, or sending the action. The action is controlled through the break of tormos (where if necessary the actor pauses in mid-action because of some obstacle – like the body of another actor) and continues, ending at toichka. The cycle arrives at stoika ready to begin again. In the process of otkaz, we see an embodied theatrical structure whereby it is recognised that in order to move forward it is necessary first to go back to gather control. In therapeutic terms it supports the necessity to sometimes stay back for a while in order to make decisions about how to go forward; that it is possible to be in charge of how this movement might take place and be able to survey the context in which it is happening and how.

Research vignette: Biomechanics workshop

In the workshop, I emphasised aspects of the biomechanical training that attuned to dramatherapeutic understandings of containment within a theatrical aesthetic. It was possible for the biomechanics to be a literal container of movement but also to operate on a metaphorical level of containing the group's explicit given narrative – the story – and individual narrative – projection onto that story. The partners (as Meyerhold called the actors) 'control' the space with an awareness of the limits of the performance area and a sense of the presence of each partner, the shape and rhythm of their movement. Each contributes to the total drama and its construction, each movement is significant and sensed by the whole group. As a dramatherapist standing in the liminal space between theatre practitioner and therapist I wanted to stay true to the integrity of the theatrical system and at the same time make it useable for a therapeutic process.

As a preliminary training I taught the participants the principles on which specific biomechanical forms are based, structuring each movement task on the cycle of otkaz, posil, toichka but without insisting on how each gesture was constructed. Thus each person determined their own otkaz before moving in any direction, sensed the posil and the appropriate moment for them and their presence in the group, to arrive at toichka. What became clear was how attention to the precision of movement created control and expansiveness. Each gesture could be repeated as an abstract form and the weight and rhythm of the movement calibrated. Applying this to a short story, the shapes and dynamics of the *mise en scène* could be explored from a rational perspective as the group moved away from the feelings of the story in order to construct the aesthetics of the enactment. In the performance it was possible to re-engage with feelings from the more distanced perspective created by the form.

Individuals spoke of how the control of the form gave them a sense of liberation. I sensed an atmosphere of calm and energy in the group. The work had taken place in the evening and the participants who had arrived tired after a long day's work appeared revitalised and to have gained stature. By working with Meyerhold's ideas through a dramatherapy process, what could seem a rather arcane system became a live functional process.

Anna Seymour

This form of theatre embraces a dialectical approach which seems to be a more serviceable concept than referring to paradox in that it incorporates the dynamic of power relations. Here opposites are held in tension, reliant on each other for existence, continually going through cycles of giving way to each other to create new dynamics.

We can see this political/philosophical idea worked out in the practice of biomechanics in the Russian theatre as well as in the work of Brecht and Dario Fo.

Research conversation with Anna Seymour

Jones: In terms of therapeutic possibilities, what processes do you see at work here? You mention, for example, projection and embodiment and a movement between 'feelings' and a 'distanced perspective'.

Seymour: There is a particular kind of embodiment going on here that is different from the more familiar Stanislavskian process. (Often it is taken for granted that this naturalistic form of acting is simply 'what acting is'.) In that system the actor's purpose is the faithful reproduction of another person, a transformation of the self to create the sense of it is 'as if I am that other'. There is an emphasis on internal processes of empathy and identification. In therapeutic terms we can say this produces the paradoxical result of dramatic distance because the client uses their feelings to produce the feelings of 'another'. But we can also say that this is a process of projection as 'the other' holds the client's feelings.

In the non-naturalistic theatre the process works the other way around, the actor begins from the external form of the body in gesture, movement, spatial relationship with fellow actors, setting, context. Rather than beginning with feeling, the emphasis is on how the *rational* construction of these aspects may produce realistic truthful representations and that feeling may be controlled and focused. In therapeutic terms there is a potential for a different kind of distancing through the distancing of the form, in this case the gestural language of biomechanics that looks at the idea of efficiency and clarity in movement.

Jones: You talk about biomechanics being 'a literal container of movement but also to operate on a metaphorical level of containing the group's explicit given narrative'. How could that be useful to a client in dramatherapy?

Seymour: Because biomechanics is like a gestural vocabulary it is possible to learn it in a literal sense – how does the biomechanical actor walk, change direction on the stage, sit down, etc. However, biomechanical actors needs to train their bodies to a high level of athleticism. In dramatherapy we are not interested in this kind of 'training'. We want to use forms that serve the client's needs. Yet through using this form we may enter into the aspect of 'training' as another means of distancing that develops the client's vocabulary of movement; in this context using a system that is predicated on rational construction and efficient reproduction, using the actor's full physical potential.

Jones: So is part of what you're saying here that it's less the capacity of the dramatic work to depict reality through image or representation (for example, in role play portraying a life event) and more the capacity of the physical work of the drama to engender bodily change?

Seymour: Yes, because the purpose of the training is to be able to 'act' in an efficient, controlled way on the stage. There is a development from the early phases of moving in the space 'as myself' listening to my own rhythms in relation to others, being responsible for filling the whole space by moving in equidistance from each other and then moving into the highly stylised forms of biomechanics. In dramatherapy terms it is like a warm-up before moving into an embodied style of action. However, the action is not predicated on emotion but on the physical needs of the task, for example, I need to move from here to there. When working with a text there is a discussion about content, motivation, feelings and then this is looked at through the movements needed to represent this using the otkaz, posil, toichka.

   Because the forms could be looked at in an abstract way – for example, 'What is the shape of my arm when I do this? – the body can take familiar actions and make them an object of enquiry by doing them in a different way. This can shift the everyday into a metaphorical realm.

Jones: I'm curious about taking the everyday into the metaphorical. Can you say more about that?

Seymour: When people in the group began to 'gather their resources' they made and took different shapes from each other as each explored how their gathering took place. These shapes could then begin to suggest narratives. However, this was not the route we took. We used a story where the elements of the setting – trees, huts – became interpreted through the biomechanic forms. This 'estranged' movement applied to a story creates some distance from the story itself, another 'space' to work in between the self and story.

In both research vignettes individuals are given opportunities to explore and develop a new relationship to their body and to the way they relate to other people through improvised movement forms and activities. Though very different from each other in terms of the activities worked with, both examples show how the dramatic body is given different permissions from their everyday body. In the Meyerhold creation of movement sequences and in the movement work in Dokter's vignette the client's everyday relationship to their own body is transformed by the enactment in dramatherapy. One way of looking at this is that the potential of the body to create meaning is intensified and freed from the usual constraints placed upon it by, for example, the repetition and patterns developed in daily life. Through the life–drama connection, the work in the dramatherapy group can affect the client's life and this enriched exploration can be brought out of the therapeutic space. The client can begin to assimilate aspects of the new relationship they are making with their body in dramatherapy into their everyday life.

Summary

The body is the main tool of communication and expression in drama and in dramatherapy. It is the chief means through which individuals express themselves and make contact with others. The use of the dramatic body in dramatherapy is typified by a series of changes:

- The physical body of an individual essentially stays the same when in and out of dramatic mode. However, when an individual enters into a dramatic act or space a change in the way the *individual experiences* their body and the relationship between their *body and identity* can occur.
- The change involves a *shift in behaviour* and *relationship* to body, self and others, due to the kinds of rules and boundaries within a drama space. These rules usually differ from those in reality outside the drama.
- The client is perceived to be in a *heightened* or *special state*. This involves an alteration of perception, a change of focus and responses, the sharpening of senses.
- The sense of identity of an individual can be *altered* by physically changing appearance and body language in dramatic activity.
- The *way others perceive and relate* to the individual's body and identity can alter. This is the case whether people are engaged directly with the individual in the drama, or indirectly as audience members.
- This change involves *transformation* due to a different language of gesture and expression being used. This language is due to training and theatrical traditions and can involve impersonation and personification within dramatherapy.
- As an individual's body becomes involved in dramatic acts it can lead to an *increased awareness of the body's range and potential*.
- By involving their body in drama an individual can become more *self-aware* in terms of being able to look at their own body, their relationship with it, and the social or personal forces affecting it.

For the dramatherapist it is important to acknowledge not only what the body can do in terms of performance possibilities, but what occurs to the individual's identity in relation to their body whilst engaged in enactment within dramatherapy.

The dramatic body as defined above seeks to describe the relationship between an individual and their body within drama. Three main ways of working have been described in this chapter: the first involves developing the 'potential body' of the client through enactment in dramatherapy; the second involves transforming the body through dramatic forms; the third concerns the way in which dramatherapy can evoke and work with memories linked to the body.

10 Symbol and metaphor

In order to believe that all these castles, trees and rocks designed in canvas and unnatural in outline and proportions are real, one must will them to be real.

Hoffman, 'Cruel Sufferings of a Stage Director'

Introduction

Some clients or client groups form relationships with dramatic symbols and metaphors quickly and spontaneously. They will be able to create, be aware of and use the richness of the symbol or metaphor. Van Den Bosch reflected this in her research vignette (p. 150) regarding Jilly's use of symbolic objects: 'it was a very powerful connection and quite immediate'. Other clients may create and use symbols within sessions but are developmentally unable to reflect and use them. For others, the emphasis in dramatherapy would usually be upon concrete and reality-based drama, rather than the exploration of metaphoric or symbolic aspects of enactment. For some clients it is necessary to introduce them to the way in which dramatic symbols and metaphors can be expressed and worked with in dramatherapy. The formation and expression of a symbol or metaphor within dramatherapy involves a particular kind of relationship with the material presented by the client. Langley referred to the ideas presented in the first edition of this book on symbol and metaphor in a way that lies at the heart of clients' vital involvement in acting. She says that within the dramatherapy space clients experience an enacted, metaphoric or symbolic reality:

> Bolton . . . describes the experience of 'it is happening to me now' as a function of dramatic play (1979: 54). Certainly the 'as if' factor is paramount in both dramatherapy and psychodrama . . . The use of a stage area indicates the presence of an audience, and with it the application of . . . a 'suspension of disbelief' (Jones 1996: 44) . . . the audience knows the events in the story being presented on stage are not really happening

in the here and now, yet are able to believe in them as if they were. The performance is real and happening at the moment.

(Langley 1998: 265)

Dramatherapy enables the creation of a symbolic and metaphoric reality that clients can explore. The symbolic and metaphoric world created can have an intimate relationship to the issues they bring to therapy. The dramatic form enables the expression and exploration of issues.

This chapter aims to describe this special relationship and to look at how it can assist the therapeutic processes within dramatherapy. Two vignettes follow which demonstrate the therapeutic potentials of metaphor and symbol in dramatherapy. The first indicates how the expressive use of dramatic metaphor can create a particular way of relating to problematic issues from life within therapy.

Vignette: The prince in the tower

The dramatherapy group took place over a two-year period at a day centre for young adults who were autistic. The group met once every week and consisted of one dramatherapist, an assistant and, initially, three young adults. The clients manifested many of the features often ascribed to autistic people, including hands being drawn up to cover the face, engagement in forms of ritualistic behaviour and resistance to any form of communication. Eye contact was limited and there was little voluntary verbal communication. Any change in the environment was experienced as extremely distressing and threatening. Having worked with and observed the clients prior to the group, I had noticed an insistence on maintaining an existing state. On one level, if a chair was not in the identical position to the one it was usually in, a client might need to put it back. On another level, if the usual progress of a day or a client's living conditions was disrupted this could result in extreme distress. Clients might self-mutilate or physically attack those around them.

The client I will focus on, Thomas, had many of the above traits. He would, for example, insist verbally on an unchanged situation when change had occurred. He would repeat over and over that a situation had not changed by listing the elements or factors around him which involved the change. When he had come to some level of acceptance in relation to the alteration, then he would list, in a similar fashion, the elements involved in the new situation. He also often withdrew from contact with people. He showed emotional affect from events in his life, such as the changing of some important component, but would not refer directly to his involvement or to any emotion.

Whilst reference to daily occurrences such as eating or day centre activities was allowed, any reference to more immediately personal matters was not permitted. Any question or reference would be met with blocking – no overt recognition that any communication had happened. This took the form of running away, covering eyes, ears or nose whilst humming, rocking, repeatedly jumping high in the air, or self-mutilation such as biting.

One of the key difficulties experienced by the individuals was that, although they were clearly distressed by events in their lives, there was no apparent way that they could communicate about any experienced problem. In discussion with staff and parents a decision was made to run a dramatherapy group which aimed to try to find a way to help the expression and exploration of difficult situations.

Two main questions emerged. The first concerned how to establish some sense of relation for individuals who seemed to exist largely in a world where relations were denied, avoided or, when present, were surrounded by difficulties. The second involved how to establish a contact, a method of communication or expression for the clients.

My aim was to see if it was possible to use the metaphoric value of story work. I wanted to see whether it would be possible to establish a metaphoric relationship between Thomas's inner experience and the outer expressions of a story.

As has been documented by authors such as von Franz (1970), Bettelheim (1976), Gersie and King (1990), the form of story can provide a useful framework for therapy. Bettelheim sees the child's desire to hear stories repeatedly as due to the fact that in the 'fairytale internal processes are externalised and become comprehensible' (1976: 27). Both von Franz and Gersie and King describe how, for adults and children alike, stories can be used within therapy for their symbolic and metaphoric value. Using this approach the characters, events, scenery and scenarios become charged with symbolic and metaphoric meaning for the client.

The potential of this approach for this particular client group was in two main areas. First, the metaphoric language (characters, story events) would mean that clients could deal with personal material without having to talk about themselves directly. Second, by acting the stories the participation would rely on physical and visual expression rather than upon the spoken word alone.

During an assessment period, the story vocabulary to which the individuals already had access was established. Assessment also considered the degree of capability group members had in order to construct and enact stories. In addition, it was important to discover the extent to which clients could make connection between the story images and the problems they encountered in their lives.

The work had three stages to it. The first consisted of developing the story vocabulary of the group. It emerged that they knew a few stories, but it was felt that a wider vocabulary would assist the range from which clients could choose to reflect inner emotional states. In addition, due to the lack of verbal skills in the group, we wanted to find a method of storytelling which did not rely on words. To develop the vocabulary and to find a way to tell stories, we devised a series of story cards. These consisted of images of characters, events, scenarios and objects. Clients also made their own images from these stories (see Plates 10.1–10.3).

The second stage consisted of group members creating their own images for story cards, creating their own sequences of images into a short story and then acting them out. At first these were simple: a

Plate 10.1 Sleeping Beauty

Plate 10.2 Open the Door for You Mother Said the Wolf.

Plate 10.3 The Bird from Tree to Tree.

prince who met another prince, for example. Another story was of a bird which flew from a tree to another tree (see Plate 10.3). As the group became more familiar with the approach, the stories became more complex and a move from stereotyped, repeated actions to more individual representations occurred. Images, characters and events from the original stories became transformed into a personal story language. The following story was made by a series of drawn images. The client then made simple statements about what was happening and completed a simple enactment of the story with the group. The story demonstrates this process: it is from the ninth month of the work. The client first created the story cards, then, by answering questions from the dramatherapist, clarified what was happening. This was followed by a brief enactment of the tale. The story shows traces of *Sleeping Beauty, Rapunzel* and the *Three Little Pigs*.

> The story is about a prince. He wants a home. The house and the tower belonged to the witch. The witch was in the house. The prince was in the tower. The prince wanted to find a house outside. The prince in the tower would be happy when he was dead. The prince could get out of the tower if he hit the witch. When the witch came to the tower he hit and killed her and got out. The prince went into the witch's house. He went back to the house and they went for a walk.

It was not possible, for reasons made clear above, to reflect upon personal connections at the end of sessions. At the close clients were taken out of the roles of any characters they'd played, the cards were put away and a simple physical closure exercise was completed. However, in the story related above, it is possible to see that story elements are not only being adapted, but could also be expressing feelings, inner dilemmas and anxieties. The process outlined above is present in the following story from the same period:

> The story is about a hand – it wanted to be stroked. First mother came to it, she stroked it, but she also nipped it. The hand went to father but he was sawing. He stroked the hand but also gave it a nip. The hand went to the telephone. The telephone stroked the hand and didn't nip it. The hand ate an apple. The hand met a dog. The dog ate the hand.

Themes began to emerge as, week after week, images or scenarios would be returned to. This return to situations started to occur from the end of the first year of the work. The stories contained variants or different treatments of the images or scenarios. I would suggest that this marked not only the discovery of the internal resonances of the story work, but also indicated that the clients were returning to areas of conflict or difficulty which needed attention. The storymaking and enactment was not only a place to make symbolic and metaphoric representations of unconscious material, but was also becoming a place to develop and explore alternatives, to make attempts to resolve and deal with those conflicts. An image and series of stories which were constantly returned to by Thomas came to be called 'The Prince in the Tower' (Plates 10.4–10.6).

For much of the work the story consisted of a prince who stayed

Plate 10.4 The Tower with the Window.

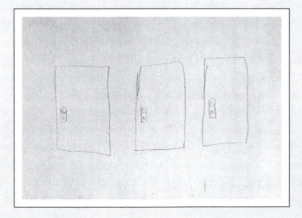

Plate 10.5 The Three Doors in the Tower.

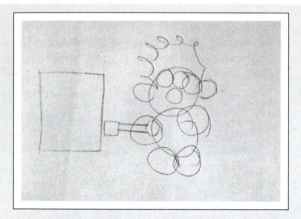

Plate 10.6 The Prince with the Door Key.

in a tower, and narratives usually concerned occurrences within the tower. A long series of stories concerned doors, locks, corridors and rooms within the tower. At first there was no window or door on the outside. Gradually, a window shape appeared behind the bricks and a window and door emerged (see Plates 10.4 and 10.5). The tower became populated with images, objects and incidents (Plate 10.6):

> The Prince is walking in a corridor. He has a key in his hand. He reaches the doors. He looks through the keyholes. The first is a dining room. There's nothing inside except a pile of knives and forks. In the second is a large bed, wardrobe and a table. In the third is a witch.

It became clear that these images were metaphoric. By this I mean that connections were being made by the clients with their lives. However, these were not directly, verbally acknowledged. Thomas was able to use the stories to look at themes and problems in his life. As the day centre was in contact with Thomas's parents we knew that themes from the individual's life were present and that the story alternatives seemed to be a way of talking about things which were not usually permitted by Thomas.

One example of this is the story of 'The Two Princes'. We knew that Thomas's brother was going to leave home. As said earlier, any change in the client's life situation was experienced as extremely distressing. His parents had alerted us to this, as on previous occasions when change had occurred Thomas had manifested a great deal of physical distress. At the same time, the prince in the tower was joined by a second prince. For a while the stories involved the princes staying together in the tower. They then went out of the tower together, one prince going on long journeys, returning to the tower. If there were any doubts in our minds about the connections which Thomas was making they were dispelled when during a dramatherapy group he momentarily referred to the other prince by his brother's name.

Thomas was not able to discuss the situation or problem concerning his brother directly. However, he seemed to be able to alleviate his anxiety by first expressing his desire that his brother should stay, then experimenting with letting his brother go, whilst reassuring himself that his brother would return. The parents reported that the distress they expected did not manifest itself to the extent they had anticipated. This could be taken as some indication that the dramatherapy group allowed Thomas to explore and express himself through metaphor and that this helped to alleviate some of his distress.

CORE PROCESS BOX

Dramatic projection

Through the creation of the images and stories Thomas is able to externalise his preoccupations and anxieties. They enable him to express and explore issues, to try to communicate them and to resolve some of the dilemmas he faces.

Distance

Because of his disability, Thomas was not able to refer directly to himself and his emotions. The images and story improvisations provided a way of creating enough distance for him to feel that he was not exposed or 'seen'.

Life–drama connection

For Thomas there seems to be no need to cognitively acknowledge the connections between the stories and his actual situation at home. Indeed, this would have been countertherapeutic, as Thomas seemed to become extremely distressed and agitated when saying 'I', or referring to life experiences directly. However, it seems as if the return to the

> stories enabled him to express his distress, and to seek some reassurance from communicating and replaying the 'brother' prince returning home. He would not, in his life outside the therapy or within the therapy room, have been able to tolerate direct reference to the situation. Hence the drama provided an oblique rather than a direct way of connecting to life experiences.

A basic process relating to the use of dramatic metaphors in dramatherapy underpins this work with Thomas. The first stage involves discovering the world of images, both verbal and dramatic, which the client or clients use or can use. Eco (1984) calls this an 'encyclopedia of reference' that someone draws upon in making a symbol or metaphor.

For the purposes of dramatherapy it is crucial to discover whether the client can connect the images to themselves, to see whether they can make personal metaphors. In the vignette this concerned whether Thomas could make the connection between the tower and himself, for example. One of the central metaphoric connections for Thomas involved the tower and himself – the metaphoric connection was that they were both 'locked in'. The other involved his brother and the second prince, the metaphoric connection being that they were both 'leaving'. Figure 10.1 summarises the metaphoric process.

The next stage involves the use of the connections made within the metaphor to explore a situation. In Thomas's case the exploration took the form of stories. These were drawn and enacted, enabling him to express and look at repressed feelings. The therapeutic effect of the metaphor lay in the way it permitted the release and expression of feelings which were repressed and censored within usual communication. As an alternative mode of relating to and describing an experience, the dramatic metaphor enabled release and change to occur.

The final stage involved the connection of the metaphoric exploration to the life situation. With Thomas this did not happen through conscious insight expressed within the dramatherapy session. There is, as described above,

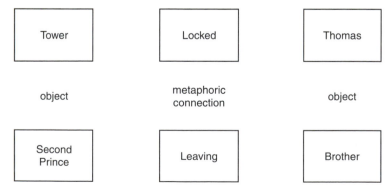

Figure 10.1 The Prince in the Tower: two dramatic metaphors.

some evidence to indicate that this was occurring for him as shown in his verbal 'slip' and in the response to the departure of his brother in real life.

The vignette involving Thomas related to dramatic metaphors within dramatherapy. The next vignette illustrates the way a dramatic symbol can be worked with in exploring a problem.

Vignette: Barbed wire circle

In a dramatherapy session within a psychiatric day centre George was making a sculpt concerning his feelings in the group. The dramatherapy part of an arts therapies programme was running as a closed group and was in its sixth week. Over the previous weeks I had established that the group as a whole was familiar with drama as a medium and able to use complex dramatic forms. Symbols and metaphors were used naturally by the group in working with individuals' experiences and in looking at the dynamics of the group.

George had sat out of many activities within the first five weeks of the group, but had said that he wanted to show us his feelings soon after the sixth group had started. The group had begun in silence, as was the custom, and people had started to talk about their feelings about working together. George took each group member and sculpted them in a circle. He put himself in the centre of this circle and placed me outside, some distance from the circle. I was placed looking towards the circle and George was looking out towards me. He then doubled each aspect of the sculpt, saying that the circle was made of barbed wire, that I wanted to get in, and that he wanted to get a rifle and shoot at me to keep me away.

I encouraged George to explore this, first by free associating with the feelings he had within the circle and then exploring the feelings, briefly taking on the roles of 'the barbed wire' and 'the person on the outside of the circle'. We then looked at whether the symbol and the feelings it contained had any associations or connections for him from other aspects of his life, his past.

He was able to discover a number of meanings in the circle. It brought back memories of his relationships with his father and with his lover, Andrew. He also made connections with the symbol as a representation of different parts of himself in a struggle. One part of himself within the circle wanted to stay isolated, alone. The circle represented the 'ill state', as he called it. The person on the outside represented the part of himself that was well and scared of the ill part of him with the gun.

George selected one area to focus upon. He chose the circle structure as a representation of the internal battle between parts of himself. By becoming the different parts of the sculpt – the ill part inside, the healthy part outside, the circle barrier and the gun – he was able to develop the exploration of his dilemma. I invited the different parts of the sculpt to enter into dialogue with each other – for the George within the circle to talk to the George outside, for the barrier to have a voice.

Group members also doubled for George when he was playing the different parts. For example, whilst George was playing the 'ill George', saying that he didn't want contact, that he wished to stay inside and would shoot the 'well George', one of the group doubled him in this role saying simply, 'It's safe here, I know what it's like. I don't want to move.' Another immediately doubled, saying, 'I need your help but I don't know how to say this to you.' George accepted both of these doubling statements.

After exploring the different parts of the symbol I asked George to step outside the sculpt and to think of anything he'd like to say to any of the parts of the sculpt. I invited him to address any specific aspects such as the barrier or either 'George' directly. He did so, expressing a wish that the barrier might have a door in it saying to the gun that it could be put down but not disposed of, and that the 'well' George should extend his arm and hand to the inner George. I asked for a new sculpt to be made reflecting these messages and we explored it as we had done the original sculpt.

At the close George and the group members in the sculpt de-roled by physically leaving the stage area, stating their identities and discussing what it was like to be in the sculpt. George and other group members talked about issues that the sculpt had raised for them, connections they had made with the symbol.

CORE PROCESS BOX

Dramatic projection

The symbol of the circle which George brought to the group was used by him to explore a number of significances. When originally creating the sculpt George had a specific attached meaning in mind: it was an image representing his feelings in the group. As the circle was a symbolic expression made by George, it was loaded with a number of other possible significances. By identifying other possible meanings and personal connections George was able to have access to the potential of the symbolic nature of the sculpt. By a way of working akin to a dramatic free association, he was able to see parallel or repressed relationships and issues present within the original sculpted circle. Once these repressed feelings and associations were acknowledged, the symbol proved a way of working with the associations. Its specific meaning changed from being a sculpt to represent the group to a sculpt representing an internal struggle within George. The dramatic symbol could contain both situations.

Embodiment

Through embodying and playing the part of different aspects of the sculpted symbols George was able to connect with the internal personal struggle. He was also able to consider a way of changing his relationship with the problematic aspects of the struggle. In addition the symbol helped George to try out what it might feel like to make the change. He did this by entering the changed sculpt and experiencing what each part felt like once the change had been made.

The work described did not aim to achieve immediate change regarding George's situation. Rather, it offered him the opportunity to deal with a part of a problem. The symbol produced many other resonances which George could go on to explore. The symbol itself and the work we did with it in the session marked a part of an ongoing process. The symbol and the themes it raised were worked on by George for the rest of the therapy.

Symbols and metaphors in dramatherapy

The symbol: a nebula of meaning

In certain theatrical traditions, such as Kabuki, the twitch of a mouth or a gesture of a hand have deliberate symbolic significance. The bodily movements and positions function primarily as symbolic signs with deliberate codes of interpretation. So, for example, a movement of the eyes would symbolise 'the moon'. One way a symbol can function, then, is as a form which represents something else. It need not have any physical resemblance to the thing it represents. A symbol can also represent a complex idea or concept: Christ symbolising compassion or the hammer and sickle symbolising communism, for example.

Symbols can also function in a more oblique way. For Jung (1959) a symbol has many potential clusters of meaning and to try to select one as final or definitive is to misunderstand the potency of the symbol. As Eco observes, the content of the symbol is a 'nebula of possible interpretations'. The symbol says that there is something that it could say, 'but this something cannot be definitely spelled out once and for all; otherwise the symbol would stop saying it' (1984: 161).

For Freud and Jung the unconscious and dreams are rich sources of symbols that can be used by individuals to gain insight into trauma or distress within analysis. Freud's influential *The Interpretation of Dreams* (1900) centres around processes of symbolic representation. As Jones has said, within Freudian thinking 'a symbol is a manifest expression for an idea that is more or less hidden, secret, kept in reserve' (Jones 1919). Miller sees the symbol as crucial to the way our unconscious mind relates to the outer world. It represents 'a sort of courier service which passes between the carriers of the internal fantasy life of the mind, and all that goes on out there' (Miller 1983: 266). So in psychotherapy the symbol is something which is expressed unconsciously, through a dream or free association or through a painting. This is seen as a communication concerning a repressed trauma or problem. The act of psychotherapy involves trying to clarify this communication and by this process the client achieves insight, which leads to therapeutic change.

Dramatherapy acknowledges the wide variety of potentials which the symbol or symbolic ways of relating offer in therapy. The symbol might be used to create and express issues. A dragon seen across a ravine within a session might come to represent a number of important meanings for a client, or for clients within a group. The opportunity to develop symbolisation within a therapy group for someone with a learning disability might have important consequences on the way they are able to relate to and understand the world. Karkou and Sanderson summarise this in a succinct manner:

> In the case of symbol formation, Jones (1996) claims that the process can be intentional or spontaneous. In the first case (i.e. intentional creation of symbols), a forest might be chosen by a dramatherapy group as a symbol to be explored in terms of discovering the role of each individual within this group. In the second case (i.e. spontaneous creation) a forest might be part of a dramatherapy enactment that eventually acquires symbolic meaning beyond its original insubstantial function as merely a component of a story.
>
> (Karkou and Sanderson 2005: 57–58)

As the research vignettes later in this chapter will show, the symbolic connection between the world of drama and the real world is crucial to the efficacy of much dramatherapy.

The metaphor: from one object to another

Linguistically the metaphor involves the bringing together of two different objects or subjects which have a particular contact in common. One is spoken of in terms of the other, as if it actually *was* the other. For example; 'My daughter is a butterfly in everything she does.' Here we are not to believe that the daughter actually is a butterfly. The statement powerfully brings together qualities of the daughter and the butterfly. One thing is spoken of *as if it is* another. The making of a metaphor acknowledges that one thing has important connections with another. The qualities of the daughter and the qualities of a butterfly are brought together so that the butterfly-like aspects of the daughter are highlighted. The reason a metaphor can be made to link these two different subjects is that they have a 'metaphoric connection' – a common quality, which in the example is the state of being unsettled.

A metaphor brings together two 'objects' and says that they are one. The two objects or subjects can be quite different from each other, but are linked through the metaphoric connection (see Figure 10.2).

Within therapy metaphors are introduced as a way into a closed situation. Often, if a client is blocked in thinking about a situation or problem, a metaphor is introduced. A family might be asked to name their familial roles as if they were kinds of creature. Skynner (1976) gives an example where the relationship between a woman and himself as therapist was illuminated by her use of the metaphor of his being a 'sea anemone'. This enabled her to talk about contradictory experiences of him, first as a warm comfortable person 'who made people trust me, but then I suddenly stung them, pulled their insides out and spat them out again' (Skynner 1976: 343). The use and exploration of the metaphor helped both therapist and client to understand the dynamics of the therapy. Langley (1998) develops the ideas about metaphor contained within the analysis in the first edition of this book by connecting it to the ideas of Jaynes:

> Jones states that it is the common quality that links the two (Jones 1996: 222). Jaynes suggests that the metaphor is a means of understanding the unfamiliar by substituting something that is familiar (Jaynes 1990: 52). He says that we create images that do not really exist in order to explain the inexplicable, and gain a sense of understanding.
>
> (Langley 1998: 264)

In this way, if something cannot be talked about directly then it may be possible to talk about it through metaphor. The distance from the original

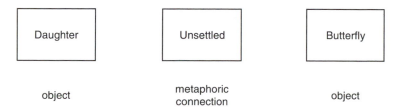

Figure 10.2 The metaphoric connection.

object created by the use of metaphor helps the client to talk about something they wouldn't be able to do directly.

Within dramatherapy the creation of dramatic metaphors performs similar functions. They allow a new perception to be brought into the therapy and can permit access to material which would not usually be allowed.

Dramatherapy practice and the connected world

In dramatherapy the therapeutic potential of symbols and metaphors is connected to dramatic scenarios – stories, improvisations, object play. It is through the scenarios that the value of the symbol or metaphor is developed. The following research vignettes illustrate ways of exploring the 'connected world' of symbol, metaphor and a client's life experiences. They demonstrate how clients can express and work with material through symbols and metaphors in dramatherapy's use of story, play, role and embodiment.

The first research vignette illustrates how play and playfulness need not only be the province of children, and the profundity of the world that can be created within the symbols and metaphors engendered by play activity. The comparative safety of playful expression through symbolic and metaphoric images compared to direct reference to real life is shown here as an essential part of the client creating access to extremely difficult material. It also illustrates how trust develops between dramatherapist and client within the playful space. Dramatherapist Ruth Goodman describes the background to a client, Bilal, in the following way:

> Bilal, a 27-year-old Somalian man, had come to the UK about three years prior to his admission. He was arrested and put into prison following a violent altercation with his landlord whom Bilal believed had committed a sexual assault on him while he was in bed asleep.
>
> In prison he suffered from severe depression and a belief that he had also been raped by his cell mate. He made a suicide attempt through hanging. Psychological assessments suggested Bilal was suffering from paranoid psychosis and the possibility of post traumatic symptoms relating to his experience of torture in Somalia. He was admitted to hospital where he attacked a member of staff, accusing him of sexually assaulting him by rape. He also experienced auditory hallucinations and flashbacks of himself being beaten and tortured.
>
> Bilal was born into a minority tribe in a small village in southern Somalia. He said that larger, more powerful tribes frequently persecuted his community during the political conflicts in his country. Frequent raids on his village by 'the rebels' resulted in houses being burnt, property taken away and people being tortured. In one such incident his father was badly beaten and soon afterwards died from his injuries. His mother and sisters were sexually assaulted and his own life was threatened. Bilal fled to Kenya, taking shelter in a refugee camp. He then undertook various

jobs until he had saved up enough money to pay for the necessary documents to come to the UK. On arrival in England he claimed political asylum and was given hostel accommodation. He enrolled on college courses and took part-time jobs, determined to make a success of his new life. But Bilal remained estranged from his family, not knowing whether they were alive or dead.'

The vignette is from a session that took place a few months into the work. Goodman says of her initial work:

My first impression of Bilal was of polite acquiescence, head held low with nervous eyes that peered at me through a fringe of heavy dreadlocks. He was evidently deeply troubled and was distrustful of staff, maintaining his belief that a male nurse had sexually abused him. His perceived sense of violation and recurring traumatic flashbacks suggested to me that here was a story urgently needing to be told.

The early dramatherapy sessions involved an introductory exploration of movement, work using objects, sculpts and image making. The 'encyclopedia' of reference was created between Goodman and Bilal exchanging a range of images, symbols and metaphoric material to draw on:

Most importantly we used story work, creating imaginary stories and working with the themes and metaphors within traditional stories that I brought in. In return Bilal related to me stories that he remembered from his childhood, of Islamic prophets and parables from the Koran. The story work encouraged the use of metaphoric language and provided a containing framework to help prepare him for the telling of his own story.

Research vignette: Bilal

Bilal arrived on time and asked if he could use the objects. He carefully made a line of animals all facing the same way. He then made another line of animals facing opposite the first line. He pointed to the first line. 'These are the meat eaters' and to the opposite line, 'These are non-meat eaters.' He then categorised them into those who were friendly to humans and those who were not. I asked him if he could create a story from the objects, prompting him with occasional questions.

'One day,' he began, 'the sheep wanders off from the herd to find water. When the sheep is drinking the water, it is attacked by a crocodile.'

'Who can help?' I ask.

'A man with a spear who can kill or chase the crocodile away.'

'What might prevent him rescuing the sheep?' I ask.

'He does not have a weapon,' he replied.

'So what will happen?' I ask.

'The only way is for them all to keep together so the shepherd can keep his eye on all the flock.'

We reflected on the story together. 'Leaving the herd makes you vulnerable to attack,' I commented. He nodded.

'I wasn't armed,' he said. 'I was defenceless, but if I'd had a weapon they would have killed me too.'

We began to talk about fear, his fear for his own life and his fear for his family that he had left behind. He also talked about his fear of telling his story, that in recalling events he might be retraumatised, provoking a relapse. I too acknowledged this concern, but I also reflected on the fear of *not* telling, of the memories and feelings that he carried alone and that might remain unheard.

Bilal became very thoughtful and said he would like to tell me his story. I would write down his words verbatim as a form of testimony. He told of being held at gunpoint while his father was beaten and his sister and mother were sexually abused. He heard their cries but was unable to intervene. When he had finished I read his words back to him. He looked tearful, shook his head and said, 'It's heartbreaking.' He talked of the guilt he felt being unable to protect his family, of his intense feelings of powerlessness and anger. I acknowledged with him his helplessness in the face of such an attack and we sat together for a long time in silence.

Ruth Goodman

Goodman comments on the core processes at work within the practice in a way that illustrates an interesting and crucial aspect of witnessing and distancing, different from that originally contained in the core processes chapter:

This somewhat unusual formal approach of taking testimony from the patient and then delivering it back enables a distance which, paradoxically, allows the patient a closer emotional identification with the material. The process became a significant aspect of our work together. It was as if, through this enactment, we were engaged in a parallel process of witnessing. I witnessed his story that was intrinsically about him having to be a witness – a witness to the atrocities committed on his family. I became the container for his story and in the dramatisation took on his role, recounting his story verbatim, in the first person.

In the process of reading back, Bilal then became a witness to his own story, but from a distance. The distancing provided a safe space for him to recognise aspects of his experience as if for the first time. He was also able to acknowledge some of the painful feelings that he had been carrying. For example, 'It's heartbreaking' was a compassionate response to his own story and allowed us both to feel the enormity of the horrors he had witnessed. In the silence that followed it felt that a bridge had been created between his world and my own. It was also the beginning of an acknowledgement of the extent of his losses and of his need to grieve.

CORE PROCESS BOX

Dramatic projection

The client projects aspects of their feelings and experience into the animals. They become an expression and a container for material which cannot be expressed directly.

Play and playfulness

The client uses the safety of the play space to express material and to represent it in a safe way. The client uses small object play as a safe way to express aspects of his life which may feel overpowering. By using small world representation of these areas he can express them in a manageable way. In addition it becomes a way of beginning to tell his story in an indirect manner. Once the safety of the play space and the relationship with the therapist have been tested this enables the client to begin to tell more of their story to the therapist.

Witnessing

The therapist becomes a witness to the client's experiences initially through being shown the animals and images, and then through the direct telling of life events by Bilal. In turn Bilal is being a witness to his own life experiences – first through the animals being external representations of his life, and then through listening to the reading or performance of his story read out by Goodman.

Research conversation with Ruth Goodman

Goodman: I think Bilal was testing the space as well me. The relationship developed through the gradual way we learned to play together and, indeed, laugh together. I tried hard to afford him respect, particularly for his determination to survive. He was filled with guilt about abandoning his family and I tried to help him recognise that he had a right to save himself.

Jones: I'm really interested in your bringing space, relationship and learning to play together in your answer. You talk about him being 'filled with guilt' and in your vignette you talk about his fear of 'telling his story', of putting his story out into the space and into his relationship with you. You talk about his use of objects to begin to 'tell.' Do you think the objects played a particular role in this change? In your vignette you seem to suggest it was a key moment in his telling?

Goodman: I believe the 'playful' use of objects certainly helped him externalise some painful material. In the spontaneity of the play and in the subsequent story he created, unconscious themes emerged. We worked with the metaphors in his story and then after my comment about leaving the herd there was recognition of a convergence between the created story and his real life story. I think it was also a significant moment of change in that Bilal began to have more of an understanding and respect for the process of play which enabled us to work more fluidly in the future.

Jones: I was very moved by your taking (what felt like for me – did it for you?) the risk to say that; to make your comment that you felt created a 'convergence'. In a way I'm wondering whether, in the story within your vignette and within your relationship to Bilal's story, you shifted from being a witness/listener to a witness/co-creator of meaning for him?

Goodman: I think essentially therapy is about the presence of a willing witness/listener. It is also a continuous creative process of trying to find meaning through and within the therapeutic relationship. The connections made between Bilal and myself enabled him to begin to reconnect with dislocated parts of himself, his feelings and experiences. The wonderful thing about dramatherapy is that as well as being witnesses we can also be co-creators, playmates, and engage creatively with whatever roles we are cast into or choose to play for a particular purpose. When someone has been traumatised, the recovery of meaning can take a long time. I believe that although my role was to help Bilal find meaning in his story, it was fundamentally to stay alongside him through the processes of telling and all the complex feelings that emerged.

Sarah Mann-Shaw's work with Kia took the form of individual dramatherapy and was self-referred to private practice. It illustrates how symbolic and metaphoric work can relate to role and embodiment in dramatherapy practice. Mann describes her client as 'a white European woman in her late twenties. Kia had experienced developmental trauma and felt that the impact of this was affecting her current relationship with herself and her partner. She said she wanted to live in spite of this trauma and not because of it.'

Mann-Shaw says that they worked with various dramatherapy structures during their 38 sessions together but the one which 'held as a common theme and which most enabled Kia to support herself in a different way was the creation of a landscape and the character which lived within it'. The research vignette exemplifies aspects of working with symbolic material in dramatherapy.

Research vignette: Kia

The landscape came from a poem which Kia brought to therapy. She explored the feelings it engendered in her: despair, death, foolishness and failure and also the contrasting feelings of hope, life, laughter and trying. From this engagement Kia spent the next few sessions creating a huge painted and collaged landscape, which I witnessed. As the landscape took shape I encouraged her to tell me its story. It was split into two definite sides. On one side there was a huge slate cliff with barren trees and a dark and dangerous cave which often flooded. This place held memories of pain and tension and a large and powerful waterfall separated it from a more gentle and containing landscape. On this side the water followed more gently and within the hills there were caves to keep a character (which we had yet to meet) safe and dry. These caves also kept the character hidden, as he or she did not like to be seen by people. On the edge of the landscape there was an area of wasteland which the character often visited. It was dirty and barren, and the water could seep into it and obliterate it. She made reference to this being like her childhood. Over the top of a landscape she created a yellow and pink sky which she said held hope.

We reflected on the creation of the story landscape and Kia said that although it contained despair and fear what she was able to clearly see was the potential for movement and hope. She felt excited by the landscape and by the prospect of meeting the character who lived it in. She felt that the character was currently hiding but that it was prepared to let itself be seen by Kia and she was excited by the story it had to tell.

As Kia's dramatherapist my role during the creation of this landscape was to act as witness, to acknowledge and support Kia's role as set designer as she created a symbolic space for the theatre of her character. My second role was to be curious about the creation of the set and its ability to contain the polarity of feelings worked on from the initial poem. The landscape/set needed to contain both the hope and the despair and the potential for movement from one space to the other.

As the dramatherapist I was also excited by the potential of this landscape and the character within. I was curious to know how Kia's relationship with this character might develop in terms of identification and projection. I felt that engagement with the character through dramatic projection may enable Kia to be expressive about her internal world. I was excited by the possibility of the story waiting to be told and that it might inspire a new way of being for Kia.

As Kia created her landscape, we talked about who might live in it, so even before the character was embodied Kia had a sense of who would inhabit this world she had created. Kia knew that the character was young and that she was fearful, that she lived in the gentle containing side of the landscape and rarely visited the cave of despair. Kia knew that the character had a level of self-sufficiency because it had to have and that it did not like the wasteland. She also knew that the character had spirit.

I asked where the character's safe place might be in the landscape and Kia created two caves high above the water level and deep in the cliffs where her character could live and sleep in safety. Having spent time exploring Kia's sense of this character, I asked how she might like to bring this character into creation, how she might create a dramatic body for it. Kia explored the therapy space and chose to create the character from pink foam. She spent time creating a limbed and jointed small figure which she then decided was too clean and so covered her in a sandy mixture so that she looked dirty and unwashed. Kia created her character with a level of tender attentiveness and as dramatherapist I witnessed this developing relationship and was curious about its identity.

Partially in response to my enquiry, partially because of her developing relationship with this character, Kia was clear that this creature had no clear gender identity and that it was named 'Scampers'. The choice of name reflected the way it moved around the landscape, which Kia showed me by operating this small puppet and demonstrating how it darted in and out of different parts of the landscape before settling into the safety of the cave.

Kia had now created a dramatic set and its central character. In the sessions that followed she created Scampers' wise helpers.

The central character's developing relationship with these wise figures enabled it to journey into a different landscape and to create a rich and vibrant ritual which enabled Scampers to fully embrace and recognise her female identity.

Kia's work on set, story, role, character and dramatic projection enabled her to engage in the reason she first came to dramatherapy with a level of aesthetic distance. We did not work interpretively, because to do so would have missed the richness and potency of the dramatic metaphor. The last time I saw Kia she was able to tell me how well and happy she was and how she was now able to fully embrace her own female identity.

Sarah Mann-Shaw

CORE PROCESS BOX

Dramatic projection

The client selects a poem, and from this springs the symbolic world she creates. The features of the landscape take on a symbolic significance, holding different meanings and significances at different times, holding 'memories of pain' or 'being like her childhood'. The client is able to project different aspects of herself and experience into the dramatic images and interactions, to explore them through the landscape and character and to integrate them back into her life.

Witnessing

At times the client becomes a witness to the symbolic world she has created. She becomes a viewer of her internal world, its split sides, and through developing a reflective relationship with it gains insight. Mann describes herself as 'witnessing' the material and inviting the stories to emerge.

Transformation

By creating and entering into the world she takes elements which are expressed and transformed through the connection between aspect of herself and the image. The creation of the hidden cave says something about a part of herself, but by meeting the character she transforms the relationship from one of being hidden and unknown to one where contact occurs and it becomes 'known'. This transformation enables Kia to express herself.

Research conversation with Sarah Mann-Shaw

Mann-Shaw: I felt that the move into the creation of a landscape, a dramatic set, would enable containment and dramatic projection of Kia's internal process on and into an external space. I was hopeful that this would enable Kia to engage with exploring the issues which had brought her into therapy with a level of dramatic distance. The time spent in, and with, the landscape and the characters enabled Kia to move significantly. Her engagement with the symbolic representation of those initial words and feelings really shifted Kia (she said). She began to feel more rooted, stronger, more empowered. She was kinder with herself and this change was also represented in the change in the central character who underwent a significant ritual of change and renewal, of fully stepping into her identity, of embracing it and having it witnessed and affirmed by others. You have, perhaps, noted that I now use the pronoun 'she' in reference to this central character rather than the initial ambiguous 'it'. This change from 'it' to 'she' was as a direct result of the ritual which took place.

Jones: You talk about 'her own creative potential' and your affirmation of that. You say as well that she became a 'narrator' – her 'ability' to do this was strengthened, and she was also gaining a sense of 'what the characters might do next'. So are you saying that witnessing actually helped develop those parts of her, and do you see that as something that transferred to her sense of her own development/her life outside?

Mann-Shaw: Yes, I do. Kia would also, in some sessions, spend time talking about life and relationships outside of therapy. What she noticed in herself, as the therapy progressed, was a real ability to hold her own space and to hold saying *no* to those relationships which had previously been unsupportive. She noted that she felt more rooted in her body and in therapy was able to embody some really powerful sculpts which seemed also to enable her to know her own ability and strength outside of therapy. I think that the movement between therapy and life was pretty transparent and therapy enabled her to make different life choices which were then reflected on in the therapy space. Kia's reflection on therapy was that it had been an immensely healing and had enabled parts of her to be resettled in a more appropriate order.

Jones: Okay, and in response to this last comment from you I'm just thinking of your words 'stepping into her identity' and 'having it witnessed and affirmed by others' – very physical this stepping, being seen. In the vignette you talk about creating this 'dramatic body' and of embodiment. How do you see this physicalising – embodying as a process?

Mann-Shaw: The physicalising of stepping into her identity was done through the character which was initially represented by a small doll that Kia had made. The process of being witnessed was again done through this character and through the symbolic creation of a host of other characters to witness and affirm this life-changing moment of the character. Kia involved herself in this ritual through her narration of it, and through her engagement with the central character whom she held and moved through the ritual with a great deal of care and gentleness. It was essential for this dramatic relationship to evolve from the set at the beginning, because it was through this process that we could engage with dramatic dialogue and movement. Kia did some embodying work through sculpting – playing parts of the landscape – which seemed to parallel the change in the character in the landscape itself. It was almost as if there was a symbiotic relationship. As one felt more rooted and explored strength, so did the other. I think towards the end of our initial aMSN conversation I was thinking about this need to sculpt and embody different positions. To have just stayed with the set might have been a very static experience for Kia. It was the dynamic relationship between dramatic projection, distance, witnessing and the central metaphor which I think really enabled Kia to experience movement and integration in herself.

In this work it is important for Kia to be able to explore the symbolic or metaphoric expressions. As the research vignette and conversation indicate, if clients are too rational and interpretive this can block such exploration. The aim should be to find a way for clients to be open to the material which the creation of the symbol or metaphor can yield. In part this is helped by ensuring that the individual or group is adequately warmed up prior to engaging with the metaphor or symbol. In part this can also be assisted by the therapist not forcing meaning or interpretation.

Mann-Shaw allows Kia to develop images and find a relationship to them, making the connection between the images and what they say to her, or what she wants to say to them – the life–drama connection. As this vignette shows, this does not need to be a conscious, verbally articulated process whereby Kia denotes that the wasteland equals a precise aspect of her life. This can be useful at some points for some clients, but it can also be mechanistic and reductive. The therapist and client must find the balance together about the way the client makes the life–drama connection. There are no rules about this. Each case must be dealt with in its own context. In a sense there is a continuum between images that speak directly and whose significance can helpfully be named and those whose meaning lies in a less conscious process.

The way the images work on a symbolic dramatic level allows processes to occur which can be worked with and embodied in a manner that allows meaning to stay within the physical, dramatic images and character. Therapeutic changes and transformations can be experienced without necessarily being cognitively analysed. This helps in the absorption of the symbols or metaphors created.

Connection and assimilation

Within dramatherapy there are a number of positions relating to the ways in which clients can connect with, and assimilate, symbolic and metaphoric material. Jennings (1987) and Mitchell (1992) state that it is not necessary for the client to reflect verbally or analyse the enactment. Their position is that the unconscious connections are made by the client within the drama. They propose that automatic verbal analysis following the work detracts from the process of assimilation by forcing rational dissection on to the experience. However, Dokter (1990) states that it is crucial to allow the unconscious images to become conscious. She suggests that this can only happen through verbal reflection and acknowledgement of the connections between the conscious self and the unconscious images and scenarios in the drama. Within this approach the connections that the clients make verbally and cognitively are crucial to therapeutic change. Some advocate an unstructured time for verbal reflection whilst others advocate structured dramatic and verbal activities to enhance the process of connection (Gersie and King 1990). The role of verbal interpretation made by the dramatherapist within the assimilation process also varies within these ways of working (Dokter 1990: 27; Jennings 1991: 4, 1992: 41).

Within the approach that stays entirely within the drama, the completion of the enactment would be followed by activities designed to de-role participants from roles or characters and to close the session. There would be no emphasis placed on a time to discuss personal connection. The work described in 'The Prince in the Tower' (pp. 247–249) is an example of this method.

Within the approach that advocates verbal and dramatic analysis, a time is left to de-role, followed by structured or unstructured activity. In an unstructured way of working the dramatherapist would allow the group members or individual to discuss their feelings in character, the responses of group members to the roles they played, and their in-role feelings towards others (see Chapter 8). This would include time to discuss any connections or insights they have in relation to their own lives. A structured approach might include specific dramatic exercises and verbal exercises such as symbolic gift giving (Gersie and King 1990: 57), pair reflection and structured sharing (Blatner and Blatner 1988b: 112).

In the following research vignette Christine Novy, in work with women who have come into conflict with the law, describes an aspect of the way connection and assimilation can take place within practice that drew on the symbolic potential of story work.

Research vignette: Beth

In my practice as a dramatherapist I have often been privy to the disempowering effects of 'expert' stories, but I have also, at times, felt ill-equipped to guide the people I work with to choose their own direction and share their own understanding. Because of the frequent gender-blind treatment of women within the criminal justice system, in the Narratives of Change project it was especially important for me to find ways to use my influence respectfully. To assist in the negotiation of meaning I combined dramatic languages from dramatherapy with narrative therapy's 'questioning approach'. I found that narrative therapy preference for questions encouraged a different quality of reflection. Questions like 'Is this a helpful image or not?' followed by an invitation to explain 'Why?' and 'Is it something you would like to explore further?' or 'Are you drawn to something else?' lead to an awareness of choice, both in the participants' experience and storytelling. Narrative therapist White (2004) employs the metaphor of a 'scaffold' to describe the use of questions in narrative therapy which, he explains, make it possible for a person to separate from 'the known and familiar' and to 'arrive at new conclusions' about their life and identity (p.60). I found similarities between the use of questions in narrative therapy and Jones' description of de-roling in dramatherapy (1996: 27–30).

The participants had created characters based on an exploration of their bodies' experience and they were now ready to give voice to this experience. Opportunities to share and listen to each other's stories were especially valued by all the participants. To further this experience of collaborative storytelling I provided interview guidelines which the group used as a script to interview each other in role. During the interview Beth spoke through her character Welcome Freedom about her preferred ways of living and relating in life. She spoke about her preference for a healthy environment and about her appreciation of sports like walking and cycling that enabled her to relax and breathe better. She also described how she took care of her body and how free she felt, now that she was no longer a prisoner of her thoughts and having worked on her problems. Following the interview I asked Beth, still in role as Welcome Freedom, to speak about her interview experience. She said that she had felt inspired. I then invited her to de-role, first by taking off a costume she had created for her character, and then by reflecting on her in-role experience. Beth explained that playing Welcome Freedom had projected her into the future she wants. She added that she wasn't quite there yet, but that the words she had chosen to describe a 'sort of freedom and well-being' were true to what she hoped to achieve one day.

It had been important for me to find ways to guide the women participants to choose their own direction and to share their own understanding about their lives and identities. The de-roling questions and structure provided helpful scaffolding that assisted me to remain decentred while at the same time influential in the negotiation of meaning with Beth. As she explained, these were her words and her evaluation of her preferred life.

CORE PROCESS BOX

Role

By creating roles, clients are able to identify and explore aspects of themselves. These roles help them to find a symbolic language to express and explore issues about their sense of self along with issues and needs about themselves and their future. The role creation is not only a way of analysing their lives, but also becomes a way to engage creatively with issues they would like to explore. The de-roling is used to help develop reflection and insight into the possible meanings of the experiences.

Life–drama connection

By using questions, the therapist invites clients to create their own sense of meaning from the experience. The richness of the images is left for the client to discover within the improvisations and interviewing, but also in the de-roling and reflection. The clients finding their own meaning seems to be a part of the process of empowerment. The client makes decisions as 'her words' and 'her evaluation' rather than the therapist imposing meaning and importance through direct interpretation of the symbolic connection to the clients' lives.

Research conversation with Christine Novy

Jones: I was very intrigued by your idea of scaffolding and de-roling?

Novy: I am interested in the politics of meaning making in dramatherapy, particularly in terms of interpreting symbol and story, and I find the de-roling process helpful for the people I work with, not only in terms of connecting and assimilating but also interpreting symbolic material.

Jones: . . . And is that connected to what you were saying about the women becoming more in touch with the artist role in themselves as interpreter of their own life experience?

Novy: Yes, because the de-roling process provides incremental scaffolding for people both to feel knowledgeable about, and to describe, their experience at each step.

Jones: In terms of scaffolding, then, and describing their experience 'at each step', what do you see as your role in this process of step taking?

Novy: Well, the structure and questions of de-roling are like the skills that I bring to the process of negotiating or co-creating meaning. So my role is influential but decentred, and that's what I love about the de-roling process as you describe it.

As this research vignette illustrates, closure contains a number of important processes. Leaving the dramatic space helps clients to de-role: physically they leave the role behind. In addition they can be asked to talk to the character out of role as themselves. This process reinforces de-roling. It asks the client to think or feel about the role from outside rather than inside the skin of the role. The physical changing of position along with the request for a message reinforce each other. This also helps the process of assimilation to begin. The clients are being asked to separate from, and relate to, the characters they played. This change can be helped by the verbal reflection of the client, by the responses of other people within the group who had been in role or who have witnessed an enactment, and by the therapist.

Whatever the stance taken on remaining within the dramatic symbol or metaphor, or upon the primacy of verbal cognitive reflection, it is clear, as Novy points out, that the assimilation of the symbolic or metaphoric expressions is crucial to the efficacy of the work. Whether this occurs within the enactment or within a prescribed period of time after the drama, the therapist must engage with the issue of how the client or clients are able to connect their lives with the symbol or metaphor. It is also important to provide space for clients to separate from the dramatic involvement with the material, and to re-engage with their usual identity. As this chapter has shown, metaphors and symbols often take fantastic, imaginative forms, and these forms are given powerful emotional investment and involvement by clients. If clients are not offered the space to differentiate at the close of work, then this can feel extremely dislocating and cause distress and identity confusion.

Summary

Work involving symbol and metaphor in dramatherapy can help clients to engage with highly problematic material. They serve both to permit expression and to give a form for exploration of the presenting problem. Langley has said of metaphor in dramatherapy that it 'disguises' reality in 'fantasy "as if" it were real . . . [it] . . . creates a distance from reality, and makes it easier to speak the truth and understand or tolerate a difficult situation' (2006: 84–85). The following summary tries to show how the dramatic symbol and dramatic metaphor operate within dramatherapy.

In dramatherapy a *symbol* is a way of encountering unconscious material and a way of negotiating between inner conflict, outer expression and potential resolution. The symbol in dramatherapy needs two things: a physical form and a particular kind of relationship. It involves the creation of dramatic expression which is symbolic. This expression is an image, action, expression or embodiment that, whilst having a specific form, has wider interpretative meaning in its relationship to the client.

Symbols in dramatherapy can either be created deliberately or can occur spontaneously within an enactment. For example, a group might deliberately use an image such as a forest to explore its symbolic value and connections for individuals. Alternatively, an enactment might contain a forest that starts out as an event in an improvisation, but which becomes a symbol as it takes on meaning beyond its original purpose as a functional part of a narrative. This dramatic symbol may have a specific interpretative value for the client. However, the expressed form of the symbol may be seen as having no single definitive meaning or significance, as a dramatic symbol can take on a wide range of meanings and significances.

The dramatic symbol might be taken from cultural symbols that already exist, it might be a representation of a symbol encountered elsewhere (e.g. in a dream), or it might be created within the therapy session. The expressed meaning of a symbol in dramatherapy may be less important than the experience of the making and expressing of the symbolic, dramatic form.

The creation or use of *metaphor* in dramatherapy involves the bringing together of two separate entities which have a common connection. The two entities are made into a composite dramatic metaphor. For example, a client might experience their father as inaccessible and cold. They might create a castle of ice within an improvisation. Though they are improvising trying to gain entry to an ice castle, through metaphoric connection, the attempted entry is to do with the client trying to gain access to the father. An ice castle and the father and are the two entities brought together into the dramatic metaphor.

This metaphor is a dramatic form or image that condenses the two entities into one form or image. The point of contact for this condensation is the common metaphoric connection. The common connection in the example above is 'cold', 'unreachable'. The client is able to deal with one thing by means of another as a result of the metaphoric connection. Hence, the client can deal with the father through the dramatic image of the ice castle.

A dramatic metaphor would usually be used in dramatherapy when the therapist perceives that a new perspective is needed by the client as they are 'stuck' with the material. The client may spontaneously create a metaphor for a problem during an improvisation. The therapeutic potential of a dramatic metaphor in dramatherapy may be as follows:

- The dramatic metaphor creates distance from the actual real-life identity of the problem.
- The distance may enable the client to relate differently to the problem by creating a new perspective.
- The creation of the metaphor brings an altered relationship with the problematic material. By connecting the problem with the dramatic form in making the metaphor the client is opening up the way they see and experience the original.
- The creation of the metaphor enables the problem to be brought into contact with imaginative, dramatic exploration and with the therapeutic potential of the dramatherapy process.

The process that occurs between the client and the metaphor during the session may help the client to work through the issue and the connecting up of awarenesses made during the exploration of the metaphor and the real-life original problem is important in the efficacy of the metaphor.

11 Dramatherapy and ritual

Man must reassume his place between dream and events.

Artaud, *The Theatre and its Double*

Introduction

A relationship between dramatherapy and ritual has been suggested by a number of theoreticians. Parallels have also frequently been drawn between theatre practice and religious or social ritual. In the twentieth century this connection ranged from experimental Holy Theatre to the work of Schechner and Boas in the anthropology of performance. The meanings given to the word 'ritual' in these comparisons and relations are extremely varied. In this chapter I intend to identify a number of these areas of meaning and to look at their relevance to dramatherapy.

In answering the question 'What is ritual?' it is important to consider the rituals and attitudes towards ritual of different cultures. Themes concerning ritual that are often considered relevant to dramatherapy cover a range of areas including:

- ritual as a means of connecting with a reality or state which is different from the everyday
- the ritual use of artifacts
- behaviours and expressions particular to ritual healing and ritual
- the relationship between dramatic enactment and ritual.

Lewis (1980) describes ritual as a fixed procedure bound by rules. Turner has defined ritual as a prescribed formal behaviour 'for occasions not given over to technological routine' (Turner 1969). Berne refers to ritual as 'a stereotyped series of simple complementary transactions programmed by external social forces . . . The form of ritual is . . . determined by tradition' (1964: 36). Haviland defines ritual as a way in which important events are celebrated and in which crises are made less socially disruptive and less difficult for the individual to deal with (1978: 342).

Douglas has described ritual's role in maintaining 'the relation between both individual psychological needs and public social needs, both expressed by symbolic acts' (1975: 61). This mediation includes the rituals of the life cycle and rites of passage at birth, marriage and death. Rituals are also used to create a relationship with the seasons such as harvest or midwinter, as part of initiations and in relation to historic events. Others have commented upon the function of rituals to bring together or unify a worshipping community (Ray 1976: 86) and the ritual's capacity to meet both individual and group needs at the same time (Scheff 1979: 144).

Scheff's writings are particularly useful in considering dramatherapy's relationship to ritual and describe 'ritual and . . . myth as dramatic forms for coping with universal emotional distress' (Scheff 1979: 115). He defines ritual as the 'potentially distanced re-enactment of situations' of emotional distress that are 'virtually universal in a given culture' (Scheff 1979: 118).

The link here between ritual form, enactment and dealing with distress is of interest when considering how ritual and dramatherapy might relate to each other. It is often argued that ritual and dramatherapy are connected as they use enactment to deal with experiences of distress. Attention in dramatherapy has often focused upon the relationship of healing to ritual. This has involved the consideration of rituals from various cultures. Discussion is mainly in terms of the role of the shaman or healer, along with the nature of the relationship between the activities within the ritual and the way healing occurs. Some see this kind of parallel as being problematic, as will be discussed later.

Drama, theatre and ritual

Drama and ritual are connected by both contemporary anthropologists and experimental theatre practitioners. Ritual space is seen by some to be akin to dramatic space. Landy, for example, says: 'Ritual activity . . . is dramatic, as it calls for the subject to create a representational world through symbolic means' (Landy 1986: 67). Douglas has referred to the way in which a number of rituals rely upon the belief that events can be changed 'by mimetic action' (1975: 23).

Artaud, Brook, Barba and Grotowski have all rooted their theatre in the notion of performance as a form of ritual. They speak of its efficacy as a means of communication, and its power to touch the performer and the audience emotionally and through religious feeling. These different theatre experimenters have linked their theories and practical work to the concepts and expressive languages of ritual. Grotowski's Theatre of Sources or paratheatrical activities, for example, have been paralleled with ritual. He describes it as 'bringing us back to the sources of life, to direct primaeval experience, to organic primary experience' (Roose-Evans 1984: 154).

Innes has linked this kind of thinking in theatre to disillusion, to a search for an antidote to an overly rational culture, a desire to turn from western materialism towards an alternative value scale. Ritual, he argues, becomes linked with a primitivist notion that in ritual, myth and in non-western cultures a pure form of theatre can be discovered which can communicate powerfully (Innes 1993: 10). He, like others, says that this desire to 'borrow' from other cultures is often 'deeply questionable'. It is often based on nineteenth-century imperialist notions of other cultures being simple, basic and pure, or on a 'superficial exoticism' where the work is valued for its surface only.

Practitioners such as Schechner (1988) have begun to develop an approach to performance and to ritual that tries to establish a model of intercultural working which is less rooted in racism and colonialism than the work of many of the theatre practitioners mentioned above. This approach stresses the importance of dialogue between cultures, between practitioners and cultural forms rather than the mere appropriation of surface elements of non-western forms by western individuals.

Efficacy and ritual

A problem often referred to in relation to ritual concerns its validity and efficacy. For some individuals ritual is felt to be effective: it has meaning for them, it is useful. For others ritual is experienced as alien, meaningless or irrelevant. Goffman, for example, says: 'Ritual is a perfunctory, conventionalised act' (1961: 62). From religion to sport, there is frequently a perception that contemporary rituals are impoverished reflections of their predecessors or those existing in other cultures. This notion is common in western responses to ritual. Scheff, for example, suggests that in modern western society the connection between strong emotion and ritual appears to have been severed, and religious rituals are perceived as having decreased emotional meaning (1979: 129).

Some see ritual as a 'negative' force or form that enables society to contain problematic elements. Viewed in this way ritual is seen as essentially conservative and a force against change.

Current studies tend to indicate two possible positions regarding ritual. One viewpoint advocates the power and usefulness of ritual, the other stresses alienation and the lack of efficacy (i.e. negative uses of ritual). One asserts that ritual can function in a number of ways which have beneficial and positive functions for group and individual processes. The other view of rituals includes the notion that they contain and oppress and that contemporary rituals are ineffective.

A research group on ritual was set up by me, working with 16 dramatherapists who aimed to explore aspects of the relationship between ritual and dramatherapy. Each participant filled in a questionnaire concerning their background and experiences of ritual prior to the start of the work. They completed a form analysing and recording their responses to the active work undertaken within the research. The practical work took the form of a number of activities designed to engage with aspects of ritual using drama-therapy. Participants came from a variety of different cultural backgrounds and racial groups and were of different religious belief systems. They were asked to identify their experiences or feelings towards ritual. In many ways the findings reflected the two positions described above. Comments on positive examples of ritual included the following:

- 'Marking significant stages in the development of the individual.'
- 'A strong container to elicit, support and carry through strong feeling.'
- 'Ritual has fulfilled an emotional or physical need which resulted in a shared experience – a coming together.'
- 'Rituals which serve a very personal purpose, where the ritual has grown out of a personal need and where it has structure and rhythm which give their own safety and boundary.'

Negative examples of experiences with ritual included:

- 'Not being initiated into rituals.'
- 'Fears of feeling, participating, being rejected, getting it wrong.'
- 'Feeling of unfinished or unconnected rituals: for example, not closing the curtains at my grandmother's cremation service.'
- 'Incomplete, insensitive, fierce, detached.'
- 'Imposing and controlling . . . imbalance of power . . . no choice.'
- 'A funeral which was cut short because of rain and improper burial equipment. There was no acknowledgement of my family's need (and right) to accompany the deceased, my grandmother, to the graveside.'
- 'Rituals which are shallow or empty because they have become stultified with time.'
- 'Those belonging to something alien to me. For example, religion. These rituals make me feel excluded. I feel as though I'm missing something at a fundamental level that everyone else understands.'

As this chapter will show, this division or ambiguity in relation to ritual's efficacy is at the heart of the way in which dramatherapy and ritual can usefully connect.

Dramatherapy and ritual

There are two main areas of connection made between dramatherapy and ritual by theoreticians. One approach says that dramatherapy is a ritual. The other approach refers to ritual as a mode of healing using enactment. This is then linked to dramatherapy's use of enactment or becomes a rationale in justifying how and why dramatherapy uses drama to heal. Others have indi-cated spiritual links between the ways in which ritual can function as an act of worship and the ways in which dramatherapy can have a spiritual component

(McNiff 1988; Grainger 1990). They often refer to the spiritual links between health, curing illness and religion that are present in other cultures and currently denied in mainstream health provision in the west. Spiritual aspects of the healing that occurs in dramatherapy are then emphasised, as if dramatherapy is an equivalent of non-western rituals.

Landy asserts that one of the key 'reasons' for applying drama to therapy concerns what he calls the 'traditional therapeutic function of theatre' (Landy 1986: 47). He goes on to connect this with a statement that the ritual and healing aspects of theatre performance have been demonstrated throughout history. This pattern of associations is not uncommon within dramatherapy. Leaps are being made between ritual and healing, theatre performance, history and therapeutic function. This approach tends to take other cultures' phenomena, groups them as a term, 'ritual' and reinterprets them as a pattern for dramatherapy. Part of this process seeks to create an ancient lineage and cross-cultural significance for dramatherapy.

Elements of these claims may be of interest when considering and practising dramatherapy. My concern is that there has been little critical consideration of the ways in which the connection of dramatherapy with ritual can be of practical use. I would argue that therapists are often unclear as to what they actually mean by ritual. Vast, vague statements are made about this other world of perceived ancient power. Dramatherapy has been too quick to claim other cultural practices as its own; too eager to draw parallels between itself and ritual. Dramatherapy is not a ritual. The dramatherapist is not a shaman. To draw links between the shaman and the dramatherapist in such a way as to say that the shaman uses role play, or that the contemporary therapist working within a completely different cultural and racial context can 'use' rituals from other cultures and races, is to ignore the complexity of this area.

As Schmais (1988) has pointed out, the shaman usually operates in a non-literate tribal society, with roots in a polytheistic, animistic philosophy. Illness is seen as a result of supernatural forces – a loss of soul, an invasion by a spirit power. In the west where most dramatherapy is practised she says that this would be classified 'as conversion hysteria and simple nuclear forms of schizophrenia' (1988: 281). The primary focus for many shamans is to intervene between spiritual forces and humans. To claim that the dramatherapist is a shaman presiding over a ritual is inappropriately to 'align ourselves with a mystical religious tradition and declare that our primary mission is to intercede between man and the supernatural' (1988: 301). She stresses the importance of considering the content and form of any process in terms of its cultural and social context. If this is ignored and elements of ritual are simply lifted and transplanted, 'we proceed at our peril'. The dramatherapist ignores crucial differences when taking techniques rooted in another time and in another social context (Schmais 1988: 283).

It is important to try to establish a clear framework to describe the relationship between dramatherapy and ritual. Schmais goes on to say that it is possible to develop a relationship to ritual and shamanic practices but that these must be carefully thought through. Below is an attempt to define a framework and relationship that is based in the practical ways in which ritual and dramatherapy can usefully connect. The approaches outlined attempt to avoid the problems noted above. The relationship between dramatherapy and ritual can be located in three key areas:

- The *reproduction of incomplete or problematic ritual experiences* from the client's past, e.g. a distressing association with a barmitzvah, and *reframing* and reworking the experience.
- The *creation of dramas using ritual forms* to deal with client's material. This might involve the creation of an improvisation using ritual language to acknowledge a life event which has been ignored. Another aspect of this area is the use of ritual form as a way of expressing and dealing with material brought to the therapy, e.g. the creation of improvisations using ritual language to mark endings or beginnings.
- Aspects of the dramatherapy group which can usefully be considered or analysed within a *'ritual' framework* (e.g. rituals which the group create), such as patterns of exercises or ways of relating at the start or close of sessions.

Dramatherapy practice and ritual

The basic relationship between ritual and dramatherapy for the client and therapist can be summarised as follows. The client in dramatherapy:

- can bring material from rituals that have featured in their lives which are experienced as problematic
- can create dramatic representations of these experiences in order to work with and resolve the problem
- can create their own dramatic rituals to deal with personal material.

The dramatherapist:

- can help clients to re-create experiences of ritual that are problematic in order to deal with the difficulty they have encountered
- can work with clients to create their own dramatic rituals using the group or individual's own cultural language of ritual.

Reframing rituals

In dramatherapy rituals may not only be referred to but can be reworked or worked through using the *language* of ritual. This means that the movements, sounds, words and interactions may be re-created within the expressive language of the therapy. In verbal therapy the ritual can be spoken about, or experiences relived or worked through in recollection or in the transference relationship. In dramatherapy the recollection or working through can be done in the language of the ritual form itself.

This active use of the language and form of ritual within dramatherapy is useful, given the area referred to earlier: that some individuals feel disenfranchised or alienated from ritual. Evreinov has pointed out the importance of individuals feeling that they connect to the rituals they experience in society, and says that it is an aspect of the theatrical instinct. Active participation in ritual allows the individual to feel that they are connected with others, have ownership and a sense of power in life. When life becomes actively reflected in the enactment of the ritual, 'it acquires a new meaning, it becomes *his* life, something he has created' (Evreinov 1927: 27).

In dramatherapy the ritual is re-created within a framework that allows the individual to explore the ritual and its relationship to them. The enactment of the ritual means that it can be used in improvisation, the individual can explore different ways of responding to the ritual, or can accommodate the ritual to themselves by adapting its form. A number of people in the research group mentioned above found that the reproduction of elements of ritual involved a powerful re-evaluation of the ritual or the problem attached to the ritual. A participant discovered, for example, just how powerfully the rage was still present with her in terms of an incomplete ritual, 'unhappiness with inadequate . . . incomplete ritual':

> Sculpt of rage. Taking mother's body after long wait for (a) dying (b) death (c) burial service to crematorium. False smile of sympathy on face of flunkey bringing flowers unburnt round to the front. Furnace not on that day. Bring to be left like so much rubbish. No guarantee what was in the box of ashes later. Powerless. Frustration.

One set of exercises involved individuals sculpting ritual experiences that had been experienced as problematic. Another involved brief improvisations of difficulties in rituals from people's lives:

> Sculpting my wedding – having talked endlessly and at length about my wedding and marriage I was amazed that the sculpt I used said it all in such a concise and powerful image. (It's a shame I didn't sculpt these feelings prior to the wedding – perhaps I wouldn't have made the mistake of going through with it.)

Opportunities were offered to improvise a different version of the ritual, to rework the ritual experience in order to reframe it. Participants could express feelings through the dramatic representation of the ritual. They could also comment about the ritual and their experience of it during and after the re-enactment. A life experience was identified and described by individuals. They then sculpted others into a depiction of the ritual, and participants were informed of the details of the situation. The individual then directed and watched the improvised version of events. The individuals could then say what they liked to those involved, could talk about the experience and rework it in a way which helped them to deal with the problem.

In this way participants could choose to rework the ritual experience to fit their specific emotional needs. If necessary they could deal with unfinished business left over from the ritual. Individuals could also gain insight into their responses by bringing the event into the here and now of the dramatherapy work and could discuss the activities and feelings with the group and facilitator. For example, one individual worked with a childhood experience in Africa concerning the pressure put upon him by ritual expectations due to his gender. Another example from a past experience of ritual involved Greek celebrations of Easter.

Vignette: Easter cake

A chair was put to one side of the performance area and Zanetta sat in it. She described the ritual experience and her problem with it. The focus was the ritual of baking an Easter cake, which in Greek culture is undertaken by the women of the house. The problem was that as an adolescent she had been forbidden to make the family cake one year as she had been menstruating. She had and still felt anger towards the situation and towards her grandmother at her exclusion.

Individuals from the group were invited to play the roles involved in the situation and were sculpted into position by Zanetta who described the kitchen where the activity took place.

The key moment of the grandmother's refusal to let her take part in the ritual was played. Zanetta talked about her feelings at this point and doubled each of the roles. She then replayed it in a way which she would have found satisfying. She chose to make her own cake in the kitchen alongside the grandmother. This, for her, meant both respecting the grandmother's feelings and attitudes toward the ritual, whilst finding a satisfying role for herself. She then addressed her grandmother and the person representing herself in relation to what the experience had revealed to her about the incident, the ritual, her relationship to her grandmother, and what she had discovered to take back to that ritual in the future.

CORE PROCESS BOX

Role

The ritual is reproduced by role playing. Zanetta's relationship to the ritual is explored through enactment and witnessing. She is able to re-experience the ritual, to alter her relationship to the experience and to the ritual itself. She chooses to confront her grandmother with words which were unspoken in the original situation and finds a way of challenging the ritual. She keeps the original ritual of the cake baking and bakes her own cake. As this chapter will later reveal, some of the group felt that this did not fully challenge the attitudes to women and to menstruation, but for Zanetta this was an outcome which satisfied her. She could satisfy her unfinished need to find words and ways to challenge the ritual and yet find a position that felt comfortable in relation to it.

Witnessing

By bringing the past into the here and now of the group, Zanetta is able to receive the witness and support of group members in looking at and reworking the original experience. The original memory of being isolated is reworked with the company of supportive group members and the therapist.

Here the original experience of the ritual is problematic. This is due to the attitude towards women within the ritual and Zanetta's response as an adolescent. Although this experience came from Zanetta's past, it is also relevant to her ongoing experience as a woman in relation to this ritual. Additional factors present within the work are Zanetta's relationship with her grandmother, her adolescent self, her own response to cultural attitudes to women, and her own feelings about menstruation. As so often in working with ritual forms, the chosen image is one which is rich in condensed meanings and issues.

Such examples of the ways in which ritual relates to dramatherapy can be seen within a clear process. I propose a way of looking at this which contains four stages concerning the reframing of ritual in dramatherapy:

1   The recollection of an issue which is connected with a ritual.
2   The use of ritual 'language' to recollect or represent the issue. This process begins to adjust and adapt the language and experience to the client's own expressive repertoire.
3   This process of adjustment and adaptation is taken further into the client's work on the issue.
4   A working through of the original stuck or incomplete experience using

the new adjusted ritual language, or the client achieving insight into the problems encountered in the ritual experience.

The creation of dramas using ritual forms

Ritual has a specific expressive form and has content which is particular to it. Dramatherapy can enable clients to use their own cultural experiences of ritual form and content to create their own rituals. It is useful to describe these as dramatic rituals as it differentiates them from social and religious rituals present in society at large. Social and religious rituals are the product of large, historic processes and have generally evolved over a period of time. The dramatic ritual is the created product of an individual or group within the space of a dramatherapy session to deal with the problems brought to therapy.

Another part of the research work involved utilising the elements of the languages and structures of people's experiences of ritual to create a form to satisfy an emotional need. This could be said to work with the notion that ritual can be seen as suited to deal in a highly effective manner with certain cultural, emotional and psychological areas. These areas are usually connected to changes in status, position or identity, or to religious contexts.

Small groups of four or five chose areas to work on and then created ritualised dramatic forms. These contained patterns of movements, repetition and chants based on their own cultural experiences of ritual. The form and type of content were seen to evoke particular kinds of responses. Strong reactions were noted by many members to vocal chants:

- 'Listening to the orchestration of sounds literally made my hair stand on end (on arms and back of neck!)'
- 'It enabled entry into another dimension of experience where voices, intentions and "conversation" became both explicit and symbolic. It was perhaps the closest I came to an "ecstatic" or "altered perception" which I feel is essential to an experience of ritual.'

Patterns of movement to express particular emotions were structured and worked with in the small groups: 'I was amazed how just by repeating the movement my emotion of being pulled in all directions became more real and accurately reflected my intense feeling of anger at being in that position.'

Vignette: Menstruation ritual

One piece of work involved a group of women who all identified a feeling of absence in their lives. This concerned the lack of acknowledgement of women's bodily changes and menstruation. For some of the women the work was triggered by the feelings of anger in

Zanetta's exclusion and denial from the Greek Easter ritual. This was seen to be an illustration of the way their bodies and selves had been denied:

> In Zanetta's experience of being excluded from the baking ritual because of menstruating, I felt so angry on her behalf and I wanted her outcome to be different. I wanted to tell her grandmother that she was continuing a cycle of oppression and to challenge it, not to accept an alternative which still accepted the old way.
>
> The new ritual gave me a chance to work with women who had similar dissatisfactions around the lack of symbolic rites of passage into womanhood; as well as culture's reticence to be explicit about bodily, emotional and psychological changes through the maturation process.

A group of four worked on the creation of a set of repeated movements, vocalisations and the use of objects to achieve a retrogressive acknowledgement:

> We were a group of four women – one grandmother, one mother and two women who did not have children. We wanted to make a ritual to celebrate the start of menstruation. This celebration had been absent from our lives. We all began by holding a long sheet of material which we threw out in front of us. As we stepped on to it each of us worked with a series of movement patterns. The use of a symbolic cloth in our new ritual was very effective as it defined a ritual space.

This group had previously worked on anger and had experienced difficulties in working with the feeling, the exercise and with each other, 'not being able to gel as a group and find the same starting point'. In the creation of the ritual they found a way of making contact, uniting in an experience and dealing with an experience that was both individual and collective. The created ritual involved the following:

- Finding a common need.
- Devising a way of working which was effective as an emotional and expressive form.
- Dealing with unfinished business.

The recollection of an absence, the anger evoked by the experience of an individual and the problem of working together were all used in the new ritual these women had created in the research group. They were able to find a group form that had individual meanings. In one sense the group's work reflected Evreinov's ideas cited in Chapter 2. These described the importance of effective rituals for individuals in owning and taking power in relation to life events. The group's witnessing each other and publicly marking the unacknowledged onset of menstruation was the basis of the therapeutic work.

Many of the group remarked upon the work's effect in validating the experience of menstruation and of being a woman. The importance here was not only in being in the ritual but the therapeutic benefits of *making* the ritual as well. One woman remarked that the silence around the onset of menstruation was still with her: 'such an important transition in my life but it went almost unnoticed, certainly not celebrated or enhanced'. To create a ritual was a 'wonderful' liberation of this material: 'something that was always treated as a whispered, frightening, unclean secret into a positive greeting of a life transition'. Another commented of this work: 'I was able to find some release and the feeling of having given/received and worked together positively.' Another participant described the experience of creating a ritual as follows:

> These experiences were all planned, meaningful and physical. I found myself very engaged with them and could have repeated them for a great deal of time with the group. I felt the experience worked at a level which was emotional, symbolic, embodied and free of language constraints.

A number commented on how the creation of a planned form using ritualistic theatre form helped to express and contain very powerful emotions:

> Amazed at how closely/intimately we related to each other . . . my anger was manageable . . . incredibly powerful and exhausting and safe . . . I was able to get in touch with my feelings of anger quickly and to reach the 'scary' point and go beyond this . . . I felt close to tears but was able to continue until I had released my feelings.
>
> We repeated a movement to work with the emotion . . . when I was reaching a point of frenzy where it might get dangerous my body automatically closed and responded to a movement which the other two in the group were also doing. We had our eyes closed and yet we were doing the same thing. It was as though the body has a memory of a response to a frantic emotion and movement.

Summary

The following summarises the use of ritual form in dramatherapy:

- In some cases a need is identified concerning the absence of a ritual in the client's life. In others a problem is expressed which might usefully be worked with through ritual, or through ritual forms of expression. Problems or issues most suited to this approach are usually related to areas with which ritual is connected in the client's culture. Examples of these include changes in status, changes in identity or in the life cycle, and religious material.

- The client or clients use ritual forms/patterns and content from their own experience as a basis for the creation of a dramatic ritual. This involves building a dramatic ritual using aspects of form and content such as repetition, chants, patterns of movement, songs, call-and-response.
- The client experiments and improvises with these forms until they arrive at a dramatic ritual which adequately deals with and expresses the problematic feeling or area.
- In some work the expression or creation of the ritual in the therapeutic work results in a change (occurring in the relationship) to the feelings or area to which the dramatic ritual refers. This is due to the use of the form to express material. The experience of the created ritual can also be 'a means of containing and reaching a different relationship to the problem or issue. Here the emphasis is upon the dramatic ritual as a way of expressing and resolving the material or issue. The creation of the 'Menstruation Ritual' is an example of this way of working.
- For other work the dramatic ritual enables the effective expression of the problematic material or issue. Once expressed, the material can be worked with as in other areas of dramatherapy as described in Chapter 5. Here the emphasis is upon the created, dramatic ritual as the best way of expressing an issue or problem.

12 Assessment, recording and evaluation in dramatherapy

> Whatever we see could be other than it is.
> Whatever we describe at all could be other than it is.
>
> Wittgenstein, *Tractatus Logico-Philosophicus*

Introduction

Vernon (1969), in his survey of assessment in therapy, has pointed out that many dramatists, writers and artists have excelled in the portrayal of character 'but seldom stopped to ask how they, or we, get to know people, or how accurate is our knowledge' (1969: 2). This is debatable. Many would argue that the arts and certainly much drama constantly engages with these very questions. However, Vernon does encapsulate the concerns at the heart of assessment, recording and evaluation. How do we know people in dramatherapy and how accurate is our knowledge? The answer to this must always be 'partially'. There are many routes to apprehending, describing and knowing oneself or another. For dramatherapy a part of the way the therapist tries to know others is through assessment. Another aspect of this process concerns the way in which we try to understand what has happened over a period of time within the dramatherapy – this is evaluation.

Assessment

A basic aim of assessment is to find out as much as possible regarding the client and the difficulties they are encountering. A further aim is to find out how they might proceed to use the dramatherapy space to work with the material they bring to therapy. Assessment gathers information. It can do so in a number of ways and from a number of sources. Usually dramatherapy is practised alongside other therapies and treatments and a dramatherapist might use the documented information which has been gathered within these other activities to support their observations. All dramatherapy, however, uses direct assessment within sessions to gain information. This might include the therapist using a variety of methods to help clients assess themselves. The dramatherapist can make use of a variety of formats and approaches to assess the clients they work with.

In some situations the process will be connected to diagnosis. This concerns the identification of the client's problem or condition according to set criteria. The assessment process might also include a consideration of a client's suitability for dramatherapy.

Assessment is linked to the formation of aims. For some groups the main aims will have been decided beforehand. A setting might decide upon an aim for a dramatherapy group as a part of its programme. Aims might be advertised in order to help individuals decide whether they wish to attend the therapy. For example, a women's dramatherapy group run in a community centre dealing with assertiveness might be advertised locally before its start. For other work the specific aims will be negotiated with the group or individual once the therapy has started. In some work the aims might be very general: 'to bring about personal change'. In other situations aims will be very specific, for example: 'to use role play to enable individuals to become more assertive in their everyday dealings with people in the community'.

Evaluation

Aims are evaluated by the dramatherapist and by clients within the therapy. Bruscia has defined evaluation as documenting 'whether the client's original status did in fact change as a result of the therapist's interventions' (1988: 5). In some work this might be formal. For example, in a dramatherapy group whose aim is to develop a particular kind of behaviour or mode of relating to others, the client might be asked to evaluate their own progress. This would entail asking each client to look back at their experiences within the group and within their lives in general. A number of headings or criteria might be used to help to focus this reflection. A group working with assertiveness might look at a series of criteria to evaluate their progress during the group. *Formative evaluation* takes place as the work is in progress and helps to orientate therapist and client. *Summative evaluation* occurs at the close of the work and looks back at the whole process.

Assessment and evaluation: the basic process

Valente and Fontana undertook research into the ways dramatherapists working in the field approach the question 'Is your client getting any better?' (Valente and Fontana 1997: 29). The following lists some of the key ways of working:

- observation of client behaviours
- client self-reports
- reports from other professionals
- projective techniques

- client's use of diagnostic dramatherapy media
- reports by other group members (Valente and Fontana 1997: 29).

This chapter considers some of these key approaches and looks at ways of approaching observation, projective techniques in assessment and the use of diagnostic approaches to dramatherapy media such as role playing. It also looks at dramatic approaches to capturing and reflecting upon processes at work within dramatherapy, including the use of play and drama activities to consider progress and change within work. Whatever methods or tools are used, the basic process often used in dramatherapy is as follows:

- referral
- initial assessment
- formulation of aims
- ongoing and formative evaluation
- review of aims
- retrospective evaluation

Referral

Referral concerns the way in which clients come to the dramatherapy group. This might be through self-referral. A setting might refer an individual to dramatherapy as part of a specific programme for a particular group (e.g. a class in a school for children with emotional or behavioural difficulties). Individuals might be referred by a key worker (e.g. a client is referred to a group by their social worker). In some settings there might be a referral assessment to establish whether a client's issues or problems are suitable to be worked with through dramatherapy.

Initial assessment

This is a period when the therapist and clients work together to obtain information on the problems to be dealt with, and on the ways in which the dramatherapy sessions might be used.

Formulation of aims

Based on the information gained in the initial assessment, a series of aims are formulated which will guide the dramatherapy. In some settings main aims might be decided prior to the group. In others they might be formulated once the group has been formed. In either case it is usual that aims reflect the initial assessment. These aims might be very specific or quite general, depending upon the context. Factors such as the dramatherapist's therapeutic orientation, the length of therapy and the nature of client group affect the nature of the aims.

Ongoing evaluation (formative)

This is an ongoing process during the therapy whereby the work is evaluated. It consists of considering the efficacy of the work according to set criteria. Again, the nature of the criteria varies according to the therapeutic orientation, nature of the client group, etc.

Review of aims

From the information gained by the ongoing evaluation, the aims are reviewed to see if they are appropriate and realistic. Following this review aims might need to be adjusted.

Retrospective evaluation (summative)

At the close of the work a retrospective evaluation looks back at the process of the dramatherapy and considers the nature of the changes which have and have not occurred. This includes a review of the aims in the light of what has occurred in the therapy.

Ethics

There are ethical considerations to be taken into account in relation to assessment and evaluation. These are set within the context of ethical guidelines of professional associations and bodies, settings and health care or education providers. The dramatherapist, for example, must bear in mind the reasons why assessment and evaluation are occurring, how the information to be gained is to be recorded and used, and who will have access to this information. The issue of consent must be engaged with in terms of whether the client has consented to assessment. If, for example, the client is severely learning disabled and cannot cognitively understand the concept of assessment, then the therapist must make sure that they deal with the situation with respect and within the ethical protocols regarding permission at work within any setting and within the position set by professional organisations such as the UK's Health Professions Council.

Ciornai (1983) has emphasised the importance of taking cultural and socio-economic factors into account within diagnosis, assessment and evaluation. She says that it is important for the arts therapist to take into account possible cultural biases and differences. The lack of acknowledgement of these areas can hinder understanding and communication within the therapeutic work. Ciornai gives an example of a therapist unfamiliar with Latino culture who may encounter values which seem to be 'symptoms of dysfunction or immaturity'. Within Latino culture these values are considered 'signs of health' (1983: 64). She asserts that understanding different cultural values is crucial to the prevention of misdiagnosis.

Approaches to assessment and evaluation in dramatherapy

A wide number of approaches to assessment and evaluation exist within the fields of psychology, psychotherapy and the arts. As Courtney (1981) has said, the form of assessment used within dramatherapy will be connected to the orientation of the therapy and the therapist. To an extent, the conclusions drawn from assessment and the framework which the assessment uses are also influenced by the orientation of the therapist and setting. Hence analytically orientated therapy will utilise a different approach to work being undertaken within a behavioural context. Projective testing using enactment, when conducted to reveal aspects of the client's unconscious world, is more orientated towards a psychotherapeutic way of working with dramatherapy. A series of drama exercises designed to show the different developmental aspects of the client's way of responding to situations can be effective within a developmental framework. McAlister, for example, has said:

> One of the most important concepts I have found useful in dramatherapy as an evaluative tool is the developmental model . . . [it] . . . describes a series of developmental stages in children's play which can be seen as a continuum. The first stage is sensori-motor play, followed by imitative and pretend play, progressing to dramatic play and finally arriving at drama (Jones 1996: 185). The value of this model lies in enabling clients to work expressively at any stage along the continuum. Therefore it allows the dramatherapist to identify areas in which the client's development is stuck or arrested. However, this developmental progression is about being able to move between stages rather than from one to another, hence its importance as a continuum.
>
> (McAlister 1999: 104–105)

Most assessment approaches, however, can be used within a number of frameworks in dramatherapy. A projective test which looks at role behaviour through role playing a series of scenarios can be useful to both psychodynamic or behavioural approaches. The way of reading the information gained in the assessment would differ. Within a psychodynamic framework the kinds of themes and content expressed during the role work would be seen as reflecting the client's feelings and unconscious material. The behavioural assessment would be looking at the particular behaviours manifested by the client in the role situations in order to see where work needed to be done in altering behaviour.

Interviews and projective testing, along with structured and unstructured participation, are listed by Bruscia as the main assessment approaches used by dramatherapists (1988: 8). Casson's (2004) description of his assessment process with clients who hear voices uses a combination of ways of working with assessment which reflect this diversity. The core of the assessment is described by him as 'an exchange of basic information (2004: 99) and occurs

over a number of sessions before a contract for a period of therapy is negotiated. His approach combines an adaptation of the Romme voice interview
(1994), a structured method including questions about the client's 'voices'
such as 'How often do you hear voices? Are you hearing voices now? What do
you feel about your voices?' (Casson 2004: 252). It involves the client in
activities such as drawing their family tree, which gives 'vital information in
understanding the development of the psychosis' (2004: 100). He offers the
client a choice in the use of projective techniques. These include a storymaking structure 'in which the client draws or writes a short story about a hero or
heroine, their mission, helper, the obstacles they encounter and the way they
overcome these', rooted in Lahad's Six Piece Storymaking structure (Lahad
1994); work with small objects such as a small human figures; and role work
'creating a friend: the client creates a real or imaginary friend and role
reverses, saying what the "friend" likes and appreciates about the client'. He
offers information about the therapy along with a copy of his professional
codes of practice. He sees this as empowering the client: 'to have some agency,
control and ownership of the process' (Casson 2004: 101).

Dramatherapy often uses profile observation within assessment: the use of
a series of observable criteria to describe a state or way of being. In dramatherapy these usually concern the way in which the client uses drama, the way in
which the difficulties they bring to therapy are manifested and how any
potential changes might be observed or perceived.

As Read Johnson (1982) has documented, some dramatherapy work is
structured around a developmental paradigm. Here a problem or disorder
can be seen as a blockage or halt in development. He identifies a number of
developmental processes especially relevant to dramatherapy (1982: 184):

- the complexity of the media of expression used
- the intensity of affect which an individual can tolerate without overwhelming anxiety
- the degree of interpersonal demand which can be experienced in interactions with others.

Read Johnson connects the assessments of these areas to the way the dramatherapy's aims are formed: 'Treatment first involves an assessment of where
in the developmental sequence the person has stopped him/herself, and then
starting the journey again with the therapist as a companion and guide'
(1982: 184).

Assessment involves a reciprocal relationship between the therapist and the
client. 'New paradigm' approaches to research, as described by Reason
(1988) and Rowan (1990), have emphasised this notion. Aspects of new paradigm ways of working can be important to consider in relation to certain
approaches to assessment. The client, for example, becomes a collaborator
rather than a subject within assessment, contributing to the planning and
operation of any assessment. The task of the dramatherapist is to design a

form of assessment which is appropriate to a particular individual or group and the setting or context of the work. As I have said elsewhere, this area 'is most alive when it is part of the creative process, a dialogue between all those involved' (Jones 2005: 215).

Why assess? The problems with assessment and evaluation

Assessment within therapy is a notoriously complex business and its use in the arts is contentious. A number of questions arise concerning the validity and appropriateness of testing and much debate has taken place in relation to how artistic experiences and products can be assessed. The nature of criteria used and the conclusions drawn from them have been much argued over. There can be no absolute criteria in artistic judgement and assessment and inevitably criteria are highly value laden and specific. Some schools of therapy have rejected the notion of assessment. In non-directive work the clients bring their own problems and 'effect [their] own re-integration of [their] conflicting perceptions and goals' (Vernon 1969: 11). The effectiveness of most forms of therapy is difficult to 'prove'.

Why assess at all? The process is intended as a way of helping client and therapist to become as clear as possible about what is needed and what occurs within the therapeutic process. Assessment aims to provide a framework through which the therapist and client can understand what is brought to dramatherapy and what occurs within the work. As acknowledged earlier, this is bound to be a partial process. Many people have asserted that what occurs within an art form is too complex to be fully encompassed by a series of criteria. Others have pointed out the inherent difficulties in trying to reduce the processes of change in therapy to a small area described through assessment and evaluation criteria. However, once these difficulties are acknowledged, it is useful for the therapist and client to find a language to consider what is initially brought to the dramatherapy and how the potential and actual changes can be described and named. It is important, though, to bear in mind that assessment is a partial process and also to be just as aware of what is not being assessed as what is being assessed.

Assessment methodologies

There are two main areas which the dramatherapist covers in an initial assessment:

- identification of the areas or difficulties which might be brought and worked with by clients
- identification of how the client might best find meaning in the dramatic expressive media within dramatherapy.

The first area focuses upon ways of helping to elicit or focus on the reasons why the client has come to therapy. The second looks at the different aspects of the dramatic media within dramatherapy and sees which is most effective for the client to work with in exploring and dealing with the material to be brought to therapy.

The following extract demonstrates one way in which a potential client can come to find out about and arrive at dramatherapy. The vignette from Genevieve Smyth shows how a dramatherapy referral is made to a Scottish National Health Service (NHS) Community Mental Health Team (CMHT) by the service user's psychiatrist. The vignette focuses upon the initial assessment process. Smyth describes the initial part of the process as follows:

> The CMHT contact person (CP) for dramatherapy, the user's community psychiatric nurse (CPN), screens the referral. This allows the CP to consider the service user's needs and to decide if dramatherapy is likely to be the most appropriate service at the right time.

In this vignette Smyth's dramatherapy practice is described by her as 'an established theatre-based, community service service for adults with severe and enduring mental illness'. It takes place in a local NHS community mental health centre.

Vignette: Assessment in dramatherapy

In a joint dramatherapist/CPN needs assessment with the service user, there is open dialogue between the dramatherapist, CPN and service user which determines dramatherapy's appropriateness. Empowered by the choice of verbal psychotherapy, art therapy or dramatherapy, the user states their preference for dramatherapy on this occasion.

   Smyth describes part of the way in which she introduces the therapy to a service user, A:

   I introduce various play objects as aids to self-expression and gaining further understanding of difficult issues. A's interest seems sustained by the objects. He observes and listens attentively. Then, spontaneously, he picks up a relaxation globe (a small, soft ball decorated with a map of the world) and rotates it gently in his hand, commenting on how small he feels on the planet. When asked by the CPN if anything could be done to make a change for the better, he reflects on how powerful it feels to hold the world in the palm of his hand for the first time. Simultaneously, he smiles and squashes the globe. Moments later, his palm opens and the globe re-forms. With direct eye contact, A talks of feeling tension relief and now

talks clearly about his need for self-control and regaining lost confidence following his last psychotic episode.

The CP completes a referral form in consultation with A. This
enables relevant information to be stored such as a user's family
background, significant relationships and life events causing notable difficulty. Details of past and current support services provided
and by whom, as well as medical conditions and treatments proscribed, are also collated, as are any warning signals of health
deterioration. Resulting from discussion with A, the CP also records
his need for symptomatic relief from auditory hallucinations, in addition to exploration of the underlying causes of psychosis and strategies for extending self-control and regaining self-confidence.

A 'dramatherapy verbal assessment' is undertaken with A, in part
dealing with risk assessment. This is a follow-on, more detailed
dialogue with me for in-depth goal setting with A, such as 'gaining
control in the way I respond to intrusive voices in my head'. The
dialogue also facilitates clarification of confidentiality boundaries,
exemplified by the need for me as dramatherapist to bring, with
service user consent, progress reports and professional queries
about the work to CMHT case management meetings and clinical
supervision.

*Smyth goes on to undertake what she calls a 'dramatherapy prac-
tical assessment' so that the service user can sample dramatherapy in working with active methods to help clarify their needs
within the therapy.*

I decided to build on the projective technique used earlier by the
A in the joint needs assessment in his exploration of the relaxation
globe. A selects further play objects to describe how he sees himself in the world. This is illustrated by how he moves across the
session room with a knee-high string puppet of vibrant colours but
with no fixed animal or human identity. A comments on the puppet's
emotional well-being: 'Look how it walks . . . unsteady like . . . been
stuck down a lot . . . it's a bit wary . . . not quite sure where it's going,
but determined to get there.' I acknowledge the puppet's experience of hurt and motivation to move on, reflecting openly how A's
walk has mirrored that of the puppet's. He grins in conscious recognition, concluding, 'Aye, I should know.'

*Such activities and dialogue help both Smyth and A to develop
three goals:*

- 'to use my creativity to understand myself more and feel better about who I am'
- 'to explore the impact of abusive authority figures on how I see myself'
- 'to gain more control in how I manage hearing voices'.

Following on from this, the unmet need of reviewing side-effects of antipsychotic medication is reported to the CPN.

Smyth communicates the assessment outcomes to the CMHT at the weekly team meeting and proposes a 36-week treatment pro-gramme of solution-focused brief dramatherapy. She says,

'This is based on the De Shazer model of brief therapy which capitalises on the service user's ability and motivation to refocus her or his perception of reality on what she or he has done already in life and can do anew or again, to help overcome the obstacle. In this case, due to the extent of the A's negative experience of family dynamics and consequent fragmented ego, therapy is offered initially on a one-to-one, rather than group, basis.

This process is developed as the therapy progresses. Weekly dramatherapy sessions of one and a half hours are contracted with A who consents to charting notes of sessions being retained in his medical file to be reviewed at CMHT meetings and during drama-therapy clinical supervision. Interim case review results in week 12 affirm A's progress in terms of symptomatic relief. Contributory factors are ego strengthening through creative exploration and interaction; greater understanding of the effects of family dynamics; and new insight into triggers of psychotic episodes and how to manage these more effectively.

This vignette illustrates the way in which therapist and client use the assess-ment process to explore the two areas noted earlier. They identify the areas or difficulties which might be brought and worked on by A, and also start to explore the art form to begin to establish how the client might best find meaning in the dramatic expressive media within dramatherapy. The next sections focus upon the relationship between the drama in dramatherapy and assessment.

The media within dramatherapy

The following two formats aim to demonstrate ways in which a client can begin to use the expressive forms or media within dramatherapy. The first focuses upon the way in which the client finds meaning in dramatherapy; the second can be used to consider the way in which clients involve themselves in the expressive forms used in dramatherapy. As Smyth's work in the vignette illustrates, dramatherapists often combine case information including material from other members of a team or who are involved with a client, along with material gained directly from working with the client themselves. Bannister (1997) gives an account of this when she combines information from carers of a child, reports from professionals such as social workers as well as projective techniques in working with play process such as object play and role work. She structures this as follows:

- the child's developmental level, 'especially play development'
- issues concerning attachment and bonding
- a child's coping mechanisms
- the child's emotional and therapeutic needs at present.

The first area, for example, involves work with a child in assessment drawing upon a developmental understanding of play and drama. Her practice uses structures around play language and processes using dolls and small objects to create a sense of the play language a child might best use in the therapy, as well as exploring how a child forms relationships and relates to the space and the therapist. This is connected with input from an 'educational psychologist, teachers, the paediatrician' (Bannister 1997: 19). This combination of information from different sources indicates the ways in which interagency information, as well as direct work between therapist and client, can be helpful in discovering where client and therapist can begin work together.

More specific models of assessment are also available and used by dramatherapists. Some of these are used directly, others adapted to fit the needs of the context. The adaptation of scales is often necessary as they are designed for drama settings not dramatherapy, or are aimed at play with children rather than play with adults in therapy. The following scale is an adaptation of the Sutton-Smith-Lazier Scale of Dramatic Involvement (1981). It seeks to give a general impression of involvement for a client's use of drama.

Jones's adaptation of scale of dramatic involvement

I Focus

(a) Within the dramatic activity as a whole

Focused	Occasionally focused	Often distracted	Distracted
❏	❏	❏	❏

(b) in engaging with 'as if' behaviours

Focused	Occasionally focused	Often distracted	Distracted
❑	❑	❑	❑

2 Completion

The degree to which the client completes tasks

Completes all tasks	Completes some tasks	Completes no tasks
❑	❑	❑

3 Use of imaginary objects

The capacity for creating and sustaining the use of pretended objects in a manner convincing to self and others

(a) Can create and sustain pretended objects   ❑

(b) Can disengage from object at end of the activity   ❑

(c) Can engage with others' created objects

Until end of the activity	During part of the activity	Momentarily	Not at all
❑	❑	❑	❑

4 Elaboration

Demonstrating the capacity to develop and initiate ideas within improvisation or play

No elaboration	Useful elaboration	Too much elaboration*
❑	❑	❑

No engagement with others' elaborations	Useful engagement with others' elaborations
❑	❑

* (detracts from enactment)

5 Use of space

Use of space within dramatic activity: movement in improvisation, games or character-based work

Uses available space easily	Uses space well in relation to others	Confines self to small space
❑	❑	❑

6 Facial expression

Use of face to depict appropriate emotions or responses in pretend or improvised activity

Appropriate and constant use of face	Some attempts to use face	No use of face
❑	❑	❑

7 Body movement

Using body effectively and appropriately to dramatic activity or character, communicating information or messages appropriately

Appropriate and effective use of the body	Some use of the body	No use of the body
❑	❑	❑

Understanding information or messages communicated by others' bodies within dramatic work

Constant	For some of the work	Not at all
❑	❑	❑

8 Vocal expression

Emotional relevance and projection within activities

Constant	For some of the work	Not at all
❑	❑	❑

9 Social relationships

Awareness and response to others within the activities

Constant	For some of the work	Not at all
❑	❑	❑

Projective techniques

Another important area of assessment concerns the use of projective devices in dramatherapy. There are two main approaches to projective testing. One sees the material as revealing the emotional conflicts, drives and unconscious motivations. The other is object relations orientated. In this approach the material is seen to indicate the patterns and constructs which the individual makes with others. Vernon says that projective techniques are seen as 'revealing covert dynamic forces in the personality through their expression in fantasy, creative activity, play or free associations to verbal or inkblot stimuli' (1969: 13).

The social atom

An early form of assessment that uses the concept of projection is Moreno's social atom, which is a way for the client to express material concerning the relationships and interactions with those around them and acts as a means of eliciting this information. The atom can also be utilised by the client to focus upon the main issues which cause them discomfort within their life. Additionally it can be employed as a means of gaining information to evaluate the changes that a client may have experienced in the course of the therapy (Figure 12.1).

The social atom can be drawn or sculpted. In sculpted form the client uses objects, empty chairs or others in the group to represent other people in their life, and they sculpt a map of their relationships. If the exercise is undertaken on paper then they use simple marks – a circle, for example – to represent the people in their lives. The client also represents themselves within the atom. The client then explains who is represented in the atom and describes the nature of the relationships, indicating what they experience as difficult or problematic.

Dramatherapist Vanitha Chandrasegaram describes the use of the atom as an assessment tool, but also demonstrates how it can act as a way of developing work. The session was facilitated by her with a group of seven abused women in a refuge in Malaysia:

> I had requested that the group drew a diagram (social atom) of a maximum of ten significant people in their lives. The distance between the objects may represent either the closeness of the relationship or physical distance. Later the clients were requested to sculpt the diagram using each other.

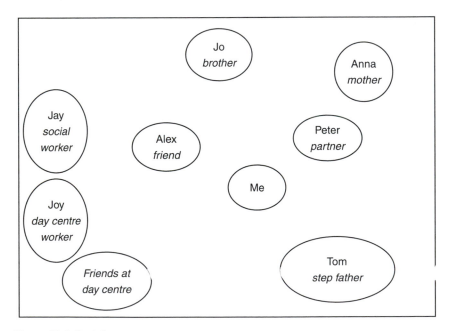

Figure 12.1 Social atom.

The following vignette concerns Chandrasegaram's description of one woman's experience in working with the social atom within this session.

Research vignette: Suraya

Suraya places Naini in the centre to represent herself. She then places Hasnah, representing her son, next to Naini, holding Naini's hand. She places Gaya, Poova and Azura at the back, left corner of Naini, representing her parents and siblings. On her right, she places Jayanthi, slightly far from her, and said that Jayanthi represents her husband, and Malathi at the far right corner of the room represents her mother-in-law.

I ask her to place her hand on the shoulder of each person or role and to say what she feels about each of the people represented. She places her hand on Naini (representing herself) and says, 'I'm now at the shelter, but I am frustrated because I can't seem to get on with my life. I've been here for five months now. However, I am thankful that my son is with me.' She then goes to her son and says, 'I love you. Everything is going to be all right . . . I will take care of you.'

When she placed her hand on the people playing her parents and her siblings, she says, 'Thank you for all of the support that you have given me – both emotionally and financially. I really do appreciate it, especially at this time.' She places her hand on Gaya, representing her father, and says, 'I know that you mean well, but I have my own plans of what I want to do once I leave the shelter.'

She places her hand on her husband and asks, 'Why did you treat me so badly? Why did you keep hitting me and putting me down? Why did you abuse me? What did I do to deserve it? I know that it was your mother who had influenced you to treat me that way . . . Even after all that, deep down, I still love you.' [She begins to sob.]

Lastly she points her hand to Malathi, playing her mother-in-law, not wanting to even go close to her, and yells, 'You bitch! You have ruined my life! I hate you for that!' Her face expresses rage. Her eyes narrow, she frowns and breathes very heavily. Looking at her reaction, I feel her fury, and let her go on, as I feel it is safe for her to fully express it. In our previous sessions, she has never really expressed anger, only sadness. Perhaps it has got to do with cultural expectations. Expressing anger is not encouraged in Malaysian society.

Next, I request that she places her hand on each role and say what she thinks they would say to her. When she placed her hand on Hasnah, playing her son, she says, 'I love you, Mom, and I want to be with you, but I miss my dad.'

When she places her hand on her parents and siblings she says, 'We will support you, and we love you.'

When she goes to her husband, she says for him, 'You are so stupid and useless. You have no right to take my son away from me.' There is anger and bitterness in her tone of voice.

When she points her finger on the character of her mother-in-law, she shouts, 'You are not good enough for my son. You are stupid and you have spoilt my son's life. I hate you.'

Every time I had done this exercise in the past, I had seen strong emotions being expressed. Therefore, I usually do this exercise only when I feel that the group is comfortable with each other and with me. This group, particularly, has been very expressive regarding their feelings about the situation that they are in.

While Suraya did this exercise, I noticed that she was really involved. This was evident to me through her facial expressions, body language, tone of voice and her tears/sobbing, especially when she was addressing her son, husband and her mother-in-law.

Later when we discussed about the session she says that she feels really bad about calling her mother-in-law a 'bitch'. In Asian culture, respect for the elderly is emphasised more than in western culture. I respond to her saying that in actuality her mother-in-law was not there and that she was only expressing her anger in a safe and acceptable way through this exercise. Even though she felt guilty for cursing at her mother-in-law, Suraya says that she feels a deep sense of relief after the exercise.

We continued our sessions for four more months. Through that time she gave up the idea of the possibility of her husband changing for the better (as she had felt that the husband abused her because he was influenced by her mother-in-law, not of his own doing), and getting back with him. Instead, she planned for a successful career and ways to take care of her son.

Vanitha Chandrasegaram

CORE PROCESS BOX

Role

Through representing aspects of her life experience by group members playing roles, Suraya is able to emotionally engage with her life experiences and bring them into the therapeutic space. This deepens her involvement with the material brought to the session.

Witnessing

She is able to offer her experiences to the group as witnesses. From a life situation where she felt isolated and victimised, she can re-experience them in the supportive situation of being with other group members and the therapist. They become witnesses with her, reflecting and gaining insight into what happened in the past and her feelings in the present.

Research conversation with Vanitha Chandrasegaram

Chandrasegaram: One of the core processes I see at work is dramatic projection, where the client has externalised her relationship with people which have influenced her life through sculpting other clients and expressing her perspective on what each of them would say to her. Her expression of words to each of them is her feelings projected on to them. Suraya was able to use drama to create access and allow the expression of showing what she was going through in life. She expressed her feelings towards different characters in her life as well as acting as director of the scene.

I see part of this in terms of a transformation that Suraya went through in this exercise. It was especially evident when she actually expressed how she felt towards her mother-in-law. In her comments later, she mentioned that doing the exercise actually allowed her to see her life as it is . . . Making it visual and lifelike made a lot of difference in bringing her into a deeper state of realisation of her life situation. The ability of seeing her relationship with each person in 3D form made a difference in the way she had perceived things, including her hope of getting together with her abusive husband.

Suraya was able to 'see' her life at the moment. That gave her further motivation on her decision of wanting to be successful and independent, proving to the world, her husband and mother-in-law, but especially to herself that she is capable of taking care of herself and her son, and capable of making her life a 'success'.

The following examples demonstrate projective assessment sessions involving small world object play. The first research vignette contains an extract from an initial assessment, along with a section of work following on from this initial contact. The assessment was within a dramatherapy department in the secondary mental health services in the UK National Health Service, and was for outpatient dramatherapy. Clare Hubbard describes the context of this assessment in relation to the client's own motives for coming to therapy:

John was referred for dramatherapy to help with his depression. He had experienced psychotherapy in the past but had not found this helpful as he had found it difficult to talk. John was offered two initial assessment sessions to see if he could use the medium of drama as a form of expression and to assess whether John could use group therapy. One of John's difficulties that emerged from the assessment was social interaction. John could find it difficult to openly talk in our sessions but expressed himself more freely through the drama. He worked especially well with objects.

Research vignette: John, second assessment session

I invited John to choose some small objects from a collection of shells, stones, toys, figures and animals, to represent parts of himself and significant people in his life. He playfully explored the collection of objects and recalled how he would have played with them as a boy. He settled on a toy bus to represent both this boy part of him and, on another level, the hard-working adult who is focused on his route and follows directions. We explored this a little further through the metaphor of the bus. John chose a cork to represent drinking alcohol in pubs. He expressed concern about his alcohol intake. He thought about the reason why he drinks, to feel more relaxed, but said it doesn't help him socialise. John selected a chimp to represent his brother. He described the characteristics of a chimp: its silly, uninhibited behaviour, but also its strength and potential for aggression. I asked John if there were any of the chimp's characteristics that he would like for himself. He identified its ability to have fun, but was adamant he didn't want to behave like it socially. The last object he chose was a figure of a man in outdoor clothes – khaki trousers, boots and a hat. John said this was a hunter, or policeman, and represented his father. The chimp and hunter were positioned in front of the cork and bus and I wondered if this suggested their dominance.

I asked John if there was another object he would like to add to the image, perhaps a characteristic he'd like to have. He chose a dinosaur, as a wished for part of himself and described this as powerful, armoured, not a predator, but it could fight back if attacked. I asked John, 'Who has the power now?' He replied that other people had. John also noticed that the dinosaur was far bigger than the bus.

John expressed more about himself through the drama than he did through purely verbal means, when he struggles to know what to say, preferring to be asked closed questions. He was animated, imaginative and, at times, spontaneous. The object work gave us something to focus on together and communicate through.

From the initial assessment John was offered 12 individual drama-therapy sessions in preparation for a group.

Research vignette: John, later session

In the previous session, using persona cards (paintings of fictional people), we had been exploring the kind of person John perceives as confident. Two of the characters he created he immensely disliked, and it materialised that they were representative of people who had bullied or shunned him.

In this session, John was talking about old buildings around his home town that he liked to explore. He would often think about the buildings. I asked John to imagine a place he would like to be, and to create this by drawing, or with objects from around the room. John used pieces of plastic wall to create a rectangular building, which he thought could be a castle, in which he placed himself as a small soldier with a gun pointed forward, and with him an old man whom he described as kind and non-judgmental. Outside the castle John placed a dinosaur and a snake to keep guard. They were loyal to the soldier. A young woman and her muscly boyfriend were trying to get in.

We returned to the scene in the following session and explored the different characters and what happened next. Eventually the soldier was all alone. The couple had given up trying to get in and left him alone. The old man had died and the guards weren't real anyway. The soldier wanted to go outside but suspected there were dangerous creatures out there and he didn't yet feel prepared enough to face them. John asked to leave the drama at this point as he didn't know how to move it forward. John didn't offer any connections with the drama but was quiet and thoughtful.

I suggested a connection with John's fear of social interactions: perhaps he did not yet feel he had the confidence or skills to relate to others, and had a fear of how they will react to him. John agreed with this interpretation. He had been very apprehensive about joining a group but now asked me to explain more about this possibility. He said he could see it was something he needed.

CORE PROCESS BOX

Dramatic projection

John projects aspects of his life experiences and sense of his identity into the materials provided. He externalises his inner concerns, and the dialogue between the cork or the chimp which he chooses and the areas of his life they represent, begins to open up and express issues which can be looked at within the therapy.

Play

Stuck issues and unexpressed material is given access to the play space within the dramatherapy session, encouraging experimentation and playfulness in exploring and changing issues and areas of his life.

Research conversation with Clare Hubbard

Jones: When John chooses the bus to represent two different aspects of himself, how do you see that?

Hubbard: John hadn't been able to tell me much about himself up to this point. He projected parts of himself onto the bus. He rediscovered a playful side to him that he had forgotten about and contrasted this with him now as an adult: his need for structure, and 'a route'.

Jones: What was behind your question about the choice of chimp as brother regarding any parts of the chimp he wanted?

Hubbard: It was a response to how he had described, very critically, the chimp's lack of self-consciousness about how he is perceived by others, and lack of social boundaries, but it was happy. John wasn't. I wondered if he envied anything about his brother, and could he think about this. The chimp appeared very different from the adult side of the bus that stuck to its route, which also wasn't desirable for John, but was closer to the boy part. I wanted to challenge John's adult bus a little and see how rigid this was: how John wanted to be.

Hubbard's analysis of the processes at work within her assessment show how the dramatherapist works with the client to develop a mutual relationship, trying to see how connections between the objects and the client's life can communicate and reveal what the client wishes to bring to therapy. The relationship between the client and therapist can also be seen to be developing within the work, as Hubbard works with the client to explore meaning and insight in a questioning and thinking *together.* This is demonstrated by her question about the chimp in the vignette, and in her analysis of her motivation in asking the question. The second part of the vignette demonstrates that another part of the assessment is to establish whether the dramatic language to work with John is appropriate, and shows how the use of the objects in assessment is deepened within the ongoing work. Assessment is not a one-off event using objects to 'test' but rather to see where to begin, and then to carry on the exploration.

The next research vignette illustrates a parallel use of projective work. It is included to show the versatility of projective assessment techniques in terms of language and process and to reinforce that assessment is an ongoing process rather than something which is useful only at the start of therapy. In relation to language it illustrates the flexibility with which a similar language or method can be adapted by therapist and client alike to express and explore their therapeutic needs. In terms of process the context of the assessment is responded to in that the meaning of the work evolves here in relation to family therapy, rather than the individual psychodynamic orientation of the vignettes about John (pp. 302–305).

Jay Vaughan describes her work with Margie and her parents who were referred to Family Futures. This was initially presented as being due to Margie's controlling and oppositional behaviour, which often culminated in violence both at home and at school. There was also an awareness that Margie, when aged three, had been removed by social services from her birth family who had visited and found her eating her own nappies whilst trapped in her cot. Following a three-month integrated multidisciplinary assessment programme, Margie and her parents began the Family Futures three-year programme. The programme devised for Margie and her family consisted of a combination of family therapy, school liaison and support as well as parent mentoring. Vaughan sets the context:

Margie and her family, as with all the families we work with, would have full days of therapy in which the usual formula would be for there to be an introductory session for the family altogether lasting usually around half an hour in which they discuss how things have been since the last session. Following this there would be an individual session for the child with an individual child therapist and a parent session with the parents' therapists. It is in this session that the parents would be prepared for the play session, the reason for the particularly activity chosen and the aims and objectives of this activity discussed with the parents. The child may well also be prepared for the family session in their individual session. Following this the main part of the therapy day would consist of a family session.

Margie and her family would therefore have had an opportunity to prepare for the family role-play session. At the beginning of the session one of the members of the therapy team would have explained the structure for the family session and the task for the family, in this instance the role play of the mountain climb expedition. At the end of the session there would be time for dismantling the 'play' space and de-roling from the play. A crucial part of this ending process would be the time given with the whole family to reflect on the whole process and to think about the key things learned from the session which can be put into practice at home.

Vaughan further contextualises this vignette by contrasting the early and later phases of the work: 'There had been considerable emphasis in the early part of the treatment programme on Margie's life story. The focus in the therapy has now been shifted to thinking about the impact that Margie's early experiences have upon her day-to-day life.'

The vignette is from a family therapy session in the first year of work and is led by all three therapy team members, an arts therapist, a social worker and a parent mentor. Vaughan provides the following information in relation to the direction and ideas behind the vignette:

> The aim of the session is to help the family think about the dynamics being played out in the family, and the role that Margie wishes to assume: of leader in the family. It has been decided by the therapy team, in consultation with their supervisor, that a session using role play would be a helpful way of exploring the family dynamics. It is already known that the family enjoys role play and that this would therefore be a good way of engaging them in thinking about the difficult dynamics in the family.

Research vignette: Mountain climb expedition

The family is asked in the session to create an imaginary mountain for a mountain climb expedition. They are then asked to devise a script consisting of five scenes portraying their adventures on their travels up and down the mountain. It is emphasised to them that during this journey anything can happen, but at the end of the journey everyone must manage to get down the mountain together alive! They are asked to act out the scenes whilst the therapy team has the power to intervene, as if they are a film crew, asking them to 'rewind', 'fast forward' 'freeze' or even 'hot seating' one of the family members to interview them. This is what happens.

Margie pouted her mouth. You could almost see her dig her heels in the carpet as she stared defiantly at her parents saying, 'I want to carry the tent, the biscuits and the map. All of them. I can manage. I know what I am doing.'

Margie began to climb precariously onto a chair and moved towards a large pile of jungle animals. Margie somehow managed to kick her mother in the face as she clambered upwards. Mrs Walker started to speak and then decided not to. She swallowed hard and picked up her woolly hat pulling it on roughly over her ears and then continued traipsing on behind her daughter. Mr Walker rolled his eyes and continued up the mountainous pile of cushions behind his wife and daughter. Margie, ahead of them, held on tightly to the map the family had drawn earlier that day and prepared to jump over a crevasse. Mrs Walker held out her hand to help Margie. Margie ignored her. The tent dangling over her shoulder almost obscured her determined little body altogether, as she made a leap to jump to the other side. For a moment she seems suspended in mid-air and then suddenly she plummeted into the crevasses of cushions below. One of the therapists said 'freeze' and everyone stopped.

Margie's eyes filled with tears of frustration and her lower lip began to quiver. Mrs Walker moved to sit beside Margie on the floor and took her little hand in hers. Margie talked while the tears streamed down her face, insisting quietly, 'I can manage all on my own, that is how I like it. I've always done everything on my own. I don't need a mum and dad.' Margie collapsed into her mother's arms exhausted and began to eat the biscuits. Mrs Walker said, 'But Margie you're only eight. You still need a mum and dad to care for you. It is not fair you had to do it all on your own for so long in your birth family. You've got us now. We can help you over the crevasse.'

The film was 'rewound' and the therapy team challenged Margie to try the jump again, now with her parents' help. This time

Margie, still holding most the family's possessions tightly to her body, managed to jump from her father balanced on a cushion on one side of the crevasse to her mother on the opposite side. Whoops of delights and cheering broke out from the therapy team as she landed triumphantly in her mother's arms. Margie beamed and took a bow. Mr Walker slid his hand into Mrs Walker's, pulling her closer to kiss her on the cheek.

At the end of the mountain climb expedition all the family were sitting around thinking about their journey. Mr Walker, who had been quiet up to this point, said, 'When I set out on this journey with my adoptive family I was really looking forward to being altogether. But the journey was hard, and terrible things happened on the way. I had no idea what I was letting myself in for. However, I would not change things and I am glad I went on the journey. It is only that I now realise how much help I need to manage all the challenges ahead.'

Mrs Walker turned to her little daughter sitting sandwiched between her and her husband on the sofa and very gently moved a strand of hair from her forehead kissing her ever so softly. Margie looked up at her and smiled.

Jay Vaughan

CORE PROCESS BOX

Dramatic projection

The mountain expedition creates a dramatic image and situation which the family enter. The journey starts to take on dynamics and emotions that hold and express feelings and patterns which exist in life outside the drama. The mountain as an image, and the clients' roles as climbers start to express issues and tensions that reflect the reasons the family have come to therapy. The dramatherapy space becomes a space to explore these dramatic reflections.

Witnessing

The therapists act as witnesses, through pausing, rewinding and commenting; they act as an active audience, as well as witnessing directors. The aim is to help increase the meaning and use of the drama, to help the family explore and gain insight into what patterns occur. In this way, they are helping the family to become witnesses to their own experience with an aim to develop insight and the capacity to try different routes in the 'journey'.

Play

By creating a playful space, the therapists are trying to enable the family to open up fixed patterns to flexibility and experimentation with new ways of relating.

Research conversation with Jay Vaughan

Jones: In relation to the space you created together, I was very interested in this choice to 'freeze' and to rewind with the challenge. Can you say a bit about freezing at that point in particular?

Vaughan: Families have really enjoyed this interactive way of working and it helps ease the sense that they are being watched, as the therapy team are very much a part of the process. Another positive aspect of this way of working is how parents feel that they are not just abandoned to be observed when things go wrong. Most parents are acutely aware of the metaphor that they are working with and of the significance of the points they are struggling with in the journey.

In our experience, the particular group of children with whom we work struggle to have positive experience, and frequently set up situations in which they fail and receive negative feedback. To build in the opportunity during a therapy session to reinforce a success is a gift in the work. In our view, whilst sometimes it is helpful to just observe as situations unfold there are occasions where it is more helpful to freeze the action and replay it in a different way.

In this instance we were very aware that Margie set up situations where she tried to manage alone and, understandably, because of her age failed. On the one hand this reinforced her pattern of struggling on her own and on the other hand it gave her no opportunity to practise doing it differently. Maybe this is a rather behavioural aspect to our model of family dramatherapy. This moment of freeze, at the point of disaster when Margie falls down the crevasse, and then giving the family an opportunity to rehearse another way of being provides an important moment to return to in the drama where we can hear from Margie and her parents what it felt like doing it differently, as well as providing them with an example of what we want them to try to do more of at home.

Jones: What aspects of playing were you drawing on to help assess or see what was happening or needed within the family?

Vaughan: Children who have been traumatised often try to unconsciously play out over and over in the therapy, and in their lives, their traumatising experiences. In this way Margie was trying to demonstrate how she had learnt to struggle on her own with unmanageable tasks for an eight year old, and how life threatening some of these situations had been for her. We are very aware of the pull in the therapy to act out the trauma so that it is retraumatising, rather than to rework the trauma in a way that helps it to be resolved. We also believe that all the research on working with trauma suggests that talking about the experiences does not help resolve them, but using alternatives ways of engaging the brain and more active forms of therapy, especially non-verbal ways of working, means that the trauma can be accessed without retraumatising the child.

Jones: How would you see the play Margie and her family engaged in as having an impact on their life outside? For example, what's there to stop Margie and her family creating a play world with the therapist where they behave in one way, and sticking to their old ways of behaving outside?

Vaughan: It is very slow process in therapy to help children like Margie take the experiences that they have learned in the therapy session and do things differently at home. We place a strong emphasis in our work on supporting parents with parent therapists into becoming part of the therapeutic team. Clearly parents spend much more time with their children than therapists and, therefore, we believe it is essential that they can take the work of the therapy session into their home and integrate it into their lives.

For Margie's family, the need for Margie to practise letting her parents look after her is key and at the end of the session some homework would be given to the family asking them to focus on this. Telephone support from the parent therapist, post the session, would help try to maintain this focus. The next session would begin by reviewing what had happened the previous session and seeing how the homework had worked for the family. The next session would usually either be a fortnight, or a month, away depending on the particular treatment plan for each family. Obviously addressing such huge changes in family dynamics and ways in which children have learnt to manage their attachment relationships would be a slow process.

Jones: I was curious about the facilitators 'whooping' with delight and cheering, and Margie bowing. How do you look at that in terms of the therapeutic process?

Vaughan: It is an interesting process being asked about one's work in this way as this has become one of the interventions we do regularly with families, and until you asked about it I had not reflected on how curious it might seem. I suppose it takes me back to the way that we set up this work for families and our original intention to engage families in the work who had had difficult experiences of therapy, feeling very observed and criticised. Families we work with very much get the message that this is a collaborative approach, which includes them in the team. There is a lot of spontaneous warmth and affection between the families the team and a very relaxed style.

The task for the therapy team, aside from being very in touch with their own process during the work is, perhaps, aside from working with all the pain and despair that is brought to the therapy but to also encourage some joy. Colin Trevarthan has done extensive work on the need for positive experiences that become shared between children and the parents. Sometimes the families that get referred to us have forgotten how to laugh together and laughter and praising them is just as important as anything else in the therapy.

The next research vignette, by way of a contrast, shows the ending of therapy. It shows how the 'same' process of dramatic projection and role playing in a journey is employed by Naomi Gardner to enable clients to use dramatic images and processes to discover and express the meaning of the work for them within a summative evaluation of dramatherapy.

Research vignette: Desert journey

For a group of 18- to 21-year-old males with schizophrenia, the theme of journeys seemed to resonate. The group, set up to help with transitions back into the community, had been running for 16 weeks in a UK mental health hospital. In the penultimate session Brian discussed having seen a film about a group of boys who go on an expedition. The group were vociferous in opening circle and I was struck by my own feelings of enthusiasm. Discussion ensued about specific moments from sessions, sharing in common the 'passage' they had experienced. Anthony said, 'I remember how scared I felt at first, I didn't want to do anything.' Anthony suggested the group go on a 'last journey' and seemed to be reflecting anxieties about the sessions ending and separation.

Brian suggested it be set in a desert, with them riding over sand dunes in a jeep. I was placed in the role of audience, to observe and freeze the action at specific points. The group also seemed to be seeking containment and boundaries. They set about creating the landscape using furniture and other materials. Anthony, usually a quieter member of the group, took the role of driver, Brian became navigator and Christopher a passenger. They seemed to be exploring alternative roles within the safety of the drama. After exploring for a while, Christopher announced that treasure was hidden under a rock close by. Using a compass Brian directed them to the rock. Together they dug until they found a box with a store of jewels. I stopped the action at this moment, asking for a word or phrase to define how they were feeling. Anthony described feeling 'alive', Brian 'together' and Christopher 'empowered'. In discussing the journey afterwards, clients began to reflect on the significance of their journey and the treasure. The group felt that the sessions had helped them to rediscover their own creativity, which had been hidden through isolation, medication and institutionalisation.

Naomi Gardner

CORE PROCESS BOX

Dramatic projection

The group create an expedition and this holds images to do with their journey. The group image enables individuals to project and explore their own experience during the session.

Role taking

The group are enrolled together as travellers. Within this specific roles are taken, seemingly reflecting aspects of the roles they had taken within the dynamics of the group, or as a part of their image of themselves.

Life–drama connection

The dramatic projection into the landscape, expedition and roles are seen to be 'significant' and the reflection enables connections between the content and process of the dramatisation and issues in their lives outside the session: for example, isolation, medication and life within the institution.

Research conversation with Naomi Gardner

Gardner: The group was able to explore and embody alternative roles. By trying out different aspects of themselves they were able to gain insight into their capacity to develop and change. Anthony was very shy and withdrawn in initial sessions. He adopted a confident and leadership role and was surprised by how others responded to him. The safety of the group enabled him to attempt such work.

Jones: You talk about insight here in relation to embodying roles. I'm very interested in that idea, especially as part of evaluation. How do you see that?

Gardner: Anthony became more aware of his physicality, particularly in relation to others. In sessions he would sit further back in group circle and eye contact would be minimal. However, in this role his physicality changed, he stood upright, used good eye contact and verbal communication was enhanced. After de-roling his eye contact remained high and his body language was strong and confident. The experience in role seemed to have impacted on the way he perceived himself in life. The clients instinctively made connections between their characters and themselves.

Jones: I would be interested to hear what kind of things. Did you see them doing this during the drama and within the drama, for example, in character, or did they make explicit comments after the enactment? Or none of these?

Gardner: During the drama, it appeared that the group was internalising the experience. It would perhaps have been difficult for them to make connections with their own lives while they were still in role. However, on discussing the differences and similarities they shared with their roles, after the drama, the group began to assimilate the different aspects of themselves as seen within their characters. Anthony in particular seemed to acknowledge that parts of himself (he described having previously been outgoing) had been affected by the illness. He was able to re-experience what it felt like to be confident, through the physicality and characteristics of the role he had adopted. This process was very emotive and the group acknowledged the loss (of their old selves) they had experienced as a result of their illness. The process had reinvigorated the group and provided insight into their 'potential' selves.

Jones: In terms of evaluation, how do you see what the group did? How were the processes at work useful to them?

Gardner: Being in hospital had left them feeling deskilled and disempowered. The group made decisions and worked together. They experienced trust and containment. The opportunity to play out roles, and experience different situations, within a safe and boundaried space helped to develop confidence and self-esteem. Using the dramatic medium seemed to reignite feelings of being creative and being 'useful'. My role was to facilitate boundaries so that the group felt safe exploring this life–drama connection. By stopping and starting the action, the group felt contained and could fully engage with the embodiment of their characters and safely be de-roled.

Jones: So, in describing the process in this way are you saying that 'safety' can be a key part of making the 'life–drama connection'? If so in what way, as I'd not thought of the process in that way before?

Gardner: Trust plays a central part in facilitating safety. If the group trusts one another and the therapist to 'hold' them, then they feel freer to explore their roles and make connections with themselves. This process requires an environment of acceptance. Without this the group, in particular the less confident or more introverted members, were unlikely to engage.

Role-playing tests

A number of assessment and evaluation methodologies have been designed which focus upon role. These vary from Satir's (1967) use of sculpting family roles in order to assess family dynamics to studies based around assessing the effectiveness of dating behaviours. The following describes two ways of framing assessment around role.

Johnson's role-playing test

David Read Johnson's role-playing test is designed to test and indicate the client's 'internal personality structure'. The individual is asked to enact a short series of roles. This improvisation is undertaken alone and 11 props are provided (table, wastepaper basket, chair, stick, cloth, paper cup, book, hat, phone, man's coat and woman's dress). Five roles are given to be enacted – grandparent, bum, politician, teacher and lover (1988: 25) – and scenes are usually one minute long. A second test follows this. The props are removed and the individual is asked to improvise three scenes, which involve action between three 'beings'. The individual describes the three beings and then improvises with them, telling the facilitator when they have finished.

The intention is to provide a sample of the client's role-playing behaviour. In turn this is seen to give information about the personality structure of the individual, along with information about their concerns bringing them to therapy and about their use of drama in terms of role play. The material is interpreted according to a series of categories to provide a framework for assessment. These include:

- role repertoire
- patterns in thematic content style of role playing
- the way the client structures space, tasks and roles
- the interactions amongst the characters in terms of complexity the degree and forms of affect (Read Johnson 1988: 26–27).

Categories are divided into criteria to assist assessment. For example, the organisation of the scene is described in Table 12.1.

All of the above role-playing tests assume that inferences about personality can be made from dramatised scenarios within the context of therapy. They select an area of behaviour and focus upon it. Each of the tests creates a fixed

Table 12.1 Diagnostic role-playing test – complexity of representations

Item	Description
Organisation of scene	1 Developed – characters and their interactions are presented in the context of a story with a plot 2 Adequate – only characters and their interaction are clearly portrayed 3 Incomplete – characters and/or plot are incompletely or vaguely portrayed 4 Incoherent – no discernible plot, characters or interaction

Source: Read Johnson (1988: 33)

structure and seeks to assess clients through their individual responses. In all the tests or assessment exercises the emphasis is upon the therapist or professional using information to make conclusions about the client. There is limited opportunity for the client to participate in their own assessment.

Play-influenced assessment

Play process and research into the assessment and evaluation of play have influenced the assessment of dramatherapy. The following present a series of frameworks for assessment which can be useful to work with both adults and children.

Lowenfeld's World Technique

Lowenfeld's World Technique can be used as an assessment technique (Lowenfeld 1970). As described in Chapter 7, it consists of miniature toys and a tray, usually made of metal or plastic, 75 × 52 cm (29 × 20 in). The toys are divided into a series of basic categories:

- human beings
- animals
- countryside objects (trees, fences, etc.)
- buildings such as houses
- transport (cars, ships, ambulances).

The work is divided into two stages: one is called 'The Bridge', the other 'Picture Thinking'. The first stage consists of the therapist informing the child that adults and children live on opposite sides of a river and there is a gap of understanding between the two. The work entails building a kind of bridge across the gap. The sandtray is introduced as a way of forming pictures in the sand. These can be anything the child wants and need not be realistic. The child can use any of the objects along with the contents of the tray. Whilst the world is being made and after its completion, the therapist tries to find out the meaning the child gives to the different objects in the world and the relationships between the different elements in the world. This is done both through asking questions, and listening and observing what the child does with the created world.

Adapting assessment methods

Parten's social participation scale

Another example of the adaptation of existing assessment methods is the way that Parten's study of young children and assessment scale was adapted to work with adolescents who had been diagnosed as autistic (Jones 1993). The dramatherapy involved an attempt to enhance clients' social skills through the use of puppetry. Elements of the Parten scale were adapted by Sanctuary (1984) in order to try to ascertain the effect of the dramatherapy upon the client's interactions outside of the therapy group. A series of criteria based on Parten's scale was used to assess certain behaviours and to evaluate the work. Eight areas were developed from the Parten scale to produce 'a continuum ... ranging from withdrawn to active and pro-social behaviours and inter-actions' (Jones 1993: 51).

Box 12.1 **Parten's social participation scale**

1 Stereotyped
2 Unoccupied/withdrawn
3 Solitary
4 Responsive
5 Aggressive
6 Initiated
7 Helping behaviour
8 Parallel activity (adaptation of Parten, Sanctuary 1984).

Each area was subdivided into more specific criteria. So, for example, the fourth area was built of a number of behaviours.

---

4 Responsive: including

Smiling or laughing in response to another
Answering when addressed
Maintaining conversation
Maintaining eye contact for at least one second
Handing or passing objects in response to another

Clients were assessed for a period two weeks prior to the dramatherapy group, during the nine-week group, immediately after the closure of the work and finally two weeks after the end of the therapy. The comparison of these assessments was then used to help evaluate the nature of behavioural change in the clients.

In adapting scales or methods from other areas of study or practice, the dramatherapist aims to meet the requirements of their own assessment needs. They do so by altering the original criteria to relate more effectively to the dramatic media at the heart of dramatherapy, or by connecting their work to the assessment strategy of another discipline. As the examples cited in this chapter show, this can be effective. However, there is a danger inherent in this form of adaptation. Payne (1993) has identified this problem in the context of research, saying that 'a sole reliance on traditional research approaches denies us access to the richness available in the processes and other phenomena intrinsic to practice' (1993: 33).

Recording sessions

Recording dramatherapy sessions will usually involve the documenting of material for the analysis of the therapist in order to communicate about the work to other colleagues in situations such as case conferences. It is not possible to document and analyse everything that occurs within therapy. However, a good recording format should aid the process of finding a language and structure to describe and consider what has occurred. Recording helps to create a space for reflection, aids the process of considering themes, patterns, key occurrences and interactions within the work. Different modalities of recording sessions are often used. These include video, forms for clients to fill in, the creation of pictoral images and still photographs of elements of enactments.

The following format, often used by dramatherapists, seeks to set up a framework for describing, documenting and analysing the session through writing. This example concerns work in a setting that encouraged clients to engage with a variety of therapy programmes; some were group psychotherapy, others took a more behaviourally orientated approach.

Written dramatherapy recording sample

Dramatherapy group

Date 22 May   **Time** 10.00–11.30 am

No. of session 10 out of 20

Present Eva, Janet, Malick, Mark, Miriam, Pete, Jo, Zina

Absent None

Pre-session notes Am informed that community meeting prior to group was argumentative, with some clients expressing anger about an outing which had to be cancelled due to staff shortage. Janet expresses reluctance to come to any sessions at the centre just within my earshot. I feel anxious as group seem quite silent and reticent about entering the room, rather like first sessions.

Overall aims within the dramatherapy group

- To increase confidence
- To improve self-image
- To increase communication skills

Intended sessional aims

1   To offer the opportunity for clients to present personal issues concerning confidence, self-image and communication skills.
2   To enable clients to explore these issues through dramatherapy.
3   Through exploring and working with the problems to enable individuals to look at the way issues from their past relate to their current problems.
4   To look at ways of achieving change in order to become more confident, to develop a more accurate relationship to self-image and to develop effective communication.

Preparation Last session a heated debate had followed the enactment created by Eva when Zina claimed to have been completely ignored in her role of Eva's mother and said that she felt angry with Eva for ignoring her. She said she felt this was something Eva did to her all the time. Eva had denied this, saying that it was her mother she was ignoring, not Zina herself. The session had ended on this note. It seemed likely that this specific issue might be returned to, along with issues around ignoring, being ignored and parents.

Rationale for sessional aims To give space for unfinished business from last time, given the heated ending. To reflect the group's aims to create opportunities to consider self-image, confidence and communication in working with whatever material group members might choose to bring.

Description Group very silent on entry. All acknowledge me and some acknowledge each other. Eva and Zina do not make any eye contact. As usual at the start of the group there is a silence and people begin to talk about the last session and how they feel now. I suggest a sculpt whereby each person places themselves in a position representing how they felt at the end of the session. In this sculpt they each can say a little about how they felt. This is followed by a partner taking up their position. They then say anything they want to that position from where they are now. The partner then says what it felt like to be in that position.

Several themes emerge. Eva says she doesn't want to talk about it any more. Zina says that she feels ignored by Eva, that she won't listen to how upset she is. I ask whether she wants to explore this further. She says that she does and I offer her a number of options. These include telling us a story about the feeling of being ignored, or showing us a situation where she has felt ignored, or exploring the relationship with those in the group by sculpting. She chooses to tell a story. A character is created, 'Jasmin', who shares three qualities with Zina and which relate to being ignored. Zina gives these as shy and unsure, used to being ignored and feeling unworthy. I suggest that we see a story where her character experiences these feelings in three events. It takes place in a desert in a small Bedouin encampment near an oasis. There is a family who live in two tents. The first event involves Jasmin trying to tell someone that she has an aching tooth, but no one will listen. In the second she is sent out to find some wood with her two sisters, but though they come back with damp wood and she returns with dry wood, theirs is chosen for the fire. The third event tells how a stranger arrives. This is someone Jasmin likes but she cannot say to him that she likes him. She is unable to make any contact with him.

Zina chooses Mark for her father, Miriam for her mother, Eva and Janet for her sisters and Malick for the stranger. She sculpts them and describes the desert for us, along with the tents. The boundaries of each tent are set up by chairs. Each character is given two qualities by Zina. The father is pre-occupied and works hard, the mother is quiet and loves her two younger daughters best, the middle daughter is hard working and jealous of Jasmin, the youngest daughter is quiet and happy. The stranger is warm and mysterious. Zina chooses to play Jasmin, though she was given the choice to cast one of the group in this role.

The story is kept to by the group. The characters then talk about what it felt like to play these roles. At the end I ask Zina what it is that Jasmin wants and how she might get it. Zina says that Jasmin wants to be appreciated more and to get what she wants more. She should push herself and rely less on others to put her forward and to feel at a loss if they didn't. At this point Zina makes a comparison between herself and Jasmin's position. She talks about the expectations around women and cultural issues concerning her Muslim upbringing and her current rejection of these traditions and her faith.

We replay the scenario. Zina is to play her role as if she could be more assertive, to rely less on others. As Jasmin, Zina manages to do this in some situations. The enactment is broken into three parts and there is a pause after each to see if Zina wants to try it again differently. At times I invite audience feedback on how Jasmin is doing and, if Zina wants it, to be given some ideas about how to handle things.

When this is completed the players speak to the audience about their experience in role and how they feel in relation to the role. Zina says that, although she had needed support, she is astonished to be able to find Jasmin being more forthcoming. She adds that the feelings she experienced as Jasmin remind her of her family situation. Some of the group talk about how they could identify with the character and her experience. Eva stays silent during this time.

Analysis The work seemed to be able to reflect the material Zina was becoming aware of in the last session. The underlying relationship between Eva and Zina is still reflected in the content and by the casting of Eva as the 'jealous' sister. The group did not engage with how the casting reflected their actual feelings or relationships between each other.

Personal response I too could recognise the feeling of being ignored. It especially reminded me of the feelings raised in the early days of the group when a number of clients did not participate or participated a little and my interventions were often ignored. I remembered how shut out I felt. I felt warm towards the group as they supported the portrayal of Jasmin.

Evaluation

Sessional aims

1 Zina was able to present personal issues concerning confidence and self-image. She was also able to practise enhancing her communication skills. Others were able to discuss their own issues in relation to the work undertaken by the group through joining in with the enactment, through witnessing and through discussion.

2 The group were able to explore these issues through dramatherapy. For Zina this was through the story and role she created. Others were able to identify with elements of the content and process. To an extent they were able to engage with their own material by witnessing and in the playing through of fears in the roles they took on.

3 Zina was able to look at issues from her past and how they related to her present situation. A specific example was how her relationship with her mother seemed to reflect the feeling of being ignored by Eva in the last session. Though this was not verbally acknowledged in the session, my opinion is that this was an important aspect of the improvisation.

4 By changing Jasmin's behaviour, Zina was able to identify how change might occur and experienced effecting that change. She had the skills to work with the family and to work in role with more assertion and with more confidence. Her communication skills were enhanced by the way she talked to the group in putting herself forward as willing to explore the situation. She also communicated to the group the ways she wanted to handle the improvisation. The feedback from the group reinforced this. The group, by identifying, witnessing, offering support and playing roles, were able to find some contact and use for themselves within the work.

Other points There were issues around the connecting of the character to reality – 'Jasmin could do it, but could I?' However, Zina seemed pleased that she could manage more assertive behaviour at all. Themes continue within the group of ignoring, lack of communication, isolation, although the ability of the group to support Jasmin was a significant change. The individuals managed to keep roles, though Mark became confused and on two occasions needed help to get back into role.

Summary

The development of methods of assessment in dramatherapy is still an area which needs research. The establishment of clear strategies that are based firmly in the theories, principles and core practices of dramatherapy is needed. As this chapter has shown, the current approaches toward assessment and evaluation in dramatherapy are usually adapted from those utilised in related disciplines – dramatic scales, methods from play therapy or psychodrama. Whilst these approaches and techniques suffice to support the work which the dramatherapist undertakes, the therapist has to adopt a way of working which must be adapted, rather than working with an approach generated by the field of dramatherapy itself. However, the chapter has illustrated the broad range of assessment and evaluation practices available to dramatherapy. A wide range of processes can be brought to the work in a way that suits the needs and context of the client involved in dramatherapy.

Appendix: Research vignettes and conversations

The approach to research contained in this book

The research project drawn on in the writing of the second edition of this book aimed to investigate the impact of the core therapeutic processes described within *Drama as Therapy* (Jones 1996: 99–129) on thinking and practice in the field. The research question was: *How are dramatherapists making use of the therapeutic core processes (Jones 1996) in analysing their practice?*

The goal was to ascertain the ways in which the original ideas described in *Drama As Therapy* (Jones 1996) were being used and adapted by therapists. Two key components of this research involved:

1   A request for vignettes from therapists making use of the therapeutic core processes in analysing their practice.
2   The submission of the vignettes followed by a reflective research conversation with each respondent based on the vignette.

The project had three phases:

1   Offer opportunity to take part in the research made to dramatherapists with an aim to involve 30 respondents.
2   To receive vignettes and to undertake a research conversation that will take the form of a joint reflection on the vignette.
3   Writing up results.

Both research vignette and conversation were conducted with care for ethical issues. A separate Ethics document was issued to respondents which drew on the UK Health Professions Council's Standards of Conduct, Performance and Ethics, Duties of Registrant (2003) *http://www.hpc-uk.org* and the British Association of Dramatherapists Code of Practice, as well as reference to Leeds Metropolitan University's Ethical Guidelines and to the University's Carnegie Faculty Research Ethics Sub Committee. A form confirming that material was submitted in adherence with the Ethics document guidelines, as well as the ethical protocols and procedures of any setting in which work had taken place, were signed and submitted by therapists submitting vignettes, to be kept by myself as researcher under the remit of Leeds Metropolitan University's Carnegie Faculty Research Ethics Sub Committee.

The brief was to offer a short vignette from practice. This could either be part of a session, or a broader description of a process through a session – something that could breathe easily in that wordage and would make coherent sense. The remit was that the participants considered it practice that had drawn on their understanding of, and use of, the core therapeutic processes as referred to above.

After supplying the vignette there would be a 'conversation' between the therapist/participant and myself. This would normally be undertaken by aMSN messenger and each participant would see the final version to agree it. No part of the introduction, vignette or analysis would be altered without their permission. The therapist/participant could withdraw at any time up to publication.

As stated in the Ethics document the participant anonymised the client work in a way that is consistent with the relevant and identified ethical protocols and that reflected good practice in this area, and which would meet all ethical requirements concerning areas such as confidentiality and permission.

During the research process I kept a research diary, reflecting on the theoretical development of the work, and a more personal diary reflecting on the process. Participants were similarly invited to keep a personal log of their experiences of the process. Some did this and agreed to make this available to help reflect upon and report on the research process.

Vignettes

Vignettes are 'narrative investigations that carry within them an interpretation of the person, experience, or situation the writer describes . . . a vignette restructures the complex dimensions of its subject for the purpose of capturing in a brief portrayal, what has been learned over a period of time' (Anzul *et al.* 1997: 70). Ely (1991) describes some characteristics of vignettes:

- stated in the first person
- include words of participants
- distilled from data in as close a likeness to the participant's mode of expression
- intention to present in miniature the essence of what the researcher has seen or heard over time.

Ely goes on to note something that has been important in my research:

> themes, social rules, and constructs/vignettes do not stand alone. They are devices that are established through analysis and offered to provide meaning, cohesion, and colour to the presentation. They serve also to

counter the danger of over abstracting by *anchoring* the findings firmly in the *field* that gave rise to them.

(Ely 1991: 154–155)

Here, for me, were some important connections. First, that the vignette should not be isolated, that it is a device of connection. There were two main elements of this. One is that the vignette is a connection with the particular, the individual situation and context whilst, and this is not a paradox, taking on the role of a selection, a presentation of 'essence' at the same time. The other is that the vignette links with the contexts it is practised in – with particular social meanings. At the same time, then, the vignette is absolutely only of its situation, but can also stretch and build a bridge through its use in the process of research with a wider meaning.

So, in a way, I am adding to Ely's image of making sure the findings stay firmly in Ely's '*field*' but also introducing the role of the vignette in building *bridges* – connecting the particular to the 'essence' of distilled general process. Like most bridges, when they are built they connect two territories and both are changed – the traffic across the bridge is normally two way. It is important for me that in this the vignettes create changes on both sides. They draw the specific experience of the practising therapists to the general descriptions of the core processes and both are changed by it.

Narratives and enquiry

The research was based in approaches rooted in enquiry concerned with narratives. Anzul *et al.* (1997) talk about narrative as 'a method of inquiry and a way of knowing – a discovery and way of analysis (1997: 64). The narratives within and around the research vignettes are both: they are ways of finding out about what the therapists recall and want to communicate, and the ways they tell themselves and myself as researcher about what matters to them in their work, how the core processes connect with how they construe, see and talk about change. In this approach to the research I am also drawing upon the ways in which 'narrative analysis' has been used within the area of my research's concern: in 'the burgeoning therapeutic culture – exploration of personal life in therapies of various kinds . . . construct texts for further analysis.select and organize documents . . .'. What I have done is akin to this approach where 'field notes and/or . . . sections of interview transcripts [are used] for close inspection. Narratives do not speak for themselves . . . they require interpretation' (Jupp 2005: 186). The therapists and myself, as researchers, are taking narratives together and working with interpretation.

Elliott says that 'a narrative can be understood to organize a sequence of events into a whole so that the significance of each event can be understood through its relation to that whole. In this way a narrative conveys the meaning of events' (2005: 3). In my research work the notion of 'narrative' and 'whole' is more problematic than that. The narratives are not intended as *wholes* in one way – whole in the sense of complete or entire. The narratives in vignettes are partial, selections, slivers and in that sense are full of *holes* – absences and omissions – highlighting their partiality and partial nature. I suppose they are self-consciously thus, and it was important to me that the presentation of the research findings needed to show this: aware – which means that they are not intended to tell *the* story of the core processes or the client work, but *a* story about the processes. By that I mean that they are selected for a purpose, and by a person in interaction with a particular circumstance (myself researching the way they see change in relation to the core processes). Like most stories or narratives, they are both specific and general. They emerge from very particular circumstances but become different as they appear in different contexts of telling. So one 'telling' is the therapist making the story in relation to the original context: the way she or he creates the story as its happening with the clients or (in a way) co-authors. The next is in recollection, in process afterwards in, for example, clinical supervision. Then in co-creation of writing it to me, and still further in the light of its new contact with the book: another narrative. Still further as the therapist and I reflect on it together, the narrative of the book changes and is changed by the act of the research and the retelling of the core processes. In this way the research and its outcomes can be framed as a chain of narratives that are interdependent but not complete. The research is communicated with a consciousness of the other elements of stories that are contingent – that are 'left out' – and these holes have their own significance.

Another theme within narrative approaches to research is that narrative concerns itself with causality, why something happened, when and how it happened: 'linked to each other as cause to effect, effects in turn causing other effects . . . [there] . . . may be some larger principle' (Chatman 1978: 46, quoted in Elliott 2005: 8). Again here is something crucial to the research work: the way in which narrative concerns cause and effect. In essence this is that causes may be multiple and can be considered in relation to the revealing of 'larger principle'. Narratives are never 'simply the reports of experiences, rather they make sense of and therefore invariably distort those experiences' (Elliott 2005: 23). In a way my interest within the research is in the distortion – the ways in which sense was made by the therapists, the ways in which the processes were used to structure narratives about change, therapeutic change and the ways in which causality was seen. These changes were helpful in seeing how the therapists involved in the research changed the original sense of the processes by what they had discovered about them in their work and in the mutual analysis of the vignettes. This example from the conversation with Secchi in Chapter 5 illustrates a part of this happening:

Secchi: I use my feelings as a guide to deciding what choice I make in the session and how to respond. My feelings take the role of witness but should not become 'infected' by the emotion too much (as may a witness). Witnesses by their nature may be over-distanced or under-distanced by the event they experience, the therapist has to try to remain aesthetically distanced.

Jones: Lovely ideas about witnessing here that stretch the ideas I put forward in the first edition. . . . I want to learn from your experience and thoughts . . . this intriguing idea about 'infection' and under-over distance . . . would be very interested to have your thoughts about how these notions connect with what was happening in the vignette?

aMSN messenger and the research conversations

The intention in using aMSN messenger within a narrative research approach was that it would allow for time to reflect in typed conversation – a mix of spontaneity and reflection different from verbal conversation. In essence aMSN is a live, typed conversation between two people using computers. This was used partly in recognition of the potential benefits of this way of working, and partly as a way of dealing with the fact that respondents needed to be communicated with whilst living as far apart as Canada, South Africa and Taiwan. One criticism of computer-assisted interviewing procedures is that it creates distance between researcher and respondent, no space for 'marginalia or evidence of answers being revised'. This critique argues that when data is captured electronically, it reduces reciprocity. This could be said to contrast with narrative interviewing which Jupp says is a 'major shift in perspective in the human sciences about the research interview itself' (Jupp 2005: 190). Question and answer give way to viewing the interview as 'a discursive accomplishment. Participants engage in an evolving conversation; narrator and listener/questioner, collaboratively, produce and make meaning of events and experience that the narrator reports (Mishler 1986). So my approach was to try and a create way of working that is more like this within aMSN messenger.

The approach I adopted was that I would aim not to be only an interviewer who asked standard questions to a 'vessel-like respondent' but would also encourage a way of working where I would try to be as responsive as possible to the material offered by the therapist, aiming to become 'two active participants who produce meaning (Gubrium and Holstein 2002: 27). The term research conversation seemed an appropriate way to mark this mutuality. This way of approaching research is seen to help explore associations and meanings, involving turn taking, entrance and exit talking, following participants down their trail: 'Genuine discoveries about a phenomenon can come from power sharing in interviews' (Jupp 2005: 190). The spontaneity inherent in this approach to narrative research – staying alert to associations and potential meanings – can be seen in many of the research conversation edits within this book. The following dialogue shows how this sensitivity is used by both myself and Van Den Bosch in the research conversation in Chapter 6 when we both respond to an error in my typing within the aMSN conversation.

Jones: Do you think there was the possibility that the connection with play, with fantasy and externalising inner material, might be problematic even countertherapeutic for Jilly? I'm thinking about that maybe in terms of attachment or being almost overwhelded to the things she projects into. Sorry – my typing mistake! 'Over whelded' – interesting typo – mixture of overwhelmed and welded!

Van Den Bosch: I think this is a fascinating word as she has become over 'whelded' to objects at times: at times she could find it frightening. Jilly would come out with some powerful connections and interpretations but then become scared by her disclosure.

This illustrates the ways in which both parties can be alert to the spontaneous, mutual discovery of meaning, and the connections between the narratives, within the vignettes and the stories we created about the ways in which the core processes work. So, as this example illustrates, in the research conversations I aimed to become a co-reader of the vignette. The research was not only about the therapist telling or reporting the vignette, but also about our reading it together. I offered a framework as a starting point, but let the research conversations evolve and reshape between us – attempting to provide mutual attention, understanding and evaluation.

My questions were often, therefore, rooted in the respondent's words, theirs in response to mine: a conversation that tried to stay with the immediacy of the meanings which were emerging together. I tried to foreground my natural curiosity about their work and to be alert for distortion or evolution, encouraging dissent and interrogation of the core processes. We were together trying to create a sense of what the processes were – the narratives the vignettes contained and how they related to our mutual narratives about the way the core processes were seen within the way the therapist and I looked at the practice.

The basic pattern was as simple as I could make it and left as much room for us to work together as two participants 'producing meaning'. The first tended to be very general: about how they were seeing the processes in relation to their account in the vignette, the rest focused on them as a reader of their own work.

To leave room for the maximising of meaning and to deepen the analysis and the conversation, we also agreed that for a period of days after the live MSN messenger conversation we could email our dialogue between us so that we could alter and continue the MSN file conversation. This was to reflect the idea of the value of narratives and the research and dialogue in the conversation were open-ended in character: 'they are always unfinished. With each retelling we discover more of what we know' (Van Meen 1988: 12). Edited versions of these extended research conversations were then sent to each participant for approval for inclusion. The edited versions of the research conversations within this book are deliberately left in more or less the form they emerged in. The editing process was one of selecting particular sections of the conversations, not polishing the words. A part of their value as a research tool was in validating the spontaneity of interaction, the improvisational properties and value of this mode of enquiry.

I wanted this unfinishedness to remain and, in a way, the presentation of the edited conversations continue this. The research in this second edition is still an open process, still living, with practising therapists reading this book and the research it contains and, in turn, retelling and discovering more about the processes in their work with clients. The words here are printed but not fixed: the conversations continue.

References

Abrams, M. (1981) *A Dictionary of Literary Terms*, London, Fontana.

Ammar, H. (1954) *Growing Up in an Egyptian Village*, London, Routledge and Kegan Paul.

Andersen-Warren, M. and Grainger, R. (2000) *Practical Approaches to Dramatherapy: The Shield of Perseus*, London, Jessica Kingsley Publishers.

Anderson, W. (ed.) (1977) *Therapy and the Arts: Tools of Consciousness*, New York, Harper Colophon.

Antinucci-Mark, G. (1986) 'Some thoughts on the similarity between psychotherapy and theatre scenarios', *British Journal of Psychotherapy*, 3, 1, 14–19.

Anzul, M., Ely, M., Downing, M. and Vinz, R. (1997) *On Writing Qualitative Research*, London, Falmer Press.

Argyle, M. (1969) *Social Interaction*, London, Methuen.

—— (1972) *The Psychology of Interpreting Behaviour*, Harmondsworth, Penguin.

Aristotle (1961) *Poetics*, trans. S.H. Butcher, New York, Hill and Wang.

Arnheim, R. (1992) 'Why aesthetics is needed', *The Arts in Psychotherapy*, 19, 149–151.

Artaud, A. (1958) *The Theatre and Its Double*, New York, Grove.

Ashley, K., Gilmore, L. and Peters, G. (eds) (1994) *Autobiography and Postmodernism*, Amherst, University of Massachusetts Press.

Association for the Anthropological Study of Play. Various leaflets. Middle Tennessee State University, Murfreeboro, TN 37132.

Axline, V. (1964) *Dibs: In Search of Self*, New York, Ballantine.

Baker, D. (1981) 'To play or not to play', in N. McCaslin (ed.) *Children and Drama*, New York, Longman.

Barba, E. and Savarese, N. (1991) *A Dictionary of Theatre Anthropology*, London, Routledge.

Barham, M. (1994) 'Dramatherapy: the journey to become a profession', paper presented at ECARTE conference, Ferrara, Italy.

Bannister, A. (1997) *The Healing Drama: Psychodrama and Dramatherapy with Abused Children*, London, Free Association Books.

Barrault, J.L. (1972) 'Best and worst of professions', in J. Hodgson (ed.) *The Uses of Drama*, London, Eyre Methuen.

—— (1974) *Memories for Tomorrow*, London, Thames and Hudson.

Barry, D. (2006) 'Dramatherapy, good practice examples', *The Prompt*, Summer, 8–11.

Becker, A.L. (1979) 'Text building, epistemology and aesthetics in Javanese shadow theatre', in A.L. Becker and A.A. Yengoyan *The Imagination of Reality, Essays in Southeast Asian Coherence Systems*, New Jersey, Ablex.

Becker, A.L. and Yengoyan, A.A. (1979) *The Imagination of Reality, Essays in Southeast Asian Coherence Systems*, New Jersey, Ablex.

Becker, E. (1975) 'The self as a locus of linguistic causality', in D. Brissett and C. Edgeley, *Life as Theater: A Dramaturgical Sourcebook*, Chicago, Aldine.

Beckerman, B. (1990) *Theatrical Presentation – Performer, Audience and Act*, London, Routledge.

Beik, J. (1987) *Hausa Theatre in Niger*, New York and London, Garland.

Benjamin, W. (1955) 'Das Kunstwerk im Zeitalter seiner technischen Reproduzierbarkeit', in *Schriften*, vol. 1, Frankfurt, Suhrkamp.

—— (1970) *Illuminations*, Harmondsworth, Penguin.

Benthall, J. and Polhemus, T. (eds) (1975) *The Body as a Medium of Expression*, London, Allen Lane.

Bentley, E. (1976) *The Theory of the Modern Stage*, London, Penguin.

—— (1977) 'Theatre and therapy', in W. Anderson (ed.) *Therapy and the Arts: Tools of Consciousness*, New York, Harper Colophon.

Berger, P. (1975) 'Sociological perspectives: society as drama', in D. Brissett and C. Edgeley (eds) *Life as Theater: A Dramaturgical Sourcebook*, Chicago, Aldine.

Bergland, B. (1994) 'Postmodernism and the autobiographical subject: reconstructing the "other",' in K. Ashley, L. Gilmore and G. Peters (eds) *Autobiography and Postmodernism*, Amherst, University of Massachusetts Press.

Berne, E. (1964) *Games People Play*, New York, Grove.

Bettelheim, B. (1976) *The Uses of Enchantment*, London, Thames and Hudson.

Bixler, J. (1949) *Play in Therapy*, New York, Wiley.

Blanchot, M. (2000) 'The original experience', in C. Cazeaux (ed.) *The Continental Aesthetics Reader*, London and New York, Routledge.

Blatner, A. (1973) *Acting In*, New York, Springer.

Blatner, A. and Blatner, A. (1988a) *The Art of Play*, New York, Springer.

—— (1988b) *Foundations of Psychodrama*, New York, Springer.

Boal, A. (1974) *Poetics of the Oppressed: Experiments with the People's Theatre in Brazil*, London, Pluto.

—— (1979) *Theatre of the Oppressed*, London, Pluto.

—— (1992) *Games for Actors and Non-Actors*, trans. A. Jackson, London, Routledge.

Bolton, G.M. (1979) *Towards A Theory of Drama In Education*, London, Longman.

—— (1981) 'Drama-in-education – a reappraisal', in N. McCaslin (ed.) *Children and Drama*, New York, Longman.

—— (1984) *Drama as Education*, Harlow, Longman.

Booth, D. and Martin Smith, A. (eds) (1988) *Recognizing Richard Courtney*, Ontario, Pembroke.

Borges, J.L. (1970) *Labyrinths*, Harmondsworth, Penguin.

Bowyer, R. (ed.) (1970) *The Lowenfeld Technique*, Oxford, Pergamon.

Brecht, B. (1964) *Brecht on Theatre*, ed. J. Willen, London, Methuen.

Bretherton, I. (ed.) (1984) *Symbolic Play: The Development of Social Understanding*, Orlando, Florida Academic Press.

Brissett, D. and Edgeley, C. (eds) (1975) *Life as Theater: A Dramaturgical Sourcebook*, Chicago, Aldine.

British Association of Dramatherapists (2004) www.badth.org.uk (accessed January 2007).

Brook, P. (1968) *The Empty Space*, Harmondsworth, Penguin.
—— (1988) *The Shifting Point*, London, Methuen.
Brookes, J.M. (1975) 'Producing Marat/Sade: theatre in a psychiatric hospital', *Hospital and Community Psychiatry*, 26, 7, 429–435.
Brown, D. and Pedder, J. (1979) *Introduction to Psychotherapy*, London, Tavistock.
Brown, N.S., Curry, N.E. and Tittnich, E. (1971) 'How groups of children deal with common stress through play', in N.E. Curry and S. Arnaud (eds) *Play: The Child Strives Towards Self Realization*, Washington, DC, National Association for the Education of Young Children.
Brown, R.P (ed.) (1968) *Actor Training*, New York, Institute for Research in Acting, Drama Book Specialists.
Bruscia, K. (1988) 'Standards for clinical assessment in the arts therapies', *The Arts in Psychotherapy*, 15, 5–10.
Buchanan, D.R. (1984) 'Moreno's social atom: a diagnostic treatment tool for exploring interpersonal relationships', *The Arts in Psychotherapy*, 11, 155–164.
Bunt, L. (1994) *Music Therapy: An Art Beyond Words*, London, Routledge.
Buhler, N. (1951) *World Technique*, New York, Wiley.
Burke, K. (1975) 'On human behavior considered dramatistically', in D. Brissett and C. Edgeley (eds) *Life as Theater: A Dramaturgical Sourcebook*, Chicago, Aldine.
Caldwell Cook, H. (1917) *The Play Way*, London, Heinemann.
Canda, E.R. (1990) 'Therapeutic use of writing and other media with Southeast Asian refugees', *Journal of Independent Social Work*, 4, 2, 47–60.
Casement, P. (1990) *Further Learning from the Patient*, London, Routledge.
Cassirer, E. (1946) *Language and Myth*, New York, Dover.
—— (1955) *The Philosophy of Symbolic Forms, Vol. 1: Language*, New Haven, CT, Yale University Press.
Casson, J. (1997) 'The therapeusis of the audience', in S. Jennings (ed.) *Dramatherapy Theory and Practice 3*, London, Routledge.
—— (1999) 'Evreinoff and Moreno: monodrama and psychodrama, parallel developments or hidden influences?', *Journal of the British Psychodrama Association*, 14, 1, 20–30.
—— (2004) *Drama, Psychotherapy and Psychosis*, Hove, Brunner-Routledge.
Cattanach, A. (1992) *Play Therapy with Abused Children*, London, Jessica Kingsley Publishers.
—— (1994) 'The developmental model of dramatherapy', in S. Jennings, A. Cattanach, S. Mitchell, A. Chesner and B. Meldrum (eds) *The Handbook of Dramatherapy*, London, Routledge.
Cave, S. (1999) *Therapeutic Approaches in Psychology*, London, Routledge.
Cazeaux, C. (2000) *The Continental Aesthetics Reader*, London, Routledge.
Cerf, K. (1972) 'Drama therapy for young people', in R.P. Brown (ed.) *Actor Training*, New York, Institute for Research in Acting, Drama Book Specialists.
Cervantes, M. (1898) *The History of Don Quixote*, ed. J.W. Clark, London, Cassell Petter and Galpin.
Chaplin Kindler, R. (2005) 'Creative co-constructions: a psychoanalytic approach to spontaneity and improvisation in the therapy of a twice forsaken child', in A.M. Weber and C. Haen (2005) *Clinical Applications of Drama Therapy in Child and Adolescent Treatment*, New York and Hove, Brunner Routledge.
Chapple, E.D. (1970) *Culture and Biological Man: Explorations in Behavioral Anthropology*, New York, Holt, Rinehart and Winston.

Chauncey, H. (ed.) (1969) *Soviet Pre-School Education, Vol. 2: Teacher's Commentary*, New York, Holt, Rinehart and Winston.

Chesner, A. (1994) 'Dramatherapy and psychodrama: similarities and differences', in S. Jennings, A. Cattanach, S. Mitchell, A. Chesner and B. Meldrum (eds) *The Handbook of Dramatherapy*, London, Routledge.

Ciornai, S. (1983) 'Art therapy with working class women', *The Arts In Psychotherapy*, 10, 63–76.

Clark-Shock, K., Turner, Y. de G. and Boree, T. (1988) 'A multidisciplinary psychiatric assessment, the introductory group', *The Arts in Psychotherapy*, 15, 79–82.

Clarkson, P. and Pokorney, M. (1994) *The Handbook of Psychotherapy*, London, Routledge

Cohen, N. (1944) 'Puppetry with psychoneurotic soldiers', *Puppetry Journal*, 4, 2, 7–9.

Cohen, R. (1969) 'Play amongst European kindergarten girls in a Jerusalem neighborhood', cited in D. Feitelson (1977) 'Cross-cultural studies of representational play', in B. Tizard and D. Harvey (eds) *Biology and Play*, Philadelphia, Lippincott.

Connor, L. (1984) 'The unbounded self: Balinese therapy in theory and practice', in A.J. Marsella and G.M. White (eds) *Cultural Conceptions of Mental Health and Therapy*, Dordrecht, Reidel.

Corsini, R.T. (1966) *Roleplaying in Psychotherapy*, New York, Aldine.

Coult, T. and Kershaw, B. (1983) *Engineers of the Imagination*, London, Methuen.

Courtney, R. (1974) *Play, Drama and Thought*, New York, Drama Book Specialists.

—— (1981) 'Aristotle's legacy', *Indiana Theater Bulletin*, 2, 3, 1–10.

—— (1988a) 'Human performance: meaning and knowledge', in D. Booth and A. Martin Smith (eds) *Recognizing Richard Courtney*, Ontario, Pembroke.

—— (1988b) 'Mirrors: sociological theatre/theatrical sociology', in D. Booth and A. Martin Smith (eds) *Recognizing Richard Courtney*, Ontario, Pembroke.

—— (1988c) 'A whole theory for drama therapy', in D. Booth and A. Martin Smith (eds) *Recognizing Richard Courtney*, Ontario, Pembroke.

—— (1988d) *Recognizing Richard Courtney*, eds D. Booth and A. Martin Smith, Ontario, Pembroke.

Cox, M. (1992) *Shakespeare Comes To Broadmoor*, London, Jessica Kingsley Publishers.

Critchley, S. (2001) *Continental Philosophy*, Oxford, Oxford University Press.

Curran, F. (1939) 'The drama as a therapeutic measure in adolescents', *American Journal of Orthopsychiatry*, 9, 215.

Curry, N.E. and Arnaud, S. (eds) (1971) *Play: The Child Strives Towards Self Realization*, Washington, DC, National Association for the Education of Young Children.

Daley, T., Case, C., Schaverien, J., Weir, F., Nowell Hall, P., Halliday, D. and Waller, D. (1987) *Images of Art Therapy*, London, Tavistock.

Davidoff, E. (1939) 'Reactions of a juvenile delinquent group to story and drama techniques', *Psychiatric Quarterly*, 13, 245–258.

Davies, M.H. (1987) 'Dramatherapy and psychodrama', in S. Jennings (ed.) *Dramatherapy: Theory and Practice 1*, London, Routledge.

—— (1992) 'Dramatherapy and psychodrama', in S. Jennings (ed.) *Dramatherapy: Theory and Practice for Teachers and Clinicians*, vol. 2, London, Routledge.

Dawson, S.W (1970) *Drama and the Dramatic*, London, Methuen.

Derrida, J. (1988) *Limited Inc.* trans. S. Weber, Illinois, Northwestern University Press.

—— (2001) 'I have no taste for the secret: Jacques Derrida in conversation with

Maurizio Ferraris and Giorgio Vattimo', in J. Derrida and M. Ferraris, *A Taste For The Secret*, trans. G. Donis, Cambridge, Polity Press.

Deutsch, N. (1947) 'Analysis of postural behaviour', *Psychoanalytic Quarterly*, 16, 195–213.

—— (1952) 'Analytic posturology', *Psychoanalytic Quarterly*, 21, 196–213.

Dokter, D. (1990) 'Acting in or acting out?', *Dramatherapy, Journal of the British Association for Dramatherapists*, 12, 2, 7–9.

—— (1992) 'Dramatherapy a psychotherapy?', *Dramatherapy, Journal of the British Association for Dramatherapists*, 14, 2, 9–11.

—— (1993) 'Dramatherapy across Europe – cultural contradictions', in H. Payne (ed.) *Handbook of Inquiry in the Arts Therapies: One River, Many Currents*, London, Jessica Kingsley Publishers.

—— (1996) 'Dramatherapy and clients with eating disorders: fragile board', in S. Mitchell (ed) *Dramatherapy: Clinical Studies*, London, Jessica Kingsley Publishers.

—— (ed.) (2000) *Exile: Arts Therapies and Refugees*, conference proceedings, Hatfield, University of Hertfordshire Press.

—— (2005) Exile: applied intercultural arts therapies research in practice with refugees, Kossolapow, *Arts-Therapy-Communication*, vol. 3, Munster, Verlag.

—— (2005/6) 'The fool and "stranger anxiety": creative and destructive possibilities', *Dramatherapy, Journal of the British Association for Dramatherapists*, 28, 4, 9–13.

Douglas, M. (1966) *Purity and Danger*, London, Arc/Routledge and Kegan Paul.

—— (1970) *Natural Symbols*, New York, Barrie and Rotkliff.

—— (1975) *Implicit Meaning*, London, Routledge and Kegan Paul.

Downing, J. N. (2000) *Between Conviction and Uncertainty: Philosophical Guidelines for the Practising Psychotherapist*, New York, State University of New York Press.

Dubowski, J. (ed.) (1984) *Art Therapy as a Psychotherapy with the Mentally Handicapped*, conference proceedings, Hatfield, Hertfordshire College of Art and Design.

Dunlop, I. (1977) *Edvard Munch*, London, Thames and Hudson.

Dunton, W.R. (ed.) (1950) *Occupational Therapy, Principles and Practice*, Springfield, IL, Charles C. Thomas.

Ebbek, F.N. (1973) 'Learning from play in other cultures', in K. Forst (ed.) *Revisiting Early Childhood Education*, New York, Holt, Rinehart and Winston.

Eco, U. (1984) *Semiotics and the Philosophy of Language*, London, Macmillan.

Eco, U., Santambrogio, M. and Violi, P (1983) *Meaning and Mental Representations*, Bloomington, Indiana University Press.

Eifennann, R.R. (1987) 'Children's games observed and experienced', *Psychiatric Study of the Child*, 42–44.

Ekstein, R. and Friedman, S.W. (1957) 'The function of acting out, play action and play acting in the psychotherapeutic process', *Journal of the American Psychoanalytic Association*, 5, 581–629.

Elam, K. (1991) *The Semiotics of Theatre and Drama*, London, Methuen.

Elliott, J. (2005) *Using Narrative in Social Research: Qualitative and Quantitative Approaches*, London, Sage.

Ellis, G.E. (1954) 'The use of dramatic play for diagnosis and therapy', *Journal of Colorado-Wyoming, Academy of Science*, 4, 57–58.

Elsass, P. (1992) 'The healing space in psychotherapy and theatre', *New Theatre Quarterly*, 8, 32.

Ely, M. (1991) *Doing Qualitative Research: Circles within Circles*, London, Falmer Press.

Emunah, R. (1994) *Acting For Real*, London, Psychology Press.

—— (2000) 'The integrative five phase model of drama therapy', in P. Lewis and D.R. Johnson (eds) *Current Approaches in Drama Therapy*, Springfield, IL, Charles C. Thomas

Emunah, R. and Read Johnson, D. (1983) 'The impact of theatrical performance on the self images of psychiatric patients', *The Arts in Psychotherapy*, 10, 233–239.

Erikson, E. (1950) *Childhood and Society*, New York, Norton.

—— (1963) *Childhood and Society*, Harmondsworth, Penguin.

Esslin, M. (1978) *An Anatomy of Drama*, London, Maurice Temple Smith.

—— (1987) *The Field of Drama*, London, Methuen.

Evans, K.R. and Gilbert, M.C. (2005) *An Introduction to Integrative Psychotherapy*, New York, Palgrave Macmillan.

Evreinov, N. (1927) *The Theatre in Life*, New York, Harrap.

Fein, G. and Stork, L, (1981) 'Sociodramatic play: social class effect in integrated and pre-school classrooms', *Journal of Applied Developmental Psychology*, 2, 267–279.

Feitelson, D. (1977) 'Cross-cultural studies of representational play', in B. Tizard and D. Harvey (eds) *Biology and Play*, Philadelphia, Lippincott.

Feitelson, D. and Landau, M. (1976) *The Home Environment of Two Groups of Pre-Schoolers in Jerusalem*, cited in D. Feitelson (1977) 'Cross-cultural studies of representational play', in B. Tizard and D. Harvey (eds) *Biology and Play*, Philadelphia, Lippincott.

Fenichel, O. (1942) 'On acting', *Psychoanalytic Quarterly*, 11, 459.

—— (1945) 'Neurotic acting out', *Psychoanalytic Review*, 32, 197–206.

Fink, S. (1990) 'Approaches to emotion in psychotherapy and theatre: implications for dramatherapy', *The Arts in Psychotherapy*, 17, 5–18.

Florsheim, M. (1946) 'Drama therapy', paper presented at American Occupational Therapy Association Convention.

Fontana, D. and Valente, L. (1993) 'Dramatherapy and the theory of psychological reversals', *The Arts In Psychotherapy*, 20, 1332.

Forst, K. (ed.) (1973) *Revisiting Early Childhood Education*, New York, Holt, Rinehart and Winston.

Fortes, M. (1938) 'Social and psychological aspects of education in Taleland', *Africa*, 1 (supplement), 272.

Foster, J. B. and Froman, W.J. (eds) (2002) *Thresholds of Modern Culture: Identity, Postcoloniality, Transnationalism*, New York/London, Continuum.

Foucault, M. (1979) *Discipline and Punish*, New York, Vintage.

—— (1986) *The History of Sexuality*, vol. 2, New York, Random House.

—— (1988) *Michel Foucault: Politics, Philosophy, Culture. Interviews and Other Writings*, ed. L.D. Kritzman, New York/London, Routledge.

Freud, S. (1900) *The Interpretation of Dreams*, London, Hogarth Press.

—— (1950) *Totem and Taboo*, London, Hogarth Press.

Frost, A. and Yarrow, R. (1990) *Improvisation in Drama*, London, Macmillan.

Fryrear, J.L. and Fleshman, B. (1981) *The Arts Therapies*, New York, Charles C. Thomas.

Garner, S.B. (1994) *Bodied Spaces, Phenomenology and Performance in Contemporary Drama*, Ithaca and London, Cornell University Press.

Garvey, C. (1974) 'Some properties of social play', *Merrill-Palmer Quarterly*, 20, 163–180.

—— (1977) *Play*, Cambridge, MA, Harvard University Press.

Gerould, D. (1985) *Doubles, Demons and Dreamers*, New York, Performing Arts Journal Publications.

Gersie, A. (1987) 'Dramatherapy and play', in S. Jennings (ed.) *Dramatherapy: Theory and Practice 1*, London, Routledge.

—— (1991) *Storymaking in Bereavement*, London, Jessica Kingsley Publishers.

Gersie, A. and King, N. (1990) *Storymaking in Education and Therapy*, London, Jessica Kingsley Publishers.

Giffen, H. (1984) 'The co-ordination of meaning in the creation of shared make-believe reality', in I. Bretherton (ed.) *Symbolic Play: The Development of Social Understanding*, Orlando, Florida Academic Press.

Gill, M. (1997) 'Different therefore equal? Dramatherapy and frame analysis with a learning disabled man', in S. Jennings (ed.) *Dramatherapy: Theory and Practice 3*, London: Routledge.

Gillies, N. and Gunn, T. (1963) 'Live presentation of dramatic scenes', *Group Psychotherapy*, 16, 3, 164–72.

Gilmore, L. (1994) 'The mark of autobiography: postmodernism, autobiography and genre', in K. Ashley, L. Gilmore and G. Peters (eds) *Autobiography and Postmodernism*, Amherst, University of Massachusetts Press.

Glaser, B. and Strauss, A. (1975) 'The ritual drama of mutual pretense', in D. Brissett and C. Edgeley (eds) *Life as Theater: A Dramaturgical Sourcebook*, Chicago, Aldine.

Goffman, E. (1959) *The Presentation of Self In Everyday Life*, New York, Doubleday.

—— (1961) *Encounters*, New York, Bobbs Merrill.

—— (1972) *Relations in Public*, Harmondsworth, Penguin.

Golub, S. (1984) *Evreinov, The Theater of Paradox and Transformation*, Ann Arbor, UMI Research Press.

Goodman, J. and Prosperi, M. (1976) 'Drama therapies in hospitals', *Drama Book Review*, 20, 1, 20–30.

Goodman, N. (1981) *Languages of Art*, London, Harvester.

Grainger, R. (1990) *Drama and Healing: The Roots of London*, Jessica Kingsley Publishers.

—— (1995) *The Glass of Heaven: The Faith of the Dramatherapist*, London: Jessica Kingsley Publishers.

—— (2005a) 'Theatre and encounter Part II – courageous theatre', *Dramatherapy*, 27, 1, 3–7.

—— (2005b) 'Theatre and encounter Part III – transforming theatre', *Dramatherapy*, 27, 1, 8–12.

Green, R. (1966) 'Play production in a mental hospital setting', *Journal of Psychiatry*, 122, 1181–1185.

Gregory, D. and Garner, R. (2000) *Paradigms and Research: Examining the History and Future of Art Therapy*, Artery International, *http://burleehost.com/artery/researchparadigm.htm* (Accessed January 2007).

Griffing, P. (1983) 'Encouraging dramatic play', *Children*, 38, 4, 13–22.

Grimshaw, D. (1996) 'Dramatherapy with children in an educational unit: the more you look, the more you see', in S. Mitchell (ed.) *Dramatherapy: Clinical Studies*, London, Jessica Kingsley Publishers.

Grolinski, S.A. and Barkin, L. (1978) *Between*, Northvale, NJ, Jason Aronson.

Groos, K. (1901) *The Play of Man*, London, Heinemann.

Gropius, W. (ed.) (1979) *The Theatre of the Bauhaus*, London, Methuen.

Grotowski, J. (1968) *Towards a Poor Theatre*, London, Methuen.

Gunn, G.R.L. (1963) 'The life presentation of dramatic scenes as a stimulus to patient interaction in group psychotherapy', *Group Psychotherapy*, 16, 3, 164–172.

Hall, S. (1996) The formation of a diasporic intellectual: an interview with Kuan-Hsing Chen', in D. Morley and K-H. Chen (eds) *Stuart Hall: Critical Dialogues*, London, Routledge.

Hampson, S. (1988) *The Construction of Personality: An Introduction*, London, Routledge.

Handke, P. (1971) *Offending the Audience and Self-Accusation*, London, Holt.

Harding, A. J. (2002) 'Subject, self, person: Marcel Mauss and the limits of poststructuralist critique', in J.B. Foster and W.J. Froman (eds) *Thresholds of Modern Culture: Identity, Postcoloniality, Transnationalism*, New York/London, Continuum.

Haviland, W.H. (1978) *Cultural Anthropology*, New York, Wiley.

Henke, S.A. (2000) *Shattered Subjects: Trauma and Testimony in Women's Life-Writing*, New York, St Martin's Press.

Henry, W.E. (1973) *The Analysis of Fantasy*, New York, Krieger.

Heymann-Krenge, R. (2006) 'The engendered spectator: a spectator orientated process in dramatherapy to reveal the inner spectator of the client', *Dramatherapy, Journal of the British Association for Dramatherapists*, 28, 2, 15–23.

Hickling, F.W. (1989) 'Sociodrama in the rehabilitation of chronic mentally ill patients', *Hospital and Community Psychiatry*, 40, 4, 402106.

Higson-Smith, C., Mulder, B. and Zondi, N. (2006) *Report on the Firemaker Project: a Formative and Summative Evaluation*, Johannesburg, South African Institute for Traumatic Stress.

Hill, C. (2005) 'The foolish dramatherapist? An exploration of the role of the fool', *Dramatherapy, Journal of the British Association for Dramatherapists*, 27, 2, 3–10

Hodgson, J. (1972) *The Uses of Drama*, London, Methuen.

Hoffman, E.T.A. (1952) 'Cruel sufferings of a stage director', in A. M. Nagler (ed.) *A Source Book in Theatrical History*, New York, Dover.

Holland, L.A. (2000) *Philosophy for Counselling and Psychotherapy*, London, Macmillan.

Holland, P. (1964) *Self and Social Context*, London, Macmillan.

Hope, M. (1988) *The Psychology of Ritual*, Dorset, Element Books.

Hornbrook, D. (1989) *Education and Dramatic Art*, Oxford, Blackwell.

Horwitz, S. (1945) 'The spontaneous drama as a technic in group therapy', *Nervous Child Journal*, 4, 252–273.

Houben, J., Smitskamp, H. and Velde, J. (eds) (1989) *The Creative Process*, Hogeschool Midden Nederland, Phaedon.

Hougham, R. (2006) 'Numinosity, symbol and ritual in the Sesame approach', *Dramatherapy, Journal of the British Association for Dramatherapists*, 28, 2, 3–5.

Howes, M. (1980) 'Peer play scale', *Developmental Psychology*, 16, 371.

Huizinga, J. (1955) *Homo Gudens*, Boston, Beacon.

Hunter, D. (1986) 'Hysteria, psychoanalysis and feminism', in S. Garner, C. Kahane and M. Sprengnether (eds) *The (M)Other Tongue*, Ithaca, Cornell University Press.

Ickes, W. and Knowles, E.S. (eds) (1982) *Personality, Roles, and Social Behavior*, New York, Springer.

Ikegami, Y. (1971) 'A stratificational analysis of the hand gestures in Indian classical dancing', *Semiotica*, 4, 365–391.

Innes, C. (1993) *Avant Garde Theatre 1892–1992*, London, Routledge.

Irwin, E.C. (1979) 'Drama therapy with the handicapped', in A.M. Shaw and C.J. Stevens (eds) *Drama, Theater and the Handicapped*, Washington, DC, American Theater Association.

—— (1983) 'The diagnostic and therapeutic use of pretend play', in C.E. Schaefer and K.J. O'Connor (eds) *The Handbook of Play Therapy*, New York, Wiley.

Irwin, E.C. and Shapiro, M.I. (1975) 'Puppetry as a diagnostic and therapeutic technique', in T. Jakab (ed.) *Transcultural Aspects of Psychiatric Art*, vol. 4, Basel, Karger.

Jacksons, S. (1988) 'Shadows and stories: lessons from the Wayang Kulit for therapy with an Anglo-Indonesian family', *Australian and New Zealand Journal of Family Therapy*, 9, 2, 71–78.

Jacques, F. (1991) *Difference and Subjectivity: Dialogue and Personal Identity*, trans. A. Rothwell, New Haven, Yale.

Jacques, J. F. (2006) 'Dramatherapy and user involvement', *The Prompt*, Autumn, 10–11.

Jakab, T. (ed.) (1975) *Transcultural Aspects of Psychiatric Art*, vol. 4, Basel, Karger.

James, W. (1932) 'A study of the expression of bodily posture', *Journal of General Psychology*, 7, 40536.

Jaynes, J. (1990) *The Origins of Consciousness in the Breakdown of the Bicameral Mind*, Boston, Houghton Mifflin.

Jennings, H.H. (1943) *Leadership and Isolation*, New York, Longman Green.

Jennings, S. (1973) *Remedial Drama*, London, Pitman.

—— (ed.) (1975) *Creative Therapy*, London, Kemble.

—— (ed.) (1987) *Dramatherapy: Theory and Practice 1*, London, Routledge.

—— (1991) 'Theatre art: the heart of dramatherapy', *Dramatherapy, Journal of the British Association for Dramatherapists*, 14, 1, 4–7.

—— (ed.) (1992) *Dramatherapy: Theory and Practice 2*, London, Routledge.

—— (ed.) (1997) *Dramatherapy: Theory and Practice 3*, London, Routledge

Jennings, S., Cattanach, A., Mitchell, S., Chesner, A. and Meldrum, B. (1994) *The Handbook of Dramatherapy*, London, Routledge.

Jernberg, A.M. (1983) 'Therapeutic uses of sensory motor play', in C.E. Schaefer and K.J. O'Connor (eds) *The Handbook of Play Therapy*, New York, Wiley.

Johnson, D.W. and Johnson, F.P. (1987) *Joining Together: Group Theory and Group Skills*, New York, Prentice Hall.

Johnson, J.E., Christie, J.F. and Yawkey, T.D. (1987) *Play and Early Childhood Development*, Illinois, Scott Foresman.

Johnson, L. and O'Neill, C. (eds) (1989) *Dorothy Heathcote: Collected Writings on Education and Drama*, London, Hutchinson.

Jones, E. (1919) 'The theory of symbolism', *British Journal of Psychology*, 9.

Jones, P. (1984) 'Therapeutic storymaking and autism', in J. Dubowski (ed.) *Art Therapy as a Psychotherapy with the Mentally Handicapped*, conference proceedings, Hatfield, Hertfordshire College of Art and Design.

—— (1989) *Dramatherapy – State of the Art*, conference proceedings, Hatfield, Hertfordshire College of Art and Design.

—— (1991) 'Dramatherapy: five core processes', *Dramatherapy, Journal of the British Association for Dramatherapists*, 14, 1, 5–10.

—— (1993) 'The active witness', in H. Payne (ed.) *Handbook of Inquiry in the Art Therapies, One River, Many Currents*, London, Jessica Kingsley Publishers.

—— (1996) *Drama as Therapy: Theatre as Living*, 1st edn, London: Routledge.

—— (2005) *The Arts Therapies: A Revolution in Healthcare*, London, Routledge.

Jung, C.G. (1959) *The Archetypes and the Collective Unconscious, Collected Works*, vol. 9, part 2, London, Routledge and Kegan Paul.

—— (1983) *Selected Works*, ed. A. Storr, London, Fontana.

Jupp, V. (ed.) (2005) *The Sage Dictionary of Social Research Methods*, London, Sage.

Karkou, V. and Sanderson, P. (2005) *Arts Therapies: A Research Based Map Of The Field*, London, Elsevier.

Kelly, G.A. (1955) *Psychology and Personal Constructs*, New York, Norton.

Kersner, M. (1990) *The Art of Research*, Proceedings of the Second Arts Therapies Research Conference, London City University.

Kipper, D.A. (1986) *Psychotherapy through Clinical Role Playing*, New York, Brunner/Mazel.

Klaesi, J. (1922) 'Einiges der Schizophrenienbehandlung', in I. Jakab (ed.) *Transculturel Aspects of Psychiatric Art, Psychiatry and Art*, vol. 4, Basel, Karger.

Klein, M. (1932) *The Psychoanalysis of Childhood*, London, Hogarth Press.

—— (1961) *Narrative of a Child Analysis*, vol. 4, London, Hogarth Press.

Knowles, E.S. (1982) 'From individual to group members: a dialectic for the social science', in W. Ickes and E.S. Knowles (eds) *Personality, Roles, and Social Behavior*, New York, Springer.

Koestler, A. (1977) 'Regression and integration', in W. Anderson (ed.) *Therapy and the Arts: Tools of Consciousness*, New York, Harper Colophon.

Kors, S. (1964) 'Unstructured puppet shows as group procedure in therapy with children', *Mental Health*, 7–8.

Kott, J. (1969) 'The icon and the absurd', *Drama Review*, 14, 17–24.

Kowzan, T. (1968) 'The sign in theatre', *Diogenes*, 61, 52–80.

Kreeger, A. (ed.) (1975) *Perspectives and Psychotherapy*, New York, Holt.

Krenger, W K. (1989) *Body Self and Psychological Self*, New York, Brunner/Mazel.

Kristeva, J. (1997) 'Revolution in poetic language', in K. Oliver (ed.) *The Portable Kristeva*, New York, Columbia University Press.

Lahad, M. (1994) 'What is dramatherapy?', in S. Jennings, A. Cattanach, S. Mitchell, A. Chesner and B. Meldrum (eds) *The Handbook of Dramatherapy*, London, Routledge.

Landy, R. (1982) *Handbook of Educational Drama and Theater*, New York, Greenwood.

—— (1986) *Drama Therapy*, Springfield, IL, Charles C. Thomas.

—— (1989) 'One on one', in P. Jones (ed.) *Dramatherapy – State of the Art*, conference proceedings, Hatfield, Hertfordshire College of Art and Design.

—— (1994) *Persona and Performance*, London, Jessica Kingsley Publishers.

—— (2001) *New Essays In Drama Therapy*, Springfield, IL, Charles C. Thomas.

Langley, D. (1989) 'The relationship between psychodrama and dramatherapy', in P. Jones (ed.) *Dramatherapy – State of the Art*, conference proceedings, Hatfield, Hertfordshire College of Art and Design.

—— (1993) 'When is a dramatherapist not a therapist?', *Dramatherapy*, 15, 2, 16–18.

—— (1998) 'The relationship between psychodrama and dramatherapy', in M. Karp, P. Holmes, and K. Bradshaw Tauvon (eds) *The Handbook of Psychodrama*, London, Routledge.

—— (2006) *An Introduction to Dramatherapy*, London, Sage.

Langley, D. and Langley, G. (1983) *Dramatherapy and Psychiatry*, London, Croom Helm.

Laurel, B. (1991) quoted in H. Rheingold, 'Reaching out to touch our fantasies', *Guardian*, 26 August, 14.

Lassner, R. (1947) 'Playwriting and acting as diagnostic therapeutic techniques with delinquents', *Journal of Clinical Psychology*, 3, 349–356.

Lefevre, G. (1948) 'A theoretical basis for dramatic production as a technique of psychotherapy', *Mental Health*, 12–15.

Leguit, G. and van der Wiel, D. (1989) 'A family plays itself better', in J. Houben, H. Smitskamp and J. te Velde (eds) *The Creative Process*, Hogeschool Midden Nederland, Phaedon.

Levinas, E. (2000) 'Reality and its shadow', in C. Cazeaux (ed.) *The Continental Aesthetics Reader*, London and New York, Routledge.

Levine, R. and Levine, A. (1963) 'Nyansorgo: a Gusii community in Kenya', in B. Whithing (ed.) *Six Cultures: Studies in Childrearing*, New York, Wiley.

Lewis, G. (1980) *The Day of Shining Red*, Cambridge, Cambridge University Press.

Lewis, P. and Johnson, D. R. (eds) (2000) *Current Approaches in Drama Therapy*, Springfield, Il, Charles C. Thomas.

Lindkvist, M. (1966) *Radius Document*, private collection of Ms Lindkvist.

—— (1977) *BISAT (British Institute for the Study of the Arts in Therapy)*, leaflet, private collection of Ms Lindkvist.

—— (1990) *The Sesame Institute (UK) Training in Drama and Movement Therapy*, information pamphlet, private collection of Ms Lindkvist.

Lindzey, G. and Aronson, E. (eds) (1968) *Handbook of Social Psychology*, Cambridge, MA, Addison-Wesley.

Loewald, E.L. (1987) 'Therapeutic play in space and time', *Psychiatric Study of the Child*, 47.

Loizos, C. (1969) 'Play behavior in higher primates: a review', in D. Moms (ed.) *Primate Ethology*, Garden City, Anchor.

Lomax, A., Bartenieff, I. and Paulay, P. (1968) 'Dance style and culture', *American Association for the Advancement of Science*, 88, 222–247.

Lorenz, K. (1966) *Evolution and the Modification of Behavior*, Chicago, University of Chicago Press.

Lowen, A. (1958) *Physical Dynamics of Character Structure: Body Form and Movement in Analytic Therapy*, New York, Grune and Stratton.

Lowenfeld, M. (1970) *The Lowenfeld Technique*, ed. R. Bowyer, Oxford, Pergamon.

Lyle, J. and Holly, S.B. (1941) 'The therapeutic value of puppets', *Bulletin of the Menninger Clinic*, 5, 223–226.

Macey, D. (2000) *The Penguin Dictionary of Critical Theory*, London, Penguin.

McAlister, M. (1999) 'An evaluation of dramatherapy in a forensic setting', in T. Wigram, (ed.) *Assessment and Evaluation in the Arts Therapies*, Radlett, Harper House Publications

McCaslin, N. (1981) *Children and Drama*, New York, Longman.

McDougall, J. (1989) *Theatres of the Body*, London, Free Association.

McLoyd, V. (1982) 'Social class difference in sociodramatic play: a critical review', *Developmental Review*, 2, 1–30.

McMillen, J. (1956) 'Acting: the activity for chronic regressed patients', *Journal Of Psychiatry*, 7, 56–62.

McNiff, S. (1986) *Educating the Creative Arts Therapist*, Springfield, IL, Charles C. Thomas.

McNiff, S. (1988) 'The shaman within', *The Arts in Psychotherapy*, 15, 285–291.

—— (1998) *Art-Based Research*, London, Jessica Kingsley Publishers.

McReynolds, P. (ed) (1978) *Advances in Psychological Assessment*, vol. 4, Washington, DC, Jossey-Bass.

McReynolds, P. and DeVoge, S. (1978) 'Use of improvisational techniques in assessment', in P. McReynolds (ed) *Advances in Psychological Assessment*, vol. 4, Washington, DC, Jossey-Bass.

McReynolds, P., DeVoge, S., Osborne, S.K., Pither, B. and Nordin, K. (1976) *Manual for the Impro-I*, Reno, Department of Psychology, University of Nevada.

—— (1977) *An Improvizational Technique for the Assessment of Individuals*, unpublished manuscript, Reno, Department of Psychology, University of Nevada.

Magarschack, D. (1950) *Stanislawski – On the Art of the Stage*, London, Faber and Faber.

Maier, N.R.F. (1953) 'An experimental test of the effect of training on discussion leadership', *Human Relations*, 6, 161–173.

Main, G. (1975) 'On projection', in A. Kreeger (ed.) *Perspectives in Psychotherapy*, New York, Holt.

Malachie-Mirovich, N. (1927) *Soviet Education*, cited in H. Chauncey (ed.) (1969) *Soviet Pre-school Education, vol. 2: Teachers' Commentary*, New York, Holt, Rinehart and Winston.

Marcuse, H. (1969) *Eros and Civilisation: A Philosophical Inquiry into Freud*, Harmondsworth, Penguin.

Marineau, R.F. (1989) *Jacob Levy Moreno*, London, Tavistock-Routledge.

Marsella, A.J. and White, G.M. (eds) (1984) *Cultural Conceptions of Mental Health and Therapy*, Dordrecht, Reidel.

Maslow, A. (1962) *Toward a Psychology of Being*, New York, Van Nostrand Reinhold.

—— (1977) 'The creative attitude', in W. Anderson (ed.) *Therapy and the Art. Tools of Consciousness*, New York, Harper Colophon.

Mast, S. (1986) *Stages of Identity: A Study of Actors*, London, Gower.

Mazor, J. (1966) 'Producing plays in psychiatric settings', *Bulletin of Art Therapy*, 5, 4.

Mead, G.H. (1934) *Mind, Self and Society*, Chicago, Chicago University Press.

Meldrum, B. (1994) 'A role model for dramatherapy and its application with individuals and groups', in S. Jennings, A. Cattanach, S. Mitchell, A. Chesner and B. Meldrum (eds) *The Handbook of Dramatherapy*, London, Routledge.

Menninger, K. (1942) *Love Against Hate*, New York, Harcourt, Brace and World.

Messinger, S., Sampson, H. and Towne, R. (1962) 'Life as theatre: some notes on the dramaturgic approach to social reality', *Sociometry*, 25–26.

Miller, J. (1983) *States of Mind*, London, BBC Publications.

Miller, N. (1973) *The Psychology of Play*, New York, Holt.

Mitchell, J. and Rose, J. (eds) (1982) *Feminine Sexuality*, New York, Norton and Pantheon.

Mitchell, S. (1990) 'The theatre of Peter Brook as a model for dramatherapy', *Dramatherapy, Journal of the British Association for Dramatherapists*, 13, 1.

—— (1992) 'Therapeutic theatre: a paratheatrical model for dramatherapy', in S. Jennings (ed.) *Dramatherapy: Theory and Practice 2*, London, Routledge.

—— (1993) *Hope and Dread in Psychoanalysis*, London, Basic Books.

Mora, G. (1957) 'Dramatic presentations by mental patients in the middle nineteenth century', *Bulletin of the History of Medicine*, 3, 3, 260–277.

Moran, G.S. (1987) 'Some functions of play and playfulness', *Psychoanalytic Study of the Child*, 42, 29–32.

Moreno, J.L. (1946) *Psychodrama*, vol. 1, New York, Beacon House.

—— (1953) *Who shall Survive? Foundations of Sociometry, Group Psychotherapy and Sociodrama*, New York, Beacon House.

—— (1983) *The Theatre of Spontaneity*, New York, Beacon House.

—— (ed.) (1960) *The Sociometry Reader*, New York, Free Press.

Moreno, J.L. and Moreno, Z. (1959) *Psychodrama*, vol. 2, New York, Beacon House.

Morris, D. (ed.) (1969) *Primate Ethology*, Garden City, Anchor.

Morton, R.B. (1965) 'The uses of laboratory method in a psychiatric hospital', in E.H. Schein and W.G. Bennis (eds) *Personal and Organisational Change through Group Methods*, New York, Wiley.

Müller-Thalheim, W.K. (1975) 'Self-healing tendencies and creativity', in T. Jakab (ed.) *Transcultural Aspects of Psychiatric Art*, vol. 4, Basel, Karger.

Murphy, G. (1944) *Human Potentialities*, New York, Basic Books.

Nagler, A.M. (1952) *A Source Book in Theatrical History*, New York, Dover.

Neubauer, P.B. (1987) 'The many meanings of play', *Psychoanalytic Study of the Child*, 42, 3–9.

Nietzsche, F. (1967) *The Birth of Tragedy*, New York, Vintage.

Nilli, I. (1984) 'On the theatre of the future' (*O teatre buduscego*), in S. Golub, *Evreinov, the Theater of Paradox and Transformation*, Michigan, UMI Research Press.

Oatley, K. (1984) *Selves In Relation*, London, Methuen.

O'Neill, C. and Lambert, A. (1982) *Drama Structures*, London, Hutchinson.

Parten, M. (1932) 'Social participation among pre-school children', *Journal of Abnormal and Social Psychology*, 27, 3–69.

Pavis, P. (1982) 'Languages of the stage', *Performing Arts Journal*, 15, 21–24.

—— (1985) *Voix et images de la scène pour une sémiologie de la réception*, Lille, Presses Universitaires.

Pavlicevic, M. (1997) *Music Therapy in Context: Music, Meaning and Relationship*, London, Jessica Kingsley Publishers.

Payne, H. (ed.) (1993) *Handbook of Inquiry in the Arts Therapies, One River, Many Currents*, London, Jessica Kingsley Publishers.

Pedder, J. (1989) 'Courses in psychotherapy: evolution and current trends', *British Journal of Psychotherapy*, 6, 2.

Pellegrini, A.D. (1980) 'The relationship between kindergartners' play and achievement in prereading, language and writing', *Psychology in the Schools*, 17, 530–535.

Pepler, D.J. and Rubin, K.H. (eds) (1982) *The Play of Children: Current Theory and Research*, Basel, Karger.

Perls, S.F., Hefferline, R.F. and Goodmab, P. (1951) *Gestalt Therapy*, Harmondsworth, Penguin.

Perlstein, S. (1988) 'Transformation: life review and communal theater', *Journal of Gerontological Social Work*, 12, 137–148.

Perry, J.W. (1976) *Roots of Renewal in Myth and Madness*, San Francisco, Jossey-Bass.

Pesso, A. (1997) 'Body-centred therapy' in C. Caldwell (ed) *Getting In Touch: A Guide to Body-Centred Therapies*, Wheaton, Theosophical Publishing House

Petzold, H. (1973) *Gestalttherapie und Psychodrama*, Nicol, Kassel.

Piaget, J. (1962) *Play, Dreams and Imitation in Childhood*, New York, Norton.

Pickard, K. (1989) 'Shape', in P. Jones (ed.) *Dramatherapy – State of the Art*, conference proceedings, Hatfield, Hertfordshire College of Art and Design.

Pitruzzella, S. (2004) *Introduction to Drama Therapy: Personal Threshold*, London, Brunner-Routledge.

Polhemus, T. (1975) 'Social bodies', in T. Polhemus and J. Benthall (eds) *The Body as a Medium of Expression*, London, Allen Lane.

Polhemus, T. and Benthall, J. (eds) (1975) *The Body as a Medium of Expression*, London, Allen Lane.

Price, H. and Nagle, L. (1943) 'Recreational therapy at the Sheppard and Enoch Pratt hospital', *Occupational Therapy and Rehabilitation*, 30.

Putnam, H. (1978) *Meaning and the Moral Sciences*, London, Routledge.

Ray, B. (1976) *African Religions*, New York, Wiley.

Read Johnson, D. (1980) 'Effects of a therapeutic experience on hospitalized psychiatric patients', *The Arts in Psychotherapy*, 7, 265–272.

—— (1981) 'Some diagnostic implications of dramatherapy', in G. Schattner and R. Courtney (eds.) *Drama in Therapy*, vol. 1, New York, Drama Book Specialists.

—— (1982) 'Developmental approaches to drama therapy', *The Arts in Psychotherapy*, 9, 183–190.

—— (1985/6) 'The developmental method in drama therapy', *The Arts in Psychotherapy*, 13, 17–33.

—— (1988) 'The diagnostic role playing test', *The Arts in Psychotherapy*, 15, 23–36.

—— (1991) 'The theory and technique of transformations in drama therapy', *The Arts in Psychotherapy*, 23, 293–306.

—— (1999) *Essays on the Creative Arts Therapies*, Springfield, Charles C. Thomas.

Read Johnson, D. and Munich, R.L. (1975) 'Increasing hospital community contact through a theatre program in a psychiatric hospital', *Hospital and Community Psychiatry*, 26, 7, 43538.

Read Johnson, D. and Quinlan, D. (1985) 'Representational boundaries in role portrayals among paranoid and nonparanoid schizophrenic patients', *Journal of Abnormal Psychology*, 94.

Reason, P. (ed.) (1988) *Human Enquiry in Action: Developments in New Paradigm Research*, Chichester, Wiley.

Reason, P. and Rowan, J. (eds) (1981) *Human Inquiry*, Chichester, Wiley.

Rehm, L.P. and Marston, A.R. (1968) 'Reduction of social anxiety through modification of self-reinforcement: an instigation therapy technique', *Journal of Consulting and Clinical Psychology*, 565–574.

Reider, N., Olinger, D. and Lyle, J. (1939) 'Amateur dramatics as a therapeutic agent in the psychiatric hospital', *Bulletin of the Menninger Clinic*, 3, 1, 20–26.

Reil, J.C. (1803) 'Rhapsodieen über die Anwendung der Psychichen Kurmethode', in G. Zilboorg (1976), *A History of Medical Psychology, The Age of Reconstruction*, New York, Norton.

Rheingold, H. (1991a) 'Reaching out to touch our fantasies', *Guardian*, 26 August, 14.

—— (1991b) *Virtual Reality*, London, Secker and Warburg.

Robertson, K. (1990) 'Cultural differences and similarities in dramatherapy theory and practice', paper presented at conference 'Arts Therapies Education – Our European Future', ECARTE.

Rogers, C. (1961) *On Becoming a Person*, Boston, Houghton Mifflin.

Romme, M. (1994) Unpublished research questionnaire for assessing people who hear voices, referred to in J. Casson, (2004) *Drama, Psychotherapy and Psychosis*, Hove, UK, Brunner-Routledge.

Romme, M. and Escher, S. (eds) (1996) *Understanding Voices: Coping with Auditory Hallucinations and Confusing Realities* Limburg, Rijksuniversitiet Maastricht.

—— (2000) *Making Sense of Voices – A Guide for Professionals who Work with Voice Hearers*, London, MIND Publications.

Roose-Evans, J. (1984) *Experimental Theatre*, London, Routledge.

Rossberg-Gempton, I. and Poole, G.D. (1991) 'The effect of open and closed postures on pleasant and unpleasant emotions', *Arts in Psychotherapy*, 20, 1, 75–82.

Rothko, M. (1948) 'The Romantics were prompted,' in J. Weiss (1999) *Mark Rothko, Catalogue*, Washington, DC, National Gallery of Art.

Rothschild, B. (2000) *The Body Remembers – The Psychophysiology of Trauma and Trauma Treatment*, New York, Norton.

—— (2006) *Help for the Helper – Self-Care Strategies for Managing Burnout and Stress*, New York, Norton.

Rotter, J.B. and Wickens, D.D. (1948) 'The consistency and generality of ratings of "social aggressiveness" made from observation of role playing situations', *Journal of Consulting Psychology*, 12, 234–239.

Rowan, J. (1990) 'Recent work in new paradigm research', in M. Kersner *The Art of Research*, proceedings of the Second Arts Therapies Research Conference, London, City University.

Rubin, J.A. and Irwin, E.C. (1975) 'Art and drama: parts of a puzzle', in T. Jakab (ed.) *Transcultural Aspects of Psychiatric Art*, vol. 4, Basel, Karger.

Rubin, K.H. and Seibel, C.C. (1979) 'The effects of ecological setting on the cognitive and social play behaviors of preschoolers', paper presented to American Educational Research Association, San Francisco.

Rubenstein, T.I. (2005) 'Taming the beast: the use of drama therapy in the treatment of children with obsessive compulsive disorder', in A.M. Weber and C. Haen *Clinical Applications of Drama Therapy in Child and Adolescent Treatment*, New York and Hove, Brunner-Routledge.

Sanctuary, R. (1984) 'Role play with puppets for social training', unpublished report, University of London, quoted in P. Jones (1993) 'The active witness', in H. Payne, *Handbook of Inquiry in the Arts Therapies, One River, Many Currents*, London, Jessica Kingsley Publishers.

Sandberg, B. (1981) 'A descriptive scale for drama', in G. Schattner, and R. Courtney (eds) *Drama in Therapy*, vols 1 and 2, New York, Drama Book Specialists.

Sarbin, T. (ed.) (1986) *Narrative Psychology*, New York, Praeger.

Sarbin, T. and Allen, V. (1968) 'Role theory', in G. Lindzey and E. Aronson (eds) *Handbook of Social Psychology*, Cambridge, MA, Addison Wesley.

Satir, V. (1967) *Conjoint Family Therapy*, Paolo Alto, Science and Behavior Books.

Schaefer, C. (1976) *The Therapeutic Use of Child's Play*, Northvale, NJ, Jason Aronson.

Schaefer, C.E. and O'Connor, K.J. (1983) *The Handbook of Play Therapy*, New York, Wiley.

Schattner, G. and Courtney, R. (eds) (1981) *Drama in Therapy*, vols 1 and 2, New York, Drama Book Specialists.

Schechner, R. (1988) *Performance Theory*, New York, Routledge.

Scheff, T.J. (1979) *Catharsis in Healing, Ritual and Drama*, Berkeley, University of California.

Scheflen, A.E. (1972) *Body Language and Social Order*, Englewood Cliffs, NJ, Prentice Hall.

Schein, E.H. and Bennis, W.G. (eds) (1965) *Personal and Organizational Change through Group Methods*, New York, Wiley.

Schmais, C. (1988) 'Creative arts therapies and shamanism: a comparison', *Arts in Psychotherapy*, 15, 4, 281–284.

Schwartz, B. (2002) 'Unspeakable histories: diasporic lives in Old England', in P. Osborne and S. Sandford (eds) *Philosophies of Race and Ethnicity*, London and New York, Continuum.

Schwartzman, H. (1978) *Transformations: The Anthropology of Children's Play*, New York, Plenum Press.

Shaw, A. (1981) 'Co-respondents: the child and drama', in N. McCaslin (ed.) *Children and Drama*, New York, Longman.

Shaw, A.M. and Stevens, C.J. (eds) (1979) *Drama, Theater and the Handicapped*, Washington, DC, American Theater Association.

Siegal, E. (1984) *Dance Movement Therapy: Mirror of Ourselves*, New York, Human Sciences Press.

Singer, J.L. (1973) *The Child's World of Make Believe*, New York, Academic.

Skynner, A.C.R. (1976) *One Flesh: Separate Persons, Principles of Family and Marital Psychotherapy*, London, Constable.

Slade, P. (1954) *Child Drama*, London, University Press.

—— (1959) *Dramatherapy as an Aid to Becoming a Person*, pamphlet, London, Guild of Pastoral Psychology.

—— (1981) 'Drama as an aid to fuller experience', in N. McCaslin (ed.) *Children and Drama*, New York, Longman.

Slade, P., Lafitte, E. and Stanley, R.J. (1975) *Drama With Subnormal Adults*, London, Educational Drama Association.

Smilansky, S. (1968) *The Effects of Sociodramatic Play on Disadvantaged Children*, New York, Wiley.

Solomon, A.P. (1950) 'Drama therapy', in W.R. Dunton (ed.) *Occupational Therapy, Principles and Practice*, Springfield, IL, Charles C. Thomas.

Solomon, A.P. and Fentress, T.L. (1947) 'A critical study of analytically orientated group psychotherapy utilizing the technique of dramatization of the psychodynamics', *Occupational Therapy and Rehabilitation*, 26, 423.

Sontag, S. (1977) 'Mast/Sade/Artaud', in W. Anderson (ed.) *Therapy and the Arts: Tools of Consciousness*, New York, Harper Colophon.

Souall, A.T. (1981) *Museums of Madness*, London, Sphere.

Southern, R. (1962) *The Seven Ages of Theatre*, London, Faber.

Stanislavski, C. (1937) *An Actor Prepares*, London, Geoffrey Bles.

—— (1963) *Creating a Role*, London, Geoffrey Bles.

Stebbins, R. (1969) 'Role distance, role distance behaviour and jazz musicians', *British Journal of Sociology*, 20, 4, 406–415.

Steger, S. and Coggins, M. (1960) 'Theatre therapy', *Hospital Management*, 89, 122–128.

Stock-Whitaker, D. (1985) *Using Groups to Help People*, London, Routledge and Kegan Paul.

Stone, G.P. (1975) 'Appearance and self', in D. Brissett and C. Edgeley (eds) *Life as Theater: A Dramaturgical Sourcebook*, Chicago, Aldine.

Stone, G.P. and Faberman, H. (1970) *Social Psychology through Symbolic Interaction*, Waltham, Ginn Blaisdell.

Strozier, R. (2002) 'Interiority, identity, knowledge: unraveling the Cartesian cogito', in J.B. Foster and W.J. Froman (eds) *Thresholds of Modern Culture: Identity, Postcoloniality, Transnationalism*, New York/London, Continuum.

Sutton-Smith, B. (1972) *The Folk Games of Children*, Austin, TX, University of Texas Press.

—— (ed.) (1979) *Play and Learning*, New York, Gardner.

—— (1981) 'Sutton Smith-Lazier Scale of Dramatic Involvement', in G. Schattner and R. Courtney (eds) *Drama in Therapy*, vol. 1, New York, Drama Book Specialists.

Tanesini, A. (1999) *An Introduction to Feminist Epistemologies*, Oxford, Blackwell.

Tizard, B. and Harvey, D. (eds) (1977) *Biology and Play*, London, Heinemann.

Travisano, R.V. (1975) 'Alternation and conversion as qualitatively different transformations', in D. Brissett and C. Edgeley (eds) *Life as Theater. A Dramaturgical Sourcebook*, Chicago, Aldine.

Tudor, L.E. and Tudor, K. (1994) 'The personal and the political: power, authority and influence in psychotherapy', in P. Clarkson and M. Pokorney (eds) *The Handbook of Psychotherapy*, London, Routledge.

Turner, V. (1969) *The Ritual Process*, Chicago, Aldine.

—— (1974) *Dramas, Fields and Metaphors*, Ithaca, Cornell University Press.

—— (1982) *From Ritual to Theater*, New York, Performing Arts Journal Press.

Valente, L. and Fontana, D. (1993) 'Research into dramatherapy theory and practice', in H. Payne (ed.) *Handbook of Inquiry in the Arts Therapies, One River, Many Currents*, London, Jessica Kingsley Publishers.

—— (1997) 'Assessing client progress in dramatherapy', in S. Jennings (ed.) *Dramatherapy: Theory and Practice 3*, London, Routledge.

Vernon, P.E. (1969) *Personality Assessment, A Critical Survey*, London, Methuen.

Von Franz, M.L. (1970) *The Interpretation of Fairytales*, London, Spring.

—— (1974) *Shadow and Evil in Fairytales*, New York, Spring.

Ward, W. (1957) *Playmaking with Children*, New York, Appleton-Century Crofts.

—— (1981) 'A retrospect', in N. McCaslin (ed.) *Children and Drama*, New York, Longman.

White, M. (2004) *Narrative Practice and Exotic Lives*, Adelaide, Dulwich Centre Publications.

Whithing, B. (ed.) (1963) *Six Cultures: Studies in Childrearing*, New York, Wiley.

Williams, A. (1989) *The Passionate Technique*, London, Tavistock Routledge.

Wilshire, B. (1982) *Role Playing and Identity*, Bloomington, IN, Indiana University Press.

Winnicott, D.W. (1953) 'Transitional objects and transitional phenomena, a study of the first not-me possession', *International Journal of Psychoanalysis*, 34, Part 2.

—— (1966) 'The location of cultural experience', *International Journal of Psychoanalysis*, 48.

—— (1974) *Playing and Reality*, London, Pelican.

Witkin, R.W. (1974) *The Intelligence of Feeling*, London, Heinemann.

Wolf, D. and Grollman, S.H. (1982) 'Ways of playing: individual differences in imaginative style', in D.J. Pepler and K.H. Rubin (eds) *The Play of Children: Current Theory and Research*, Basel, Karger.

Woltmann, G. (1940) 'The use of puppets in understanding children', *Mental Hygiene*, 24, 445.

—— (1964) 'Diagnostic and therapeutic considerations of nonverbal projective activities with children', *Mental Hygiene*, 24, 445.

Wundt, W. (1896) *Foundations of Psychology*, Leipzig, Engleman.

Yalom, I.D. (1970) *The Theory and Practice of Group Psychotherapy*, New York, Basic Books.

—— (1985) *The Theory and Practice of Group Psychotherapy*, New York, Basic Books, 3rd edition.

—— (1990) *Existential Psychotherapy*, New York, Basic Books.

Zilboorg, G. (1976) *A History of Medical Psychology, The Age of Reconstruction*, New York, Norton.

Name index

Abrams 94
Ammar 162, 168
Andersen-Warren 212, 230, 231
Antinucci-Mark 16
Argyle 204, 227
Aristotle 24, 26, 137
Artaud 29, 30, 32, 119, 272, 273

Barba 31, 273
Bannister 295
Barrault 31
Barry 8, 138
Benjamin 226
Benthall 227
Berger 40, 41, 42
Berne 272
Bettelheim 243
Blanchot 69
Blatner 118, 161, 162, 163, 206, 266
Boal 7, 29, 31, 75, 207, 228
Bolton 162, 163, 241
Bowyer 1146
Brecht 29, 31, 95, 207, 237
Brook 7, 29, 30, 32, 152, 273
Brookes 27, 47, 140
Brown 40, 155
Bruscia 286, 289
Burke 40

Canda 17, 18
Cassirrer 192
Casson 14, 24, 27, 34, 38, 83, 84, 289, 290
Cattanach 89
Cerf 48, 49
Chandrasegaram 298, 299, 301
Chaplin Kindler 17
Chesner 40
Ciornai 17, 18, 288
Cohen 168

Colkett 4, 156, 159, 160, 161, 199, 202, 203
Courtney 12, 20, 25, 56, 75, 114, 118, 137, 179, 225, 289
Cox 137
Critchley 61, 66, 70, 71, 72, 73
Curran 48
Curry 155

Derrida 69
Dokter 17, 19, 76, 77, 232, 238, 266
Dooman 6, 126, 132, 133, 138
Douglas 227, 273

Eco 250, 253
Elam 113, 227
Elsass 16, 25
Emunah 8, 14, 165, 213
Esslin 3, 153
Evreinov 6, 23, 24, 26, 32, 33, 34, 35, 38, 44, 119, 155, 161, 206, 278, 283

Feitelson 164, 168
Fleshman 25, 27
Florsheim 24, 49
Fontana 16, 70, 78, 286, 287
Foucault 74, 227
Freud 15, 16, 75, 83, 140, 144, 226, 254
Fryrear 25, 27

Gardner 13, 311, 312, 313, 314
Garvey 207
Gersie 85, 153, 243, 266
Gill 64, 65
Goodman 14, 24, 256, 257, 258, 259, 260
Grainger 61, 63, 69, 70, 212, 276
Green 46, 47
Grimshaw 66, 67, 68
Gropius 223, 224

Grotowski 7, 17, 29, 30, 32, 273
Guarnieri 107, 109, 110, 111, 112, 205
Gunn 47

Hall 74
Heathcote 43
Heymann-Krenge 103, 1104, 112
Hickling 45
Hornbrook 42, 43
Horwitz 49, 50
Hougham 17
Hubbard 193, 195, 197, 198, 199, 207,
   208, 302, 304, 305

Innes 25, 31, 273, 274
Irwin 176, 177, 1181

Jennings 25, 31, 32, 40, 45, 50, 51, 54, 55,
   56, 63, 70, 74, 76, 113, 206, 213, 230,
   266
Jernberg 178
Jung 16, 17, 51, 52, 75, 149, 253, 254, 307

Karkou 8, 9, 24, 34, 38, 57, 82, 254
Klein 16, 144, 146
Koestler 120
Kors 48
Kristeva 62, 63, 64, 65

Lahad 58, 290
Landy 17, 20, 24, 25, 31, 34, 40, 42, 63,
   70, 74, 75, 81, 94, 101, 134, 139, 140,
   168, 193, 203, 204, 212
Langley 9, 12, 14, 40, 58, 82, 193, 241,
   242, 255, 269
Lassner 47
Lefevre 48
Levinas 63
Levy 13, 193, 212, 217, 220, 221, 225
Lewis 7, 9, 272
Lin 114, 117,
Lindkvist 50, 51, 52, 54, 55, 56
Loizos 165, 166
Lorenz 227
Lowenfeld 145, 146, 315
Lyle 27

Mann 6, 140, 260, 261, 263, 264, 264
McAlister 289
McCaslin 43
McNiff 70, 276
Marcuse 226
Maslow 75
Mast 207

Mazor 27, 46, 47
Mead 40, 75, 203, 204
Meldrum 42, 204, 213
Meyer 5, 18, 19, 95, 96, 99, 100, 235, 236,
   238
Miller 144, 146, 254
Mitchell 32, 71, 213, 227, 266
Mora 25, 26
Moreno 23, 24, 26, 28, 29, 32, 38, 39, 40,
   44, 51, 53, 54, 55, 75, 161, 203, 297

Novy 10, 15, 121, 124, 125, 126, 266, 268,
   269

Parten 316
Pavlicevic 71
Payne 317
Pedder 40
Petzold 34
Piaget 166
Pickard 47
Pitruzzella 14, 166
Polhemus 227
Powis 11, 88, 184, 185, 187, 188, 189, 190
Putnam 72

Ramsden 107, 109, 110, 111, 112, 205
Read Johnson 47, 61, 120, 166, 213, 290,
   314, 315
Reason 290
Robertson 45
Rogers 169, 173, 174, 175, 212
Roose-Evans 273
Rothko 59
Rowan 290

Sanctuary 156, 316
Sandberg 184
Sarbin 204
Satir 314
Schattner 56, 179
Schechner 7, 17, 119, 166, 203, 206, 227,
   272, 274
Schmais 276
Schwartzman 168, 176
Secchi 103, 146, 192, 209, 210, 211, 212
Singer 169
Skynner 255
Slade 24, 43, 49, 50, 51, 53, 54, 55, 56,
   1161, 168
Smalinsky 55
Solomon 25, 46, 48, 119
Stanislavski 30, 31, 37, 44, 52, 206, 237
Stirling Twist 104, 105, 106, 107

Sutton-Smith 163, 168, 295

Turner 25, 41, 75, 204, 227, 272

Valente 16, 70, 78, 286, 287
Van Den Bosch 5, 10, 84, 86, 88, 148,
    150, 151, 241
Vaughan 89, 91, 92, 93, 228, 305, 306,
    309, 310

Von Franz 243

Ward 43
Wilshire 206
Winnicott 16, 118, 163, 206

Yalom 82, 139

Zilboorg

Subject index

active witness see witnessing
artistic process 61–3
adolescents 66–9, 95–101, 104–17
aesthetics 26, 60, 236
aims 8, 11, 25, 43, 49, 63, 68, 156, 167,
    169, 199, 217, 286–8, 290–1, 306,
    317–18, 320
anthropology 16, 25, 137–9, 165–6, 227,
    272–8
Antony and Cleopatra 137–9
Apollonian 226–7; see also Dionysian
archetype 75; see also Jung
Art therapy 53, 55–6, 76, 96, 292
Arts Therapies 9, 17–18, 20, 24, 45, 57,
    62, 73, 77, 82, 251
assessment 37, 47–8, 66, 70, 84, 89, 92,
    97, 107, 161, 167, 176, 179, 185, 191,
    215, 217, 244, 256, 285–321
Atari research 14
audience 30–2, 39–41, 47, 81, 95–8,
    101–4, 107–12, 118–19, 126–33, 153,
    199, 206–7, 211, 216, 225, 235, 239,
    241, 308, 311, 319
autism 185–91, 242–50, 316–17

Babylon 25
basic sessional shape 9–13, 168–9, 212–17
Bauhaus 223–5
Black theatre 31–2
body; 76–8, 102–17, 123–4, 146–8, 180–1,
    219–20, 223–40, 264; see also Dance,
    Dance Movement Therapy, Dramatic
    Body, mime
boundaries 9, 63, 88, 102, 112, 131–3,
    164, 199–200, 202–3, 217, 219–21, 239,
    293, 305, 311, 313, 319
Brazil 228
British Association of Dramatherapists
    8, 56–7, 230

British Medical Association 24

catharsis 24–5, 39–40, 192, 212, 222
censorship 28–9
Charenton 27
child drama 51–2
children and Dramatherapy 4, 5, 18–19,
    33, 39, 42–4, 48–51, 54, 57, 66–7, 88,
    90–3, 101, 105–7, 126–33, 138–44,
    155–91, 207, 228, 248, 256, 289, 295
    305–11, 315–16
closure 9, 11, 13, 18, 28, 85, 96, 99, 116,
    150, 246, 269, 317
cognition 118, 166, 191, 205–7, 222
cognitive behavioural therapy 17
communication 13, 223–40
computers 14, 195
confidentiality 131, 293
core processes; see distancing; dramatic
    body; dramatic projection; empathy;
    life-drama connection; playing;
    transformation; witnessing
costume 5, 137–43
creativity 7, 8, 15–16, 35, 46, 49, 121, 126,
    189, 192, 201, 294, 312
cross-cultural issues 17–18, 65, 113,
    126–33, 157–63, 168, 176, 204, 256–61,
    272–6, 288, 300
culture 15–17, 23–6, 65, 74, 118, 161–4,
    168, 225, 227, 279, 282–4, 288, 300

dance 52–3, 157–9, 223–4, 233–5
Dance movement therapy 52–3, 226,
    230–1
defence mechanisms 139
de-roling 12–13, 108–12, 197, 201, 207–22,
    266, 269, 306, 313
developmental approach 166, 176
developmental drama 166–8

diagnosis 47, 286, 288
Dionysian 226–7; see also Apollonian
disability 29, 31, 169, 174, 218, 249, 254
discrimination 17, 95–101
distancing 31, 81, 86, 95–112, 132, 150,
   174, 237, 249, 273–4
doubling 39–40, 102, 215, 252
drama 3, 4, 6, 7–20, 23–30, 34–6, 38–40,
   43–60, 74–6, 81–4, 86–8, 114–26,
   133–4, 150–4, 160–6, 170–8, 184,
   190–1, 198, 213–14, 238–9, 250, 289,
   302, 312–13; see drama in education,
   performance, play-drama continuum,
   theatre
drama in education 42–3, 54
dramatherapist 9, 13, 217, 276–7
dramatherapy; history 23–58; basic
   format 10–13; definitions 3, 7–9; as a
   profession 23–4 see Core processes
dramatic body 146–8, 223–40
dramatic projection 10, 83–8, 126–33,
   137–54, 173–4, 194, 210–12, 249, 263,
   304, 308, 312
dramaturgy 40–3, 204
dreams 15, 45–50, 254; and the origins of
   Dramatherapy 52–4

eating disorders 76–8
European Consortium for Arts
   Therapies Training and Education 57
ecstasy 206–8, 226–7
elderly clients 4, 53, 83–8, 105–7, 300; see
   also intergenerational work
embodiment 112–17, 122–5, 126–33, 159,
   198, 210–12, 219–20, 223–40
empathy 31, 95–101, 108–12, 150, 174,
   192–4, 202–22, 270–6
Epic theatre 31
ethics 9, 70, 288–9
evaluation 66, 68–70, 96, 116, 126, 268,
   285–9

Family therapy 17, 40, 88–94, 255,
   305–11
fantasy 13, 242–50
Feast of Fools 24
feminism 227, 281–3, 297–302
Forum Theatre 31

gay politics 29, 31
gender 74, 122, 196, 227, 262, 267,
   279
Gestalt 44, 76
Greece 45, 57, 212, 279–82

Greek Theatre 222
group therapy 9, 18, 44, 49–50, 192, 232,
   302

Hamlet 110; see also Antony and
   Cleopatra; Two Gentlemen of Verona
hiv 3, 18–19, 58, 95–101
healing 15, 16, 24–7, 44
health 24–7, 31, 78, 100–01, 276–7
hospital theatre 7, 27–9, 45, 46–8

identity 40–1, 61–4, 73–8, 121, 192–4,
   204–8, 211–12, 226–30
ideology 62–71
imagery 220, 231
improvisation 13, 35–8, 126–33, 157–9,
   165–6, 168–74
individual Dramatherapy 5, 36–7, 48,
   126–33, 149
insight 194–8
intergenerational work 19, 105
interpretation 25, 36, 38, 141, 153, 211,
   231, 253–4, 265–6, 304

Julio de Matos Hospital, Lisbon
   28–9
Jung 16–17, 51–2, 75, 149, 253–4

Kabuki 253
Kathakali 227–8

learning disability 64–6
life drama connection 14–15, 33, 117–19,
   148, 197–8, 220–2, 249–50, 268,
   312–14

mask 5, 6, 125, 129, 137–41, 152–3, 170,
   209, 210, 215, 225
meaning 13, 15, 41, 69–71, 78, 103, 130,
   153, 111–16, 174–7, 184, 210, 251–4,
   260, 265–74, 305
mental health 27–8, 54, 83–8, 148–51,
   195–203, 232, 235, 235, 231–53, 292–4,
   311–13
metaphor 66–8, 217–22, 241–71
mime 26, 184, 194, 206
mimesis 13, 14, 207–8, 273
Monstrous Regiment 31
Moscow Arts Theatre 30
music 33, 53, 56, 71, 160, 170, 173,
   233–4
Music Therapy 53, 71
myth 11, 17, 25, 31, 83, 118, 192, 273–4,
   292–5

narratives 110, 121–7, 266–7
National Health Service 58, 69, 107, 292, 302
Netherlands 38, 50
Netherlands Society for Creative Expressive Therapy 56
National Institute for Clinical Excellence 58

objects 11, 76–8, 83–8, 88–94, 114–17, 120, 138, 146–51, 179–80, 182–3, 209–10, 241, 256–61, 302–6
object relations theory 297
occupational therapy 24, 27, 44, 48, 52–5

Padstow horse 24
pathology 11–18
performance 3, 7, 13, 16, 24–5, 126–33
performance art 209
personification 94–101, 229
philosophy 59–78
play 4, 5, 10, 13, 26, 32, 42–3, 88–94, 126, 144–91, 197, 202, 241–2, 256–81, 295–7, 315–16
play-drama continuum 11, 88–94, 126, 155–91
playback theatre 29, 115
playing and playfulness 11, 16, 88–94, 126, 155–91
Play therapy 56, 321
politics 7, 33, 60–64, 74, 268
political theatre 29, 30–2, 118
Poor theatre 30–1
primitivism 25
prisons 9, 27, 39, 54, 105, 107–12, 256,
projection 126–33, 137–40
psychiatric hospital 23–6, 34–8, 44, 46–9
psychoanalysis 16–17, 25, 35, 44–5, 48, 62–3, 71, 226
psychodrama 26, 39–40, 44, 51–3, 55, 208–9
psychological disturbance 16–18
psychosis 58, 150, 256, 290, 293
psychotherapy 7, 8, 16–18, 26, 40, 44, 48, 59–60, 71, 139, 244, 289, 292, 302
puppetry 11, 152, 204

racism 126–33, 274
referral 285–88
research 3–6, 9, 11, 13–16, 18, 27, 29, 58, 81–4, 88–9, 91–7, 99, 103–9, 112, 115, 117, 157, 163–4, 169, 192–5, 207–10,

225, 230–54, 261, 264–9, 290, 302–6, 311, 312, 317, 321; see research vignette
ritual 16, 25, 265, 272–8
role 10, 13, 39–42, 77–8, 101–12, 122–7, 147, 182–222, 266–8, 280, 301–6
role play 5, 94–101, 122–33, 143, 192–222, 303–12
role playing tests 314–15
role reversal 39, 86–7, 102, 104, 215, 222
Russia 29–38, 52, 237

scenery 5
script 11, 31–2, 50, 110, 111, 114, 116, 125–6, 130, 144, 153–4, 215, 307
Sierra Leone 126–33
social atom 297–302
socioeconomic issues and dramatherapy 17–9, 40–1, 229
Somalia 256–7
South Africa 18–19, 95–101
Sri Lanka 3–4, 157–61
story 83–8, 153–4, 242–50, 290
structure 27, 145, 168–9, 212, 215–16, 230–31, 266, 268–9, 281, 290, 304, 314–15
symbol 15, 30, 66–8, 83–8, 118, 217–22, 241–71

Taiwan 3, 114
theatre 3, 7, 13, 16, 24–5, 27–38, 119, 273–4, 276
therapeutic paradigms 16–18
therapeutic performance process 126–33
therapeutic relationship 8, 14, 16–18, 27, 29, 58, 81–4, 88–9, 91–7, 99, 103–9, 112, 115, 117, 157, 163–4, 169, 192–5, 207–10, 225, 230–254, 261, 264–9, 290, 302–6, 311, 312, 317
therapeutic space 16–18, 88–94, 118, 126, 132, 138, 147–8, 156–9, 163, 168–76, 191, 196, 229, 262, 285, 308
Therapeutic Theatre 26–8, 34–8
Transformation 10, 31–3, 119–27, 176, 189, 213, 228, 239, 263
transitional space 18, 206

United States of America 8, 34, 42, 43, 50, 56–7

verbal communication and reflection 47, 48, 74, 92–3, 108–11, 125, 140, 250–1, 266, 269, 277, 292–3, 303, 310, 313

video 104, 114–17, 317
voice 52, 63, 81, 94, 113, 122, 138, 300;
    hearing voices 148–51, 289–94

warm up 11–13, 35–6; see also structure

witnessing 13–15, 95–112, 126–33, 188,
    207–22, 234, 256–61, 263, 280, 301,
    308
world technique 88–94, 144–51,
    315–16

ABOUT THE AUTHORS

Jeffrey G. MacIntosh is Professor of Law at the University of Toronto where he specializes in Corporation Law, Corporate Finance, Securities Regulation, Law and Economics, and Small Firm Financing. He holds a B.Sc. from M.I.T., an LL.B. from the University of Toronto, and an LL.M. from Harvard University. His publications have been principally concerned with Corporation Law, Securities Regulation, and Small Firm Financing. Professor MacIntosh served as an Assistant Professor at Osgoode Hall Law School in 1982-83 and was appointed a John M. Olin Fellow at Yale Law School in 1988-89.

Christopher C. Nicholls is Professor of Law at Dalhousie University. He holds an LL.B. and LL.M. from Osgoode Hall Law School and an MPA from Harvard. Prior to joining the faculty at Dalhousie, Professor Nicholls practised corporate law in Toronto and in Hamilton, Bermuda. He also taught Corporate Finance and Securities Regulation at Osgoode Hall Law School and Business Law at the Bar Admission Course for the Law Society of Upper Canada. His teaching and research interests include Business Associations, Commercial Law, International Trade, Financial Institution Reform, Corporate Finance, and Corporate Governance.